DWAPAR
KATHA

Praise for *Dwapar Katha*

'Sudipta Bhawmik breathes life into every character of the epic Mahabharata with deep insights into their mind. A must-read.'

—**Anand Neelakantan**, bestselling author

'Sudipta Bhawmik is a master storyteller. Over the years, this account from Dvapara Yuga has been retold numerous times, as it deserves to be, in non-English languages too. (Like the author, I too grew up with Rajsekhar Basu's Bengali retelling.) For a new generation, it deserves to be retold again, from the beginning to the final journey. Based on the widely acclaimed podcast, the style of narration is engrossing. Few have the patience and perseverance to read the unabridged Mahabharata, which runs into some 2.5 million words. Any abridged retelling focuses on characters and incidents, leaving aside rich sections on geography and governance. With that lens, this is one of the best renditions in recent times.'

—**Bibek Debroy**, author and chairman, PM's Economic Council

'A grand story told without grandiosity. Epic Indian storytelling meets Aristotelian sequencing of events.'

—**Mahesh Dattani**, playwright and director,
Sahitya Akademi Award winner

Praise for *The Stories of Mahabharata* podcast

'I'm a Zulu lady from South Africa ... and I have found so many similarities in this rich [Indian] culture with ours.'

—**Khanya Dlomo**

'Thank you so much for doing this podcast. It is so precious ... Your podcast helps me to understand a bit of my [own] culture.'

—Jyotsna Milky Jay Zilab

'Your podcast is so well-crafted. The hard work and research put into each episode is really admirable.'

—Dr Aditya Sharma

'I grew up watching Mahabharata on TV ... but this one is special. The way you speak ... I can clearly imagine it [happening]. I feel like I am in that era. Beautifully written and expressed.'

—Rashmi Chopra

'I have listened to this entire series over the course of two days, and I am hooked! What an incredible story, I am so envious of those who have grown up with this tale!'

—Peter Griffith

'It is an explosion of my imagination every time ... and Mr Sudipta Bhawmik, your storytelling skill is god-gifted!'

—Udara Abeysundara

'The way it's planned and narrated is amazing. @ssrajamouli sir if you have time listen to this podcast, this might be of help for your dream project Mahabharata.'

—Sreeram Golconda

'This is simply outstanding ... It's one of the best podcast series out there ... I'm just addicted to it.'

—Akhil Mohnot

DWAPAR KATHA

The Stories of the Mahabharata

SUDIPTA BHAWMIK

HarperCollins *Publishers* India

First published in India by HarperCollins *Publishers* 2024
4th Floor, Tower A, Building No. 10, DLF Cyber City,
DLF Phase II Gurugram – 122002
www.harpercollins.co.in

2 4 6 8 10 9 7 5 3 1

PISBN: 978-93-5699-569-7
EISBN: 978-93-5699-570-3

Typeset in 13.5/16.5 ArnhemFine at
Manipal Technologies Limited, Manipal

Printed and bound at
Replika Press Pvt. Ltd.

This book is produced from independently certified FSC® paper to ensure
responsible forest management.

To Shiladitya, Ridhima, Omkar, Emily, Anisha, Ankit, Debjit

and

Their generation for carrying the story forward

Contents

Author's Note

WHEN I WAS A CHILD, MAYBE FOUR OR FIVE YEARS OLD, MY PARENTS GOT me an illustrated book—one could possibly call it an illustrated novel—on the Mahabharata. The text covered the entire epic in less than a couple of dozen pages. Since then, I have been in love with the Mahabharata. I still remember those pictures vividly, especially the cover picture which showed a depressed Arjun sulking on his chariot and Krishna trying to raise his spirits with his sermons—a depiction of the scene where the Bhagavad Gita was delivered by Krishna to Arjun. Later, I read other books on the epic, especially those in Bengali, such as the one by Kaliprasanna Singha. But the sheer volume of the book, and the archaic language were a huge turn off. The book I liked the most and got hooked to was an abridged Bengali version of Vyasa's Mahabharata, translated by Rajsekhar Basu. A popular writer and scholar, Basu wrote the book in a language that was easy to read and enjoy. I read the book multiple times, and it never failed to fill me with awe. With every read, I discovered something new, something enlightening and inspiring.

By then, I had read many other books and studied world literature, but the Mahabharata never bored me. I found the characters with their virtues and flaws so human, so real, that I could empathize with them and understand their motives, their passions and their perspectives. I couldn't pick a side, for I felt each side—the Pandavas as well as the Kauravas—had perfect reasons to demand their right. To me, the Mahabharata is not a religious text. It is the story of humanity—the greatest one ever told.

When I moved to the United States in 1989, the one book that I carried with me was *Krishna Dwaipayana Vyasa's Mahabharata* by Rajsekhar Basu.[1] I often wondered how I could make others, especially my American friends, appreciate the Mahabharata. B.R. Chopra's *Mahabharata* videos were available in the libraries, but non-Indians hardly bothered to watch them. Just a year before I landed in the USA, the famous theatre director Peter Brook had staged his nine-hour long *Mahabharata* production in New York. It did create a stir, but the enthusiasm died down with the wrapping up of the production. Later, a shorter, six-hour video version was telecast by PBS, which very few people watched. I was also keen to help our future generations growing up in the USA appreciate the Mahabharata, part of the rich heritage of our country.

In 2014, I got an opportunity to host a talk show in a local AM radio station—EBC Radio. Besides hosting regular talk shows, I thought, why not use the radio to tell the stories of the Mahabharata to the listeners? I began the journey quite casually, when my colleague and friend Avi Ziv—who's also a sound engineer and musician—one day offered help not only with recording the episodes in his home studio but also volunteered to enrich the audio content with sound

---

1   Rajsekhar Basu, *Krishna Dwaipayana Vyasa's Mahabharata* (M.C. Sarkar & Sons Private Limited, 1986.)

effects and background music. Avi, being a native of Israel, had no prior knowledge about the Mahabharata. Listening to a few episodes, he got interested in the great epic and has been a key contributor to each episode ever since.

Soon, a new medium surfaced in the digital entertainment world—podcasts, which began to gain popularity, especially among the tech-savvy youth. More and more digital media creators and distributors were entering the fray, creating a wide range of content. From the beginning, I had wished to reach out to younger audiences, and a podcast was the best medium to reach out to them. We soon pivoted and decided to distribute our content through podcasts. I wrote the script for each episode, narrated the epic in a dramatic story telling form, and Avi did the sound design and audio engineering.

This book is mostly a compilation of the scripts of the podcast episodes. Many of our listeners have been asking for a book based on the podcast—even a transcript. So, I felt that the book version will serve as a tangible companion to read at their convenience. A book opens the imagination like nothing else.

In writing the book and the podcast scripts, I had the following objectives:

1. I will try not to impose my interpretations of the characters or their actions in any way. I will try to stick to the narrative as per the reference text by Krishna Dwaipayana Vyasa and not invent any incidents or characterizations of my own. This sometimes has raised questions from the listeners because, several times, the narrative contradicted common beliefs and tales that we've learnt while growing up. Although I have used several texts as references, there were two key books that I consulted. The first one was *Krishna Dwaipayana Vyasa's Mahabharata* by Rajsekhar Basu. I found this abridged version (in Bengali) of the Mahabharata

to be the most accurate translation of the original Sanskrit version (translated into the English by Kisari Mohan Ganguli). The second book I referred to was the ten-volume translation of the BORI (Bhandarkar Oriental Research Institute) critical edition of *The Mahabharata* by Bibek Debroy.[2] These two served as my references to cross-check against when I came across any controversial issue or contradictory version.

2. Being a dramatist, my purpose right from the beginning was to highlight the drama of the Mahabharata and keep descriptions to the minimum. Hence, the book is rich in dialogues and conversations, rather than descriptive narratives. I wanted the audience and the reader to recreate the scenes in the theatre of their mind and enjoy the stories as a live experience.

3. The language should be simple, and the text should have a high readability such that readers of all ages, including those from non-English-speaking communities, can easily understand and follow the story.

I tried my best to stick to these principles and I hope my readers like the way the narrative is structured and flows.

The creation of the podcast, and then the book, required help and support from several people. First, I must thank Avi Ziv, my creative partner for the podcast. Avi has been working on this project from the very beginning. Without his technical and musical help, the podcast wouldn't have been possible. I'd also like to thank my son Omkar and nephew Debjit for helping us with the podcast production. Thanks to my niece Anisha and my son Shiladitya for being the early listeners and approvers of the podcast. Thanks to my wife, Mitali, for supporting and promoting this project all along.

---

2   Bibek Debroy, *The Mahabharata* (Penguin, 2015).

Thanks to Ridhima Kumar from HarperCollins India for being a patient and diligent editor and for asking the right questions. I'd also like to thank Onkar Fondekar for his beautiful illustrations, which add a captivating visual dimension to these stories.

And, finally, I'd like to thank the millions of listeners around the world who not only listened to the podcast, but also encouraged us with their comments and feedback. Without their love and appreciation, this project wouldn't have been successful.

1

The Beginning

IT WAS THE DWAPAR YUGA. RISHI VYASA, THE GREAT SAGE, COMPOSED AN epic poem which he called the Mahabharata. Rishi Vyasa was the son of Satyavati (daughter of Dasharaj, the king of the fishermen) and Rishi Parashara. Since he was of dark complexion and was born on an island, he was also called Krishna Dwaipayana Vyasa. Vyasa had composed the poem but couldn't write it down, for his thoughts ran faster than his pen. So he sought a scribe who could write the verses at the speed at which he recited them. However, he could find none. Vyasa invoked Lord Brahma. Those were times when, if anyone called upon a god with sincerity, they would be graced by the deity, who would appear to listen to, and often grant, their prayers. Brahma appeared before Vyasa and asked, 'Why did you call me, Vyasa? What do you want?'

Vyasa said, 'O Lord, I have composed this wonderful poem—an epic. It is the story of humankind, the story of our humanity. But I need someone who can write it while I recite the verses. Could you recommend someone?'

Brahma replied, 'Ganesha would be the best person for this job. Why don't you ask him?'

Vyasa invoked Ganesha, the elephant-headed god. Ganesha appeared and enquired, 'I understand you are looking for a scribe for your poem?'

'Yes, I am.'

'I can write your poem for you,' said Ganesha. 'But I have a condition. My pen should never stop. If you ever hesitate while reciting and my pen pauses, it will not start again, and I will leave right away.'

Vyasa thought for a while and replied, 'I agree. But I have a condition too. You cannot write a single word or verse without understanding it fully.'

Ganesha pondered over this but decided that it was an easy condition to commit to. After all, he was a god and Vyasa a mere human being. How could Vyasa write something that he wouldn't understand? Hence, he agreed to Vyasa's condition and sat down to write.

Vyasa began dictating the poem. But whenever he ran out of material and needed some time, he would compose a verse with difficult words and complicated phrases. Even Lord Ganesha had to stop and think to decipher those phrases, while Vyasa composed few more in his mind. Thus, the great story of the Mahabharata began to take shape.

Long ago, a king named Shantanu ruled over a vast kingdom in northern India. Hastinapur was the capital city of his kingdom. One day, King Shantanu was strolling along the riverbank, enjoying the cool breeze and listening to the soothing gurgle of the flowing water.

Suddenly, he saw a beautiful maiden rise from the water and walk towards the riverbank. Shantanu was awestruck by her exquisite beauty—it was love at first sight. He felt an irresistible force pull him towards the lady. 'Whoever you are, my lady, I am deeply in love with you and cannot live a single moment without you. Please marry me and save my life. I, King Shantanu of Hastinapur, beg for your mercy,' he beseeched the gorgeous woman.

The lady smiled and replied, 'I am flattered, O king! But I have a couple of conditions for any suitor who wants to marry me. If you can agree to my conditions, I will marry you. I must warn you, these conditions are not easy to keep, especially for a husband.'

'For you, I can agree to any condition,' came the reply.

'Listen to them before you agree. First, you can never ask or inquire about who I am, or where I come from. Second, you can never stop me or demand an explanation for any of my actions—*whatever* they may be. If you ever break your promise, I'll leave you at once. Can you agree to these conditions?'

Love crazed, Shantanu didn't think the conditions through and replied, 'I agree! I will never ask you who you are, and will never stop you from doing anything. Now will you please marry me?' The lady agreed. Shantanu took her to his palace in Hastinapur and married her in a grand wedding ceremony. The couple spent a splendid year together until their first child, a boy, was born.

When Shantanu heard the news that his wife had given birth to a beautiful little boy, he left his court and ran to the birthing chamber. As he entered the room, he saw his queen pick up the newborn baby, wrap him in a shawl and walk out of the room. Shantanu was about to ask where she was going, but remembered his promise and kept quiet. He followed her as she left the palace and went to the bank of the river where they had met. And there he saw his queen drop the baby into the river. Within moments, the boy sunk into the deep waters. Shantanu was horrified. How could a mother do such a thing to her own child? He wanted to shout at and berate his wife, but again, he remembered his promise and kept his mouth shut.

After about a year, when he had all but forgotten the trauma of losing his first son, the queen gave birth to another child. And this time too, the shocked king saw his queen drown the baby in the river right after birth. Shantanu could neither protest, nor demand any explanation for her horrific behaviour.

And so, one after the other, the queen gave birth to seven sons, and each time she took the baby and drowned him in the river. The king, bound by his promise, stood silent and watched the tragic events.

When the eighth son was born, and the queen was about to drown the baby, Shantanu couldn't take it anymore. He shouted, 'Stop! Stop this murder! I won't tolerate this any longer.'

The queen halted midway and said, 'But you had promised ...'

The angry king hollered, 'I don't care for my promise anymore. How could you be so cruel? How could you kill your own children? I have kept my mouth shut all these years, but I won't let you kill this child of mine too.'

The queen smiled and said, 'You have broken your promise. Hence, I must leave you. But before I do that, I will reveal to you the reason for my actions. I am Ganga, the river goddess. These eight sons, seven of whom I have drowned, are the eight Vasus of the heavens. Once, the Vasus visited Rishi Vashishta's ashram. Provoked by their wives, they stole Vashishta's cow, Nandini. Vashishta was furious and cursed them that they would be born as humans and suffer, as any human does. The Vasus were scared. They cried and prayed for his mercy. Only Prabhas, the eighth Vasu and the one who had stolen the cow, stood defiant. Finally, Vashishta calmed down but he couldn't take back his curse. He revised the curse to mean that the Vasus would have to be born as humans but the seven who had been remorseful and begged for his mercy would live very short lives. I was assigned to be their mother, and I had to relieve them of their curse by drowning them right after their birth. But the eighth Vasu, Prabhas, would live a long life on earth and endure the sufferings of human life. This eighth son of yours is the eighth Vasu—Prabhas.'

Shantanu was amazed to hear this story. He pleaded with Ganga, 'Please don't leave! How will our son grow up without a mother?'

Ganga remained unmoved, 'I am sorry. My job is over. I must go now. I'll take this child and train him to be a worthy son to you, after which I'll return your son to you.' Saying so, she disappeared into the river with the newborn baby.

Shantanu was heartbroken. Sad and depressed, he somehow managed to run his kingdom, but kept cursing himself for not keeping his promise.

Every day, he would go back to the river bank with the hope of seeing Ganga return with their son. Days passed, months passed, years too, but Ganga didn't appear. Finally, one day, while he was taking his usual stroll along the river bank, Shantanu spotted a handsome young boy playing. He felt a strange affinity towards the boy. As he walked towards him, Ganga emerged from the river and said, 'O King, here is your son, the eighth child whom I took away with me. He has grown up and has mastered the art of warfare from the great Rishi Parashurama, and is as skilled and powerful as his guru. He has learnt all the scriptures and holy texts from the great Sage Vashishta and has become the wisest of the wise. His name is Devabrata. As I had promised, I have come to return him to you. Please accept him.'

Shantanu was ecstatic. He embraced Devabrata and took him to his palace in Hastinapur. Soon, Devabrata became the most popular prince of Hastinapur. His gentle and kind behaviour, his courage and strength, his wisdom and knowledge made him the obvious choice as the heir to the throne.

One day, Devabrata was riding his horse in a meadow nearby, when he saw a huge army approaching. It was King Shalya's army, marching to attack Hastinapur. The eighteen-year-old Devabrata fought the entire army alone and defeated it. He captured King Shalya and brought him as a captive to his father's feet. Devabrata's courage and heroism impressed King Shantanu, leading him to anoint Devabrata the crown prince of Hastinapur.

Devabrata's Promise

Shantanu, although happy to have his son by his side, felt lonely at times. He missed Ganga and would often walk along the river side, thinking of her. During one such walk on a spring afternoon, Shantanu breathed in an intoxicating fragrance. It mesmerized him and drew him towards the river, where he saw a beautiful woman on a boat. Once again, the king was struck by Kamadev's arrow. Thoughts of Ganga vanished from his mind and he felt that this woman was his destiny. Shantanu walked up to the maiden and asked her, 'Who are you, my pretty lady?'

The woman smiled and said, 'I am Satyavati, daughter of Dasharaj, the king of the fishermen tribe.'

Shantanu gently held her hand and said, 'Satyavati, I am King Shantanu of Hastinapur. Your beauty has cast a spell on me and has made me your slave. I cannot live without you. Will you please marry me and be my queen?'

Satyavati replied coyly, 'O King, I am deeply honoured by your proposal. But you'll have to ask my father for my hand. If he agrees, I will have no objection.'

As the great king of Hastinapur, how could someone not agree to give his daughter in marriage to him, thought Shantanu, before saying, 'So be it!'

The confident king went to the fishermen's village and met Satyavati's father, Dasharaj. 'O king of the fishermen,' he said, 'I am King Shantanu of Hastinapur. I am in love with your beautiful daughter Satyavati. I would like to marry her and make her my queen. Would you please give me your permission and your blessings?'

Dasharaj welcomed Shantanu with joined hands and said, 'King Shantanu, I am honoured to hear your proposal. Satyavati is fortunate that a great king like you is her suitor. But as a father, I have my responsibility towards my daughter, and that's what's keeping me from accepting your proposal. I hope you'll pardon my insolence.'

Shantanu was taken aback. 'What is it that's bothering you? Tell me, and I'll try to quell your fears to the best of my ability,' he said.

Satyavati's father kept quiet for a while, and then continued politely, 'O King, we all know that you've proclaimed prince Devabrata the crown prince of Hastinapur. No doubt, Prince Devabrata deserves to be king. But then, if you marry my daughter, what will happen to her son? Powerful Devabrata will overshadow him and he would have no role to play in the palace. As a king myself, I cannot let that happen to my grandson.' He paused a while and continued, 'If you can promise that after you, Satyavati's son would be made king, then I'll have no objection to giving my daughter's hand in marriage to you. Can you promise me that?'

Shantanu was shocked to hear this. He was keen to have Satyavati by his side as his consort and queen, but this time he did not lose his head. He said, 'That's impossible. I can never promise such a thing. Devabrata will rule Hastinapur after me.'

With folded hands, Dasharaj said, 'Then please forgive me, O King. I cannot agree to your union with my daughter.'

King Shantanu returned to the palace with a heavy heart. Devabrata had never seen his father so despondent. He asked, 'Father, what's the matter? Why are you so unhappy these days? Please let me know and I'll try my best to resolve the issue.'

Shantanu sighed, 'I am not worried about myself. I am worried about our kingdom. We have been constantly attacked by intruders from all directions and you have been fighting them all. I know you are invincible. But accidents happen. If something ever happens to you, what will happen to this kingdom? Who'll protect the people of Hastinapur? What will happen to our Kuru dynasty? Wise men say, having only one son is the same as having none.'

Devabrata sensed that the problem ran deeper. He inquired with the ministers and other well-wishers of the king. Finally, Shantanu's charioteer gave Devabrata the real cause of his father's despair. He told Devabrata about Satyavati and how her father Dasharaj had rejected Shantanu's proposal to marry her. Devabrata mounted his chariot and dashed to Satyavati's father. He asked Dasharaj, 'O King Dasharaj, I hear you've rejected my father's proposal to marry your daughter Satyavati. Tell me, what can I do to make you agree?'

Dasharaj said, 'I have already told your father my precondition. I am concerned that if your father marries my daughter, my grandchildren would be deprived. You are the crown prince of Hastinapur, and after your father, you'd be the king, while my grandchildren will have no chance at ascending the throne.'

Not wasting another breath, Devabrata said, 'Is that all? Then, I Devabrata, son of Ganga, promise that I will never claim the throne of Hastinapur. I will never become the king. Satyavati's son—your grandson—will be king. Will that satisfy you?'

Dasharaj was still not satisfied. He said, 'That's really kind of you, Prince Devabrata. But even if you renounce the throne, what about your children? When they grow up, they'd certainly stake their claim to the throne. And this could result in a terrible feud in the family. I cannot allow this to happen.'

Devabrata thought for a while. Then he spoke, 'O king, I stand before you, before the gods, and promise that I'll never marry and that I will stay celibate forever.'

Hearing this mighty vow, the gods showered flowers on Devabrata. They chanted 'Bhishma! Bhishma!' in his praise. Henceforth, for this 'bhisam' or profound vow, he was named 'Bhishma'.

Bhishma's vow quelled Dasharaj's fears and he agreed to give Satyavati's hand in marriage to King Shantanu. The young prince took Satyavati in his chariot and brought her to the palace, where her arrival washed away Shantanu's misery. The happy king embraced his son in gratitude. Soon, the wedding was held and Satyavati became the queen of Hastinapur.

When Shantanu came to know of his son's terrible promise, he was distraught. Bhishma consoled him, saying, 'Father, your happiness is priceless to me. I can give up my life to see a smile on your face. This vow is nothing in comparison.'

Shantanu blessed his son and said, 'My dear son, I give you this boon that you will have the power to decide your time of death. No one would be able to kill you unless you want to die.'

This boon, just short of immortality, made Bhishma invincible to everybody but himself.

2

Amba's Plight

AFTER THE WEDDING, KING SHANTANU AND SATYAVATI SETTLED DOWN in the palace and enjoyed their conjugal life, while Bhishma got busy fighting wars and defending the kingdom from invaders. In due course, Satyavati gave birth to two boys—Chitrangad and Vichitravirya. Chitrangad grew up to be a handsome young prince and soon joined his brother Bhishma in the battlefield, but lost his life in one of the battles. The pain of losing Chitrangad was too much for Shantanu to bear. Besides, he was suffering from health problems, leading to his death. Vichitravirya was still a child. But he had to be crowned the king of Hastinapur since Bhishma had promised to never ascend the throne. Bhishma took up the responsibility of looking after the day-to-day affairs of the kingdom on behalf of his young brother.

When Vichitravirya came of age, his mother Satyavati started to think about his marriage. She summoned Bhishma and said, 'My dear Devabrata, you have taken the vow of celibacy and relieved yourself of the responsibility to preserve the Kuru lineage.

Chitrangad also left us without leaving an heir. I am worried ... what if something happens to Vichitravirya too? I think we should get him married soon.'

Devabrata replied, 'Mother, I understand your concern. But finding a bride worthy of becoming the queen of Hastinapur is not easy. She must not only be of royal heritage, but must also be of unparalleled beauty. Let me engage our spies and the royal matchmakers and see what they can come up with.'

Soon, the spies came back with news that made Bhishma quite upset. The king of Kashi had three beautiful daughters—Amba, Ambika and Ambalika. It was said that their beauty even surpassed the splendour of the apsaras, the celestial maidens of the heavens. Men could only dream of having such beauties as their bride. The spies revealed that the king of Kashi had arranged a swayamvara for his three daughters. A swayamvara is an event where a woman could select her husband from a line-up of eligible men, using any criteria she preferred. They also reported that the Kashi king had invited all the major kings and princes to the swayamvara, but skipped the Kurus. Bhishma was enraged. This was an outright insult to the Kuru dynasty. Indeed, there was some animosity between Kashi and Hastinapur, but who would dare not invite the mighty Kurus? Bhishma decided, even though not invited, he would attend the swayamvara and bring the three princesses to Hastinapur by force. This was accepted practice in the Kshatriya tradition and he would exercise his rights as a Kshatriya and teach the king of Kashi a good lesson.

On the day of the swayamvara, Bhishma arrived in Kashi on his golden chariot. As he stepped into the swayamvara hall, the invited kings were surprised to see him. They knew Bhishma had vowed never to marry. Then why was he there? Were the Kashi princesses so attractive that even Bhishma couldn't honour his promise? The king of Kashi was taken aback too. It was not customary to attend a swayamvara without an invitation and the king had made sure that the Kurus were not on the invitee list. Soon, the three princess, Amba, Ambika and Ambalika entered the hall, and all attention shifted towards them. The invited kings and princes were awestruck by their beauty. The three princesses began to sashay around the hall, glancing swiftly at their suitors, while the men held their breath in awe. Suddenly, Bhishma stepped in front of the princesses and, blocking their path, said, 'I am Bhishma of the Kuru dynasty. I am here on behalf of my brother Vichitravirya. I want to take you to Hastinapur. So come with me in peace, else I'll have to take you by force.' Then he turned to the king of Kashi and said, 'O King, you have insulted the Kuru dynasty by not inviting my brother Vichitravirya to the swayamvara. As per the Kshatriya tradition, I am taking them with me by force. Stop me if you can.'

The kings and princes in the hall started shouting in protest. 'You cannot do this, Bhishma. We will not let you get away with the princesses.'

Bhishma didn't pay any heed to the protestations. He firmly gripped the hands of the three princesses and dragged them to his chariot. Startled, the king of Kashi started shouting at his guards, 'Stop him! Stop Bhishma!' The guards chased after the prince. Frustrated, the king of Kashi berated the guests, 'What are you doing here? Go stop Bhishma. How dare he steal my daughters right in front of your eyes?'

As if breaking out of a trance, the assembled princes picked up their weapons and ran after Bhishma who was, by then, already on his chariot, accompanied by the princesses. He picked up his bow and commanded his charioteer, 'Let's go! Now!' and his chariot shot out of the grounds, leaving a cloud of dust behind.

The guards and warriors of Kashi mounted their chariots and began to chase Bhishma. They fired arrows at him, but Bhishma deflected them all and mounted a ferocious counterattack. Soon, they began to give up. Only Prince Salwa kept up the chase, determined to get back the princesses. But Bhishma broke the desperate king's bow, destroyed his chariot, killed his horses, and left him humiliated and stranded in the middle of nowhere.

Soon, Bhishma's chariot arrived at the palace of Hastinapur. He escorted the princesses to Satyavati and said, 'Mother, here are the Kashi princesses—Amba, Ambika and Ambalika. Please accept them as Vichitravirya's brides.'

Satyavati was delighted to see the beautiful princesses. She called Vichitravirya, who was ecstatic to see them. The women were way beyond his expectations. Before he or Satyavati could react, Amba, the oldest of the three sisters, spoke. 'O queen mother, if you'd permit, I'd like to say something.'

Satyavati said, 'Sure, Amba. Tell me, what do you have to say?'

'Mother, I had chosen Prince Salwa as my husband. We are in love with each other. Today, at the swayamvara, I had planned to garland him as my husband. So, as per the tradition, I belong to Salwa. I thought I should let you know this before you decide anything.'

Bhishma now realized the reason for Salwa's valiant attempt to stop the kidnapping. He felt ashamed.

Satyavati replied, 'Amba, I am glad you mentioned this to me. Yes, of course, you belong to Salwa and you must return to him. Devabrata, please make arrangements to send Amba back to Salwa, honourably. She must be treated with care and respect while she is our guest here.'

Bhishma arranged for a comfortable chariot and a dozen armed guards to escort Amba back to her lover. He instructed the charioteer to take Amba to Salwa with care. Then he turned to Amba and said, 'Amba, please accept my apology. If I had known about your relationship with Salwa, I would have never brought you here. Please go back to Salwa and forgive me if you can.'

When Amba entered Salwa's palace, she didn't receive a warm welcome at all. She was made to wait in a private chamber. After several hours, the prince came to meet her. He asked, 'Amba, what brings you here?'

Amba was surprised to hear his cold voice. 'I am back, Salwa. I have come back to you.'

Salwa looked the other way and said, 'You shouldn't have. Bhishma has won you at the swayamvara and I couldn't stop him. You belong to Bhishma, not me.'

Amba couldn't believe her ears. 'Salwa, are you asking me to return? You know Bhishma's vow. He would never marry me. How can I go back to him? Besides, I love you. I have always seen you as my husband. And that's why the Kurus sent me back to you. You cannot do this to me now.'

Salwa didn't budge. 'I'm sorry, Amba. I cannot accept you. Please go away.' Salwa refused to listen to Amba's pleas and left the room.

The young princess was stunned. She didn't know what to do. She walked out of the palace and requested the charioteer to take her to Kashi, to her father. But her father also refused to accept her. 'Amba, you do not belong here any more. You belong to the Kurus. Go back to them.' The Kashi king slammed the door at her face. Humiliated and enraged, Amba returned to Hastinapur.

Bhishma was busy making arrangements for his brother's wedding, so when he saw Amba, he was surprised to say the least. 'Amba, what happened? Why have you returned?'

Amba replied, 'Bhishma, Salwa sent me back to you. Do you know why?'

'No, I don't.'

'Because you won me from him. Because you brought me to Hastinapur after defeating my father and Salwa.' Amba paused a while, and said, 'Bhishma, you must marry me.'

'What?' Bhishma was shocked. 'How can I marry you? You know, I vowed not to marry ever in my life.'

Amba looked right into his eyes and said, 'I don't care. You are responsible for my situation today. So you must suffer the consequences. You must marry me now!'

'That's not possible. But let me ask Vichitravirya if he wishes to marry you.'

Vichitravirya refused his brother, saying, 'Brother, I cannot marry a woman who has already accepted another man as her husband.'

Bhishma went back to Amba with the sad news. 'Amba, I am sorry. I cannot help you. I suggest you return to your father in Kashi.'

Amba was furious. 'Don't you think I tried it already? My father refused to take me. My lover rejected me. All because of you. I won't leave you. You must accept me as your wife.'

Bhishma was firm in his resolve. 'Amba, I sympathize with you. Please don't ask me to do the impossible. I cannot break my vow. Please forgive me.'

'Then what am I supposed to do now? Tell me? What should I do?' cried Amba.

Bhishma was at a loss for words. He could only say, 'I don't know!'

Amba was seething in anger. With bloodshot eyes, she said, 'People say you are the bravest and the most gallant warrior of all. I say, you are a coward! You have shunned your responsibility under the garb of your ridiculous vow. You'll pay for this dearly. You'll die for this injustice. I will kill you, Bhishma.'

'You cannot kill me,' Bhishma responded with a faint smile that reeked of arrogance. 'Nobody can kill me, unless I wish to die.'

Amba looked at him with deep hatred in her eyes. 'But I will. I will find a way to kill you. You can be sure of that. Till then, you just wait.' Amba turned around and walked out of the palace doors.

As Bhishma watched her leave, he muttered, 'I will wait, Amba. I will wait for you.'

3

Birth of Dhritarashtra, Pandu and Vidura

WITH GREAT POMP, VICHITRAVIRYA GOT MARRIED TO AMBIKA AND Ambalika. But their married life was cut short by the sudden death of Vichitravirya. Satyavati was grief-stricken. Not only was she saddened by her son's death, she was also worried about the future of the Kuru dynasty. Vichitravirya did not leave a son who could be the torchbearer of the Kuru legacy. Is this the end of the Kuru lineage, she wondered.

In those days, if a husband didn't have the ability to produce a child, it was acceptable to use the services of a virile man to ensure that the wife was with child. The man could be someone from the family, or a Brahmin, considered to be of noble origin. This practice was known as niyoga. Satyavati was convinced that if the Kuru dynasty had to be preserved, she had no other option than to invoke the practice of niyoga. She called Bhishma and said, 'My son, the fate of the Kuru dynasty now lies in your hands. I would like you to use the practice of niyoga and father a son with Amba or Ambalika.'

Bhishma was shocked. 'Mother, how could you say such a thing? You know of my vow.'

'I know, my son. But difficult times call for difficult measures. The fate of our dynasty is in jeopardy. We cannot let the lineage die with us. You must break your promise for the sake of your race, of your ancestors' legacy.'

Bhishma was adamant. 'Forgive me, mother. I can never break my promise. You'll have to find some other option.'

Satyavati was desperate. 'What other option? Tell me if you have a better idea.'

Bhishma thought for a while and said, 'Why don't you ask brother Vyasa to do the job? He is your son; hence belongs to the family. Besides, he is the most learned and the wisest person we know. I can think of no better person to help us in this crisis.'

The moment Bhishma mentioned Vyasa, memories flooded Satyavati's mind. She remembered the days when she was a young, unmarried girl who rowed her father Dasharaj's boat across the Yamuna to ferry passengers. One day, Rishi Parashar came by to cross the river. Satyavati's beauty mesmerized the great sage. He held Satyavati's hand and said, 'Come to me, my dear. I wish to give you a son.'

'O great rishi, it will be my honour to bear your child,' she said. 'But, I am afraid, if I lose my virginity, I would never get married.'

'Don't worry, my dear,' replied Parashar. 'You will remain a virgin even after you bear my child.'

Parashar held her and drew her close. Satyavati was uncomfortable. 'Please stop,' she pleaded. 'There are people around, the gods above. I can't do this with them watching.'

Parashar laughed. Using his magical powers, he created a dense fog around the boat to screen off curious onlookers and pulled Satyavati to his chest.

In due course, Satyavati gave birth to a boy in an island on the Yamuna River and he was named Krishna Dwaipayana. When Dwaipayana grew up, he left his mother to become a hermit and a sage. His knowledge and analysis of the Vedas earned him the name Vyasa.

Satyavati liked Bhishma's idea and summoned Vyasa, who appeared before her and said, 'Mother, I am glad to see you after so long. Please tell me, what can I do for you?'

Satyavati explained her predicament and asked Vyasa to father a child with Ambika. The hermit replied, 'Mother, I understand your situation and I will do as you ask. But do you think Ambika would agree to this proposal?'

Vyasa had a reason for asking this question. Although he was respected by everybody, even the gods, he was an ugly and grotesque-looking man. He never cared for his looks, and was always covered in dirt and filth, and smelled awful. No woman would dare to come close to him.

Satyavati comforted him. 'Don't worry about that. I will explain everything to her. She is aware of the crisis and would do her best to keep the Kuru lineage alive. You just go and wait in the bedroom. I'll send Ambika to you.'

'So be it,' said Vyasa.

Satyavati went to Ambika and told her about the plan. Ambika didn't object to the idea of having a child with a rishi, but when she heard of Vyasa, she was scared. She had heard of his appearance and shuddered at the thought of sleeping with him. Besides, she was aware that the rishi was short-tempered, and if he was not satisfied, he could punish her with a horrible curse. But Satyavati was insistent, and she had to agree. Satyavati asked the maids to dress Ambika in her best clothes and jewellery. When she was ready, Satyavati took Ambika to a bedroom and closed the door. Ambika was so scared that she kept her eyes closed. Vyasa got up from the bed and pulled

Ambika close. But she didn't open her eyes even for a single moment the whole night. The next morning, Vyasa told Satyavati, 'Mother, I have obeyed your command. Ambika will give birth to a strong and handsome son, but he would be born blind.'

Satyavati was shocked. 'How could a blind man be the king?' she asked. 'You must give us a normal, healthy child. Go back to the bedroom. I will send Ambalika in. You must give her a son, too.'

Vyasa agreed.

Satyavati went to Ambalika and told her, 'Ambalika, I want you to give the Kuru dynasty a son from Vyasa. Go to him. But remember, do not keep your eyes closed.'

Ambalika was scared too. When she entered Vyasa's room, she forced herself to keep her eyes open. But she was so afraid that the blood drained off her face. Her face turned pale as Vyasa pulled her to his chest.

The next morning, Vyasa said to Satyavati, 'Mother, Ambalika's son won't be blind, but he would be pale and frail looking. But don't worry, he will be strong and powerful.' Saying so, Vyasa left Hastinapur.

In due course, Ambika gave birth to a blind boy who was named Dhritarashtra. A few days later, Ambalika gave birth to a pale-looking boy, just as Vyasa had predicted. He was named Pandu.

Satyavati was not happy. She wanted a handsome grandson, without any physical blemish. So she called Vyasa again and asked Ambalika to have another son with him. But the princess didn't want to face Vyasa again. She dressed up her pretty maid in nice clothes and jewellery, put lots of makeup on her and sent her to Vyasa's chamber. The maid was not afraid of Vyasa. She greeted him with due respect and accepted him with love and dignity. Vyasa was very pleased. He told the maid, 'You'll have a great son, who would be the wisest and the most learned of the princes.'

In due course, the maid gave birth to a beautiful little boy, perfect in all aspects. He was named Vidura.

Dhritarashtra, Pandu and Vidura grew up together in the palace of Hastinapur. Dhritarashtra, though blind, was very strong and became skilled in using many weapons; Pandu grew up to become a great archer; while Vidura grew up learning all the sacred texts and scriptures, and was the most learned and wisest of all. Although Dhritarashtra was the eldest of the three brothers, he couldn't become the king because of his blindness. So, Pandu was installed as the king of Hastinapur. Vidura, the son of the maid, was appointed the prime minister.

Pandu proved to be a great ruler. He conquered many kingdoms and expanded Kuru rule far and wide. He amassed huge amounts of wealth from the vanquished kings and became the richest ruler of the land. The people of Hastinapur were pleased to have a ruler like Pandu who took good care of them. Soon, Pandu came to be known as the best king the Kuru dynasty ever had.

Gandhari, Kunti and Madri

When Dhritarashtra came of age, Bhishma arranged for him to be married. Subala, the king of Gandhara, had a beautiful daughter named Gandhari. Bhishma sent Subala the marriage proposal and the Gandhara king agreed. The marriage would give him the opportunity to build an alliance with the mighty Kuru dynasty and it was too attractive a proposal to pass. Gandhari too was quite pleased. But when she heard about Dhritarashtra's blindness, she decided to share the fate of her husband. Taking a piece of dark cloth, she tied her eyes in a permanent blindfold. Gandhari's brother Shakuni was not happy with the union. He resented the fact that the Kurus, especially Bhishma, had offered his sister the blind Dhritarashtra and not the handsome King Pandu. Besides, his bitterness grew every time he saw his sister in a blindfold. He vowed to take revenge on Bhishma, Pandu and his clan for their unfair treatment of Gandhari.

Kunti, the adopted daughter of King Kuntibhoj, selected Pandu as her husband at the swayamvara arranged by her father. Kunti was also known as Pritha and she happened to be the aunt of Lord Krishna, who plays an important role in this story. But Kunti had a little secret, and we'll learn about it later.

Later, Pandu also married Madri, the beautiful sister of King Shalya of the Madra kingdom.

4

Birth of the Kuru Princes

AFTER FIGHTING MANY WARS AND AMASSING GREAT AMOUNTS OF RICHES for his kingdom, Pandu wanted to take a break. So he requested his brother Dhritarashtra to take care of the kingdom and went on a long hunting trip to the forests with his two queens, Kunti and Madri. They travelled to many countries and forests, and were having a great time.

One day, Pandu went hunting in a dark and dense forest. He left his entourage behind with the hope of enjoying the thrills of hunting alone. Suddenly, he heard a rustle in the bushes ahead. He tiptoed towards the source of the sound. And there, behind the thickets, he saw a deer couple playing with each other and making love. Without making a noise, he raised his bow, aimed, and shot his shabd-vedi ban or the sound-guided arrow. Pandu was an excellent archer, and he made no mistake. He heard a cry, but the voice was of a human. He ran towards his target, the deer couple. There he found struck with his arrow a man and a woman in each other's embrace. The man was Rishi or Sage Kindama and the woman was his wife. Kindama was alive but was bleeding profusely. His wife was already dead.

Pandu was intensely remorseful for having killed a rishi and his wife while they were making love. He knelt beside the dying sage and said, 'O Rishi, I made a grave mistake. I thought I saw a deer couple! And I shot you without the knowledge that it was you. Please forgive me.'

The rishi raised his head a little and said, 'Pandu, how could you be so cruel? How could you kill a couple making love, be it human or deer or any other living being? It is the most heinous crime one can commit and I cannot forgive you for that. I, Rishi Kindama, hereby curse you: you too will die a painful death if you try to make love to a woman.' And saying this, he breathed his last.

Pandu was devastated. He was terrified. He knew a rishi's curse was bound to come true. He didn't know what to do. He went back to his wives and told them about the incident. Kunti and Madri were shocked to hear of the curse, for it implied that they could never have a child with Pandu. But they still tried to console Pandu. Kunti said, 'Please don't worry. We will never demand any physical affection from you. We will never ask for a child from you.'

Pandu was still upset. He decided to give up his kingdom and the luxury of his palace life and live in the forests like an ascetic, a hermit. He believed it would be the right penance for his crime. Maybe his sacrifice will not go unnoticed by the gods and one day they might release him from the curse. Pandu sent a messenger to Hastinapur informing Dhritarashtra of his decision, and asked him to take care of the kingdom with the help of Bhishma and Vidura. He asked his queens to return to the palace, but Kunti and Madri didn't agree. They said, 'O King, we are your wives and we have the right to share your fate. We cannot go back to the palace without you.'

So the three started their life of penance and hardship in the forests along with the other hermits and sages who lived there.

Days passed, weeks too, then months. Pandu, Kunti and Madri were getting used to their life in the forest. Living off the land, in the lap of nature, seemed quite enjoyable now. Pandu was still unhappy. A disturbing thought kept bothering him: that he could never father a child. The thought of leaving the world without an heir was horrifying to him. According to the Hindu way of life, a man can achieve salvation only when his son performs his last rites. Besides, leaving no heir also meant the end of his line.

One day, he called Kunti in private and said, 'Kunti, I just cannot bear the thought of dying without leaving an heir behind.' Kunti remained quiet. Pandu continued, 'Kunti, you know, if a man cannot father a child, his wife can get one with the help of a family member or a Brahmin. It is accepted in our tradition.' He even gave the example of his and his brother Dhritarashtra's birth. 'Kunti, you and Madri must do the same. I insist!'

Kunti replied, 'O King, if you permit me, let me tell you a secret. Long ago, when I was a teenager, Rishi Durvasa came to visit my father's palace, and I had the honour of taking care of him. He was pleased with my hospitality and granted me a boon. He gave me a mantra which empowered me to invoke any god and have a child with him. So, if you desire, I can use the mantra and have a son from any god you'd like me to have the child with.'

Pandu was ecstatic with joy. He said, 'Kunti, you must use your boon and beget a son for me. Please invoke Dharma, the god of righteousness and religion, so our son would be the wisest man of all.'

Kunti went into the hut and chanted the mantra to invoke Dharma. Dharma appeared before her and in due time Kunti gave birth to a beautiful boy named Yudhishthira. Yudhishthira means one who can stay calm and steady in the midst of a battle.

Pandu wanted more. He asked Kunti to invoke the god of the winds. Kunti obliged and Bheem was born of their union. Next she called upon Indra, the king of the Gods, and had a son named Arjun with him.

Watching Kunti give birth to three sons made Madri want a child too. She asked Kunti, 'Would you please share your mantra with me? I too would like to bear a son with a god.'

'But Rishi Durvasa didn't give me permission to share the mantra with others,' Kunti replied.

Pandu intervened, 'Please Kunti, please be kind with Madri. Please let her have a child too.'

Kunti said, 'O King, your wish is my command. Madri, I will share the mantra with you, but you can use it only once!'

Kunti gave her the mantra. Madri then invoked the twin gods, the Ashwins, the celestial physicians, and of them were born Nakul and Sahadev, the beautiful twins.

Kunti was not happy at all. She said, 'Madri, you tricked me. I permitted you to use the mantra once to have one child, but you invoked the twins and abused the power. Now I withdraw the mantra forever. Neither of us would be able to use the mantra any more.'

Pandu was happy with five sons—Yudhishthira, Bheem, Arjun, Nakul and Sahadev. As sons of Pandu, they came to be known as the Pandavas.

Meanwhile, in the palace of Hastinapur, Dhritarashtra and his wife Gandhari were not happy. When Yudhishthira was born, Gandhari was already pregnant. But she did not give birth to any child for almost two years. When she heard that Kunti has given birth to a boy, she grew impatient. She called a maid and asked her to bring an iron rod. She commanded her, 'Hit my belly with this rod! Hit me hard!'

The maid was scared. How could she hit the queen? She hesitated, but Gandhari yelled at her, 'I told you, hit me! I don't want to stay pregnant any longer. Hit my belly. Hit it hard!'

The maid hit her hard, several times. Gandhari screamed in pain and went into labour. Soon, something dropped out of her womb. Gandhari was in her blindfold and couldn't see. She asked her maid, 'What is it? A boy?' The maid remained quiet. She asked again, 'Tell me, what it is? A boy or a girl?'

The maid said, 'Oh Queen, it is neither! It is a ball of flesh, hard as a rock.'

Gandhari was devastated. She cried out loud and asked the maid to throw the ball of flesh into the river.

Just then, Vyasa appeared. He told the maid, 'No, don't throw it away!'

Gandhari said, 'Rishi Vyasa, your boon didn't come true. You once blessed me that I'll bear one hundred sons. See what I have given birth to! A ball of flesh!'

Vyasa said, 'Gandhari, don't despair. My words will come true.' He called the maid and said, 'Take this ball of flesh and put it in a jar of fresh water. Soon, it will break up into one hundred foetuses. Then place each foetus in a separate jar filled with ghee.'

The maid followed his instructions and, after a few months, one hundred boys were born in the jars filled with ghee and other nutrients. First was born Duryodhan and next Dushasana followed by ninety-eight more sons. Gandhari also gave birth to a girl named Dushala. The hundred sons of Dhritarashtra and Gandhari were known as the Kauravas.

Back in the forest, Pandu was happy spending his days with Kunti, Madri and their five sons. He was no longer depressed, and maybe the thought of Rishi Kindama's curse was fading away.

It was a beautiful spring morning. Pandu and Madri were roaming in the forest, picking fruits and berries for their mid-day meal while back home Kunti took care of the boys. Laden with the fragrance of spring blossoms, the air was intoxicating. Madri looked gorgeous in the golden sunshine falling on her through the new leaves and branches of the trees above. Pandu, walking next to her and watching her beauty, felt something stir in him. Suddenly, he felt an irresistible urge to make love to her. For a while, he tried to hold himself back, but soon his desire overwhelmed him and, with uncontrolled lust, he embraced his wife. Madri was shocked. 'Stop it! Stop it, O King! You cannot do this! Don't you remember the curse?' But no words reached Pandu's ears. He was too excited to remember Kindama's curse. He embraced Madri and showered her with kisses, while she tried her best to escape from his clutches. Right then, Pandu felt a shooting pain in his chest: he couldn't breathe. Clasping his chest, he dropped down. The next moment, he was lying dead on the ground next to Madri. Kindama's curse had come true.

'Why? Why did you do this?' cried Madri!

Hearing Madri's cries, Kunti came running and found Pandu lying dead with his head on her lap. Madri was crying hysterically. Kunti knew right away what had happened. She screamed in rage, 'Madri, how could you let this happen? How could you do this to our husband? Why did you have to lure him to his death? Did you forget his curse? '

'Believe me, Kunti, I tried ... I tried my best to stop him. But he didn't listen.'

Soon, Kunti realized, this had to happen. A rishi's curse could never go unfulfilled. It was Pandu's destiny. Once she had calmed down, she told Madri, 'Well, in a way, you are lucky and I envy you. You at least saw his happy face before he died. Now let's go and inform the boys and our neighbours. His funeral needs to be arranged.'

Madri said, 'Kunti, I have one request. I want to give up my life and follow my husband to the next world. I couldn't satisfy his desire in this world; maybe I could do so in the next world. Please take care of Nakul and Sahadev as your own sons. I know they will not miss their mother in you.'

Kunti tried to deter her from her decision, but Madri was adamant. When Pandu's funeral pyre was lit, she stepped into the fire to sacrifice herself with the hope of joining her husband in the next life.

The sages and hermits dwelling in the forest, who were the neighbours of the Pandavas, advised Kunti to return to Hastinapur with her five sons. 'They are the rightful heirs of Hastinapur. There, they will receive the best training under the guidance of Bhishma and Vidura, and grow up to be the future rulers of the land,' they said. So, Kunti returned to Hastinapur with Yudhishthira, Bheem, Arjun, Nakul and Sahadev. Bhishma greeted them with open arms and tears in his eyes. And so the Pandavas started the next phase of their life in Hastinapur.

5

Childhood of the Kuru Princes

THE PANDAVA BOYS STARTED THEIR NEW LIFE IN THE PALACE OF Hastinapur along with their one hundred cousins, the Kauravas. The good-natured Pandava brothers soon became the favourites in the palace. Their gentle behaviour, their kindness, their respectfulness and humble attitude not only pleased the Kuru elders, but also made them popular among the people of Hastinapur. It became quite clear that the throne of Hastinapur would soon belong to Yudhishthira. He was not only the eldest of the brothers, but also the son of Pandu, the rightful king of Hastinapur. Dhritarashtra was nothing but a caretaker. But this did not please the Kaurava brothers, especially Duryodhan, whose ambition was to ascend the throne of Hastinapur as the next Kuru king. Being the son of the present King Dhritarashtra, he believed he was the rightful heir to the throne. A grave injustice had been done to his father when his younger brother Pandu was made the king of Hastinapur, for Dhritarashtra had proven his mettle after Pandu had passed. This logic reinforced his justification to claim the throne even more.

Bheem was the other cause for the Kaurava brothers' annoyance. Being the strongest and the most powerful of the lot, Bheem would always bully the Kauravas, even if in good humour. He would challenge them to wrestle with him and proceed to thrash and toss them like feather pillows. Sometimes, the Kauravas would climb right up to the highest branches of a tree to escape Bheem. However, Bheem would hold the trunk of the tree and shake it so vigorously that they would drop like ripe fruits. Duryodhan knew that they had to do something about Bheem, else he had the capacity to decimate all the Kaurava brothers. So he came up with a devious plan to get rid of Bheem.

One day, he and Dushasana invited the Pandavas to a picnic by the riverside. 'It's so hot these days. Let's go to our riverside resort and have a nice picnic. We can swim, play and eat the delicious meals prepared by the royal cooks,' he said. The Pandavas happily agreed.

Soon, the cousins went to their grand riverside palace. The Pandavas played in the gardens, swam in the cool river and had a wonderful time. However, the Kauravas had a rough time—Bheem sometimes flung them in the water, held them underwater as they gasped for air on occasion, and sometimes created huge waves in the water which tossed the brothers out of their rafts. The angry brothers went to Duryodhan and complained. Duryodhan replied, 'Bheem will be out of our way forever. You just wait and watch.'

After enjoying all the fun and frolic, the boys would enjoy a grand feast. The royal cooks would prepare umpteen delicious dishes for the princes. The princes were hungry, and they enjoyed every bit that was served to them. Bheem was a glutton and could finish a feast meant for twenty men in one go. Soon, he finished all the food the chefs had prepared for them. Just as he was scraping off the last morsel from his plate, Duryodhan said to him, 'Brother Bheem, you must still be hungry. How could this insufficient food satisfy your appetite? I have made some special arrangements for you and asked our private

cook to make some extra food for you. Come with me. I will serve you myself.'

Being quite naïve, Bheem didn't suspect anything at all and was, in fact, elated. He went with Duryodhan to a secluded spot behind the resort, where Dushasana brought him plates full of delicious food. Little did Bheem know that the dishes had been laced with a deadly poison that could kill a person in seconds. Any other man would have died after a single bite. Astonishingly, nothing happened to Bheem. He finished all the poisoned food given to him and it seemed to have no effect. Duryodhan and Dushasana realized that the poison would take some time to work on a person as hefty as Bheem. So they said, 'That was a grand feast! Perfect time for an afternoon siesta. Why don't you take a little rest under this tree?'

Bheem yawned and agreed to take a quick nap. He lay down in the shade of the banyan tree by the river bank. Duryodhan was relieved that the poison has started to take effect. Soon, Bheem sunk into a deep coma, while Duryodhan and Dushasana watched from a distance. When they were sure that Bheem was not waking up anytime soon, they tied his hands and feet together using strong ropes. Then they dragged him down the bank and threw him into the river. Bheem sank like a heavy rock.

Duryodhan and Dushasana went back to their brothers who were getting ready to leave. Yudhishthira was looking for Bheem. Duryodhan said, 'Bheem has already left for the palace. The son of Vayu challenged that he would beat our chariots and reach there well before us. Now let's go and try to prove him wrong.' They all leapt into their chariots and left for Hastinapur.

In the Land of the Nagas

As Bheem sank into the deep waters, the river currents took him via the underwater channels, through the crevasses in the river floor, down to the land of the Nagas or the celestial serpents. As his body rolled into the river bank, it crushed some of the serpents there. In anger, they struck Bheem several times with their deadly, venomous fangs. The serpent venom acted as an antidote to the poison in Bheem's body and soon he woke up from his coma. Bheem flexed his muscles to break the ropes tied to his arms and legs and stood up. The snake bites made him furious and he went on a rampage. He thrashed the Nagas, trampled them, and beat them to the ground. The serpents had no option but to flee. They went to their king, Vasuki, and complained, 'O King Vasuki, a human being has arrived in our lands. He is huge and strong. He is beating us up, and if this continues for long, none of us would survive. Please do something.'

The Nagas had the power to change their forms whenever they wished. Vasuki and his deputy, Arka, assumed human forms and went to meet Bheem near the river bank. When Arka saw Bheem, he recognized him to be his distant grandson. Once upon a time, Arka lived as a human being and had a regular human family. Kunti happened to be his niece. Arka introduced himself and embraced Bheem. Vasuki was also pleased to meet the great Kuru prince and invited him to his palace.

Vasuki said, 'Arka, we must treat our esteemed guest to our famous elixir. We must offer him a drink of our rasa.' Rasa was a delicious and intoxicating drink that gave the Nagas their super strength.

Arka said, 'Yes of course! Come with me, my dear grandson. Let me treat you to some rasa.'

The Nagas served Bheem a big pot full of rasa, and he drank it up in one long swig. They served him another pot, and he drank it all too. Plied with unending pots of rasa, Bheem drank eight pots of the intoxicating drink and he couldn't keep his eyes open any longer. Vasuki took him to a beautiful room in his palace, where he lay down

on the luxurious bed and went to sleep right away, not to wake up for
eight long days.

Meanwhile, in Hastinapur, Kunti and the Pandavas were extremely
worried for Bheem. As soon as they arrived at the palace from the resort
and found that Bheem was missing, they knew Duryodhan had lied.
Still, they waited for some time with the hope that he might turn up.
But he didn't. Kunti was afraid that Duryodhan had done something
evil to her son. Without any proof, she couldn't question him either.
She went to Vidura and said, 'Vidura, I think something bad has
happened to Bheem. He never goes anywhere without informing us.
I am afraid Duryodhan has harmed him.'

Vidura tried to console her: 'Don't worry, Kunti, no harm can
come to Bheem. He is the strongest of the brothers, and Duryodhan
wouldn't dare to do anything to him. Besides, Vyasa himself has
prophesied that your sons will enjoy a long life. I am sure, Bheem will
be back soon.'

Vidura was right. On the ninth day, Bheem returned to the palace.
When he woke up from his sleep, the rasa had given him immense
strength and he felt invigorated. He thanked Vasuki and Arka, and
asked for permission to go back home, which was heartily granted.

Kunti and the Pandava brothers were shocked to hear what
had transpired. They knew Duryodhan and Dushasana were evil-
minded, but they could never imagine that the Kauravas could stoop
so low. Yudhishthira advised, 'We should not talk about this and
not complain to anybody either. But we should always be vigilant
because, I am sure, Duryodhan will strike again.' So they went about
their life as if nothing had happened. Duryodhan and Dushasana
were also surprised to see Bheem back in the palace. But they kept
their mouths shut and began cooking up other plots to eliminate
their rivals.

6

Guru Dronacharya Arrives

$\mathbb{B}$ HISHMA HAD APPOINTED KRIPA, A BRAHMIN, TO TRAIN THE ROYAL princes in the art of warfare and weaponry. Kripa was doing his best and the brothers, especially the Pandavas, were fast in picking up the skills. Bhishma knew that the boys would soon need someone who could teach them the use of the most advanced weaponry and skills of warfare, and began looking for a new guru. Bhishma himself would have been the best teacher, but he was too busy with the administrative affairs that he handled on behalf of Dhritarashtra. Soon a strange incident happened, and Bhishma availed of the services of the greatest weapons teacher one could hope for.

One day, the Kuru princes were playing with a wooden ball in a meadow not far from the royal palace. Midway through the game, the ball rolled into a deep and unused well. It was dark inside and the boys could only see the tip of the ball floating in the water below. They were sad to lose the ball and kept blaming each other for this loss. Suddenly, a Brahmin in tattered clothes appeared. He saw the quarrelling boys and laughed at them: 'Aren't you the Kuru boys? You

can't even pick up a ball from a well? What kind of arms training did
you get from your guru?'

One of the brothers replied, 'Sir, do you see how deep the well is?
And what does our arms training have to do with it?'

'If you knew how to use your bows and arrows, you could have
picked up the ball,' smirked the Brahmin. He then took off a ring
from his finger and dropped it into the well and said, 'Here, not only
can I pick up the ball, I can also pick up this ring with my bow and
arrow. Would you like me to show you how?'

Yudhishthira was curious. 'Sir, please do. And we'll give you
whatever you want.'

'All I want is a good meal.'

'Sir, if you can do what you said, then not only a meal, we
will arrange for a permanent livelihood for you in the palace of
Hastinapur.'

The Brahmin smiled. He looked at the tall grass field around and
told the boys, 'Go and get me some reeds from those grasses.'

The boys ran to get the reeds. When they returned, the Brahmin
took the reed and sharpened one end of each reed using a knife.
Then he stood next to the well, concentrated for a while, and then
shot a reed into the well. The reed pierced the top of the floating
ball and stood vertical in perfect balance. He then took another reed
and shot it the same as before, but this reed hit the rear of the first
and remained stuck there. One after another, the Brahmin shot the
reeds, and they stuck to each other and formed a long chain which
soon reached the top of the well. He then pulled the chain of reeds
and retrieved the ball from the well. The boys applauded and cried
out in joy. The Brahmin said, 'Wait, I still have to recover my ring.'
He looked at Arjun and said, 'Give me your bow and an arrow.' Arjun
complied. The Brahmin aimed down the well, chanted a few mantras

and released the arrow. The arrow went in and flew back to him with the ring attached to its tip.

The boys were awed to see the Brahmin's skill.

'O Sir, who are you?' asked Yudhishthira. 'You cannot be a simple Brahmin.'

The Brahmin laughed. 'I am Drona, son of Rishi Bharadwaja. Go to your granduncle Bhishma and tell him about me. I am sure he'll know.'

The boys ran to the palace and narrated the incident to Bhishma. As soon as he heard this, Bhishma realized that the teacher he had been looking for had himself arrived at his door. He knew of Drona quite well, for like him, Drona too had received his arms training from Parashurama. Besides, the fame of Drona as one of the most skilled warriors had reached his ears through his spies and informers.

Bhishma came out to the meadow and welcomed Drona with open arms. 'Drona, we are honoured to have you here. I'd like to offer you the position of the royal weapons trainer of Hastinapur. You can have whatever honorarium you'd like for your services. Please grant us the privilege.'

Drona had no reason to reject the offer. It was for this specific reason that he had come to Hastinapur. Although he was a great archer and a warrior, as a Brahmin, it was difficult for him to earn a livelihood from his skills in weaponry. Drona was desperate to find a job that would pay him well and give him the respect he deserved. He had another motive too, about which we will learn later.

Drona settled down in the palace with his wife Kripi and his son Aswathama, and began training the Pandavas and Kauravas the advanced art of warfare and weaponry. Although he taught the princes the use of many weapons, he made each of his students specialize in a single weapon. Yudhishthira used the spear, Bheem

the mace, Arjun was an archer, while Nakul and Sahadev wielded the
sword. Duryodhan also picked up the mace as his weapon of choice.

The Test

Drona had an unorthodox teaching style. He'd often test his students
for their focus and skills. One day, he built a small wooden bird and
placed it on a distant branch of a tree. He then called the princes and
challenged them to hit the bird's eye using their skills with bows and
arrows. First he called Yudhishthira and asked him to aim for the
target. As Yudhishthira got ready to shoot, Drona asked, 'What do you
see, Yudhishthira?'

Puzzled, the young prince replied, 'Well, I see the meadow, I see
you, I see my brothers, I see the tree, I see the bird ...'

Drona stopped him and said, 'Put down your bow. You don't have
to shoot.' He called Duryodhan next, and as Duryodhan aimed, he
asked him the same question, 'What do you see?'

Duryodhan said, 'I see the tree, I see the trees behind the trees, I
see you, I see ...'

Drona said, 'That's all right, put down your bow.' One by one, he
called upon each of the princes to aim and asked the same question,
and they all gave the same answer—they saw the tree, the bird, the
meadow, the brothers, etc. And he let no one shoot the arrow. Then
Arjun came up to the spot. He engaged the arrow to his bow and
aimed at the bird. Drona asked him the same question.

Arjun kept quiet for a moment, still focusing on the target, and
then replied, 'I see the eye!'

Drona asked, 'Are you sure? What else do you see?'

Arjun replied again, 'I see only the eye of the bird.'

Drona smiled and said, 'Shoot!' Arjun released the arrow which
went straight and pierced the eye of the wooden bird. Drona was
delighted at his student's success. He embraced Arjun and said

to all his pupils: 'This is what your concentration should be like. When you aim at a target, that's the only thing you are supposed to concentrate on, nothing else.' He then turned to Arjun and said, 'Arjun, keep practising like this and I will make you the greatest archer of all!'

As a matter of fact, Arjun never tired of practising. He practised his archery skills from dawn to dusk with no break. One evening, when he was having his dinner, the lamp in the room went out in a gust of wind and the dining room became pitch dark. Arjun realized that he was still able to eat his food. In the darkness, he could pick up the food from his plate and take it to his mouth with no effort at all! He realized that if he practised long enough, he could shoot his target even in the dark. From then on, he practised during the night and soon became skilled in hitting his target in total darkness.

Ekalavya's Guru Dakshina

One day, while Drona was teaching archery to his royal students, a young boy walked in. From his looks and his clothes, it was quite evident that the boy was of tribal origin, a Nishaad. He was carrying a crude bow made of bamboo and a few arrows with him.

The boy walked up to Drona, knelt in front of him to pay his respects and said, 'I am Ekalavya. I long to become a great archer and have always wanted to learn the skill from you. Please accept me as your student and teach me the art of archery.'

Drona raised his hand to bless the boy and said, 'I am glad you want to learn the art of archery from me. But my duty binds me to accept students only of royal origin. Are you of royal lineage?'

Ekalavya bowed his head and said, 'No, Sir. I do not come from a royal family. I am a tribal—a Nishaad. I live in the forest.'

'Then I am sorry, Ekalavya, I cannot teach you. Please go back and find yourself a good teacher.' Disappointed, Ekalavya walked away while the Kuru princes mocked his audacity. Drona scolded them: 'Stop it and get back to practice.'

A few months later, Drona took his students on a hunting trip to the forest. The royal entourage comprised a huge team of servants, guards, cooks, cattle and a few hunting dogs. They set up camp and Drona started to train them in forest warfare between hunting trips. One day, a hunting dog went astray and ran deep into the forest. It came upon an opening next to which was a small hut. Beside the hut stood a clay statue of Drona. In front of the statue, a young boy was busy practising his archery skills. It was Ekalavya. He looked fierce in his leopard skin loin cloth and tribal jewellery and body paintings. Scared, the dog began to bark at Ekalavya. Annoyed by the dog's incessant barking, Ekalavya tried to shoo it away a couple of times. But the dog refused to leave and continued to bark. Impatient, Ekalavya shot seven arrows inside the dog's mouth and stopped it from barking: all without hurting him. The dog ran away and returned to the Kuru camp. When Drona and his students saw the dog, they were astonished. Only an immensely skilled archer could quieten a dog this way. Even Arjun couldn't pull off such a feat. Inquisitive, they followed the dog to Ekalavya's hut and were surprised to see the clay statue of Drona. Ekalavya was ecstatic to see Drona at his door. He knelt in front of the teacher and paid his respects. Drona asked, 'Ekalavya, what are you doing with my statue?'

Ekalavya replied, 'Gurudev, I was not fortunate enough to have you as my teacher in real life. I have always considered you my teacher, my guru. So I made this statue of yours and have been practising archery in front of your form to perfect my skills.'

Drona was elated to find such a talented student whom he had never taught in person. He noticed Arjun looking mortified. Drona pulled Arjun to one side and asked, 'What's the matter, Arjun? Why are you so despondent? Anything wrong?'

Arjun replied, 'Gurudev, you had promised me that I would be your best student in archery. No other student of yours could surpass me. I guess that's not true any more.'

Drona realized that it would be a strategic mistake to let Ekalavya surpass his favourite student, Arjun. He came back to Ekalavya and said, 'Well, Ekalavya, if you consider me your guru, then you must pay me your guru dakshina—my fees.'

'Gurudev, I'll be honoured to pay you my dakshina if it is in my power to do so. Please let me know, what can I offer you?' said Ekalavya with joined hands.

Drona glanced at Arjun standing next to him with a gloomy face. He then turned to Ekalavya and, with a stern voice, said, 'Ekalavya, I would like to have the thumb of your right arm as my dakshina. Can you give me that?'

Ekalavya regarded Drona's face for a few moments. He knew what the teacher who had never taught him was asking for. Cutting off his right thumb would mean he could never shoot an arrow again in his life. But Ekalavya didn't protest. He pulled out a knife from his belt and, with no hesitation, he cut off his right thumb and placed it on Drona's feet. Drona was stunned and overwhelmed by Ekalavya's devotion. But he expressed no emotion. He accepted the boy's dakshina and raised his arm to bless him. Then he turned away and left the forest with his students.

7

A Show of Strength

AFTER A FEW YEARS OF RIGOROUS TRAINING, DRONA WANTED TO showcase the talent of the Kuru princes. He went to King Dhritarashtra and said, 'O King, I have taught the Kuru princes how to use the most advanced weapons and they have successfully completed their training. If you permit me, I would like to display their talents in front of the royal family as well as the citizens of Hastinapur. It will not only please the audience, but will also carry a message to the enemies of Hastinapur that the Kuru throne will be in capable hands for years to come.'

Dhritarashtra was pleased to hear this news. He held Drona's hands and said, 'Oh, how I wish I could see this exhibition of my sons' talents and skills. Drona, please go ahead with the arrangements for this grand event. I will watch the event through the eyes of my brother Vidura.'

With Dhritarashtra's blessings, Drona had the royal architects build a huge arena stadium on the outskirts of the city. It was a grand stadium, the likeness of which had never been built before.

The tiered seats of the stadium reached high into the sky. The royal boxes were decorated with luxurious silk and jewels. Colourful flags fluttered on top.

On the day of the event, people from all over the kingdom poured into the stadium and took their seats early in the morning. Later, the royal family arrived and sat in the royal box. Dhritarashtra was accompanied by Vidura, who described the grandeur of the stadium and the surroundings to his brother. Kunti did the same for Gandhari.

Before the main event, the priests sought blessings from the gods for the successful completion of the event. Then arrived Drona, accompanied by his son Aswathama. The old warrior's white beard and white silk robe billowed in the winds and the crowd erupted in a loud cheer. Drona sat down on his special seat on the sidelines and gestured to the guards at the entrance. They opened the gates, and through them entered the princes, led by Yudhishthira. They were all dressed in gorgeous costumes, jewellery, ornate armours and helmets. The entire stadium stood up to cheer the Pandavas and Kauravas who walked in and stood at their marked positions. Soon, the show started and the princes began to exhibit their prowess in different kinds of arms and weaponry. As a group and individually, they displayed their skills using spears, bows and arrows, swords and maces. Sometimes they galloped around the stadium on horseback, sometimes they chased each other on roaring chariots, and sometimes just barefoot. The enthralled crowd broke into thunderous applause.

Then Drona called upon Bheem and Duryodhan to a mock fight with their favourite weapon, the iron mace. The arch rivals faced each other, growling and snarling like two fierce lions and then broke into an all-out fight. The maces clanged against each other, making a loud noise while sparks flew all around the arena. The crowd went wild. Soon, the stadium was divided into two groups.

One supporting Bheem and the other Duryodhan. They cheered their favourite prince on, while hurling insults at the opponent. The event ceased to be a match to demonstrate the readiness of the young boys and turned into a bloody battle. Drona realized that things will soon go out of control. He called Aswathama and said, 'Go, stop this nonsense. It is an exhibition match and not a real fight.' Aswathama stepped into the arena and somehow managed to break up the fight. The two brothers, although unhappy to stop their battle, went back to their seats hurling insults at each other. The Kuru seniors sighed in relief.

Drona then stood up and addressed the crowd. 'My dear citizens of Hastinapur, now I present to you my favourite student, and the best archer in the world, the third son of our late King Pandu—Arjun.'

Arjun stepped into the arena with his weapons. He bowed to his guru, to his elders, to the crowd, and began to display his skills and expertise in the use of mystical weapons and archery. The crowd gasped when he made a huge fire erupt in the stadium using the Agni or Fire missile. Soon he doused the fire in a thunderous downpour using Varunasthra or the water missile. Next he fired the Vayuasthra or the wind weapon and forceful winds blew through the stadium, blowing off the audience's turbans and other garments. He then fired his Parvatasthra or the mountain weapon and a huge mountain appeared in the stadium to quell the winds. One after another, Arjun demonstrated his skills with a variety of weapons. And each time, the crowd exploded in thunderous applause to cheer their hero. Arjun also showed his skills in archery by hitting a variety of almost impossible targets. The city of Hastinapur realized that Drona's claim was not in vain. Arjun was indeed the best archer and warrior in the world.

Right at that moment, a handsome young man entered through the gates and the eyes of the entire stadium turned towards him.

Although the man wore simple clothes, he had a natural armour on his chest that was an integral part of his body. The bright and glowing earrings on him also seemed to be fused to his ears. He stepped into the arena and called out to Drona, 'O great guru Dronacharya, I am Karna. I can prove to you that I am a better archer and a better warrior than your favourite student Arjun. Whatever skills he demonstrated, I can perform them all—even better. So please permit me!'

There was such confidence in his voice that it amazed the audience as well as Drona. His bold stance and his defiant attitude in front of the mighty Kuru princes drew the attention of the entire stadium. The excited crowd began to cheer Karna and called upon him to display his skills. Drona had to give in to this demand. Standing on the sidelines, Arjun felt a tinge of jealousy creeping into him. He didn't like his moment of glory being challenged and possibly overshadowed by the stranger.

Karna stepped into the centre of the arena and began to show his mastery over various weapons. He displayed the same feats displayed by Arjun; some even better. Soon, the audience realized that Karna was indeed a great warrior, a worthy opponent to Arjun. They cheered Karna on as he concluded his demonstrations. The Pandavas felt the limelight shifting from them to Karna.

Duryodhan realized that Karna might be the only person who could counter Arjun in the battlefield, and befriending him would be in his interest. He walked up to Karna, embraced him, and said, 'Karna, you have amazed us with your skills. What can I do for you?'

Karna was overwhelmed by this kind gesture. He said, 'O Prince, all I desire is your friendship.'

Arjun was fuming with jealousy and anger. He knew Duryodhan wanted to make friends with Karna only to annoy him. Duryodhan glanced at Arjun and smiled, while Arjun glared back at him and growled in anger.

Karna could sense this rivalry between the cousins. He took this opportunity and asked Duryodhan: 'O Prince Duryodhan, if you permit, I have one more request. I want to challenge Arjun to a duel—a one-on-one combat.'

According to the Kshatriya tradition, a warrior can never decline a challenge for a duel. Arjun too was eager to fight Karna and end his arrogance once and for all. He picked up his weapons and stepped into the arena. Duryodhan escorted Karna to the centre of the arena where the two rivals faced each other. The crowd went berserk. The stadium exploded with thunderous shouts, screams, roars and cries of the people. Everybody stood up on their feet to watch this unprecedented battle.

In the royal box, Kunti suddenly felt dizzy. She fainted and fell off her seat.

To know the reason for Kunti's sudden illness, we need to go back to her past, when she was just a teenager. We know already that she had earned a boon from Rishi Durvasa for her kindness and hospitality towards him. The rishi gave her a mantra to invoke any god and have a child with him. Kunti was too young to appreciate the seriousness of this boon. One morning, while watching the sunrise on the eastern horizon, just out of sheer curiosity, she recited the mantra and invoked the Sun god. And, lo and behold, the Sun god, Surya, appeared before her. He said, 'Kunti, you called me and here I am. I will give you the most beautiful child one could possibly ask for.'

Kunti was flabbergasted. She was just a child. 'No, no, I don't want a child. It was a mistake. Please go back!' she protested.

The Sun god smiled and said, 'I cannot go back without fulfilling my task. The mantra obligates me to give you a child. You must accept me.'

The scared princess said, 'But I am not married. How can I have a child out of wedlock?'

'Don't worry, Kunti. Even if you have a child with me, you'll remain a virgin.' Saying so, he embraced Kunti.

A few months later, Kunti gave birth to a beautiful little boy. The newborn displayed a strange phenomenon. He seemed to wear a hard armour on his chest as well as a pair of glowing earrings. Being an unmarried girl, Kunti didn't have the courage to keep the child. She placed the baby in a basket and set it afloat in the flowing waters of the Ganga. She returned to the palace teary-eyed, knowing she'd never see her child again.

Meanwhile, the basket floated down the river for miles till it reached the outskirts of Hastinapur. Adhirath, the royal charioteer, was taking a bath in the river when he saw the basket with the beautiful boy floating by. He picked up the child from the basket and brought him to his wife who was ecstatic with joy to get a son. The childless couple thanked the gods for being so kind to them. They named the boy Karna.

So, the moment Karna stepped into the arena with his natural armour and earrings, Kunti knew that he was none other than her firstborn. She was overwhelmed with mixed emotions. She was happy to see her son grown up to be a handsome young man. But she was also racked by the awareness that she could never embrace him as a mother. She tried hard to control herself and keep calm.

But when she realized that Karna was about to fight Arjun, which could result in the death of one of her sons, she couldn't take it any more. Her head began to spin and she fell off her seat, unconscious. The royal maids and nurses rushed to help her and Kunti regained her consciousness soon.

'I am alright! It must've been the heat,' she mumbled and returned to her seat to see what was going on in the arena.

The duel between Arjun and Karna was about to begin. Kripa, Arjun's previous teacher, stepped into the arena to introduce the duellists. He first introduced Arjun, giving the details of his glorious ancestry and lineage. Then, he asked Karna to announce his lineage. 'Karna, please tell us about your lineage. Whose son are you? Which kingdom do you hail from?'

Karna remained silent. He looked quite embarrassed. From his attitude, it became quite evident that he was not of royal origin. Kripa asked again, 'Karna, you must be aware that duels can only be fought between equals. So please tell us who you are and which noble heritage you come from. Else, we cannot permit you to battle with Kuru prince Arjun.'

Karna felt humiliated. As he was about to step out of the arena, Duryodhan came forward and said, 'Kripacharya, a hero's identity is defined by his strength and valour, not his birth! Karna has proven that his capabilities are no less than Arjun's. That alone should be enough to prove his credibility. However, if it is royalty you seek in Arjun's challenger, so be it. Here, right now in front of the whole of Hastinapur, I proclaim Karna the king of the state of Anga.' He called the Brahmin priests and, in the middle of the amphitheatre, in front of thousands of people, he crowned Karna as the ruler of the kingdom of Anga.

Karna was overwhelmed with emotion. Hands joined, he asked, 'Duryodhan, how can I ever repay you?'

Duryodhan held his arms and said, 'I only desire your friendship, dear Karna. Nothing else.'

With the question of Karna's royalty being resolved, the duel with Arjun was about to start again. As the two fighters got ready to fight, an old man holding a charioteer's staff walked into the arena. The moment Karna saw the old man, he bowed down to his feet.

'This is my father, Adhirath,' Karna said to Duryodhan, who was curious to know who the man was. 'He had adopted me when I was an infant.' Then he turned to Adhirath and said, 'Father, thanks to my dear friend, prince Duryodhan, your son is now a king.' Adhirath was not able to control his emotions. Tears rolled down his cheeks while he embraced his son and kissed his forehead several times.

In the sidelines, the Pandavas were laughing. Bheem jeered, 'Hey Karna, it would be better if you went back to driving chariots. A son of a charioteer does not belong here and does not deserve to die at the hands of Arjun.'

The insults hurt Karna, but he didn't utter a single word. Duryodhan lashed back at Bheem: 'Shut up, you moron! Don't you dare insult my friend Karna! His birth may be mysterious, but no one can doubt his skill. Besides, who are *you* to question him about his birth? We all know that neither *you* nor *your brothers* are Kuru by birth! What gives *you* the right to question Karna?'

Soon, an argument broke out between the Pandavas and the Kauravas, each hurling the choicest of insults at the other. The crowd went wild and soon the verbal volleys were about to turn into a physical skirmish. The sun was about to set on the western horizon. Drona blew his conch shell to announce the formal conclusion of the day's proceedings. Kunti sighed in relief as Karna left the arena holding Adhirath's hand and with his new friend Duryodhan by his side. As the crowd filed out of the stadium, it discussed the day's events and speculated about the future of Hastinapur and the Kuru dynasty.

8

Drona's Revenge

SOON AFTER THE SHOW, DRONA CALLED HIS STUDENTS AND SAID, 'BOYS you have completed your formal training and I have taught you all I could. You have demonstrated your skills to your elders and to the citizens of Hastinapur, and from their applause and cheers it was quite evident that they were more than satisfied with your performance and they have passed you with honours. But, to graduate, you have one more task to complete. You must pay me your guru dakshina, my fee.'

Yudhishthira said, 'Gurudev, please let us know what you want. We'll scour heaven and earth to fetch it for you.'

Drona said, 'Well, then, here is what I want from you. Go to the kingdom of Panchal and bring me King Drupad as a captive.'

Yudhishthira was surprised at this strange request. Drona explained, 'When I was a young boy and a student at Rishi Agnivesh's school, Drupad, the Panchal prince, was there too. We were good friends. In fact, he was my best friend. One day, while we were strolling in the meadows, Drupad said, "Drona you are my best friend, and there is nothing in the world that I won't do for you. I promise you, when I become the king of Panchal, I'll give you half of my kingdom." I laughed and replied, "Drupad, you are being too emotional. I am sure you don't mean it." He stopped me and said, "Drona, I am Drupad, prince of Panchal. I always mean what I say." I replied, "Well then, maybe one day I will take you up on your offer."

'After we graduated, we parted ways. Drupad became the king of Panchal. And I went on to learn advanced military skills. But my skills failed me in making money. I was so poor that I couldn't even manage to feed my family. I remembered my friend Drupad's promise. I went to the Panchal court and said to Drupad, "My dear friend, I have come to accept my share." Drupad looked surprised. He asked, "Who are you? What share are you talking about?" I was shocked. "Drupad, don't you recognize me? It's me, your friend, Drona!" Drupad looked at me for a while and said, "Yes, indeed. It's you, Drona the Brahmin. What have you done to yourself? I could hardly recognize you." I replied, "My friend, I am going through a difficult time and poverty must have had an effect on my appearance." Drupad said, "That's possible. What brings you here? What share were you talking about?" I reminded him of his promise at Rishi Agnivesh's school. Drupad laughed and said, "I promised you half of my kingdom? Are you out of your mind?" I was surprised. "You forgot your promise, my friend?" Drupad stopped me and said, "No, I never promised you anything. And don't call me a friend. Yes, we were students at Rishi Agnivesh's school, but you were never my friend. You were a poor Brahmin boy, and I was the prince of Panchal. How could we be friends? Remember, only equals can be friends." Saying this, he laughed again, and the entire court joined him in laughter. Those sounds fell on my ears like hot molten lava. I felt so humiliated and insulted that I could barely stand on my feet. Trembling with rage, I said, "Drupad, one day you'll have to pay for this humiliation," and left the court. From that day, I have been looking for an opportunity to avenge my insult and give Drupad the punishment he deserves. And today is the day. I know you can fulfil my wish, and that will be my guru dakshina.'

Duryodhan stomped the ground in rage and said, 'Acharya, your wish is our command. I will bring that arrogant King Drupad in chains and make him kneel in front of you in no time.' Duryodhan jumped up on his chariot and sped towards Panchal with his brothers.

The Pandavas followed the Kauravas towards the Panchal kingdom. Before entering the city, Arjun said, 'Let's wait here and watch what happens to Duryodhan. Drupad is not a weakling, and I am sure our arrogant cousin will get a good thrashing from him and his army. Let's watch their strategy and their war tactics, and then we'll attack at the opportune moment.'

As the Kauravas entered the Panchal capital, they were stopped by the huge Panchal Army consisting of thousands of infantrymen, hundreds of horse-mounted cavalry and hundreds of elephant-mounted soldiers. The efficient spies of Drupad had alerted the king of the impending attack, and Drupad was waiting to face the Kauravas on his golden chariot. Soon, a fierce battle ensued and Duryodhan was overwhelmed by the Panchal Army. Drupad attacked him with such violence that Duryodhan was not able to counter him at all. The citizens of Panchal joined hands with the army to defend their homeland. Duryodhan had no other option but to retreat.

The Pandavas have been watching from a distance. When they saw Duryodhan backing off, Arjun said, 'Brother Yudhishthira, we should strike now. You wait here. The four of us should be good enough to defeat the Panchal Army.' Saying so, the four brothers—Bhima, Arjun, Nakul and Sahadev, attacked the Panchal Army. Bhima, spinning his huge mace, began to destroy the Panchal Army like a bulldozer. Nakul and Sahadev attacked with their swords, while Arjun sped through the army on his chariot to attack Drupad. The endless stream of arrows from his bow killed thousands of soldiers along the way. Failing to counter this fierce attack, the Panchal Army started to flee the war field. Soon enough, Arjun faced Drupad and a fierce battle broke out. Drupad fired a barrage of arrows to Arjun, but the young prince destroyed them all, mid-flight. Some of Drupad's soldiers were crushed to death by Bheem's deadly mace. Drupad's elephant army tried to protect him, but Bheem struck them down, killing some while the others fled. Arjun, with a quick succession of arrows, killed Drupad's horses and his charioteer. He then cut off his flagstaff and bow, and left Drupad standing helpless on his broken chariot. Arjun then dropped his bow, picked up a sword and jumped off his chariot and ran towards Drupad. Holding his sword at Drupad's throat, he said, 'King Drupad, in the name of our Guru Dronacharya, I capture you. Please come with me.'

The Pandavas tied King Drupad in chains and brought him to Hastinapur and offered him as their dakshina to their guru. Drupad stood there in front of Drona with his head bowed in humiliation. Drona smiled and said, 'So, Drupad, it seems now I own your entire kingdom and all your wealth. What do you have to say about that?'

Drupad remained quiet. Drona came close, held his arm and said, 'Don't be afraid. I am a Brahmin and I forgive you. I would still like to be your friend, but as you said, how could unequal people be friends? So, I will give you half my kingdom and we can continue to be friends. Do you accept?' Drupad swallowed his pride and replied, 'Drona, it is kind of you to forgive me. Yes, I accept your offer with all humility, and I hope to stay your friend forever.'

Drupad regained half his kingdom while Drona took over the other half. Smarting under the humiliation, the defeated king kept his eyes open for ways to get back at Drona and the Kuru dynasty.

9

The Varanavata Conspiracy

As DAYS PASSED, THE PANDAVAS GREW IN STRENGTH AND POPULARITY. They kept busy defending Hastinapur from external attacks, conquering kingdoms all around, amassing huge amounts of wealth for the royal treasury and donating large sums to the poor and needy of the kingdom. The citizens of Hastinapur knew that good governance and prosperity awaited them as soon as the Pandavas ascended the throne of Hastinapur.

The Kauravas did not like this at all. It pained King Dhritarashtra to think that soon he might have to hand over the throne to his nephew Yudhishthira, instead of his son Duryodhan. In his heart, Dhritarashtra knew that Yudhishthira was indeed the most eligible prince to inherit the throne. He was the most learned, the most righteous and the wisest of all the Kuru princes. His ministers, his advisors and even Bhishma were urging him to anoint Yudhishthira the crown prince. But he kept stalling the inevitable.

Then one day, Akrura, a close associate of Krishna, visited Hastinapur and said, 'O King Dhritarashtra, I hope you realize that

Yudhishthira is the rightful heir to the throne. You have been serving as a caretaker and you've served well. But the time has come to hand over the reins of the kingdom to your nephew. Remember, Kunti's sons enjoy the support of their cousin Lord Krishna and of the entire Yadava family.'

Dhritarashtra, though blind, was smart enough to get the hint. Krishna, it is said, is the reincarnation of God Vishnu himself. Krishna had slain his uncle, the vicious King Kans of Mathura, with his bare hands. He was also known to have killed the ferocious demon Putana as well as the monstrous serpent Kaliya, apart from many others. Nobody in their right mind would dare antagonize Krishna. The Yadavas were too powerful to be ignored. Dhritarashtra thought it would be prudent to go with the will of the people. Hence, with great reluctance, but with much pomp, he announced Yudhishthira the crown prince of Hastinapur.

Furious Duryodhan barged into his father's room and hollered, 'How could you do such a thing? You are the rightful owner of the throne, and as your son, I should have been the crown prince!'

'My son, control your anger,' Dhritarashtra tried to console his son. 'I know I have done a disservice to you. Believe me, I had no other option. If I hadn't made Yudhishthira the crown prince, the citizens of Hastinapur would have revolted against me. They would have thrown us out of the palace and made Yudhishthira the king. The Pandavas enjoy the support of the Kuru elders, the Yadavas, and most of all, of Krishna.'

Duryodhan was still fuming. 'Father, the way things are going, soon we the Kauravas will have no stake in this kingdom. People will forget us and we'll have no legacy to leave behind.'

'My dear son, I understand your concern and I don't disagree with you. But you must also understand that I cannot disregard the law of the land. I cannot disregard our age-old traditions and customs. But ...' he paused.

'But what?' Duryodhan was anxious to hear what his father had to say.

Dhritarashtra, said in a whisper: 'Remember, Yudhishthira is not the king yet. He is only the crown prince.'

A faint smile appeared on the edges of Duryodhan's lips, which the blind king couldn't see. He only heard his son's footsteps fade away as he left the room. Dhritarashtra stood alone in the centre of his chamber and stared at the eternal darkness ahead.

Accompanied by Dushasana, Duryodhan went to see his uncle Shakuni, who was a gold mine of evil ideas. Shakuni said, 'My dear nephews, you must understand one thing. The Pandavas enjoy the trust and support of the people of Hastinapur. They are the favourites of Bhishma, Drona, Kripa and Vidura. If you try to harm them, they won't forgive you.'

Duryodhan was frustrated. 'You suggest we sit idle and watch the Pandavas enjoy the throne? I'd rather die than go through this humiliation!' he thundered.

Shakuni held Duryodhan by his shoulder and said, 'Who says you'd have to go through this humiliation? Not while I am alive.' Duryodhan and Dushasana were curious to know more. Shakuni continued, 'Duryodhan, you must win the trust and the support of the people of Hastinapur. But with the Pandavas around, that's impossible. So, we must arrange to send them away ... far away, from Hastinapur. Out of sight from the people of Hastinapur. And as you know, out of sight is out of mind.'

Dushasana said, 'You mean send them into exile?'

Shakuni smiled, 'No, not to exile—a vacation. A long vacation to a nice place. And while they are away, you garner the support of the people of Hastinapur.'

Duryodhan was restless. 'What about when they come back? They'd claim their throne again, wouldn't they?'

Shakuni smiled, 'Don't accidents happen these days? What if an accident befalls our beloved Pandavas while they are on vacation? People can't blame you for that, can they?' Duryodhan's eyes lit up as he grasped the potential of Shakuni's evil plan. He continued his discussion with Shakuni to finalize the details of their devious plan and its execution.

Dhritarashtra was still racked by guilt. His heart was torn between his love for his son and his obligation as a king. He called upon his trusted advisor Kinaka and confided in him, 'Kinaka, I can't bear the fact that I had to crown Yudhishthira the future king of Hastinapur while my son Duryodhan stands in the sidelines. Tell me, what should I do?'

Kinaka was a shrewd politician and a close confidante of Duryodhan. He said, 'O King, one must bear the burden of an enemy like a fragile earthen pot until the right moment. And when that moment arrives, don't hesitate to unburden yourself by crashing it to the ground. One who wants to become great and powerful must exhibit kindness on the exterior but should be sharp and ruthless like a sword at heart. A fisherman kills thousands of fish to build his fortune. Similarly, one cannot become rich and powerful without being cruel and vicious. O Kuru king, you are the most powerful person now. Protect yourself and your family while you can. Do what you must, and make sure you don't have to repent later.'

Kinaka's advice swayed Dhritarashtra towards Duryodhan. So when his son came asking him to send Yudhishthira and his brothers on a vacation to the city of Varanavata, he didn't refuse. He knew

Duryodhan was up to something evil, but he didn't press for the details. He only asked, 'Why would they agree to go to Varanavata? I need to give them some justification.'

Duryodhan was ready with his answer. 'Tell them, the city of Varanavata is celebrating a grand festival. People from all over the country and delegations from all the major kingdoms are visiting the city to join in the festivities. The Pandavas should visit Varanavata as the representatives of Hastinapur. If you request them, they won't refuse. Once they reach Varanavata, I'll take care of the rest.' Saying so, Duryodhan left the king's chamber, and Dhritarashtra sat down to prepare his proposal to the Pandavas.

The Flaming House of Varanavata

Dhritarashtra called upon Yudhishthira and said, 'Dear Yudhishthira, you and your brothers have been busy fighting wars and hardly had any rest. I think you should take a vacation. Why don't you visit the beautiful city of Varanavata? I hear that a great festival is underway there. All the nearby kings and their representatives are attending. Why don't you and your brothers go and spend a few days in Varanavata as representatives of Hastinapur? You can take your mother Kunti with you. You'll get some rest and also enjoy the festivities.'

Yudhishthira was surprised to hear this proposal. He suspected that something must be wrong. But he couldn't decline the offer either. He bowed to his uncle and said, 'Uncle, your wish is our command. We'll leave for Varanavata soon.'

Duryodhan was delighted to hear the news. He never expected his plan to get such a great start. He called upon his trusted confidante Purochana and said, 'Go to Varanavata and build a house for the Pandavas. Build it with highly flammable materials ... but don't make it too obvious. A palace that would burn to ashes within minutes when exposed to a tiny spark. When it's built, invite the Pandavas to stay there. And when they settle down ...' Duryodhan mimed the act of lighting a fire with his hands.

Evil Purochana knew right away what his master was asking for. He said, 'Don't worry, Prince Duryodhan, I'll make sure your mission succeeds.'

'Please do, and I promise you, you'll have no dearth of wealth. Now go and begin your work.'

Purochana hired a few skilled artisans and left for Varanavata. Soon, they built a beautiful house using wood, sawdust, lac and wax. When the Pandavas and their mother Kunti arrived, Purochana welcomed them to their new house. The moment Yudhishthira entered the house, he knew he was stepping into a death trap. The faint but indistinguishable odour of lac and wax told him that Vidura's warning was not unfounded.

Just before the Pandavas were about to leave for Varanavata, Vidura came to know of this conspiracy through his spies in the palace. It was too late for him to do anything else but to warn Yudhishthira. As the Pandavas were about to mount their chariots, Vidura spoke to Yudhishthira in a language that only the two of them knew. He said, 'One who knows the enemy's plans should work on ways to counter them. Remember, there are many ways to kill one's enemy. A fire can burn down a forest but can hardly touch those who live underground. A mole can escape a fire by tunnelling underground. A person who can navigate by reading the stars can find his path and can not only protect himself but his family too. Do you understand?'

Yudhishthira replied, 'I understand.'

On their way to Varanavata, Yudhishthira looked concerned and thoughtful. Kunti asked him, 'What are you thinking, son? What did Vidura say to you?'

Yudhishthira said, 'Vidura warned us of a conspiracy and suggested that we plan our escape.'

Inside the house, Yudhishthira explained the situation to his brothers. Bheem was quite upset. He asked, 'Why did you agree to live in this house when you knew of Duryodhan's plan? Let's go back to Hastinapur and demand an explanation from the vile man.'

Yudhishthira urged him to calm down. He said, 'We have no proof yet. If we confront them now, they'd deny the accusation and blame us for suspecting them and causing ill feelings in the family. I suggest we play along. At the opportune moment, we'll burn down the house ourselves and escape.'

The same day, a man arrived to meet Yudhishthira. He was sent by Vidura to dig a tunnel out of the house. And soon, the tunnel digger dug a deep and long tunnel from inside one bedroom, leading out into the forest. At night, the Pandava brothers and Kunti would sleep in the tunnel while one brother stayed awake on guard. During the day, the Pandavas would explore the city of Varanavata and plan an escape route. Purochana was clever too. For almost a year, he showed no signs of antagonism towards the Pandavas. He served them like a loyal servant to earn their trust. He stayed in one room and took care of all the household tasks.

One day, Yudhishthira called his brothers and said, 'Now is the time to make our move. I have learnt from Vidura that Duryodhan has sent his signal. We need to act before Purochana does.'

That evening, the Pandavas arranged for a grand feast. Sumptuous food and drinks were served to the guests. Purochana helped himself to quite a few pitchers of wine and soon fell asleep in his room. A little after midnight, when the entire city was in deep slumber, the Pandavas set the house on fire and slipped out through the tunnel under the house. The house, made of lac, wax and wood burst into flames. Within minutes, there was nothing left, except a huge pile of smouldering ashes. Purochana too was burnt alive in his sleep. And along with Purochana died a group of five tribal men and their mother. The night before, after attending the feast and downing a few bottles of wine, they lay down in a corner of the house and were fast asleep when the fire swallowed them. The next morning, when the people of Varanavata found the charred bodies of the five men and the woman, they thought the Pandavas had died in the fire.

The news soon reached Hastinapur and a deep sorrow engulfed the city. Bhishma, Drona and Kripa couldn't believe their ears. How could such gallant warriors be killed in a petty fire? Dhritarashtra, Duryodhan and his brothers, while lamenting the loss of the Pandavas in public, were elated. They declared a month-long mourning and donated large amounts of wealth to the Brahmins and the poor, who praised the glory of the Kurus. In fact, Duryodhan had set his plan in motion and had begun appeasing the citizens of Hastinapur right after the Pandavas left. The death of his cousins gave him the opportunity to win their sympathy. Only Vidura knew that the Pandavas were safe and sound. But he kept his mouth shut and patiently waited for their return.

The Pandavas, along with Kunti, came out of the tunnel into a dense forest outside the city. They followed the stars and ran towards the south. Not accustomed to walking through the forest, and that too at night, Kunti was getting tired. She often tripped and fell on the uneven ground. Bheem said, 'Mother, please let me carry you.' She didn't even have the strength to object. Bheem lifted Kunti on his shoulders. He then said, 'Brothers, let me carry you too. Then we can move much faster.' With his superhuman strength, Bheem lifted his four brothers on his two arms. The son of the wind ran through the forest, bulldozing through the trees and boulders along the way to carve his path. Soon, they were miles away from the city. At dawn, they reached the banks of River Ganga. They walked down the riverbank to find a shallow spot to cross the river. Suddenly, they saw a large boat on the river with the boatman waving at them.

The boatman introduced himself to Yudhishthira and said, 'Vidura had instructed me to wait for you and I have been waiting here for months. He asked me to take you down the river to any destination you want.' The boatman was speaking the same language that Vidura had used earlier with Yudhishthira. The Pandavas had no reason to distrust him. The boat took them down the river and dropped them off at the other side, next to a deep forest. Bheem once again picked up Kunti and his brothers and trampled through the forest.

At dusk, Kunti asked him to stop. 'I am thirsty, my son. Can you arrange for some water?'

Bheem gently put her down and said, 'Mother, wait here with my brothers. I'll get some water for you.' Bheem wandered through the forest until he found a lake. When he came back with water, his mother and siblings were fast asleep. He didn't wake them. He sat on a rock nearby and stayed awake to guard them.

Bheem and Hidimba

In that forest lived the ferocious demon, or rakshasa, Hidimb, with his sister Hidimba. Ferocious and powerful beings possessing various mystical powers, they could change their shape and form at will, had the power to fly and could perform many magic tricks. The rakshasas hated humans but loved their flesh. Hidimb was deep asleep. But the sweet smell of human flesh woke him up. He got up from his bed and ordered his sister, 'Ummm ... Hidimba, I smell human flesh. Some human beings must have come to our forest. Go and get them for me. Tonight, we will have a grand feast.' Hidimba was excited to have human flesh after a long time. She followed the scent and soon found Bheem sitting next to his sleeping mother and four brothers. Looking at the handsome prince Bheem, Hidimba was struck by a thunderbolt, and fell in love with him right away. If she could accept someone as her husband, it could only be Bheem. So Hidimba, with her magical powers, took the form of a beautiful maiden, dressed herself in gorgeous clothes and jewellery and came to seduce Bheem. She asked, 'Who are you, my dear? And who are these men and woman sleeping next to you?'

Bheem was quite surprised to see such a pretty woman in a dense forest like this, and grew suspicious. So, instead of answering her question, he asked, 'Who are you, lady? And what brings you here?'

With a coy smile she replied, 'I am Hidimba, sister of Hidimb, the demon who rules this forest. He wants to devour you all and has sent me to fetch you. But I have fallen in love with you and would like to marry you. Come with me. I will take you far away from my brother and we can live happy ever after.'

Bheem was not impressed. He said, 'You horrible creature! How dare you make such a proposal? I would never abandon my family here to be eaten by your rakshasa brother.'

Hidimba said, 'I can save them too. Wake them up, and I'll fly you all to safety.'

Bheem replied, 'They have had a long day and need the rest. I can't wake them now. And let me tell you, I am not afraid of demons and rakshasas. Go back and send your brother. I'll teach him a lesson he'll never forget.'

Hidimba didn't have to call her brother. Hidimb was hungry and couldn't wait any longer. He followed the human scent and arrived in front of Bheem and Hidimba. When he saw Hidimba in human form flirting with Bheem, he was furious. He growled at her and said, 'You bitch! I will kill you too, along with these humans.' He ran towards the Pandavas to attack them.

Bheem stopped him and said, 'Hey, coward, why do you blame your sister? Whatever she did was because she is in love with me.

And don't you dare awaken my mother and brothers. Come here and fight me if you dare.' Bheem pulled Hidimb to one side, so as not to disturb his mother and brothers, and soon a fierce battle began. Hidimb pounced upon Bheem only to be tackled and thrashed on a large boulder. Hidimb cried out in pain, but he didn't give up. He got up and attacked Bheem again, and this time Bheem picked him up and hurled him away. Hidimb crashed into a huge tree, breaking it in two.

The noise of the battle woke up Kunti and the brothers. Hidimba was standing next to Kunti. Kunti asked her, 'Who are you, girl?'

Hidimba introduced herself and said, 'Mother, I am in love with Bheem and would like to marry him. Please bless me and grant me my wish.'

In the meantime, Arjun told Bheem, 'Brother, please finish this soon. The sun is about to rise, and during this twilight period, these demons can multiply their power.'

Bheem lifted Hidimb over his head, spun him around a few times, and then threw him to the ground. Hidimb's bones were shattered by this powerful blow. Bheem then struck his torso with a powerful kick and broke his spine to kill him.

He then came to Hidimba and said, 'Rakshasas cannot be trusted. I must kill you too.'

Yudhishthira came forward and stopped him. 'Brother, you shouldn't hurt a woman, let alone kill her. She hasn't done us any harm, and she'll never be able to do so.'

Hidimba kneeled in front of Kunti and said, 'Mother, I have abandoned my family for the sake of my love. If you turn me back, I'll have no other option but to die. Please accept me as your daughter-in-law. Please let me marry Bheem and take him with me. I promise, I will return him whenever you want me to.'

Kunti looked at Yudhishthira for advice. Yudhishthira said, 'Hidimba, since you love my brother so much, we can permit you to marry him, but with one condition. Bheem can spend the days with you, but he must come back to us every evening.' Hidimba agreed.

Bheem interjected, 'Well, I have a condition too. I'll marry you, but will stay with you only until you have a son.' Hidimba agreed again.

Bheem and Hidimba got married following the Gandharva tradition of exchanging garlands. After the wedding, Hidimba flew them all to a nice place in the Himalayas and the couple began their conjugal life. In due course, Hidimba gave birth to a son. The son, being a rakshasa, grew up to adulthood almost immediately. He was named Ghatotkach. Ghatotkach was as strong and powerful as his father Bheem. He also had magical powers like his mother Hidimba. Ghatotkach asked Kunti and the Pandavas, 'What can I do for you, Grandma? What can I do for you, Uncles?'

Kunti smiled and said, 'Dear Ghatotkach, you are my first grandson. We don't need anything now. But do help us when we need your help.'

Ghatotkach said, 'Call me whenever you need any help. I'll arrive in a moment's notice.' Saying so, he and Hidimba flew off to the northern Himalayas.

The Pandavas continued their journey. They had grown long beards and long hair. They wore clothes made of tree bark and looked like the sages residing in the forest. One day, they met their grandfather Vyasa. Vyasa advised them to stay in hiding for some more time. He took them to the village of Ekachakra to a Brahmin's house. There, the Pandavas lived disguised as Brahmins and waited for further instructions from Vyasa.

10

Draupadi's Swayamvara

THE PANDAVAS AND THEIR MOTHER KUNTI WERE LEADING A PEACEFUL life in the village of Ekachakra. During the day, the brothers would go from door to door, begging for rice and vegetables, which they would bring to their mother. Kunti would cook the food and give half of it to Bheem, while the remaining would be divided amongst the rest. Life was quite uneventful, except when Bheem killed the demon Baka Rakshasa who was terrorizing the villagers. But he had to be careful not to reveal his identity and hence had to do the job in secret.

One day, a Brahmin visited their home. He was coming from Panchal, the kingdom of Drupad. He told the Pandavas that Drupad was arranging a grand swayamvara for his beautiful daughter Draupadi. Kampilya, the capital city of Panchal, was getting ready for this great event. The Pandavas were curious to know more.

The old man said, 'Well, the daughter was not born of Drupad and his queen. Her birth, if you may call it, is quite a story. You must have heard of Drona, the great arms teacher of the Kuru princes? King Drupad had a nasty encounter with Drona ...' The man then narrated the story of how Drona had humiliated Drupad with the help of his students, the Kuru princes. The Pandavas didn't utter a word. The old man continued, 'Since then, Drupad has been seeking revenge. He knew he wouldn't be able to fight Drona and his students alone, and needed a strong and powerful son who could avenge his father's humiliation. After a long search, he met great sages, Yaja and Upayaja. Drupad begged them to do something so he could procure a powerful son. The seers were reluctant at first, but on Drupad's persistence broke their resolve. On behalf of Drupad and his wife, they started a sacrificial fire ritual or yagna. They lit a huge fire and poured offerings of ghee and butter, while chanting mantras on behalf of the king and the queen. A little later, a handsome and powerful young man with a shining armour emerged from the fire. He was named Dhrishtadyumna. It was prophesied that Dhrishtadyumna would destroy Drona. Then emerged from the fire a beautiful woman, fragrant like the lotus flower. The woman had a dark complexion. Hence, she was named Krishnaa. It was prophesied that this woman would cause the destruction of the Kauravas, and thousands of men would die for her. King Drupad and his wife adopted Dhrishtadyumna and Draupadi as their son and daughter. As Drupad's daughter, she was also named Draupadi. And as the princess of Panchal, she was also called Panchali by the subjects.'

Hearing about her incomparable beauty, the young Pandavas felt an irresistible urge to see her and win her at the swayamvara as their bride. But they hesitated to express their wish to their mother.

Kunti noticed the change in their behaviour and said, 'You know what? We have lived in Ekachakra for quite a long time. Our collections have dropped too. I think it is time for us to move. How about moving to Panchal?'

Yudhishthira was hesitant. 'But grandfather Vyasa told us to stay here until further instructions. How can we move without hearing from him?'

No sooner had Yudhishthira uttered these words than Vyasa appeared and said, 'My dear Pandavas, Kunti is right. Now is the perfect time for you to move. You must move to Panchal, and you must take part in Draupadi's swayamvara. For it is Draupadi's destiny to be your wife.'

The brothers didn't quite grasp the significance of this prophecy, and each of them thought that Draupadi would be his. The excited brothers packed their belongings and began their journey towards Kampilya on foot along with Kunti.

The Pandavas were advised to retain a priest for themselves, one who could serve them as their religious guide. On the way to Panchal, they stopped by the village of Utkacha and requested the revered Sage Dhaumya to be their priest. Dhaumya agreed. So, with Dhaumya and Kunti by their side, the Pandavas arrived in Kampilya.

There, they took shelter in a potter's house in the outskirts of the city. The entire city was in a festive mood. King Drupad had built a huge hall, decorated with gold and precious stones, for the swayamvara. Rows of thrones were placed for the kings and princes from near and far, while special arrangements were made for the Brahmins to sit and watch the proceedings.

On the day of the swayamvara, kings and princes dressed in expensive garments, golden armours and helmets walked into the hall and occupied their designated seats. Duryodhan and his brothers were there too. Karna accompanied them. They had heard of Draupadi's magnificent beauty and longed to win her in the contest. Lord Krishna of Dwarka and his brother Balram were in the audience too. But they hadn't come to participate in the contest. King Drupad had invited them as special guests to witness the proceedings. The Pandavas, along with Dhaumya, arrived and found their seats among the Brahmins. The hall was bustling with excitement. The royal band was playing joyful music with flutes, trumpets and drums. As the band reached its crescendo, King Drupad entered the hall with his son Dhrishtadyumna. The audience stood up to cheer the king. Chants of praise for the king reverberated throughout the hall.

King Drupad took his throne, raised his hand, and requested everyone to sit down. Drupad looked around at the kings, princes and Brahmins seated in the stands and said, 'Respected sages and Brahmins, respected kings and princes, I am honoured to see you all at my daughter Draupadi's swayamvara. Draupadi is no simple woman. Born of sacrificial fire, she is not only the most beautiful woman, but also the wisest and smartest woman on earth. Whoever wins her as his wife would be the luckiest man alive. My son Dhrishtadyumna would explain to you the rules of the contest. May the best man win.'

Dhrishtadyumna then stood up and said, 'O kings and princes, before I explain to you the rules of the contest, I would like to invite my beautiful sister Draupadi to come to the hall and take her seat.'

As soon as he uttered the words, the sound of trumpets and conch shells rang through the hall. Thundering drum rolls reverberated through the auditorium while Princess Draupadi entered, escorted by two maids. The entire hall gasped in disbelief when the audience saw Draupadi. She was more beautiful than they had imagined. The lotus fragrance emanating from her perfect body intoxicated the princes and the kings. They all lusted for her and started shouting like hooligans, shedding all sense of dignity!

'You are mine, Draupadi!' shouted some. 'No, she's mine!' shouted another. Some participants broke into fistfights and the guards had to intervene to break them up. Once Draupadi took her seat, the crowd calmed down a little.

In the meantime, Krishna was looking around, searching for some familiar faces. He noticed five handsome men with long hair, long beards, and wearing simple clothes, seated amongst the Brahmins. He instantly recognized them as the Pandavas. He drew Balram's attention and whispered into his ears, 'Look at that corner. Don't you think those five Brahmins look like our cousins, the Pandavas?'

Balram smiled and said, 'Yes, indeed. I am quite sure they are our beloved cousins. They survived the fire after all.'

'I had no doubts about that,' came the cheerful reply.

Dhrishtadyumna stepped into the centre of the hall and stood next to a small, circular reflecting pool filled with clear water. He addressed the seated kings and princes: 'O kings and princes, as you have seen, my sister Draupadi is no ordinary woman. Her beauty is unparalleled in the universe. To win her as your bride, you will have to pass a test that is worthy of her.' He pointed to the ceiling and said, 'Look above. Do you see a golden fish hanging there? And below the fish, can you see that disc rotating? The disc has a hole in it and, as it rotates, it passes over the eye of the fish. Your challenge is to shoot an arrow that would pass through the hole in the disk and strike the eye of the fish. But you cannot look up at the target while you aim. You can only use the reflection of the target in this pool to help you aim.'

Dhrishtadyumna paused while the contestants tried to grasp the complexity of the challenge. Then he continued, pointing to a huge bow and a few golden arrows placed on a pedestal next to the pool: 'And here is the final condition. You cannot use your bow and arrow. You can only use this special bow constructed for this purpose. You'll have to string this bow, and then shoot the target using one of these golden arrows. By the way, you will have only one chance to hit the target. Good luck; and may the best archer win.'

Dhrishtadyumna finished his speech and, as he walked back to his seat, a murmur went through the seated audience. The magnitude of the difficulty was beginning to hit home. Some of the participants left the hall, not wanting to be humiliated in front of so many people. Some complained about the unfairness of the competition. Why set up a test that no one could pass? But Draupadi was too beautiful for most of the kings gathered there to give up without giving it a shot. One by one, the contestants came down by the pool to try their luck. Most couldn't even lift the heavy bow, let alone string and shoot. Those who managed to lift it, failed to bend the bow to string it. Some who managed to bend it a little were thrown away by the spring action and had to go back to their seats tending to their sprained arms and injured backs.

When his turn came, Duryodhan stepped up to the plate and, to the amazement of the audience, he picked up the bow and strung it with little effort. He then picked up a golden arrow and engaged the arrow with the bow. Then he knelt by the poolside with his bow and arrow pointed at the target above his head. He looked down at the reflected image of the target in the pool, made his aim and released the arrow. With a loud twang, the arrow passed through the hole in the disc. But to Duryodhan's disappointment, it missed the eye of the fish. Duryodhan stomped his foot in frustration and went back to his seat. Draupadi sighed in relief. She had heard about Duryodhan and his arrogant attitude, and didn't wish to be his wife.

Karna knew very well that if anyone could succeed in this test, it was he. Draupadi's beauty impressed him too, and deep inside, he wanted to have her as his bride. But he wanted his friend Duryodhan to try first. When Duryodhan failed and returned to his seat, Karna asked, 'My dear friend, can I give it a try?'

Duryodhan said, 'Yes, of course. Go ahead and show them who you are!'

Karna walked down the aisle to the centre of the hall and stood below the target. Then he picked up the heavy bow as if it was nothing but a piece of straw. With equal ease, he strung the bow. As he was getting ready to aim, Draupadi cried out, 'Stop! Don't shoot! I cannot accept a charioteer's son as my husband.'

Karna froze in his stance. Draupadi's words entered his ears like molten lava. For a moment, he felt like he would explode in anger. He took a deep breath to control himself. Then he placed the bow back in its place and walked back to his seat without uttering a single word. Duryodhan stood up to protest, but Karna stopped him. 'Let go, my friend. Draupadi has exercised her discretion, and she has the right to do so. It is her swayamvara after all,' he said.

No one was left to complete the challenge. Drupad and Dhrishtadyumna felt frustrated. All these arrangements for nothing? Were the pomp and grandeur to go to waste? Was the test so difficult to pass? Just then, Drupad noticed a tall and handsome young man stand up from the Brahmins' seating area. He spoke to another man sitting next to him and walked towards the royal stand. It was Arjun.

When nobody came forward to attempt the test, Yudhishthira and priest Dhaumya asked Arjun to try. They knew very well that only Arjun could pass the test with flying colours. The young man addressed Drupad: 'O King, would you permit a Brahmin like me to try?'

Drupad smiled and said, 'Sure you can. Brahmins are of higher order; and if you pass the test, I'd have no objection to giving my daughter's hand to you.' Arjun bowed to him and stepped down to the pool below the target. With utmost ease, he picked up the bow and strung it in seconds, as if it were a simple toy. He then placed an arrow on the bow, pulled the string, pointing the arrow up to the target, looked down at the reflection on the waters of the pool, and aimed for the eye. Silence fell on the hall as everybody held their breath to see what happened next. Suddenly, a twang was heard, followed by a loud clatter. Arjun's arrow had gone straight through the hole in the disc, hit the eye of the fish, and broken it into pieces. A loud roar rumbled through the audience as the Brahmins shouted and danced in joy at the success of one of their boys. The royal band played a merry tune as Draupadi walked down to Arjun and placed her garland on his neck, accepting him as her husband.

11

Draupadi's Marriage

As Draupadi garlanded Arjun, Drupad stood up and applauded from the stands. A thought kept brewing in his mind. Who is this young Brahmin? Is this, by any chance, Arjun in disguise? Although he had heard of the Pandavas' death in Varanavata, he was never convinced that heroes like Arjun and Bheem could die in a simple house fire. He had encountered Arjun in battle and knew very well how skilled and powerful a warrior he was. In fact, he had designed this contest with the secret motive to find Arjun. For he knew that very few people on earth could pass such a difficult test, and Arjun was one of them. But this Brahmin ...?

Drupad's train of thought was shattered by angry shouts and protests. The invited kings and princes were furious with Drupad for allowing a Brahmin to participate in the contest. 'We were the real, invited contenders for Draupadi's hand. The Brahmins were supposed to be mere spectators.' 'Don't you have any respect for royalty?' 'This was nothing but your crude attempt to insult the illustrious kings gathered here.' 'You ought to be punished.' The growing clamour reached a crescendo and the gathered kings picked up their weapons to attack Drupad.

Yudhishthira called Arjun and said, 'Arjun, King Drupad is now your father-in-law. We must protect him. You and Bheem go and defend the king while we take Draupadi to safety.'

Arjun picked up the bow and stood ready to defend Drupad, while Bheem uprooted a tree and used the trunk as his weapon and waited for the kings to attack him. Although the kings were taken aback to see Bheem uproot a tree with his bare hands, they were too angry to think logically. With uncontrolled frenzy, they pounced upon Bheem, who brushed off his attackers with one swift blow of the trunk. King Shalya of the Madra kingdom was a great wrestler. He pounced on Bheem and tried to pin him down. Bheem shook him off, then lifted him over his head and threw him down on the marble floor.

In the meantime, provoked by Duryodhan and the other kings, Karna attacked Arjun with a barrage of arrows. Arjun destroyed them all mid-air. A fierce battle ensued between Karna and Arjun. Karna used all his skills and weapons to attack Arjun, but not a single weapon could touch Arjun. He countered them all and stood defiant, laughing at Karna. Karna realized that his opponent is no ordinary Brahmin. He stopped attacking Arjun and asked, 'Who are you, Brahmin? Your skills are impressive. Only a few people, like my guru, Parashurama, Lord Indra, Lord Vishnu, or prince Arjun could counter my weapons. Are you any of them?'

Arjun laughed and said, 'I am only a poor Brahmin. Attack me and defeat me if you dare.'

Karna knew it would be impossible to defeat the Brahmin. He put down his bow and said, 'Pardon me, Brahmin. I shouldn't have attacked you. You have won Draupadi with your skills. Hence, you deserve to be her husband.' Karna turned and walked away from the hall.

The other kings were still trying to fight the Pandava brothers, especially Bheem.

By this time, Krishna had no doubt about the identity of the two Brahmins. He was sure that they were none other than Bheem and Arjun. He turned to Balram and said, 'Brother, I think we have seen enough of this fight. This needs to stop now.'

Krishna stood between the kings and the Pandava brothers, and said, 'Friends, please lay down your arms. You are fighting for nothing. This young Brahmin has passed King Drupad's test and won Draupadi as his bride with his might and valour. Why don't you accept this fact and go home? I think it would be best for your health as well as your kingdoms.'

The kings didn't have the courage to argue with Lord Krishna. They put down their weapons and dispersed from the swayamvara hall. Arjun and Bheem didn't wait either. They slipped out unnoticed and met Yudhishthira, who was waiting outside with Draupadi, Nakul and Sahadev. Without wasting time, they walked back to the potter's home, where Kunti was waiting for them.

As they left the palace premises, Drupad called Dhrishtadyumna aside and said, 'Follow these Brahmins and find out who they are ... where they come from.' Dhrishtadyumna covered himself in a shawl and followed the Pandavas at a distance.

When the brothers reached home, Kunti was busy in the kitchen preparing dinner. Hoping to surprise his mother, Arjun called out, 'Mother, look what we've brought for you today!'

Kunti thought that her boys must have brought their usual fruits and vegetables from their door-to-door begging. Without looking up, she said, 'Whatever it is, divide it equally amongst yourselves.'

The brothers were shocked to hear this. Bheem said, 'But mother, first see what we've brought! Arjun has won King Drupad's daughter Draupadi's hand in marriage at the swayamvara!'

Kunti came out and the moment she saw Draupadi, she knew she had made a grave mistake. 'Oh no, what a terrible thing I have uttered!' said the horrified mother who always spoke the truth. But this time, she failed herself. How could Draupadi be divided amongst the five brothers? The anxious queen looked at her son and said, 'Yudhishthira, today I have fallen from my path of truth. I have sinned.'

Yudhishthira held her hand and said, 'No, mother, you have not sinned. You have always spoken the truth, and what you've uttered now will come true. All of us brothers will marry Draupadi. Grandfather Vyasa predicted this long ago. This is our destiny, and this is Draupadi's destiny.'

The brothers' eyes lit up in joy. Yudhishthira knew that all his brothers longed for Draupadi. If Arjun married her, there was a distinct possibility that Bheem, Nakul and Sahadev would be jealous of him. This could threaten the unity of the Pandavas.

Right then, Krishna and Balram entered the hut. The Pandavas were overjoyed to see them. Krishna bowed to Kunti, his aunt, and Yudhishthira, his cousin, and paid his respects. Yudhishthira asked, 'How did you recognize us? We thought we had a pretty good disguise.'

Krishna smiled and said, 'Fire cannot be kept hidden even if you try. We were so happy to see you. I knew, a petty house fire couldn't destroy heroes like you. Seeing you at the swayamvara hall, I felt much better. Soon your days of hardship will be over, and your fame and prosperity will spread like wildfire. We should leave, else people might become suspicious.'

After Krishna and Balram left, the five brothers sat down to have their dinner while Draupadi served them. As usual, half of the food was served to Bheem while the rest was divided amongst the rest of the brothers, their mother and Draupadi. After dinner, the brothers lay down to sleep on a straw mat on the floor. Kunti slept at their head, while Draupadi slept at their feet. The brothers talked about the day's proceedings and about warfare and weapons, and fell asleep.

Hiding outside the hut, Dhrishtadyumna had been listening to all that was going on. He had been convinced that the brothers were not Brahmins but Kshatriyas, the warrior caste. From their discussion and demeanour, he was convinced that the brothers were of some royal order, possibly even the Pandava brothers. He went back to the palace and shared his observations with his father. Drupad suppressed his excitement and said, 'Well, then, let's invite them to the palace tomorrow and arrange for the wedding. Tomorrow we'll know for sure who these Brahmins are!'

The next day, Drupad sent a priest to the Pandavas' hut with the proposal. The priest said to Yudhishthira, 'Dear Sir, our great king Drupad is overjoyed to see her daughter being won by a skilled archer. But he is anxious to know his son-in law's identity. He suspects that you are the great Pandavas. Is that true?'

Yudhishthira smiled and said, 'Your princess has been won by the most eligible person. Please tell your king not to worry.'

The priest said, 'Our king has invited you to a great feast in the palace. The royal chariots are waiting outside. Please do come with me. We would also like to finalize the details of the wedding ceremony in the palace.'

Yudhishthira agreed.

The Pandavas, along with Draupadi and Kunti, mounted the chariots and arrived at the palace, where the king had arranged for a grand reception. As the Pandavas arrived, conch shells rang out, flowers were showered from the skies, and hundreds of courtesans sang and danced to welcome them.

The king had arranged for a feast, where the Pandavas, along with other guests, were treated to sumptuous food and drinks. After the meal, the king took the Pandavas to a huge chamber filled with gifts and presents. To ascertain their identity, he had arranged the gifts in a special order. On one table, he placed utensils, books and scriptures which are preferred by Brahmins. The next table had goods that are of interest to traders and business people. On the third table were heaps of weapons and armour that could only interest a Kshatriya. Drupad invited the Pandavas to pick whatever gifts they liked. The brothers walked to the table full of weapons and examined them as expert warriors would. Watching this, Drupad had no doubt that these men were not Brahmins. They must be Kshatriyas. He walked up to the Pandavas and said, 'If I may trust my judgment, I'd say you are not Brahmins. Rather, you are Kshatriyas of royal order. But I cannot say that for sure. So, please do help me understand this. Who are you?'

Yudhishthira smiled and said, 'You are right, O revered king! We are indeed Kshatriyas of the royal order. We are sons of the great king Pandu, the late king of Hastinapur. I am Yudhishthira, and these are my brothers Bheem, Arjun, Nakul and Sahadev. Arjun, the great archer, was the one who passed your test and won your daughter Draupadi. So please rest assured, your daughter is in good hands. She is the future queen of Hastinapur. And you are our revered father-in law.'

Drupad was overwhelmed with emotion. His dreams had come true. Tears of joy ran down his cheeks. He managed to control himself and said, 'Oh, what a lucky man I am! How I longed to see this day! We heard about the fire in Varanavata and feared the worst. To see you all in good health is great news. And now to have you, the great Pandavas, as my in-laws is a great honour and a matter of pride for the Panchal kingdom.' Looking at Arjun, Drupad said, 'Today is an auspicious day. I'd like the wedding ceremony to be held today.'

Yudhishthira said, 'Sure. But as the eldest brother, I'll marry Draupadi first.'

The king was taken aback. However, he soon regained his composure and said, 'If that's what you desire, so be it. I'll be glad to give my daughter to you or to any one of your brothers.'

Yudhishthira smiled and replied, 'O King, you don't understand. All of us brothers will marry Draupadi. I'll marry her first, then Bheem, followed by Arjun, Nakul and Sahadev.'

King Drupad was flabbergasted. Yudhishthira's humiliating proposal made him furious, and it took some time for him to gather his wits. With great effort, the king controlled his anger and said, 'Yudhishthira, how is this possible? You are said to be the incarnation of Dharma himself. You are the most righteous and virtuous man alive. How could you think of such an outrageous and blasphemous proposal? As per the scriptures and traditions, a man can have multiple wives. But how can a woman have multiple husbands?'

With a calm voice, Yudhishthira said, 'It's uncommon, but not unprecedented. Our mother has approved of this marriage, and what the pious queen approves of cannot be blasphemous. You can rest assured that we won't do anything that is not in line with virtue.'

Drupad was not convinced. He consulted his spiritual and legal advisors, but none of them could give him any satisfactory reasoning to justify Yudhishthira's claim. A crisis developed and Draupadi's wedding was now in jeopardy.

At this moment, when things were falling apart, the great Rishi Vyasa arrived in Drupad's chamber. He called Drupad and said, 'Dear king, I will try to clarify your doubts. Come with me.' He took Drupad to a private chamber and told him a story.

Vyasa said, 'In their past life, the Pandavas were the five Indras, or the gods of heaven. Once, the ruler of the heavens, Indra, along with his four compatriots and their consorts, angered Lord Shiva with their arrogance. Shiva cursed them to be born as human beings. Shiva ordered their consort, a beautiful celestial maiden, to be born in the world as Draupadi and marry the five Indras. King Drupad, this marital arrangement was pre-ordained. Such a marriage may not be admissible among humans, but as I said, the Pandavas and Draupadi are not normal human beings—they are gods and are obeying the commands of none other than Lord Shiva.'

Vyasa's story convinced Drupad. He had no more concerns. He ordered his ministers to arrange for the wedding ceremony. The entire city of Kampilya was decorated with flowers and garlands. The citizens joined in the festivities that continued for five days. On each of the five days, Draupadi was given in marriage to each of the five brothers, starting with Yudhishthira, followed by Bheem, Arjun, Nakul and Sahadev. After the wedding, the Pandavas continued to live in Drupad's palace along with their mother Kunti and their bride Draupadi.

12

Dhritarashtra's Dilemma

THE NEWS OF THE WEDDING FESTIVITIES REACHED DURYODHAN WHILE HE was travelling back to the palace. He was furious. Not only did the Pandavas survive the fire, but they also won Draupadi's hand in marriage. He cursed Purochana, 'I should have never trusted that fool!'

'The Pandavas now have a powerful ally in King Drupad. They can challenge us any moment. We must think of a strategy to finish them as soon as possible. Let's talk to father about this,' he said to Dushasana.

Meanwhile, Vidura was ecstatic. He went to King Dhritarashtra's chamber and said, 'O King! I have great news for you. By the grace of god, the glory of the Kurus has reached new heights.'

The blind king thought that his son Duryodhan had succeeded in winning the hand of Draupadi. He stood up in joy and said, 'Vidura, what great news you have brought me this morning! Oh, I am so happy! Arrange to welcome the Panchal princess with the finest of jewels and gifts. Welcome Duryodhan and Draupadi into the city with great pomp and honour. Let no expense be spared.'

Vidura realized that the king had misunderstood him. With a calm voice, he said, 'Brother, I spoke in haste and I think I should clarify my statement. It was Arjun who won Draupadi at the swayamvara, not Duryodhan. Contrary to our belief, the Pandava brothers have survived the fire. To keep their mother Kunti's word, they have all married Draupadi and are now living in King Drupad's palace in Kampilya.'

Vidura saw how all happiness drained away from Dhritarashtra's face. The king sat down and tried to force a smile. 'That's ... eh, wonderful news!' he said. 'Brother Pandu's sons are as dear to me as my own. My heart fills with joy to know that they are alive and have succeeded in winning the princess of Panchal.'

Vidura knew that Dhritarashtra was not being truthful. Still, he said, 'I am happy for you, my brother. May this thought stay with you forever.' Saying so, Vidura left the chamber.

In the meantime, Duryodhan, Dushasana and Karna had arrived at the palace and overheard his conversation between Dhritarashtra and Vidura. The moment Vidura left, they stormed into the room.

'Father, how could you be happy with the Pandavas' success? How could you tell Vidura to welcome our enemies? Don't you have any feelings for your sons?' asked Duryodhan.

Dhritarashtra's face was distorted in pain. He said, 'Son Duryodhan, why don't you understand? How can I express my real feelings to Vidura? After all, I am the king of the Kuru dynasty. You tell me, what should I do?'

Duryodhan walked up to Dhritarashtra. 'Father, the Pandavas have survived the fire and now the people of Hastinapur would be more sympathetic to them. They have also become more powerful by acquiring an ally like Drupad. We must do something soon to get rid of them. Else we would lose everything we have.'

Dhritarashtra asked, 'What do you have in mind?'

Duryodhan thought for a while and said, 'The only way to beat them is to break the unity between the five brothers. We can send some shrewd Brahmins to Kampilya to sow dissent and jealousy amongst the Pandavas. Or maybe we can incite Draupadi against her husbands. For a woman with five husbands, that should not be a problem. We can also use some beautiful nymphs to seduce the Pandavas and make Draupadi resent her husbands.'

Dushasana added, 'We can also bribe the Panchal king with lots of gold and silver and make him abandon the Pandavas. Or maybe we can use our spies to convince the Pandavas to live in Kampilya for ever and never come back to Hastinapur.'

'Bheem is the root of all our problems,' said Duryodhan. 'If we could eliminate him, the Pandavas lose their power. I am not worried about Arjun. Karna can take care of him. However, killing Bheem will be difficult. Why not send some assassins? They could enter Drupad's palace in secret and kill Bheem. I have another idea. Maybe we should invite them to Hastinapur and when they enter the city and drop their guard, we could ambush and kill them with the help of some sharpshooters. We can use any method, but we must keep trying until we succeed in neutralizing them. Karna, what do you say?'

Karna shook his head and said, 'My friend, I am afraid I do not agree with any of your suggestions. They are of no use against the Pandavas. You will never be able to break their unity by any sly means. They are five bodies, but of a single soul. Else, why would they agree to marry the same woman? You have been trying to kill Bheem since your childhood days. Did you ever succeed? When you yourself have failed, do you think a petty assassin would succeed in killing him? Besides, I hate any form of covert and deceptive tactics. Only cowards refuse to face their enemy. In my opinion, we must amass a huge army with the help of our allies and attack Panchal. We have no dearth of gallant warriors on our side. We should be able to defeat Drupad and the Pandavas easily.'

Duryodhan was excited. But before he could say anything, Dhritarashtra spoke. 'Karna, you've spoken like a real hero—like a proper Kshatriya. However, I think I should also consult Bhishma, Vidura and Drona, for we cannot fight the Pandavas without their support. Come to the assembly hall and I'll take a decision after listening to them.'

Karna glanced at Duryodhan, who grimaced in frustration. The elders would never support any plan against their favourites—the Pandavas. However, they kept their thoughts to themselves and followed Dhritarashtra to the royal assembly.

There, in front of Bhishma, Drona, Vidura and others, Dhritarashtra explained the gravity of the situation. 'When we came to know that my beloved nephews were killed in the fire of Varanavata, we were heartbroken. Then with a heavy heart, and with your permission, I announced Duryodhan the crown prince of Hastinapur. God only knows how glad I am to know that Pandu's sons have survived the fire and they are alive and well. But if the Pandavas come back and stake a claim to the throne, which now belongs to Duryodhan, it can blow up into a major conflict. The Pandavas are not alone either. They have the Panchal king Drupad by their side. We would have no other option but to fight, and I shudder to think of the consequences. How can we prevent such a destructive war? Karna suggested that we launch a pre-emptive strike and eliminate the problem before it surfaces. However, I cannot take such a drastic measure without your approval. I seek your counsel. Please guide me.'

Bhishma stood up and said, 'I can never support a war against the Pandavas. To me, the sons of Pandu and Dhritarashtra are all the same. Just as Duryodhan considers Hastinapur to be his ancestral home, so do the Pandavas. I suggest you give them half the kingdom. That'll be the best course of action, and one that is most appropriate of a Kuru descendant.' He paused for a moment and then continued, 'We are lucky that the Pandavas are alive and well. When I heard of their death in Varanavata, I was not only heartbroken, but also ashamed of myself. The people of Hastinapur don't blame Purochana as much as they blame you, the king of Kuru! Now that you have a chance, do the right thing and redeem yourself.'

As Bhishma got back to his seat, Drona rose to address the king. 'O King, a true friend is one who, when asked for counsel, speaks the truth and guides you towards the right path. Our wise friend Bhishma has given you the right advice and I agree with him with all my heart. Share the kingdom with the Pandavas. That will benefit all. I suggest you send a messenger to Panchal with precious gifts for King Drupad and his family. Let the messenger tell him how glad you are to know that the Pandavas are alive and safe under his guardianship. Let him also tell Drupad how glad you are with this new alliance with the Panchal kingdom. The messenger should seek Drupad's permission to bring the Pandavas back to Hastinapur. When the Pandavas arrive at the gates of Hastinapur, let Dushasana and Vikarna greet them and escort them to the palace. There, you would receive your nephews and your daughter-in law Draupadi with proper rituals and affection. Then give the Pandavas their fair share of the kingdom and install Yudhishthira as the king.'

No sooner had Drona finished his speech than Karna jumped up on his feet and said, 'O King, Bhishma and Drona have been living a life of luxury thanks to your wealth and generosity. Now they give you advice that does not serve your interest. What can be more ironic?

Please keep in mind, a person's happiness or misfortune depends on his fate and destiny and not on his friends. If it is your destiny to remain the king of Hastinapur, then nobody can take it away from you. If not, then it doesn't matter how hard you try or who you have as friends, you won't be able to keep your throne. Now it is for you to decide whose advice you should accept and whose to ignore.'

'Karna, you are an evil person, and that's why you consider our advice as evil,' retorted an angry Drona. 'King Dhritarashtra, one thing I can tell you for sure. If our advice is not followed, I warn you, the Kurus would be exterminated in no time.'

Karna was about to get up again, but Vidura interrupted. 'O King, your friends have indeed spoken in your best interests. However, it is of no use if you don't pay heed to them. You will find no better well-wisher than the great Bhishma and Drona. They are impartial and they are the wisest friends you will ever have. You should realize that it is impossible to defeat the Pandavas by force. Not only are they the most powerful warriors in the world, they also enjoy the support of the mighty Balram and Satyaki. Lord Krishna is their adviser. King Drupad is their father-in law, and they have the gallant prince Dhrishtadyumna as their brother-in law. They have the might and the resources to defeat any enemy. I urge you not to listen to the evil advice of Duryodhan, Karna and Shakuni. They are foolish and devoid of decency.'

The ministers in the court greeted Vidura's comment with loud applause. Dhritarashtra realized that this was not the time to go against the elders. He stood up and said, 'Bhishma, Drona and Vidura have spoken wisely and keeping the interests of the Kuru dynasty in mind. Yudhishthira and his brothers are as much my sons as they are Pandu's. Vidura, I request you, go to Panchal and bring our beloved Pandavas back to their home with dignity and honour.'

Soon, Vidura left for Kampilya with carts full of gold and other precious gifts for King Drupad and the Pandavas. Drupad welcomed Vidura with open arms. The Pandavas and their mother were delighted to see Vidura after so long. Krishna and his brother Balram, who were in Kampilya as guests of Drupad, also greeted Vidura and paid their respects.

Vidura then approached King Drupad and said, 'O King, I come here as the emissary of the great Kuru King Dhritarashtra. He has asked me to tell you how happy he is with this alliance with you and your family. He welcomes you to the greater Kuru family and wishes for an everlasting friendship.'

Drupad replied, 'The feeling is mutual. I feel proud and honoured to have the mighty Kuru family as an ally.'

Vidura smiled: 'Our king, the Kuru family and the people of Hastinapur have missed our dear Pandava princes for a long time. With your kind permission, I'd like to take them back to Hastinapur, their home. The Kuru women are also eager to meet their daughter-in-law, Panchali.'

Drupad replied, 'Vidura, I have no objection at all. If Yudhishthira and his brothers wish to go and if Krishna and Balram agree, you are most welcome to take them with you.'

Krishna, of course, had no objection. Soon, with a heavy heart, King Drupad and the city of Kampilya began to prepare for the departure of their daughter Draupadi to her in-laws' house.

After a long journey, the Pandavas, along with Kunti and Draupadi, arrived at the gates of Hastinapur. At the request of Yudhishthira, Krishna and Balram also accompanied them. Drona, Kripa, Vikarna and many other Kuru ministers greeted them at the gates. They escorted the Pandavas in a royal procession. Colourful flags fluttering in the air decorated their path from the gate to the royal palace. A band of musicians followed them, playing joyful music. The citizens of Hastinapur greeted their long-lost princes with loud cheers along the road. They showered flowers on them and bowed in respect when Krishna and Balram's chariot passed by. As they entered the palace, the Pandava brothers touched Dhritarashtra's feet to pay their respects. Dhritarashtra pulled them to his chest in a warm embrace. Tears flowed from his blind eyes. The Kuru women greeted the new bride Draupadi with garlands and gifts. Gandhari greeted Draupadi with an affectionate embrace. As she smelled Panchali's fragrant body, she remembered the prophecy—Draupadi would be the cause of her son's death. She shivered inside, but retained the smile on her face. Duryodhan, Dushasana and Karna received the Pandavas with a cursory greeting. They were more concerned about the action Dhritarashtra would take regarding the inheritance of the throne. However, Dhritarashtra made no statement about the future of the kingdom. And everybody, although happy, was anxious to know what the fate of the Pandavas would be in Hastinapur.

13

Indraprastha, the New Kingdom

Two days after the arrival of the Pandavas, Dhritarashtra summoned them to the royal assembly. Dressed in white silk, the five brothers took their seats in the hall. Krishna and Balram were invited to sit on golden thrones next to the king. Bhishma, Drona, Kripa and Vidura sat in their respective seats. Duryodhan and his brothers were seated opposite the Pandavas. The hall was buzzing with anticipation.

After everybody had settled down, Dhritarashtra stood up and said, 'Words cannot express the joy I feel to have the sons of my dear brother Pandu back with us again. I feel blessed.

'But we must ensure that peace prevails in the family. We must ensure that the Kuru kingdom does not become the cause for conflict between the Pandavas and the Kauravas. Hence, I have decided to divide the kingdom between the brothers equally.' He looked at Yudhishthira and added, 'Dear Yudhishthira, I give you the vast land of Khandava. Go there, establish your kingdom and live in peace.'

The assembly hall was stunned to hear this. Bhishma, Drona and Vidura glanced at each other, shocked. Dhritarashtra had followed their suggestion to offer half the kingdom to the Pandavas. But Khandava? It was a piece of barren land filled with deserts, marshes and forests. No human being could live there.

Duryodhan and Dushasana were quite happy, though. Sending the Pandavas to Khandava was nothing more than banishing them from civilization.

Bheem was mad with rage. 'Khandava? He gives that godforsaken piece of land to us to build our kingdom?' he whispered in Yudhishthira's ears.

Yudhishthira stopped him from saying any more, for he noticed Krishna smile and nod in agreement when Dhritarashtra made his announcement. Besides, Yudhishthira was happy with any proposal that ensured peace. He stood up with folded hands and said, 'O King, we are grateful for your kind gesture and accept your offer with all humility. Tomorrow, at daybreak, we will leave for Khandava.' That afternoon, Dhritarashtra crowned Yudhishthira as the king of Khandava. Rishi Vyasa himself arrived to perform the rituals.

The next morning, the Pandavas departed for Khandava. Krishna and Vyasa accompanied them. When they reached Khandava, the brothers were quite disheartened to see the vast, barren land with not a human being in sight. Krishna smiled and asked Vyasa, 'O Rishi, please find us an auspicious location where my dear friends can build their city.'

Vyasa looked around and selected a place. Krishna then summoned Indra. 'Lord, please bless this land and make it rich and fertile. Then build a great city for the Pandavas,' Krishna requested the king of the gods.

Indra summoned the celestial architect Vishwakarma and entrusted him with the job. In no time, Vishwakarma constructed a fabulous city, full of large mansions, wide roads and beautiful parks. Lakes and canals were built to make the land rich and fertile. Since Indra built the city, it was named Indraprastha. Vishwakarma built a beautiful palace for the Pandavas using marble and precious stones. It was as gorgeous as the house of the gods in heaven. The Pandavas moved into the palace and began their royal duty as the rulers of Indraprastha, ensuring quality of life for their subjects. Soon, people from other areas started coming to the new city of Indraprastha in the hope of living a peaceful and prosperous life.

The Conjugal Arrangement

One day, the revered celestial sage, Rishi Narada visited Indraprastha to meet the Pandavas. The brothers greeted him with due respect. Yudhishthira offered the rishi his own grand throne to sit. Draupadi cooked several delicious dishes and served him with her own hands. Draupadi's enchanting beauty caught the attention of the great rishi. He also noticed how enamoured her five husbands were of their common wife.

After Draupadi left, Narada called the five brothers and said, 'Boys, let me tell you a story. In the olden days, there lived two powerful demon brothers named Sunda and Upasunda. Just like you, their fraternal bond was so strong that they were almost inseparable. They did everything together, and whatever they earned, they always shared between themselves. They wanted to conquer the heavens and the earth. To ensure their success, they began a long and arduous worship of Lord Brahma to ask for a boon of immortality. Lord Brahma was pleased with their worship, but he said, "I cannot give you the boon of immortality because you want to conquer the heavens. Ask for something else."

'The demon brothers replied, "Then give us the boon that nobody or nothing in the universe would be able to kill us. We can only die at the hands of each other." Brahma agreed.

'Powered by the boon which made them almost indestructible, Sunda and Upasunda began their rampage. They marched towards the heavens and destroyed whatever came in their path. The gods were scared. They went to Lord Brahma and asked for a solution to the problem he had created. Brahma called upon Vishwakarma, the celestial artisan, and told him, "Build a woman so beautiful and attractive that nobody would be able to resist her."

'Vishwakarma then collected, bit by bit, the best things available from all over the universe and built a gorgeous woman. Her name was Tilottama. She was so pretty that when she walked around Lord Brahma, he couldn't stop looking at her and a face popped out on each of the four sides of his head. Hence, he is also known as Chaturanana or the four-headed Brahma. Indra grew a thousand eyes to enjoy her beauty. Brahma told Tilottama: "Go and seduce Sunda and Upasunda."

'The demon brothers were enjoying themselves in the foothills of the Vindhya Mountains when Tilottama appeared before them. The drunk brothers were awestruck by her incredible beauty. Sunda held her right arm and pulled her to his side. Upasunda jumped in, grabbed her left arm, and pulled her to his side. They started a tug of war with Tilottama between them.

'Sunda said, "Brother, please let go of her. I want to marry her. She is like your sister-in law. Treat her with respect."

'Upasunda growled, "No, she'll be *my* queen. *You* let go of her."

'Thus, a fight broke out between them. They pounced upon each other with their mace and soon they lay dead, each killed by the other.'

Narada paused, looked at the Pandavas, and said, 'You have also married one of the most beautiful maidens on earth. You must ensure that she does not become the cause for your mutual destruction, like

Sunda and Upasunda. I suggest you come up with a rule such that no conflict can arise regarding the companionship of Draupadi.'

After Narada left, Yudhishthira thought about his suggestion. He then consulted his brothers and came up with a plan. They decided that Draupadi would live with each brother for a period of one year. During this period, if any of the other brothers entered the couple's room and saw them together, he would have to leave the palace and go into exile for a period of twelve years. In addition, during these twelve years, he'll have to stay celibate. With this arrangement in place, the Pandavas made sure that Draupadi would never be the cause for any disagreement between them.

One evening, a group of Brahmins came to the palace and complained to Arjun that a group of bandits had been stealing their cattle. 'Arjun we pay you, the rulers of Khandava, a share of our crop as taxes. It is your duty to protect your citizens. You should go right away to catch the bandits and get our cattle back.'

Arjun assured them, 'Don't worry, I will get back your cattle.'

Arjun went in to get his weapons, but he realized that his weapons were stored in a room where Yudhishthira was spending time with Draupadi. He was in a fix. If he went into the room to get his weapons, he would have to go into exile for twelve years. If he didn't, Yudhishthira would have to suffer the consequences for not serving his duty as the ruler of Khandava. Finally, he thought, he could never let his brother down. He'd rather go into exile than let Yudhishthira fall from grace. He barged into the room and asked Yudhishthira his permission to take his weapons. Yudhishthira was surprised, but he didn't object. Arjun went out with his weapons, and in no time, captured the bandits and returned the cattle to the subjects. The Brahmins praised Arjun for his prompt action and praised Yudhishthira for being a great ruler.

Arjun came back to the palace, knelt in front of Yudhishthira and said, 'Brother, I broke the rule. I should be punished. I will leave for my exile right now. Please permit me.'

Yudhishthira was overwhelmed with emotion. 'Arjun, you have done nothing wrong. A younger brother can always enter his elder brother's room. Besides, I wasn't unhappy to see you. Whatever you did, you did it for my benefit. You should not have to go into exile.'

Arjun replied, 'Brother, I learnt from you that a rule is a rule, and breaking it under any circumstances is against virtue. I must have my punishment.'

With heavy hearts, the Pandavas bade Arjun goodbye. Draupadi stood at the doorway and watched Arjun as he vanished into the horizon. Her eyes filled with tears, while her heart pained at the thought of his indifference towards her.

14

Arjun's Twelve-Year Exile

ARJUN WANDERED THROUGH MANY COUNTRIES UNTIL HE REACHED THE source of River Ganga. He wished to take a dip in the holy waters and pray for his deceased ancestors. As he stepped into the water, something caught his feet and dragged him down. It was Ulupi, the princess of the Nagas or the celestial serpents. When Arjuna woke up, he found himself lying in a bed in a beautiful palace with a gorgeous maiden. He asked, 'Who are you? And where am I?'

The woman smiled and said, 'I am Ulupi. Daughter of Kauravya, the king of the Nagas. You are in my palace.'

Surprised, Arjun asked, 'Why did you bring me here?'

'Pardon me, my prince. When I saw you by the riverside, I was overcome with love and desire. I couldn't resist myself and I brought you here. Please accept me and fulfil my desire,' Ulupi said.

Arjun got up from the bed. 'I am sorry, lady. I cannot do that.'

Ulupi was hurt. She moved close to Arjun and asked, 'But why? Don't you find me attractive? Am I not pretty enough?'

'You are beautiful, Ulupi. Any man would die to be your lover. But I have vowed to stay celibate for twelve years during my exile. I cannot break my promise.' Arjun then explained to Ulupi the cause for his exile.

Ulupi replied, 'Your vow of celibacy only applies to Draupadi, since she was the cause for your exile. That should not prevent you from being *my* lover. If you do not please me, I will kill myself and you'll be responsible for my death. As a Kshatriya warrior, it is your duty to save a damsel like me.'

Her argument convinced Arjun. Besides, Ulupi was too attractive to be ignored. He smiled and pulled Ulupi into his strong arms.

Later, the satisfied Naga princess kissed Arjun and said, 'My prince, you have fulfilled my desire and saved my life. I give you this boon—you'll be invincible in water. No amphibious creature would be able to conquer you.'

Chitrangada of Manipur

After taking his leave of Ulupi, Arjun continued his journey towards the east. On his way, he visited many holy places and pilgrimages. He spent some time in the Mahendra Mountains and then proceeded along the eastern seashores until he reached the kingdom of Manipura. While strolling through the charming parks and gardens of the city, he saw a gorgeous woman riding by on a horse. She was in men's clothes and sported an armour, but her radiant beauty didn't go unnoticed by Arjun. He asked a passerby: 'Who is this lovely maiden?'

The man smiled and said, 'That is Chitrangada, the daughter of our king, Chitrabahana.'

Arjun walked away, but he couldn't get Chitrangada's image off his mind. Her poise, her strength and her demeanour were strangely attractive. Arjun knew that he was in love and Chitrangada was his destiny.

The next morning, he walked into the palace and bowed to King Chitrabahana. 'O King, I am Arjun, son of the great Kuru King Pandu. I am in love with your daughter Chitrangada and would like to request her hand in marriage,' he said.

The king replied, 'Arjun, I am honoured by your proposal. But there is a complication. Many moons ago, one of my ancestors named Prabhanjana worshipped Lord Shiva and prayed for a son. The satisfied god gave him a boon that ensured each of his generation would have but only one child. Each of my ancestors had a son. I was blessed with a daughter—Chitrangada. So I brought her up like a son. You can marry her if you promise me that her son would be my descendant and continue my lineage.'

Arjun was so enamoured of the princess that he was in no condition to think. 'I promise, King Chitrabahana, I promise. Chitrangada's son will be the descendant of your line and will be the ruler of Manipura. I will have no claim over him.'

King Chitrabahana was delighted to hear this and arranged the wedding. In due course, Chitrangada gave birth to a son and named him Babrubahana. After three years in Manipura, Arjun handed over Babrubahana to his father-in-law and said, 'O King, as promised, here is your grandson, Babrubahana.' He then bid goodbye to Chitrangada.

Chitrangada's eyes filled with tears. Arjun consoled her, 'Don't be sad, Chitrangada. For now, you must stay here to bring up our son, Babrubahana. When he grows up, come to Indraprastha where we can live together forever.'

Saying so, Arjun bade goodbye to Chitrangada, Babrubahana and Chitrabahana, and began his long journey to the western shores of India.

The Abduction of Subhadra

After visiting several pilgrimages on the western seashores, Arjun arrived in the city of Prabhasa. There, he met his dearest friend and cousin, Lord Krishna. After spending some time in Prabhasa, Krishna took Arjun to the beautiful Raivataka Mountains, where a grand festival of the Vrishni and the Andhaka tribes was taking place. Thousands of people from Krishna's capital Dwarka had travelled to the mountains to enjoy the festivities. Mighty warriors like Pradyumna, Sambya, Akrura, Sarana and Satyaki arrived with their families. Krishna's brother Balram went around drunk and was having a great time along with his wife. Krishna and Arjun walked around the festival grounds and enjoyed the joyful atmosphere.

One day, a beautiful woman caught Arjun's attention. She was dressed in gorgeous silk and gold ornaments, and looked as pretty as an apsara. Arjun just couldn't keep his eyes off her. Noticing Arjun's distraction, Krishna said, 'It seems the great ascetic's mind has been flooded with desire.' Arjun was embarrassed.

Krishna added, 'By the way, the lady you are smitten with happens to be my half-sister, Subhadra. She is my father's favourite. If you like her, I can talk to my father on your behalf.'

Arjun said, 'O Krishna, it will be an honour to have your sister Subhadra as my wife. How do you suggest I win her?'

'Well, if I tell my father, he can arrange for her swayamvara. But do you want to take that chance? A woman's mind is unpredictable, and there is no guarantee that she'd pick you as her husband. I think, the most assured way is to abduct her.'

'Abduct her? Your sister?' Arjun was quite surprised to hear this.

'Why not? This is an acceptable option for a Kshatriya to win his bride. You aren't committing any crime.'

Arjun still couldn't believe what he was hearing. 'What about your family? Won't they be upset? And I am not sure how my family, especially Yudhishthira, would take this.'

'Let me worry about my family. I am sure I can handle them. You take care of your family. Send a messenger to Indraprastha and ask Yudhishthira for his opinion. I am sure he won't object.'

Right away, a messenger was sent to Indraprastha, and he came back with the good news—Yudhishthira had granted him permission.

Krishna then told Arjun, 'Prepare yourself. Arrange for a fast and robust chariot and load it with weapons. You may face a stiff challenge from Subhadra's guards and the other Vrishni warriors. Tomorrow morning, when Subhadra finishes her morning prayers at the temple in Raivataka, you take her on your chariot and drive off to Indraprastha.'

Arjun did as instructed. The next morning, as if going on a hunting trip, Arjun left Krishna's palace in a golden chariot loaded with weapons and driven by four horses. Reaching the top of the Raivataka Mountains, he hid behind the temple. The moment Subhadra finished her worship and came out of the temple, Arjun leapt from his hiding place, grabbed her hand and pulled her into his chariot. And before her startled bodyguards could do anything, he sped off with Subhadra.

The guards ran to the chief officer in the court of Sudharma and complained about Subhadra's abduction. The panicked officer blew the trumpet calling all to arms. The Yadavas were enjoying their sleep after a long night of wining and dining. The sound of the trumpet woke them up. They scrambled to pick up their weapons and arrived at the court of Sudharma. When they heard that Arjun had taken away Princess Subhadra by force, they were furious.

'The Kuru prince has insulted us. He must be punished!' shouted some of them.

'Our honour is at stake. We cannot let this happen!' shouted others.

'The Pandavas must pay for this humiliation. Let's declare war on Indraprastha!' a few others chimed in.

Balram and Krishna also arrived in the court. Krishna sat in one corner of the room and watched the pandemonium as it unfolded. Noticing Krishna's indifference, Balram raised his hand to stop the Yadavas. 'Stop shouting, you fools! Do you know what Krishna has to say about this? Why is he silent? It is because of him that we had treated Arjun with so much love and respect. But that ungrateful brute did not deserve our hospitality. Arjun has disgraced us by stealing Subhadra and I won't tolerate this insolent behaviour. I will wipe out the Kuru dynasty from the face of the earth.'

The Yadavas supported him wholeheartedly.

Krishna rose from his seat and said, 'You are making a huge mistake. Arjun didn't insult us. Rather, his action could only bring us honour. Arjun didn't expect that we'd sell our woman for wealth; neither did he want to take any chances with a swayamvara. He did what is right for a Kshatriya—abduct the woman he loves. That is an acceptable option in our tradition.' He paused for a moment and then continued: 'Arjun is born of the great Bharata Shantanu race. He is the son of Kunti, our Kuntibhoj's daughter, and hence belongs to our clan too. He is indomitable in the battlefield and is the greatest warrior on earth. Who wouldn't want him as a groom? I suggest you go and try to bring him back with nice words. If you try to fight him, he'll defeat you and that would only bring us infamy and dishonour. But if you ask him politely and accept him as Subhadra's husband, it would bring us honour. Arjun is our cousin and I am sure he'll be nice to you.'

Krishna's advice made sense. The Yadavas sent a small team to bring the couple back to Dwarka and got them married in a gala ceremony. Arjun spent one year in Dwarka with his newly wedded wife. He spent the rest of his exile period in Pushkar before returning to Indraprastha.

After arriving in Hastinapur, Arjun and Subhadra paid their respects to Yudhishthira and the other elders. Then Arjun went in to see Draupadi. He stepped into the room and saw Draupadi standing near the window, gazing outside. Arjun went close to her and said, 'Draupadi, I have come back to you. Won't you greet me?'

Draupadi didn't even look at him. In a calm voice, she replied, 'You'd rather go back to Subhadra. You know, an old knot loosens when you tie a new one.'

Arjun felt ashamed. 'Forgive me, Draupadi,' he said. 'When I met Subhadra, I was tired and lonely. I couldn't control myself and I married her—because that was an honourable thing to do. Believe me I could never forget you. You were always in my heart and will always remain there. Please forgive me.'

Draupadi didn't give an inch. Arjun went back to Subhadra and told her, 'Subhadra, you'll have to win Draupadi's heart.'

And so, Subhadra went to Draupadi, dressed in a poor farmer woman's clothes. She knelt in front of Draupadi and said, 'O Queen, I am here to serve you. Please accept me as your maid.'

Draupadi smiled and pulled her to her breast in a warm embrace. 'May your husband have no enemies,' she blessed Subhadra.

A few days later, Krishna and Balram arrived in Indraprastha to visit their sister Subhadra and her in-laws, the Pandavas. They brought with them carts full of precious gifts and presents. They had a great time in Indraprastha for a few weeks. Later, Balram and the rest of their entourage returned to Dwarka, while Krishna stayed back to enjoy a few more days with his best friend, Arjun. Together, they strolled along the banks of River Yamuna. They discussed various political, social and military issues, and hunted wild game in the nearby forests. The duo built a bond so strong that it shaped the future in more ways than one.

A few weeks later, Subhadra gave birth to a handsome little boy. He was named Abhimanyu—one who is fearless and powerful. Krishna performed all the rituals for the new-born baby. Soon, Arjun realized that the boy would become as brave and powerful as his uncle Krishna. In the meantime, Draupadi had also given birth to five boys, one from each of her husbands. They were named Pratibindhya, Sutasoma, Shrutabarma, Shatanik and Shrutasena. They also grew up to be as powerful as their illustrious fathers.

The Pandavas were happy and content with what they had, but the future had something else in store for them, which we will soon discover.

15
The Burning of the Khandava Forest

ONE DAY, KRISHNA AND ARJUN ALONG WITH THEIR FRIENDS AND FAMILY
went on a trip to the banks of the Yamuna near the Khandava
forest. While the women and the children were swimming and
playing in the river and having a great time, Krishna and Arjun
walked to the edge of the forest. They sat down under the shade of a
tree and were in a deep discussion. Just then, a Brahmin appeared
in front of them. His skin glowed like molten gold. His copper-hued
beard flowed down to his chest, and the locks of knotted hair on his
head fluttered in the breeze. He was no ordinary Brahmin. He said
to Krishna and Arjun: 'I am Agni, the god of fire. I need your help.'

The friends stood up with joined palms. Arjun said, 'O lord of
fire, it will be an honour to help you. Please tell us, what do you want
us to do?'

'I want to devour this forest. Please help me do so.'

Surprised by this unusual request, Krishna asked, 'Lord, if you
want to devour the forest, you can do so at any moment. Why would
you need our help?'

Agni replied, 'Krishna, I am suffering from a loss of appetite. King Swetaki has been conducting a fire sacrifice for twelve long years. All these years, the king has been feeding me pure ghee and nothing else. Consuming such huge quantities of ghee has caused an appetite disorder. I asked Lord Brahma for a cure. He laughed and said that if I burn down the Khandava forest and eat the flesh of the creatures living here, I will be cured of my illness. But whenever I try, Lord Indra extinguishes me by sending torrential rains to protect his friend.'

'Lord Indra's friend? Who is he?' asked Arjun.

'He is a serpent named Takshak. Indra would never let me burn down Takshak's home and kill him. But if I don't consume this forest, I won't be cured of my illness. Please help me by stopping Indra from extinguishing me while I devour the forest,' Agni urged.

Arjun replied, 'We can help you, but I'm afraid we are not carrying weapons suitable to fight Lord Indra. Krishna is unarmed too.'

Agni mulled over this and said, 'Let me arrange for your weapons.' He summoned Varuna, the god of the oceans, and asked for some special weapons. Varuna brought the Gandiva and offered it to Arjun. The great bow was made from the spine of a rhino and was studded with precious jewels. Along with the bow, he gave Arjun a pair of quivers that had an inexhaustible supply of arrows. Agni also gave Arjun a grand chariot, named Kapidhwaja, driven by four powerful white steeds. Krishna received a huge mace named Kaumadiki and a spinning disk named Sudarshana Chakra that could sever anything at the command of the owner.

Arjun said, 'O lord Agni, we are now well-prepared to defend you from any obstacle. You may now devour the Khandava forest.'

'I will. But make sure I consume all the living creatures in this forest. Let no one escape me,' Agni said.

Agni then lit up in a huge blaze and began to burn the forest. Arjun and Krishna rode the divine Kapidhwaja chariot and circled the forest. As the fire raged through the huge trees and thick foliage, the animals and birds ran for their lives. As they tried to escape, Arjun's arrows stopped them on their tracks while the fire roasted them to their death. The ponds and lakes in the forest boiled in the tremendous heat, killing all fish and amphibious creatures in them. The cries and roars of the animals, merged with the loud crackling sound of the burning forest, struck fear into the hearts of men and women living miles away. As the towering inferno touched the sky, the gods in heaven became worried about the consequences. They went to King Indra and said, 'Lord, aren't you aware of what Agni is doing to the Khandava forest? If he continues for long, no creature in the forest would stay alive. You must stop him.'

Indra consoled them: 'Don't worry, I will stop Agni. We cannot let him burn down everything he wants.' Indra was also worried about the safety of his friend Takshak. He commanded the rains to pour on the forest, but the water evaporated due to the intense heat before it could reach the trees. Enraged, Indra attacked Arjun from the heavens with his thunderbolt and other weapons. The gods, the asuras and the gandharvas, all joined Indra. Arjun's arrows and Krishna's chakra defeated them all. Indra then lifted a huge peak of the Mandara Mountain and hurled it at Arjun. Arjun's arrows broke the mountain into thousands of pieces that rained on the forest and killed many more animals. Arjun's skills impressed Indra. After all, he was his son, and as a father, he felt proud. Still, he kept fighting to stop Agni from destroying the forest and killing Takshak.

At that moment, a voice rang out from the heavens, 'Indra, give up your fight with Arjun and Krishna. Nobody can defeat them in war. They are the reincarnations of the gods Nara and Narayana.

Don't worry about your friend Takshak. He is safe in Kurukshetra.'
Hearing this, Indra gave up his fight, congratulated Arjun for his
gallantry and returned to the heavens.

An asura named Maya used to live in the forest. As he was trying
to escape the fire, Krishna spotted him. Just when Krishna was about
to hurl his Sudarshana Chakra to kill Maya, the giant threw himself at
Arjun's feet and cried, 'O Prince, I am Maya. I harmed no one in my
life. Please save me from Krishna's wrath.'

Arjun felt pity for this gentle giant. He asked Krishna, 'Friend,
this man has surrendered and is begging for his life. Please spare
him.'

Krishna retracted his chakra and said, 'How can I ever deny your
wish, Parth? Maya, you are spared.'

The fire raged for fifteen days, killing all creatures in the forest.
Agni consumed to his heart's content the fat and flesh of the
animals and birds of the forest, and was cured of his disease. He
said to Krishna and Arjun, 'Thank you for curing my illness. I am
pleased with your service. You may now go back to your picnic and
get some rest.'

Arjun and Krishna went back to the river bank. As they sat, they
saw Maya standing in front of them with his palms joined. He said,
'Arjun, you have saved me from the wrath of Agni and from the discus
of Krishna. Please let me know how I can pay you back.'

Arjun smiled and said, 'You don't have to pay me back. You
may go.'

Maya was adamant. He said, 'Just as Vishwakarma is the chief
architect and craftsman of the gods, I am the chief architect of the
Asuras. It'll be an honour if you would let me build something for
you.'

Arjun replied, 'Thank you for your offer. Since I saved your life,
I cannot accept any favours from you. But I don't want to dishearten

you either. Why don't you do something for Krishna? That will make me happy.'

Maya asked Krishna what he could build for him. Krishna thought for a while and said, 'If you'd like to do something for us, I'd like you to build an assembly hall for King Yudhishthira. A magnificent hall that is one of a kind and has nothing comparable on heaven or earth.'

Maya agreed.

The Palace of Illusions

Over the next fourteen months, Maya built a grand assembly hall that was nothing less than an architectural marvel. It was a magical palace built with crystals and marbles, and decorated with the finest of jewels, paintings and drapery. The hallways merged into flower gardens and lakes in a wonderful blend of nature and architecture. Transparent crystal floors decorated with lotus blossoms were often mistaken for real pools, while the clear, still waters of actual pools looked like dry marble floor. People mistook the clear crystal walls to be doorways, and doorways as walls. It was a palace of illusions, and the clueless visitors were often fooled by Maya's designs. Eight thousand ferocious demons named kinkaras, whom Maya had brought from the mountains, guarded the halls.

When the assembly hall was completed, Yudhishthira inaugurated it on an auspicious day. He invited ten thousand Brahmins, treated them to delicious meals of rice, meat and sweets, and gave them expensive gifts such as jewellery, clothing and herds of cattle. The Brahmins praised Yudhishthira for his generosity. Then, with great pomp and fanfare, Yudhishthira ascended the throne of the assembly hall. All the invited guests broke into applause while the royal band played joyful music.

A few days later, Rishi Narada, along with his associates, came to visit the Pandavas and to see the new assembly hall. Yudhishthira and his brothers welcomed him with due respect and offered him generous gifts as honorarium for gracing their palace.

Narada then offered Yudhishthira some advice on administration and governance. He asked, 'Yudhishthira, while you think of increasing the wealth of your kingdom, do you also keep spiritual matters in mind? Do you manage your time well and serve your duties towards justice, religion, wealth and your family's needs with equal priority?' Narada further questioned and advised Yudhishthira on how to treat his subjects fairly and with compassion.

Yudhishthira bowed to Narada and said, 'You have enriched me with your advice. I will try to follow these principles to the best of my ability.'

'Yudhishthira, you have the power to conquer the world. I advise you to perform the Rajasuya fire sacrifice and declare yourself the emperor of the world. This would make your ancestors, especially your late father Pandu, proud of you.' Saying so, Narada and his associates left the palace of Indraprastha.

Yudhishthira continued his rule as the king of Indraprastha. He freed himself of any anger or pride and based his governance on the principle of Dharma or righteousness. The people of Indraprastha looked upon Yudhishthira as their father. Everybody loved him, and he earned the title of Ajatshatru, one who has no enemies.

The Rajasuya Preparation

Rishi Narada's advice about performing the Rajasuya sacrifice kept coming back to Yudhishthira's mind repeatedly. The sacrifice was no easy task and it implied declaring oneself the emperor of the world. Hence, before he could even start the sacrificial ritual, he would have to gain the allegiance of all the kings and rulers of the land. If any of them refused to accept Yudhishthira as their emperor, it would mean war. Yudhishthira's ministers, advisors and his brothers were in support and highlighted to him his eligibility as well as it being the right time to perform the sacrifice. The sages and priests gave their consent too. Yudhishthira wished to know what Lord Krishna had to say and sent a messenger to Dwarka to invite Krishna to visit Indraprastha.

No sooner did Krishna receive the message than he arrived at Yudhishthira's palace. After listening to the details of the proposal, Krishna said, 'Yudhishthira, you deserve to perform the Rajasuya sacrifice and become the emperor of the world. But before you decide, I should warn you that your claim to the throne will not go unchallenged. All the kings will accept you as their emperor, except one—the vicious King Jarasandh. He has terrorized many kings and has captured eighty-six of them. Once he captures fourteen more, he'd sacrifice the hundred kings to the goddess. Jarasandh is the father of my uncle Kansa's wife, Asti. You know, Kansa was also an evil king and he terrorized his people, which is why I killed him. Asti asked her father Jarasandh to avenge her husband's death. Since then, Jarasandh has been trying to kill me. We fought him for a while, but he has such a huge army that we realized we won't be able to destroy him even if we fought for 300 years. We fled Mathura and went to the western shores. Jarasandh knows that I am your cousin and friend. He'd never let you succeed in your Rajasuya sacrifice. If you want to succeed, you must kill him.'

Bheem said, 'If Krishna and Arjun join me, we should be able to kill Jarasandh.'

Yudhishthira was anxious. He said, 'Bheem and Arjun are as precious to me as my two eyes, and you, Krishna, are my heart. How can I risk your lives? If anything happens to you, I could never forgive myself. It seems even Yama, the god of death, can't defeat Jarasandh. I think it will be prudent to give up any plans for the Rajasuya.'

Arjun stood up and said, 'I believe in strength and prefer to use it when needed. If you give up your plans for the sake of our safety, it will be seen as your weakness. If you want to live the life of a peace-loving ascetic, you may do so later. For now, be the emperor you deserve to be, and let us fight for you.'

Krishna was happy to see Arjun's confidence. He said, 'Arjun is right. I haven't heard of anybody gain immortality by staying away from war. However, a clever man always avoids an all-out war against a powerful enemy. He tries to defeat his enemy by other means. I think we should adopt the same policy against Jarasandh. We should enter our enemy's palace in disguise, and then when he is alone, we'll attack him and fulfil our mission. Our objective is to free our friends, the eighty-six kings, from the dungeons of Jarasandh. If we get killed in the process and fail to accomplish our mission, we'd at least be assured a place in heaven for attempting this good deed.'

16

The Slaying of Jarasandh and the Rajasuya Sacrifice

YUDHISHTHIRA WAS CURIOUS TO KNOW MORE ABOUT JARASANDH. HE asked Krishna, 'Who is he? How could he terrorize *you* and still live on earth?'

Krishna said, 'Let me tell you the story of Jarasandh's birth. In the kingdom of Magadh, there lived a king named Brihadratha. He had married the twin daughters of the king of Kashi and promised he'd always treat them as equals. But he failed to sire a son with either of his wives, and the king was getting old. One day, the great sage Chanda-Kaushik came to visit King Brihadratha. The king treated the ascetic with due respect and the sage was pleased with his hospitality. Chanda-Kaushik offered to give the king something in return. The king told the sage of his wish to have a son. The sage then gave the king a blessed mango fruit and said, "Go and give this mango to your queen. By God's grace, you'll have a handsome son soon."

'Staying true to his word, King Brihadratha cut the mango into two halves and offered the pieces to his queens. When the time came, each queen gave birth to half a child, as if the boy was split from head to toe into two equal parts. Each half had one eye, one arm, one foot, and a divided torso. The queens were scared to see such a grotesque offspring. They asked the maids to abandon the body parts outside the palace. The maids did as they were instructed, and the two halves of the infant lay in the trash by the roadside. A little while later, a demoness named Jara was passing by when she spotted the two halves of a baby lying beside the road. Curious, she picked them up and put the two halves together to see how the baby looked. As soon as she did that, the halves joined to form a complete human child, and the baby boy cried out in a loud roar. Hearing the loud cry, King Brihadratha and his wives came out to see the baby in Jara's arms. By then, Jara had taken the form of a beautiful woman. She held the baby and said, "Brihadratha, your maids had abandoned your child, but I saved him. Take him and rear him well. He will grow up to be a powerful king and rule the earth." Since Jara the demoness had given life to the boy, he was named Jarasandh. He grew up to be a powerful king. He was blessed by Sage Chanda-Kaushik to rule over other kings and gained the power to witness Lord Shiva. But he developed an animosity towards me since he is the father-in-law of my evil uncle, Kansa.'

Krishna paused for a while and then continued, 'Balram and I killed two of Jarasandh's associates, Hansa and Dimbhaka. His time has come now. However, nobody can defeat Jarasandh in conventional warfare. The only way to kill him is to fight him in a hand-to-hand combat. The three of us, Bheem, Arjun and I, should be able to kill Jarasandh. I can come up with a strategy, Bheem could fight him, while Arjun can protect us from external attacks. We must meet Jarasandh alone and challenge him to wrestle any of us. I am quite certain that the arrogant king of Magadh would pick Bheem as his opponent, for he wouldn't consider Arjun or me to be worthy enough to fight him. Then, Bheem could kill Jarasandh for sure. So, if you can trust me, please permit them to go with me.'

Yudhishthira was ashamed to hear this. Joining his palms, he said, 'O Lord, please forgive me. How can I not trust you? You are our greatest friend, philosopher and guide. We are privileged to be blessed by you. With your guidance and advice, I am sure we would succeed in killing Jarasandh, freeing the captive kings, and finally performing my Rajasuya sacrifice too. Please prepare to leave for Magadh with Arjun and Bheem.'

Disguised as Brahmin students, Bheem, Arjun and Krishna left for Magadh. They travelled through the Gangetic plains and arrived at the gates of Girivraj, the capital of Magadh. But they didn't enter.

'Let's enter the city through the Chaitaka mountains. The terrain is rough, but it will lead us straight to the rear entrance of the palace,' advised Krishna.

They entered the palace through the back door, which wasn't guarded. Inside the palace, they walked through the hallways almost unnoticed and entered the royal chamber with nobody stopping them. Standing in front of Jarasandh, they said, 'O King, let peace be with you.'

Jarasandh was observing a fast to perform a ritual. He was surprised to see the strange Brahmins. Still, he paid his respects and asked them to sit down. Bheem, Arjun and Krishna took their seats.

Jarasandh said, 'You look like Brahmins and you've dressed like them. You wear garlands and sandalwood paste like Brahmins too, but I see you carry the marks of bowstrings on your arms. You also avoided the royal entrance to the palace and came through the back door. That raises questions about your identity. Tell me the truth, who are you?'

Krishna looked straight into Jarasandh's eyes. In a calm voice, he said, 'Brahmins, Kshatriyas, Vaishyas, all may wear garlands and sandalwood paste. However, you are right. We are Kshatriyas and our skills are with weapons rather than words. Clever people enter their enemy's house through the back door, and their friend's house through the main door. You are our enemy; so we preferred to use the rear entrance.'

'I don't recall you as my enemy. I have done no harm to you ... why do you take me to be your enemy?' asked Jarasandh.

Krishna replied, 'You have captured and imprisoned eighty-six Kshatriya kings and you plan to sacrifice them to Lord Shiva. We are here to stop you from doing such evil and to free the kings from their bondage. You have no right to offer human beings as sacrifice. We have come here to kill you and save the kings. I am Krishna and these are the two sons of late King Pandu—Bheem and Arjun. We ask you to free the kings and surrender to Yudhishthira. Else you die at our hands.'

Jarasandh laughed and said, 'Krishna, you know that a conqueror can do whatever he wants with the loot he conquers. That is the norm. I defeated and captured those kings in legitimate battle and I wish to offer them to my Lord. I cannot set them free. If you want to fight, so be it. What kind of combat do you prefer? A formal war in the battlefield with soldiers and armies or a hand-to-hand duel?'

Krishna said, 'We prefer hand-to-hand combat, and you can choose any of us to fight you.'

Jarasandh examined the three and said, 'You and Arjun are too weak to fight me. I can crush you in seconds.' He looked at the muscular and heavy-set Bheem and said, 'Bheem is the right person to fight me. I choose him.'

A proper place for wrestling between Bheem and Jarasandh was identified. Priests and Brahmins blessed Jarasandh as he arrived in the arena. Krishna blessed Bheem.

Jarasandh took off his crown, tied his long hair into a knot and stepped into the arena to face Bheem. The two giants looked at each other and circled the arena, growling like two angry lions. Then they pounced upon each other, slapping and kicking the other while howling and grunting like wild elephants. The ground beneath them shook as they stomped the earth. Sometimes Bheem would hurl Jarasandh to the ground, but he'd get back on his feet and throw a thundering punch at Bheem's torso. A large crowd assembled to watch the great fight, which continued for days and nights. On the fourth day, Jarasandh felt tired and took a break. Krishna approached Bheem and said, 'You should not press an enemy who is tired, for the pressure might kill him. Fight him with your arms and use as much force as he can tolerate.'

Bheem understood that Krishna was pointing out the weakness of Jarasandh. He said, 'Krishna, this evil man has killed many of your beloved friends. He does not deserve your kindness.'

Krishna said, 'Bheem, it is time to show him the strength you have inherited from your father Pavan Deva, the god of the Winds.'

When the fight resumed, Bheem growled and picked up Jarasandh above his head and spun him a hundred times and then threw him to the ground. He then held Jarasandh's feet with his two arms and, with a powerful tug, tore him apart at the seam where Jara the demoness had joined him. Jarasandh's death cry and Bheem's roar rang through the city and the people of Magadh shuddered in fear.

Krishna, Bheem and Arjun then proceeded to the dungeons to free the captive kings. The grateful kings bowed to Krishna and said, 'We cannot thank you enough for saving our lives. What can we do to repay our debt?'

Krishna smiled and replied, 'Yudhishthira is planning to perform the Rajasuya sacrifice. I'd request you to pledge your allegiance to emperor Yudhishthira.'

The kings agreed and left the palace. Krishna then installed Jarasandh's son, Sahadev, as the king of Magadh and returned to Indraprastha along with Bheem and Arjun. Yudhishthira prepared for the great sacrifice while Krishna took his leave and returned to Dwarka with the promise to return for the Rajasuya ceremony.

Arjun called upon Yudhishthira and said, 'Brother, we've got rid of Jarasandh. However, we still need to secure formal allegiance from all the kings before you can start the ritual. If you grant us permission, we, your brothers, will go to each kingdom and demand their allegiance and ask them to pay us taxes. If they don't accept, we'd declare war against them and force them to yield to you.'

Yudhishthira knew that this was the next step before he could start the sacrifice ritual. He granted them his permission to begin their conquest. Each of the four brothers took along a huge contingent, consisting of elephants, horses, cavalry and foot soldiers. Arjun went north, Bheem headed towards the east, Sahadev to the south and Nakul set out westwards. As Krishna had predicted, the brothers hardly met with any resistance. Most of the kings agreed to accept Yudhishthira as their emperor and offered gold and jewels as taxes. The mighty Pandava brothers and their army crushed those who refused to surrender. Soon, the four brothers returned from the conquest to Indraprastha with huge amounts of wealth for the new emperor, Yudhishthira.

The Rajasuya sacrifice is a long and expensive ceremony. The performer of the sacrifice must offer expensive gifts and pay honorariums to the thousands of invited Brahmins and other dignitaries. Arrangements were made to host the royal guests who were to stay for weeks. Thousands of men and women were employed to serve the guests and take care of their needs. Halls, mansions and dormitories were constructed for their lodging. Huge kitchens were built to cook their food. Performers and musicians were hired to entertain them. The scriptures mandate that the rituals of the Rajasuya sacrifice must be performed with absolute perfection. Any mistake renders the sacrifice worthless. Hence, hundreds of learned priests and sages were deployed to conduct the yagna. A huge hall was built for the fire sacrifice.

Satisfied with the arrangements, Yudhishthira sent out invitations to the guests. Krishna arrived from Dwarka along with his family. Yudhishthira bowed to him and said, 'O Krishna, without your blessings, I cannot perform this huge ceremony. Please give me your blessings and your permission.'

Krishna held Yudhishthira's hand and said, 'You are the most deserving person for this title. Please go ahead with your duties and let me know how I can serve you.'

Vyasa arrived to serve as the main priest. From Hastinapur came Bhishma, Vidura, Drona, Kripa, Aswathama, Shakuni and many others. Duryodhan and his ninety-nine Kaurava brothers accompanied them. Karna came from the kingdom of Anga. Drupad and Dhrishtadyumna arrived from Panchal. Hundreds of kings and royal personages poured into the city from all directions. Soon, the city of Indraprastha was teeming with rulers from all over the country.

Yudhishthira addressed Bhishma, Drona, Kripa and the other elders: 'I have undertaken a huge task and won't succeed without your blessings and co-operation. Please bless me.'

He then delegated several of the tasks to his relatives and friends. Dushasana was in charge of the food, while Aswathama had to receive and greet the Brahmins. Bhishma and Drona were to take care of contingencies while Kripa would manage the royal treasury. Vidura was tasked with making all financial disbursements while Dhritarashtra's charioteer, Sanjay, was to serve the royal guests. Duryodhan was asked to receive gifts on Yudhishthira's behalf. Krishna took it upon himself to cleanse the feet of all the Brahmins.

The royal guests offered huge sums of gold and silver as donation for the ceremony. When one king saw the other pour his wealth into the donation counters, he'd put in more to show off his riches. Soon, the coffers overflowed, and the amount collected was sufficient to bear the expenses of the Rajasuya ceremony.

Accompanied by the blowing of conch shells and the ringing of gongs, Narada, Vyasa and the other sages entered the hall. The guests followed them. When everybody had taken their seats, Yudhishthira and his brothers approached the stage and bowed before the guests to seek their permission to begin the Rajasuya sacrifice. The sages raised their hands and said, 'Let the great sacrifice begin.'

17

Krishna Kills Shishupal

SAGE VYASA SUPERVISED THE PROCEEDINGS AS THE GREAT RAJASUYA sacrifice began. Priests sat around six huge pyres and poured ghee into the fire while chanting hymns from the Sama Veda. Another set of priests watched over the proceedings with a keen eye to detect any mistakes. The third team listened to the chants for mispronunciations of the mantras, for any mistake would ruin the yagna. The royal guests who sat around the sacrificial grounds to watch the ceremony discussed the intricacies of the rituals. Some tried to find flaws, while some praised the Pandavas for their attention to detail. Some argued about the theological aspects of the sacrifice, while some talked about the political consequences.

By the end of the first phase of the sacrifice, Bhishma called upon Yudhishthira and said, 'Now you must pay homage to the most important person in the audience by offering him your first worship.'

Yudhishthira looked at Bhishma and said, 'O Grandsire, you are our guardian, and the wisest man amongst us. You tell me, to whom should I pay my homage?'

Bhishma smiled and said, 'Just as the sun is the brightest amongst the stars, so is Krishna among the guests assembled here. You should select Krishna as your best man and pay him your respect and offerings.'

Yudhishthira was glad to hear this, for he too had Krishna in mind. He called upon Sahadev to make the announcement of his decision.

Sahadev walked up to the stands and addressed the guests, 'Respected Brahmins, kings and guests, to conclude the Rajasuya ceremony, it is customary to pay homage to the most important person living amongst us. My brother, the great king and emperor, Yudhishthira, has chosen Vasudeva Krishna as the best man worthy of his first worship.'

The crowd broke into applause and greeted the announcement with loud cheers. But one man sat still in the audience and, as the crowd praised Yudhishthira for his wise decision, his face turned red in anger. It was Shishupal, the king of Chedi. As Yudhishthira and his brothers proceeded towards Krishna to worship him, Shishupal stood up and yelled, 'Stop! Stop this nonsense! How dare you worship Krishna when so many other deserving kings are present in the audience?'

Yudhishthira was startled to hear this. He knew Shishupal had a bitter relationship with Krishna, for Krishna had abducted and married his bride-to-be, Rukmini. Since then, Shishupal has been looking for an opportunity to get back at Krishna. But nobody could guess that he would use the Rajasuya sacrifice as an excuse to insult Krishna.

Shishupal came down from the stands and said, 'Yudhishthira, are you out of your mind? How could you select Krishna as the most important man in this gathering? Has your grandfather Bhishma turned senile to suggest Krishna's name? Krishna is not even a king.

Why would you want to worship him? If you consider seniority to be your criteria, then why not Vasudeva, Krishna's father? He's present here. Or, if it is a friend you want to worship, then why not King Drupad? If you consider Krishna to be your guru who deserves your respect, then why not Guru Dronacharya? The great sage Vyasa is here; why not him? Why not Bhishma? He is the wisest and the most gallant warrior alive. Even death cannot touch him without his permission. There are many others in this hall whom you could have selected as the candidate for your first worship. Why did you have to select Krishna? He is a cunning and evil man. That fraud killed my friend Jarasandh by deceit. If Krishna was always your choice, why invite us to this farce of yours? To insult us? Remember, I paid you my taxes not in fear or to receive any favours. I paid you my taxes because I thought you are righteous and would make a good emperor. Now I feel I have made a grave mistake.'

Krishna sat calm in the midst of the storm. He didn't even look at Shishupal, who started feeling ignored. He turned towards Krishna and said, 'Krishna how dare you accept this worship? The Pandavas may have lost their senses, but you should know better! There are many present in this hall who deserve the honour more than you do. Or, are you like that mangy dog who feels like a king when he finds a piece of food in the trash bin? You don't even realize that the Pandavas are making a laughing stock of you.' He then turned to the assembled guests and said, 'Friends, today we have seen how low the Pandavas can stoop. We have seen what kind of a man Bhishma is, and the kind of person Krishna is, who only lusts for fame and honour. We should not spend another moment on this sinful ground. We should all leave at once. Come with me.'

Yudhishthira stopped Shishupal and said in a calm voice, 'O King of Chedi, I am afraid you are not thinking straight. You cannot ignore

Bhishma's words. There are many kings and warriors assembled here today who are older and wiser than you in all respects. They all have accepted our decision to worship Krishna. Then why do you object? Bhishma knows Krishna better than you do.'

Bhishma came to Yudhishthira and touched his shoulder. 'My son, one who objects to the worship of the person who is worshipped by all in the heavens and earth is not worthy of your kind words. Krishna is the creator and destroyer of the universe. He is omnipresent in all beings. If that fool Shishupal cannot grasp this truth, then you must ignore him and proceed with your duty.'

Sahadev came forward and said, 'On behalf of my elder brother Yudhishthira, I worship the greatest of all human beings, Lord Krishna. If any of you dare to challenge this decision, come forward and fight me.'

Saying this, Sahadev proceeded towards Krishna and worshipped him by paying homage to his feet while the priests chanted some mantras.

Shishupal was furious. He called upon all the kings who were sympathetic to him: 'Friends, we should not tolerate this insult any more. Let us attack the Pandavas and the Vrishnis and ruin their ceremony. They don't deserve our reverence.'

Shishupal's inflammatory words stirred up the dissident kings, and great mayhem ensued.

Yudhishthira asked Bhishma, 'O Grandsire, these kings have lost their minds in anger and now our Rajasuya sacrifice is in jeopardy. Tell me, what should we do?'

Bhishma said, 'Don't worry. Like a pack of dogs who bark at a sleeping lion, these kings are screaming at Krishna for no reason at all. That fool Shishupal has arranged to send them to their death. When Krishna wishes to destroy someone, the unfortunate person loses his mind like this.'

Hearing this, Shishupal yelled at Bhishma, 'You good for nothing old man, how dare you threaten the kings? Aren't you ashamed of yourself? You, who's supposed to be the wisest of all, have become a sycophant of Krishna. You want to worship that foolish herdsman? Why? Because Krishna killed a weak woman, Putana? That makes him a woman killer and not a god! He killed the weak and feeble Aswasura and Brishavasura who weren't even capable of fighting— what's so great about that? They say, Krishna held the Govardhana Mountain on his finger for a week—but that mountain was nothing more than a molehill. Krishna killed his own uncle Kansa, to whom he owed his life. How can you condone such a heinous act? He is the greatest sinner of all.'

Shishupal stopped for a while to breathe and then lashed out at Bhishma again: 'Bhishma, you claim to the most righteous man. Then why did you steal Amba, the princess of Kashi, who was engaged to another man? Was that the right action for a Kshatriya? Your sisters-in-law were impregnated by another man in front of you and you claim to be the wisest of the wise? Your vow of celibacy is also fake. You have become celibate only to hide your impotence.'

Bheem couldn't sit still any longer. He turned red with anger and was about to pounce upon Shishupal. Bhishma stopped him. Shishupal laughed and said, 'Let him come. Let everybody witness how I crush this arrogant brute.'

Bhishma stood up and addressed the audience in his deep and solemn voice: 'Dear guests, I think it is time I shared a secret about Shishupal with you. This man was born with three eyes, four arms and brayed like a donkey. His parents were scared and thought of abandoning him. But then a voice from the heavens said, "O King, rear the child, for his time of death is yet to come, although his killer is already born." Shishupal's mother asked, "Please tell me who his killer would be!" The voice responded, "The man on whose lap Shishupal would lose his extra arms and his third eye would slay him." Since then, Shishupal's father placed his son on the laps of thousands of kings and warriors, but nothing happened. Then one day, Krishna and Balram came to visit their aunt, the queen of Chedi. The queen mother placed baby Shishupal on Krishna's lap, and right then the child's extra arms dropped off and his third eye vanished from his forehead. Shishupal's mother grew anxious. She said, "Krishna, promise me you'll pardon my son for all his transgressions."

'Krishna soothed his aunt, saying, "Don't worry, I will pardon one hundred of his crimes." This fool Shishupal is causing this ruckus, for he knows he'd be pardoned. It is because of Krishna that he dares to say such atrocious things. I'd say, if it is Krishna he hates, then why doesn't he challenge him to a combat?'

Hearing this, Shishupal turned to Krishna and yelled, 'Krishna, I challenge you to fight me. Today I'll kill you and your sycophants, the Pandavas. You are not a king, you are nothing but a servant of Kansa and do not deserve any kind of worship. I will kill you and rid the world of a fraud.'

Krishna couldn't stay seated any longer. He stood up and said, 'Dear kings, we the Yadavas have never done any harm to Shishupal. Still, he keeps attacking us. Shishupal is my cousin, my aunt's son, but he prefers to be my enemy. The list of his crimes and transgressions is endless. When we went to visit Pragjyotishpura, Shishupal attacked our city of Dwarka and burnt it down to ashes. When the king of Bhoj came to visit the Raibatak Mountains, Shishupal killed his entire contingent. He ruined my father's Ashwamedha sacrifice by stealing his sacrificial horse. He stole Babhru's wife while she was travelling from Dwarka to the Saubir kingdom. This odious man came in disguise and stole my uncle's daughter, Bhadra. He wanted to marry Rukmini, but he is not worthy of a great woman like her. So, I saved her from this monster. I have been tolerating all his crimes because I had given my word to my aunt, his mother. But today you have seen, and you have heard, how he insulted me in front of you all. I cannot pardon him any more.'

Shishupal laughed and said, 'Aren't you ashamed to talk about my engagement with Rukmini? You dare discuss your wife's ex-lover in a court filled with men? How shameless are you? Listen, I don't care whether you pardon me or not. Neither do I care for your anger, nor your kindness. You cannot bend a hair on my body.'

Krishna's eyes lit up in anger. He held out his hand and said, 'Enough is enough! You have surpassed your hundred transgressions and I cannot pardon you any more. Prepare to die.'

Krishna closed his eyes and summoned his weapon, the Sudarshan Chakra. In a moment, the Chakra flew in, spinning like a tornado, and settled on Krishna's right forefinger. The moment he uttered the command, the fiery disc flashed out of his finger towards Shishupal, severed his head from his body, and disappeared into the sky. Shishupal's decapitated body crashed into the ground like a huge oak tree, and the ground shook under the feet of the kings and visitors. They stood dumbfounded and stared at the mighty Krishna who stood calm, with a faint smile on his face. Some were scared, while some bowed to Krishna and hailed him for destroying a tyrant.

Yudhishthira ordered his men to arrange for Shishupal's funeral at the earliest. After the funeral, Yudhishthira, along with the other kings, installed Shishupal's son as the king of Chedi.

Finally, the great Rajasuya sacrifice came to an end under the protection of Lord Krishna. The guests congratulated Yudhishthira on the successful completion of the ceremony. They said, 'Yudhishthira, we are glad that you are our emperor now. You have performed your Rajasuya sacrifice with due diligence, and we are pleased with your hospitality and care. Please don't hesitate to call us if you need any help. Now, with your permission, we'd like to return to our homes.' Yudhishthira thanked them and made all arrangements for their departure.

Krishna also wanted to return to Dwarka. Yudhishthira held his hand and said, 'O Govinda, it was only because of you that I was able to complete my Rajasuya sacrifice. All the Kshatriya kingdoms have come under my empire only because of your blessings and help. How can I say goodbye to you?'

Krishna replied, 'My dear friend, I am always at your disposal. Call me whenever you need me. Now I must go back to Dwarka. My people are waiting for me.'

After bidding farewell to Subhadra and Draupadi, Krishna mounted his dark, cloud-like Garuda chariot and departed for Dwarka. The Pandavas stood at the gates with tearful eyes and the hope that they'd see him again soon.

18

The Game Plan

AT THE BEHEST OF THE PANDAVAS, DURYODHAN DECIDED TO STAY BACK in Indraprastha for few more days after the conclusion of the Rajasuya sacrifice. Dushasana, Shakuni and Karna also stayed back to give him company. As Duryodhan walked down the streets of Indraprastha, the beauty of the city and its opulence amazed him. The barren land of Khandava had been transformed into a fantastic city. It was beyond his wildest dreams. When Duryodhan stepped into the assembly hall and palace built by Maya, he was dumbfounded. The illusionary designs fooled Duryodhan again and again. At one spot, he mistook the clear crystal floor for a pool of water and lifted his clothes before treading carefully. But the moment his foot hit the hard floor, he realized his mistake and felt embarrassed. He moved on to another, similar area with crystal clear still water and lotus blossoms. Determined not to be fooled again, he stepped into it and everybody around heard a loud splash. It was a real pool and Duryodhan sat in the water soaked to the bone. Dushasana and Karna pulled him out while the servants turned around to hide their laughter. Duryodhan was glaring at the corridor above, where Bheem and Arjun, along with Draupadi, split their sides laughing. The sound of their laughter, especially that of Draupadi, fell on his ears like hot lava. His blood boiled in rage but he could do nothing.

Hearing the commotion, Yudhishthira came out and scolded his brothers: 'Go and help Brother Duryodhan.' He called out to the servants: 'Why are you standing there? Get some dry clothes for him.' The servants rushed to bring fresh dry clothes for him. Arjun and Bheem came to assist, but Duryodhan refused to accept any help. He wore the dry clothes and walked away towards what he thought was a doorway. Instead, it was a wall made of transparent crystal and Duryodhan banged into it and broke his nose. He sat down holding his bleeding nose while the servants ran to get some first aid. Duryodhan again heard Draupadi's laughter ring through the halls. Shakuni and Karna pulled him up, but the insulted prince shook them off and walked towards the door leading to the corridor outside. Duryodhan pushed the door hard to open it and fell face down onto the ground, for the door was only an illusion. The laughter. Again. Frustrated, he turned around and looked for an exit to get away from the bizarre palace. He approached another doorway but as he neared it, he stood rooted to the ground, hesitant to proceed. He looked at it for a while but couldn't tell whether it was real or an illusion. Afraid of being fooled again, he turned around in search of another doorway. Dushasana, Shakuni and Karna followed him. Tough luck. The great Kaurava prince of Hastinapur was embarrassed and humiliated to the core. Again and again. He left for Hastinapur in a rage. The fire of envy burned in him like a huge furnace and he vowed to extract revenge for this humiliation.

Shakuni lived in a small room in a corner of the palace in Hastinapur. The room was dark, with occasional shafts of light illuminating some parts from time to time. Decorated with black and grey drapery, the room was filled with taxidermy snakes and vultures which cast large shadows on the walls. Sitting in one corner of the room, Shakuni was practising his favourite board game—the game of dice. After years of practice and skilful tampering of the dice, Shakuni was now an expert in the game. He could command the dice to roll into any pattern he wished. Shakuni picked up a pair of dice, closed his eyes and, after a quick shake, threw them on the board. His eyes gleamed to see the dice roll down and stop at the exact pattern he wished for. Just then, he heard footsteps approaching his room. Shakuni turned around and saw Duryodhan waiting at the door.

Shakuni stood up to greet him: 'Welcome, my dear nephew! Come in, come in, please.'

Duryodhan didn't care to return the greeting. Walking in with a gloomy face, he sat down in one of the chairs next to a dead python mounted on a tree branch. Shakuni knew what was plaguing Duryodhan. He feigned ignorance and asked, 'What happened, my dear nephew? Why do you look so melancholy? What's bothering you?'

'Don't act dumb, Uncle Shakuni. You know perfectly well what's bothering me.'

Shakuni closed the door behind him and went close to Duryodhan. 'Well, I can guess, but I cannot read your mind. And one should not be so bold as to guess the intentions of the future king of Hastinapur. So, why don't you tell me?'

'The wealth and prosperity of the Pandavas is killing me. I cannot take it any more,' growled Duryodhan. 'With Arjun's help, Yudhishthira has conquered the whole world. After completing the Rajasuya sacrifice, he is now "emperor of the world", and you ask what's bothering me? Uncle, I am burning inside, burning in envy. I haven't had a minute of peace since I left Indraprastha. Didn't you see how they treated us in Indraprastha? Those imbecile kings, they lined up like peasants to pay these pretenders their taxes. None had the courage to stand up and protest when Krishna killed our dear friend Shishupal. Every day, the Pandavas are growing in power, growing in strength ... and I am sitting here, doing nothing. Shame on me! It's better to die than live this humiliating life.'

Shakuni placed his hand on Duryodhan's shoulder to comfort him. 'Is that any reason for you to die? The Pandavas are enjoying their good fortune. They have received their share of the kingdom and have prospered because of their might and valour. Why do you feel bad about that? Arjun pleased Agni to receive his Gandiva bow and the inexhaustible pair of quivers along with other divine weapons. With the help of those weapons, he forced the kings to surrender to Yudhishthira. That's nothing to sulk about. And why do you feel insulted and humiliated by the deceitful and clever designs of Maya? The palace of illusions was built to please the Pandavas, and not to trick you. Shake off your malaise and be the man you are. You are not alone. You have your gallant brothers with you. You have mighty warriors like Drona, Aswathama, Kripa, Karna and me by your side. You too can conquer the world if you desire.'

Shakuni's inspiring speech lifted Duryodhan from the doldrums. He said, 'Uncle, if you so advice, and with the help of our gallant Kuru warriors, I want to conquer the world and force all the kings to submit to my rule. Even the Pandavas.'

Shakuni smiled. 'My dear nephew, even the gods can't defeat the mighty Pandava brothers who enjoy allies like Vasudeva Krishna, King Drupad and his courageous son Dhrishtadyumna. But I know how to conquer Yudhishthira. Would you care to listen?'

Duryodhan was eager to hear any plan that would help him extract revenge. 'Please tell me, Uncle. I am open to any suggestion.'

Shakuni pulled a seat and sat down facing Duryodhan. In the dark room, his face looked as vicious as the stuffed vulture that perched behind him. 'Listen to me carefully,' he almost whispered into Duryodhan's ears. 'Yudhishthira loves to play the game of dice and is quite addicted to it. If you challenge him to a bout, he won't refuse you. I will play on your behalf, and you know very well, nobody can beat me in this game. I will defeat him with ease and win all his possessions for you.'

Duryodhan's eyes sparkled in greed. He said, 'What if he refuses to play?'

'Trust me, he won't. Especially, if your father invites him. All you need to do is, ask your father.' A smug smile flashed on Shakuni's face.

Duryodhan was sceptical. He wasn't quite sure that his father would approve of this devious plan. 'I can't ask him. You'll have to do this.'

Shakuni stood up. 'All right! I will ask him. Meet me in his chamber tomorrow morning.'

The next morning, Shakuni and Duryodhan visited Dhritarashtra in his chamber. The blind king had just finished his breakfast and was getting ready to leave for the royal court. Shakuni greeted the king and said, 'O King, I have a complaint. My nephew Duryodhan is suffering from severe depression. He has lost weight, his face looks pale, and if this sickness continues for long, I'm afraid we might lose him forever. I don't know what's bothering him. You are his father, why don't you enquire and do something about it?'

Shakuni's blunt words worried Dhritarashtra. He called Duryodhan to his side and asked him: 'My son, why are you miserable? I made you the crown prince and have given you immense wealth to cover all your expenses. Your mother and I, your brothers and your friends, everybody loves you. You have everything that a man could ask for, and you enjoy all the luxuries a person could imagine. And you are still unhappy. Why?'

Duryodhan sat down next to his father's feet and said, 'Yes, Father, I have all that one could ask for. However, like a coward, I am enjoying those sumptuous meals, wearing these expensive clothes, enjoying the company of beautiful women and passing time doing nothing. While our enemies are busy growing in strength and increasing their wealth, we are becoming weaker and poorer with every passing day. Father, this futile existence makes me angry—it makes me sick to the core. I have seen the wealth and prosperity of Yudhishthira during the Rajasuya ceremony. Thousands of kings and Brahmins poured in carts full of gold, silver and precious jewels into his coffers. When Vasudeva Krishna coronated Yudhishthira as the emperor of the world, I felt like puking. I shuddered when the conch shell rang out each day, announcing the completion of the daily meals of one million Brahmins. He employs thousands of educated men, millions of servants and guards in his palace. I am sure Yudhishthira's riches surpass the wealth of Indra, Yama, Varuna and Kuber taken together. Father, since I witnessed the prosperity of the Pandavas, I have been racked with envy and jealousy. We must do something. Or else I'll kill myself.'

Dhritarashtra was worried. 'No, no—don't even entertain such ominous thoughts. Tell me, what would you want me to do?'

Duryodhan replied, 'Uncle Shakuni has a plan to win all of Yudhishthira's possessions in a game of dice. Uncle is unbeatable in this game, and I trust him. Please grant us permission to go ahead.'

Dhritarashtra was taken aback when he heard this. 'I will consult Vidura about this and then decide. He is wise and will suggest the right path that would be in the best interests of both the parties.'

Duryodhan stood up and said, 'Father, we all know Vidura would never approve of this plan. It's fine. I will kill myself ... and you can live happily with your stepbrother, Vidura.' Duryodhan began walking towards the door.

Dhritarashtra was alarmed. 'Stop! Don't go. Let's discuss this before we arrive at a conclusion. Yudhishthira does not hate you. He and you have the same grandfather—you are descendants of the great Kuru dynasty. Why do you want to acquire your cousin's wealth? You are no less than him in wealth or power. If you wish to earn more wealth, acquire more power and influence, then do the right thing. Call the priests and sages, perform some fire ceremony, conquer kingdoms, and you'll have just as much wealth as the Pandavas. Refrain from doing what is unjust and immoral,' he said.

Duryodhan was not in the mood to hear lectures on morality. He snapped back at Dhritarashtra: 'Father, why do you want to impose the thoughts of others on me? One who cannot think for himself can never understand the real meaning of the scriptures. O King, listen to this—for a Kshatriya, winning is everything! That's his only goal. He shouldn't cloud his thoughts thinking of what is moral and what is not. Nowhere it is defined who is a friend and who is a foe. I understand only one definition—the person who inflicts pain on me is my enemy.'

Shakuni added, 'Yudhishthira's wealth, which is causing you so much pain, can be yours. Invite him to a game of dice and I will win for you all that is his. Trust me, Yudhishthira has no chance against me. Not a drop of blood will be shed, yet, victory will be yours. I promise.'

Dhritarashtra was still hesitant. 'This is a serious matter. Any misunderstanding can result in grave consequences, even an all-out war. I have always consulted Vidura in matters like this—'

Duryodhan interrupted him and said, 'Father, you know very well that Vidura has always favoured the Pandavas, and if you ask him, he'll do so again. Why are you so concerned about a simple game of dice? People have been gambling since the ancient times. It has never resulted in a war. It involves luck, which can favour either of the parties. The odds are the same for both sides. Just stop overthinking and invite the Pandavas to the game.'

Dhritarashtra had no other option but to succumb to his son's demands. He ordered his architects to build a special hall for the game to be played. When it was completed, he called Vidura and said, 'Vidura, go to Indraprastha and invite the Pandavas to visit us and inaugurate the assembly hall by playing a friendly game of dice with Duryodhan.'

Vidura could guess what the king had in mind. He said, 'O King, I must warn you, gambling is a dangerous sport and it can result in a nasty feud amongst your sons and nephews.'

Dhritarashtra replied, 'It is only a game, Vidura. Besides, who are we to control our destiny? If conflict is our destiny, it will happen, whether the game is played or not. Stop thinking negatively and carry out my orders. I'd love to meet Yudhishthira after all these years.'

19

The Game of Dice

Following Dhritarashtra's command, Vidura arrived in Indraprastha. The Pandavas were delighted to see their uncle after a long time. They greeted him and offered him their respects by washing his feet with perfumed water. Yudhishthira invited Vidura to his private chamber and offered him his seat. The maids brought food and drink for the tired guest. Yudhishthira noticed that Vidura was not his usual self and enquired, 'Uncle, you look melancholic. What's bothering you? Is everything fine in Hastinapur? Please tell me.'

Vidura rose from his seat. 'Yudhishthira, I come here as the emissary of King Dhritarashtra of Hastinapur. He has built a new assembly hall which is just as beautiful as yours. He invites you and your brothers to visit Hastinapur and inaugurate the hall by playing a friendly game of dice with Duryodhan.'

Yudhishthira felt something was not quite right. 'Uncle, gambling always results in controversy and dispute. An intelligent man should always stay away from such games. Wouldn't you agree?'

Vidura sighed. 'Gambling always leads to misery and destruction. I tried to dissuade Dhritarashtra from this dangerous game, but he didn't listen and forced me to come here. You are a wise and learned man. Do whatever you think is best.'

Yudhishthira thought for a while and then said, 'Whatever maybe the consequence, I cannot refuse an invitation from my uncle. We will leave for Hastinapur tomorrow. Draupadi will accompany us.'

The following day, when the Pandavas arrived at the Hastinapur palace, conch shells were blown, and beautiful maidens showered flower petals and sprinkled rose water on them. The ministers greeted them with flower garlands. Bhishma embraced the five brothers. Drona and Kripa hugged their favourite pupils too. Duryodhan, Dushasana and Shakuni also extended a warm welcome to their rivals with their palms joined. As the Pandavas walked by, Duryodhan felt the pang of jealousy once again. The sight of Draupadi reminded him of her humiliating laughter in the palace of illusions.

The Pandava entourage proceeded to meet Dhritarashtra and Gandhari in their private chambers. Dhritarashtra rose to welcome them. 'Come, my dear nephews. How I missed you all. I am glad you accepted my invitation.'

Yudhishthira touched his uncle's feet, followed by Bheem, Arjun, Nakul, Sahadev and Draupadi. Dhritarashtra blessed them by kissing their foreheads. Yudhishthira said, 'Uncle, how could we not accept your invitation? Besides, Hastinapur is our home and you are our family. It always feels good to come back to our home.'

The Pandavas also paid their respects to Gandhari, the queen mother. She blessed them and asked the maids to show the Pandavas their quarters. Dhritarashtra said, 'Boys, you must be tired after this long journey. Get some rest. Tomorrow, we will inaugurate the assembly hall with your game of dice.'

The next morning, Yudhishthira arrived at the assembly hall along with his four brothers. The hall was spectacular indeed. Built with marble and precious stones, it included an arena in the centre, where sports activities could take place. This area was surrounded by ornate thrones for the spectators to sit and watch the games. Huge columns supported the crystal roof, through which the bright sunlight flowed in and washed the interiors. The Pandavas were impressed by the craftsmanship. They stepped into the arena and found Duryodhan and Shakuni waiting for them. Duryodhan led Yudhishthira to the centre of the stage, where a dice board and a pair of dice lay waiting. Yudhishthira said, 'The game of dice is wrought with treachery and sin. The game doesn't demand any Kshatriya valour, and is unethical and immoral. There is no glory in deceit. I request you, please do not try to defeat us by unfair means.'

Shakuni smiled and said, 'Yudhishthira, one who is skilled in the game can handle its idiosyncrasies, including the tricks employed by artful players. You are an experienced player, and it is Duryodhan who runs the risk of losing the game because of your skilful play. But we would still like to play.'

Yudhishthira replied, 'I do not want to gain wealth or happiness by unfair means. A skilled and clever player should never indulge in deceit and fraud.'

Shakuni countered, 'Yudhishthira, even learned pundits use deceit and clever tricks to defeat their opponents in a debate. Such trickery is acceptable and is never looked down upon. But if you feel uncomfortable ... *scared*, you can withdraw from the game.'

Sensing the mockery in Shakuni's voice, Yudhishthira's eyes bore into Shakuni's when he said, 'Once I accept a challenge, I never withdraw. Whom am I supposed to play with? Duryodhan, you'll play against me, right?'

Duryodhan nodded. 'Yes, I'll make the bets. But Uncle Shakuni will roll the dice on my behalf.'

When he heard this, Yudhishthira suspected foul play, but it was too late to do anything about it. He only said, 'I don't think it is appropriate for someone to play the game on behalf of another person. Anyway, if that's what you want, so be it.'

Yudhishthira sat down in front of the board. Bheem, Arjun, Nakul and Sahadev sat behind him. Opposite Yudhishthira sat Duryodhan and Shakuni. Dushasana and the other Kaurava brothers sat behind them.

In the meantime, the Kuru elders entered the hall. Dhritarashtra sat on the huge golden throne in the centre of the hall. Vidura, Bhishma, Drona and Kripa took their respective seats too. None of them looked happy and it was obvious that they were just following orders against their will. Dhritarashtra raised his hands and said, 'Let the game begin.'

Yudhishthira was given the honour of declaring his bet first. He took off a necklace from around his neck and placed it on the board. 'My necklace is adorned with this precious gem that was procured from the depths of the sea. It is invaluable. I bet this necklace. What do you bet, Duryodhan?'

'I bet all my gems and jewels.'

Shakuni picked up the pair of dice from the board, closed his eyes and rolled them in his palms. Then he threw them on the board and yelled, 'I win!'

Indeed, the dice had stopped rolling with the winning number facing the top.

Yudhishthira said to Shakuni: 'Uncle, you have tricked me this time. But you can't do this forever. Now I bet a thousand chests filled with gold. Let's see if you can win this.' Shakuni rolled the dice again and yelled, 'I win!' And Yudhishthira lost his bet.

Yudhishthira then said, 'Now I bet my golden chariot that brought me here, along with the eight powerful horses that pull it.' With a flick of his wrist, Shakuni won them all.

With the series of losses, Yudhishthira was sucked into the game. One by one, he bet all his possessions: one hundred thousand of his most beautiful and skilled maids, one hundred thousand skilled servants, one thousand elephants, ten thousand war chariots with their charioteers, sixty thousand soldiers, and many other riches. Shakuni got it all and, like an addict, Yudhishthira continued betting.

Vidura couldn't keep quiet any longer. He stood up and said, 'King Dhritarashtra, I implore you to stop this farce. A sick person hates taking his medicines on his deathbed. Similarly, you'd also hate my words. Still, I would say what I must. Your son Duryodhan is about to usher in the greatest misfortune for your family. Just as the Vrishnis and Bhojas abandoned their evil King Kansa and engaged his nephew Krishna to kill him, you should order Arjun to kill Duryodhan right now. The death of this sinner can only bring peace and prosperity to the Kauravas. Sacrifice your evil son and win over the Pandavas. O King, remember, it is better to sacrifice a member of the family to save the entire clan. Give up a family to save the village, give up a village to save the country, and give up the world to save oneself. I know you are rejoicing at your son's victory. Let me warn you, Duryodhan's actions will result in a devastating conflict. The Pandavas are calm now, but when they lose their patience, how would you stop them from destroying your family? Save yourself, O King. Don't turn the Pandavas against you.'

Duryodhan was inflamed by Vidura's words. He thundered, 'Uncle Vidura, you never liked us and have always been critical of us. You think we are fools, and we don't know what's right for us?

You are wrong. And don't you try to guide us. We are only guided by the Almighty who controls every being in this universe, no one else. We have been patient with you, but now you must stop acting like our guardian. It is said, one should not give shelter to someone who favours the enemy. Uncle, if you hate us, you may leave Hastinapur and go wherever you like.'

Vidura replied, 'Prince Duryodhan, I know you hate me just as much as a young bride hates her old husband. Fair enough. I won't give you any more advice. From now on, when you require advice, go to the fools who always try to please you. It is rare to find someone who listens and speaks the unpalatable truth. King Dhritarashtra, I have always wished well for the descendants of King Vichitravirya. I will not speak any more. Let matters take their inevitable course.'

Vidura sat down and looked the other way while Duryodhan and Shakuni resumed their game. Shakuni said, 'Well, King Yudhishthira, you have lost a lot of your wealth. Do you have anything left to bet?'

'I have a lot more. I will bet again and win back everything I lost. I bet all the livestock I own, all my properties on the eastern side of River Sindh—villages, town cities, agricultural land—I bet everything.'

Once again, Shakuni swept the board. Yudhishthira then bet the jewellery and expensive costumes of all the Pandava princes. Shakuni won them all and laughed at Yudhishthira: 'So, Yudhishthira, would you like to quit now?'

Yudhishthira looked up. He was trembling in humiliation, his eyes bloodshot. With a cracked voice, he said, 'No, I don't quit so easy. I will win.'

Shakuni guffawed: 'But do you have anything left to bet? You've lost everything.'

Yudhishthira said, 'No I didn't.' He touched the shoulder of his youngest brothers, Nakul and Sahadev. He said, 'Shakuni, you see

my gallant brothers, Nakul and Sahadev. They are like my two eyes.
I bet them.'

Shakuni glanced at Nakul and Sahadev. 'Very well,' he said as he
picked up the dice and rolled them on the board. And once again he
yelled, 'I win!'

Yudhishthira sat stunned, while Duryodhan and Dushasana
broke into a loud applause and cheered Shakuni for his unbeatable
skills. Shakuni picked up the dice and said, 'Yudhishthira, I have won
your dear brothers Nakul and Sahadev. But Bheem and Arjun must
be dearer to you than the twins? After all, Nakul and Sahadev are only
your half-brothers.'

Yudhishthira said, 'You devil, you want to cause a rift between us
brothers, don't you?'

Shakuni grinned: 'Pardon me. The game has intoxicated me and
I have lost control over my tongue. People say the darndest things
when they gamble—never mind them. Would you like to continue?'

Yudhishthira glanced at Arjun and said, 'The one who leads us
to victory in battle, who is the most gallant warrior and the sharpest
archer of all, the one who should never be placed as a bet, I bet him—
my dear brother Arjun.'

Shakuni rolled the dice and yelled, 'I win! I win prince Arjun.'
The Kauravas broke into a thunderous applause. They jumped out of
their seats and came down dancing to the arena. Shakuni raised his
hand to stop them and said, 'What next?'

Refusing to quit, Yudhishthira said, 'Now I bet the strongest
man in the world, one who can destroy an entire army with his bare
hands ... who is beyond any bet—my dear brother, Bheem.'

Once again Shakuni rolled the dice and won Bheem. Silence
fell over the hall. Was this the end of the game? The great emperor
Yudhishthira had lost everything. He was a pauper now. What *could*

he bet next? Shakuni smirked: 'Shall we call it a day now? Or do you have anything left to bet?'

Yudhishthira said, 'I have myself. I bet myself. Try and win me.'

And Shakuni won him too. The crowd went berserk. Yudhishthira and the Pandava brothers were Duryodhan's slaves now. This was beyond their wildest dreams. Bhishma, Drona and Kripa sat like stone figures. They lost the ability to speak or comment. The five disgraced brothers sat with their heads down and waited for the command from their master. Only Bheem kept growling in frustration and anger, but the wild cries of the Kaurava brothers drowned his faint protest. Shakuni eyed Yudhishthira like a vulture. When the cries died down a little, he said, 'Yudhishthira, it is unfair to lose yourself in a bet when you still own something precious.' Yudhishthira didn't quite grasp what Shakuni meant. Shakuni continued, 'You have not lost your beautiful wife Panchali as yet. Why don't you bet her and free yourself?'

For a while, Yudhishthira didn't speak. He stared at the dice board in front of him with a vacant look while the audience sat still, holding their breath. Something ominous seemed to be unfolding right before their eyes. A little later, Yudhishthira raised his head and said, 'The one who is neither too short, nor too tall; who is neither too dark, nor too fair; neither thin nor fat; who has the most beautiful curly hair; whose eyes are like lotus petals; who is as fragrant as the lotus flower. She who is as beautiful as goddess Lakshmi, who is the most erudite and articulate of all—I bet her—our wife, Draupadi.' The audience gasped. How could Yudhishthira bet his wife? Yudhishthira, who was the wisest of all, who stayed calm and steady in the fiercest of battles, had he lost his mind? Bhishma, Drona and Kripa were sweating on their seats, while Vidura covered his face with his hands. Only the blind King Dhritarashtra couldn't contain himself. He kept asking, 'Who won? Who won?'

Shakuni picked up the pieces and looked around: Duryodhan, sitting next to him with a smug smile on his face; Dushasana drooling lustfully. Opposite him, behind Yudhishthira, sat the Pandava brothers with their heads hanging low, eyes closed, and their faces flushed in shame and disgrace. Yudhishthira sat with his eyes fixed on the board, as if he were willing the board to favour him one last time. Shakuni raised his hand and rolled the pieces in his palms. The pieces rattled as Shakuni shook them in his hand. And then, with a loud crash, they landed on the board and rolled off to the edge before stopping. Shakuni yelled, 'I win!'

The joyous Kauravas erupted in a huge cry. Duryodhan embraced Shakuni to express his gratitude. Dushasana and Karna placed garlands on Duryodhan's neck to congratulate him.

Duryodhan called Vidura and said, 'Uncle, go and fetch Draupadi to the court. She doesn't belong to the royal chambers any more. Let her get busy working with the maids to clean the floors.' His brothers broke into a rapturous laughter.

Vidura said, 'Only an evil man like you can utter such disgusting words. Draupadi cannot be your maid, because Yudhishthira lost his rights as a husband when he placed her as his bet. Duryodhan, let me warn you once again: stop this and return everything to Yudhishthira. Else, death won't be far for you and your brothers.'

Duryodhan ignored Vidura. He turned towards one of his attendants and said, 'Pratikami, go to the palace and bring Draupadi to the court. Tell her that her lord Duryodhan wants her.' Pratikami stood up, bowed to Duryodhan and left the hall to fetch Draupadi.

20

Draupadi's Humiliation

PRATIKAMI, DURYODHAN'S ATTENDANT, ENTERED THE INNER QUARTERS OF the palace. He walked up to Draupadi's room and knocked on the door. Draupadi was preparing for her bath. She wore a long piece of white silk draped loosely around her body. A maid massaged her arms and legs with aromatic oils. She gestured the maids to stop and asked, 'Who's this?'

'It's me, Pratikami. Son of the royal charioteer. May I come in?'

'Come in,' said Draupadi. Pratikami entered the room with his eyes to the ground. The intoxicating lotus fragrance emanating from Draupadi made her presence quite conspicuous. She asked, 'What do you want, Pratikami.'

'O Queen, King Yudhishthira bet his brothers and himself in the game of dice and lost to Duryodhan. He bet you too ... and lost. You are now Duryodhan's property and he has ordered me to fetch you to the assembly hall.' Pratikami's voice trembled as he uttered these words.

Draupadi couldn't believe her ears. She felt as if the ground under her feet were shaking. A surge of anger ran through her veins and she tried hard to control herself. With an imperious look, she said, 'Pratikami, go back to the hall and ask Yudhishthira, whom did he lose first? Me or himself?'

Pratikami went back to the assembly hall and asked Yudhishthira the question. Yudhishthira couldn't find the courage to open his mouth and sat still, like a dead man. Duryodhan said, 'Go back and tell Draupadi, she must come here and ask her question.'

Pratikami went back to Draupadi and passed on the message. Draupadi said, 'Ask the wise and learned seniors in the court what I should do. I'll do whatever they suggest.'

Pratikami asked, but the seniors kept silent, their eyes boring into the floor. Duryodhan was getting impatient. He yelled at Pratikami, 'Do as I say! Bring Draupadi to the assembly floor.'

Scared, Pratikami said in a feeble voice, 'What should I tell her?'

Duryodhan turned to Dushasana: 'Brother, this fool is scared to bring Draupadi because he is afraid of Bheem. You go and bring her to the hall. If she doesn't obey my orders, don't hesitate to use force.'

Dushasana stormed through the halls and entered Draupadi's chambers. He stood at the door with his arms on his hips and roared: 'Draupadi, your husband has lost you in gambling. You are now our slave, and you must obey our orders. Shed your pride and come with me to the court. Your lord awaits you.'

Alarmed, Draupadi tried to flee. She ran towards the adjoining room, where the other Kaurava women lived. Dushasana blocked her path and grabbed her by her hair. 'How dare you try to escape me! Come with me, you filthy slave.' Dushasana yanked Draupadi by her hair and dragged her out of the door.

Draupadi screamed in pain. 'Let me go, you heartless brute! I am not in proper attire to appear in the court ... Let me go, I say!'

Dushasana laughed and said, 'I don't care if you're dressed or undressed. You are our slave, and your duty is to please us! Come with me.'

Dragging Draupadi to the assembly hall in her dishevelled clothes, Dushasana threw her down to the floor. Draupadi tried her best to cover her body as she stood up in front of the assembled kings and ministers. By now, her shame and humiliation had transformed into pure rage. With fiery voice, she said, 'Dushasana, you'll pay for this with your life. Even if the gods want to protect you, the Pandavas will never spare you.' She looked at the seated Kuru seniors and said, 'I have been humiliated and dragged by my hair in front of you, the great heroes of the Kuru dynasty. Why didn't I hear a single voice of protest? What happened to the great Bhishma, Drona, Vidura? What happened to the great King Dhritarashtra? Are you all dead? Are you blind? Can't you see how morality and decency have been abandoned by this court, this family? How could you sit still and tolerate this inhuman behaviour? Is this what you've been taught by your scriptures?'

Dushasana pushed her to the floor again and jeered, 'Stop squealing, you slave!' Karna joined the laughter; so did Shakuni.

Not everybody in the audience enjoyed this brutal humiliation of their dear princess Panchali. Many hid their tears but couldn't say anything. They were either too afraid to protest, or didn't have any solid logic to support her. After all, she had been lost in the game by her husband.

Bhishma coughed a little to clear his voice and then said, 'My dear Draupadi, the laws of morality are complex and subtle. I am afraid, I won't be able to give you the right answer to your question. Yudhishthira, who always followed the path of truth, himself accepted his defeat. It was Shakuni's skill that motivated Yudhishthira to accept his challenge and play the game. And I see no reason to believe that Shakuni used any unfair means to defeat him.'

'That's not true,' said Draupadi. 'Yudhishthira didn't want to play with Shakuni. He was asked to play the game against his will. Yudhishthira is pure-hearted and couldn't see through Duryodhan's conspiracy and Shakuni's deceptive tricks. That's why he was defeated. But you, the wise Kuru seniors, I ask you to use your judgement and tell me whether I was "won" by Duryodhan or not.'

Bheem was seething in anger. Till now, he had controlled himself because of Yudhishthira. But Draupadi's humiliation broke his restraint. He jumped up from his seat, and in a thunderous voice he yelled at Yudhishthira: 'Even the worst of gamblers won't bet his concubine, let alone his wife, in a game. At least they have some morals, humanity and kindness in them; but you don't! Our enemies stole our kingdom and our wealth by trickery and deceit. That didn't anger me since you were the owner of it all. Draupadi is the wife of the mighty Pandavas. She shouldn't have to suffer this insult and misery. These cruel and low-life Kauravas had the audacity to torture her only because of you. I will set to flames those hands of yours which played the evil game of dice. Sahadev, fetch me some fire!'

Everybody in the hall grew anxious seeing Bheem's anger. Arjun rose to calm him down. 'Brother Bheem, please control yourself. Yudhishthira is our elder brother. It is our duty to follow him and support him in whatever he does. You know very well, Yudhishthira would never do anything immoral. Trust me, we will have our chance to get back at them later.' Arjun pulled Bheem back to his seat.

Just then, Vikarna, one of Duryodhan's ninety-nine brothers, stood up to say something. He was panting with excitement and was continuously rubbing his hands. Vikarna said, 'Since nobody wants to answer Draupadi's legitimate question, let me say what I feel is right and justified. Hunting, drinking, gambling and womanizing are the four worst addictions of a king. A man who suffers from these vices strays from the path of righteousness and virtue. And a man's action under the influence of his addiction can never be considered to be valid or justified. Yudhishthira was addicted to gambling and he bet Draupadi under the influence. Hence, his action cannot be valid. Besides, Yudhishthira bet her after losing himself. So, Draupadi could not have been lost in the game. She is free.'

Vikarna's comments raised a storm in the hall. Many agreed with his logic and praised him while criticizing Shakuni and Duryodhan. Enraged by Vikarna's disloyalty, Karna yelled at him: 'Vikarna, stop babbling like a moron. You are a child, and you don't know the first thing about morality and virtue. The seniors are not commenting because they have a justified reason to do so. Yudhishthira had lost Draupadi when he bet all his possessions, which included Draupadi. Still, with a clear and unambiguous voice, he gambled her again. None of the Pandava brothers raised their voice in protest. With their silence, they too gave their consent. So what are you complaining about? As per the Vedas, a woman can only have one husband. Draupadi has many; so she is nothing more than a prostitute. Now stop lamenting for her and show your support to your brother Duryodhan. Shakuni has won the Pandavas along with all their belongings, including Draupadi. They are now nothing more than slaves. Dushasana, remove their clothes. Let's see how our slaves look naked.'

The Pandava brothers took off the scarves that covered their upper body while Draupadi stood clenching the silk robe that covered her. Dushasana walked up to her and grabbed one end of her robe. Draupadi looked at her husbands helplessly, hoping they would rise from their trance and do something. But they sat still with their heads hung low. The rowdy laughter of Dushasana and the Kaurava brothers didn't reach their ears. Dushasana pulled one end of Draupadi's robe and she spun around, exposing large portions of her skin. With her palms joined, she cried out: 'O Lord Vishnu, O Lord Krishna, save me from this insult. Protect me from this unbearable humiliation.' Her cries and tears didn't stop Dushasana. He tugged at Draupadi's robe again, but this time, she did not spin around. Dushasana continued pulling her robe, but the fabric seemed to expand in a continuous stream without exposing an inch of Draupadi's body. Dushasana kept pulling and the fabric kept flowing. Soon, the assembly floor was covered in piles of silk drawn by Dushasana. The audience was amazed to witness this miracle. Everyone got on their feet and hailed Draupadi while rebuking and cursing Dushasana. Exhausted, Dushasana finally gave up and sat down to catch a breath.

Bheem was grinding his teeth in frustration and rage. He couldn't keep quiet any longer. He yelled, 'Listen all who are present here today. If one day in the battlefield I don't tear open the chest of this scoundrel Dushasana and drink his blood, then I won't attain the abode of my ancestors. This I promise.'

Hearing Bheem's terrible oath, the Kauravas shuddered in fear. Vidura said, 'Dear assemblymen, why are you not responding to poor Draupadi's question? Say something. Vikarna has spoken from his heart. You should too.' The men in the assembly didn't respond.

Karna said, 'Dushasana, take your slave Draupadi to her slave quarters.' Dushasana got up on his feet and once again grabbed Draupadi's hair and yanked her. Draupadi screamed in pain. 'Let me go! Didn't you hear what Bheem said?' Dushasana laughed and dragged her through the floor. Draupadi looked at the Kuru seniors and said, 'How could you sit still and watch your daughter treated with such cruelty? Are the glory days of the Kuru dynasty over? What evil spirit has clouded your judgement? Tell me, am I a slave or not? Answer me!'

Bhishma, with tearful eyes, said, 'I told you, my dear, justice and morality are too complicated to decipher. I cannot answer your question with certainty. But one thing I can say for sure: the Kauravas have succumbed to greed and malice, and their days are numbered. No one can stop their destruction. As for your question, I think only Yudhishthira can give you the right answer.'

Duryodhan laughed at Draupadi and said, 'All right, let Bheem, Arjun and the other brothers proclaim that Yudhishthira is not your husband. Let them say that Yudhishthira is a liar, and I will grant you freedom. Or let the son of Dharma himself say whether he is your husband or not. Maybe that'll clarify your doubts?'

Bheem stood up and raised his powerful arms. 'If Yudhishthira, our guru and leader, hadn't restrained me, I would have never tolerated your insolent behaviour,' he yelled at Duryodhan. 'If he permits, I can kill you all with a single blow of my fist.'

Yudhishthira did not bat an eyelid. He sat there in a dumb stupor, as if he had no consciousness. Duryodhan looked at him and said, 'Your brothers are waiting for your command. Why don't you say something? Why don't you answer your beloved Draupadi?'

Karna walked up to Draupadi and said, 'Pretty slave, it seems Yudhishthira has no interest in you. I say, forget him. Find a new husband—or husbands—for yourself. You'll find many men in the slave quarters.' The Kauravas broke into derisive laughter at Karna's mockery.

Duryodhan uncovered his thigh and, with a vulgar gesture, he slapped it and winked at Draupadi, who closed her eyes in disgust. Bheem roared in anger. Bursting with rage, he said to Duryodhan, 'You scoundrel! How dare you show such disrespect to Draupadi? One day, if I don't break that thigh of yours with a blow of my mace, let the doors of heaven be forever closed to me.'

Bheem's open threat made shivers run through the spines of the men assembled. Vidura said to the Kauravas: 'You sons of Dhritarashtra, beware of Bheemsen. He can cause immense pain to you all. Great danger that you cannot even imagine right now awaits you. You have disregarded the rules of the game of dice. You have gone beyond all bounds of decency by dragging a lady from your family into the court and violating her dignity in the worst possible way. This court has lost all its credibility, for here justice and morality have been corrupted.'

Just then, a jackal cried from near Dhritarashtra's fire temple. Donkeys brayed and vultures screamed in the sky. Hearing the horrible ominous sounds, Gandhari, Drona and the other Brahmins got worried. They warned Dhritarashtra that something terrible would happen soon unless he stopped the Kauravas from going too far.

As if waking up from a deep slumber, Dhritarashtra cried out, 'You fool, Duryodhan, you have insulted Draupadi, the wife of my beloved nephews, the Pandavas. Death awaits you for your unpardonable sin.' Then he turned to Draupadi and said, 'Panchali, you are the best amongst my daughters-in-law. You are the most faithful and virtuous woman in our family. Ask anything you want from me.'

Draupadi sat down in front of Dhritarashtra's feet and said, 'O King, if you'd like to grant me a wish, then please release Yudhishthira from his slavery.'

Dhritarashtra raised his hand and said, 'I grant your wish. Yudhishthira is free. What else do you wish for?'

'Please release Bheem, Arjun, Nakul and Sahadev from their slavery.'

'So be it. They are all free now. But two wishes are not enough for you. Tell me, what more do you want?' Dhritarashtra was feeling extremely generous.

Draupadi bowed and said, 'Thank you, O King. I don't want anything more. My husbands are free. They can reconstruct their life with their own deeds.'

Karna was surprised at Draupadi's magnanimous gesture. He said, 'I have never heard of any woman do what Draupadi did just now. She has rescued the Pandavas, just as a boat rescues a drowning man.'

Bheem came to Yudhishthira and said, 'Allow me, brother. Let me crush these evil Kaurava brothers right away.'

Yudhishthira stopped him. 'Bheem, please stay calm. This is not the time.' He knelt before Dhritarashtra, and said, 'O King, we are always at your service. Tell me, what should we do now?'

Dhritarashtra said, 'My dear Yudhishthira, I give you back your kingdom, your wealth and all your possessions. Go back to Indraprastha and rule as you've ruled before. Forget this evil day and do not hold any grudge against Duryodhan. I had agreed to this game only to meet you and to watch you play once again with your brothers. I never thought it would turn out to be so ugly. But you have retained your calm and acted well, following the path of truth and righteousness. With you as an emperor and Vidura as a minister, the Kuru dynasty has nothing to worry about. Remember, you and your brothers are always in our minds, and we always wish you well. Go back to Indraprastha and live in peace with your brothers forever.'

21

One Last Game

As the Pandavas sped towards Indraprastha in their golden chariot, Duryodhan, Dushasana and Karna assembled in Shakuni's chamber. The outcome of the day did not please them at all. Dushasana banged his fist on the wall and said, 'Oh, we were so close. We had them—we had them pinned to the ground. We won all their wealth, their kingdom, everything! But the old man ruined it all!' Duryodhan didn't utter a word. He sat still with his head down. How much more humiliation must he tolerate, he thought.

Karna came up to him and said, 'My friend, I have never supported deceit and trickery in winning over the enemy. I suggest we chase the Pandavas on their way back to Indraprastha and attack them by surprise. I can assure you, I will kill your enemies and make you the emperor.'

Shakuni said to Karna, 'You are a great warrior, Karna. But don't underestimate the combined strength of the Pandavas. You may be as skilled as Arjun, but remember he has Bheem by his side, not to mention Nakul, Sahadev and Yudhishthira. So, give up your dreams of fighting Arjun and listen to my plan.'

Shakuni's words caught Duryodhan's attention. But he was still sceptical. 'Another plan, Uncle? What do you have in mind now?'

'I'll tell you.' Shakuni sat next to Duryodhan. 'First you'll have to bring back the Pandavas.' And as Shakuni began to outline his plan, Duryodhan's eyes lit up once again. He could see the light at the end of his tunnel of misery and realized that all was not lost.

Dhritarashtra was preparing to retire to his chamber. The day's excitement had left him too tired. He was relieved that he had been able to control the damage and the Pandavas left without any hard feelings. At least that's what they sounded like. But again, he thought, was he being too optimistic? He wished he had interfered and stopped the game much earlier. The humiliation the Pandavas had to bear was too much for any self-respecting man to handle. What if they wanted to extract revenge? What if they returned with a huge army and attacked Hastinapur with full force? It would be a disaster. The Pandavas had powerful allies, and with their help they could destroy the Kauravas in a matter of days.

No, Yudhishthira wouldn't do such a thing, he thought. After all, he is a Kuru descendant and he would never destroy the kingdom of his father, Pandu. Dhritarashtra tried to shake off his negative thoughts and rose from his throne.

Just then, he heard footsteps. His keen sense of hearing told him it was his dearest son, Duryodhan. His heart trembled in anticipation—what was it now? What evil proposal did he have for him this time?

Duryodhan entered the room and said, 'Father, Lord Brihaspati once said, "One who hurts you either in war or in peace is your enemy. And he must be destroyed at any cost."'

Dhritarashtra could guess what his son was alluding to, but feigned ignorance. 'What do you mean?'

'Father, a serpent who's about to strike should never be spared. After what we did today, the Pandavas would never forgive us. They'll seek revenge for sure. If we don't act soon, they'll surely annihilate us.'

Dhritarashtra felt dizzy. He grabbed the hand rest of his throne and sat down. Duryodhan's words had suddenly made the possibility take concrete shape in his mind. Maybe it was foolish to have let the Pandavas go.

He asked, 'What do you have in mind?'

Duryodhan knew he had his father's attention. He said, 'Father, bring back the Pandavas. We want to play a final game of dice with them.'

'No, not again!' cried Dhritarashtra.

'Listen to me before you decide. This time, we will not wager any wealth or material possessions. This time, we'll banish them from their kingdom for a long, long time.' Duryodhan explained the details of his plan.

'And then what?' Dhritarashtra asked while trying to control his trembling voice.

Duryodhan smiled and said, 'During this time, we will amass a huge army and become the most powerful kingdom on earth. When the Pandavas return, we will fight and destroy them forever.'

Dhritarashtra thought for a while. Whatever control he thought he had of the situation, it was slipping out of his hands like fine sand. Nothing he could do would prevent the inevitable. He raised his head and said, 'So be it. Make arrangements to bring back the Pandavas.'

Duryodhan called his trusted charioteer Pratikami and said, 'Take the fastest horse from the stable and stop the Pandavas on their way. Tell Yudhishthira, the great King Dhritarashtra has asked them to come back to Hastinapur and play one last game.'

Dhritarashtra staggered back to his room. As he was taking the heavy crown off his head, Gandhari approached. She took the crown, put it aside and said, 'When Duryodhan was born, Vidura advised you to get rid of him. You should have followed his advice.' Dhritarashtra didn't answer. He felt his way to the couch next to his bed and sat down.

Gandhari said, 'O King, I implore you. Please do not listen to your evil sons. The Pandavas have accepted your offer and left Hastinapur in peace. Why do you want to infuriate them again? Listen to me, else your blind love for Duryodhan will soon destroy your dynasty.'

Dhritarashtra's face distorted in pain. He turned his face away from Gandhari and said, 'I know my dynasty will be destroyed, but I am helpless. I cannot stop the inevitable. Let my sons do whatever they wish.'

The Pandavas sat gloomy and miserable in their chariot as it raced through the plains towards Indraprastha. They hadn't recovered from the insult and humiliation heaped upon them by the Kauravas. Draupadi sat with her eyes closed. Dushasana's laughter still rang in her ears. Bheem, Arjun, Nakul and Sahadev gazed into the distant horizon and wondered if there was anything at all that could help them wash off the horrible memories. Yudhishthira looked back at the vanishing skyline of Hastinapur and wondered what he had done wrong. Why couldn't he stop playing the game and leave the assembly hall? Shakuni gave him the option to quit, but he didn't accept the offer. Why? Was it his pride? Or did he succumb to his addiction?

Just then, he saw a cloud of dust approaching his chariot. It was Pratikami riding his horse and waving his hand. Yudhishthira asked his charioteer to stop. Pratikami stopped next to the chariot and dismounted from his horse. Panting with exhaustion, he bowed in front of Yudhishthira and said, 'King Dhritarashtra has called you back to the palace of Hastinapur. He wants you to play one final game of dice.'

The Pandavas were outraged to hear this. 'How dare the Kauravas ask us to play again? Don't they have any shame?' thundered Bheem.

'A man's destiny is in the hands of his creator. We cannot change anything,' said Yudhishthira. 'Our old uncle Dhritarashtra has summoned and I must obey his orders even though I know that danger awaits us.'

'But why?' asked Arjun.

Yudhishthira replied, 'My dear brother, Lord Rama knew that no living creature could be made of gold. Still, he went to hunt the golden deer for his wife Sita. When danger looms, even the wisest man loses his head.' He looked at his charioteer and said, 'Turn back the chariot. Take us back to Hastinapur.'

When Yudhishthira arrived at the assembly hall, Duryodhan, Shakuni, Dushasana and all the Kuru elders were waiting for them. Dhritarashtra was in his throne. Shakuni came up to Yudhishthira and said, 'It was magnanimous of King Dhritarashtra to return your kingdom and your wealth to you. And to honour his gesture, we won't bet any material possessions in this last game. Instead, this is what our wager would be: if we lose this game, we will wear deerskin and go into exile in the forests for a period of twelve years. Once the twelve years get over, we'll spend the thirteenth year in hiding. During the thirteenth year, if anybody finds us, we'll have to remain in exile for another twelve years. If you lose, you must do the same. During these thirteen years, Duryodhan would take care of your kingdom. After the thirteenth year, you can return to Indraprastha and claim your kingdom back. If you agree to this challenge, let's play.'

A murmur went through the hall. The assembled audience were surprised to hear of this peculiar bet. Why aren't the Kuru seniors stopping this game? Why aren't they warning the Pandavas? And what about the Pandavas? Have they lost their mind again? Don't they realize that they are stepping into a dangerous trap?

Yudhishthira was calm. He addressed Shakuni, 'You know, I never retreat when challenged. I accept your bet. Let's play.' He sat down in front of the dice board and gestured his brothers to sit behind him. Shakuni sat across the board with Duryodhan, Dushasana and Karna next to him.

Shakuni said, 'Yudhishthira, why don't you roll the dice first, this time?' Yudhishthira picked up the pair and rolled them in his palms and threw them on the board. But the winning numbers didn't show up. Shakuni looked at them and said, 'Sorry, my dear nephew. Let's see how they behave in my hands.' He rolled the dice in his hands and threw them on the board. And even before the dice touched the board he yelled, 'I win!'

The jubilant Kaurava brothers burst out in a wild cry. They jumped off their seats and danced around Shakuni and Duryodhan. Dushasana threw a few deerskins in front of the Pandavas. 'Take off your royal clothes and wear these instead. This is the appropriate costume for forest dwellers,' he laughed.

Yudhishthira and his brothers took off their clothes and put on the deer skins and began their preparation to leave for the forests. Dushasana addressed the audience: 'From now on, Duryodhan becomes the emperor. The Pandavas will spend the next thirteen years in hell.' Turning to Draupadi, he said, 'Your father King Drupad was foolish to marry you to these impotent imbeciles. Leave them and find some better men.'

Bheem couldn't control his anger and said to Dushasana: 'You brute! Remember those words when I tear open your chest in the battlefield.' Dushasana couldn't care less for his threats. He danced around the Pandavas, mocking and hurling cruel insults at them while the Kaurava brothers laughed at his antics.

As the Pandavas walked out of the hall, Duryodhan couldn't hold himself back. He too joined Dushasana and mocked Bheem, mimicking his walk. Bheem turned around and roared, 'Listen to me, you fool. Not only will I kill Dushasana and drink his blood, but I will also kill you with my mace. I will smash your face with my feet. Arjun will kill Karna and Sahadev will kill your wicked uncle Shakuni.'

Arjun said, 'Words don't mean anything unless they are executed. Let the thirteen years pass, and then you'll see what happens. Brother Bheem, to honour your words, I promise, I will kill this foul-mouthed and arrogant Karna in the battlefield.'

Sahadev added, 'Shakuni, I too will do exactly as brother Bheem said. You will die at my hands.'

Nakul turned to the assembled Kaurava supporters and said, 'You who have insulted Draupadi to please your evil prince Duryodhan, listen to me. I will kill you all. Nobody will be spared.'

Yudhishthira addressed Dhritarashtra, Bhishma, Drona, Kripa, Vidura and the other Kuru elders and said, 'With your permission, we now want to leave for the forest. Please give us your blessings. We hope to see you all when we come back after thirteen years.'

The elders hid their face in shame. They didn't have the strength to utter any words of grace. Only Vidura said, 'Kunti will not be able to bear the hardship of living in the forest. She can live in my house with full honour.'

Yudhishthira bowed to him and said, 'Uncle Vidura, you are like our father. Before we leave, bless us, and share with us your words of wisdom.'

Vidura replied, 'Yudhishthira, there is no disgrace in losing an unfair game. Go into your exile with your head held high. Your love for each other is unparalleled in the universe. Nobody can break your bond. Take care of each other during times of duress and discuss amongst yourselves before arriving at any decision and taking any action. I wish you the best. Come back a winner in due time. I'll be waiting for you.'

Draupadi visited Kunti and asked for her blessings. Kunti said, sobbing, 'My dear, I have nothing to tell you. The Kauravas are lucky that your anger didn't burn them to ashes. You leave in peace. I will always pray for you and wish you well. Look after my youngest son, Sahadev. See to it that he doesn't feel depressed by this misfortune.'

Then she hugged her sons and cried: 'I don't know why this misfortune came upon you who are the most righteous of all. Your late father Pandu is lucky he didn't have to witness this unbearable moment. So is your late mother, Madri. Why am I alive to go through this suffering?' The Pandavas tried their best to console her. Vidura said, 'Sister Kunti, have courage. Your sons will come back in no time. Now smile and bid them farewell.'

With a heavy heart, the Pandavas began their journey.

Dhritarashtra was tormented by his inability to go against his son's wishes. He blamed himself for his failure to stop this injustice. He called Vidura to his side and said, 'I want to know how the Pandavas are going into their exile. Tell me what you see.'

Vidura said, 'Yudhishthira is walking with his face covered in a white scarf. He has kept his eyes shut, for his sight may burn down your evil sons. Bheem is walking with his arms spread wide, as if to say that one day he'll use these powerful arms to destroy his enemy. Arjun is throwing sand in the air to warn his enemies how his arrows would shower on them one day. Sahadev is walking with his face

hidden, while Nakul has his body covered in dust. Draupadi has her face covered with her hair and she is following her husbands with eyes filled with tears. Priest Dhaumya is chanting slokas from the Vedas. The people of Hastinapur are crying: "How unfortunate we are. Our saviours are leaving us." O King, the sun has been eclipsed, streaks of lightning are piercing the cloudless skies, and the grounds are shaking under our feet. O King, I am afraid, these are unholy signs, and they foretell something ominous is going to happen soon.'

Duryodhan could sense that the tide was flowing against him. He, along with Karna and Shakuni, asked Drona to take over the kingdom of the Pandavas. Drona said, 'I will honour your request. But stay assured, the Pandavas will come back and avenge themselves. So enjoy these thirteen years for, in the fourteenth year, nobody will be able to save you from destruction.'

22

The Pandavas in Exile

THE PANDAVAS LEFT HASTINAPUR AND PREPARED TO TRAVEL NORTH. BUT they were stopped by thousands of citizens of the city. 'Where are you going, leaving us with these evil Kaurava princes?' they asked. 'You are the most righteous rulers one could wish for. Take us along. We want to leave Hastinapur and come with you.'

Yudhishthira was overcome by emotion. With a heavy voice, he said, 'We are honoured and blessed to receive so much love and affection from you. We are grateful for the compassion you are showering on us. But please listen to me. Our dearest relatives, our grandfather Bhishma, King Dhritarashtra, Uncle Vidura and our mother Kunti are all grief-stricken. They need your support more than we do. Please do us a favour. Go back to Hastinapur and look after them. We entrust their welfare to you.'

The crowd realized that the Pandavas would never go back on their word. They bade farewell to them and returned to the city with a heavy heart.

The Pandavas mounted their chariot and moved away from the city. By dusk, they arrived at the banks of the Ganga. As they dismounted their chariot, they saw a group of Brahmins arrive. They had been following the Pandavas. They lit a huge fire and sat around it, chanting hymns from the Vedas, and prayed for the welfare of Pandavas.

When Yudhishthira woke up the next morning, the Brahmins were still sitting there. He realized they wished to accompany them to the forest. Yudhishthira walked up to them and said, 'O Brahmins, we have lost everything and we are about to begin our twelve years of exile in the forests. It will be twelve long years of severe hardship. The forests are dangerous and it is no place for Brahmins like you. Please go back to the city.'

Shaunak, the leader of the Brahmins, said, 'King Yudhishthira, you don't have to worry about us. We'll take care of ourselves. Please don't send us back. We'll worship the gods, chant hymns and pray for you.'

Yudhishthira saw that the people had made up their minds and were not going to listen to him. He walked back to his brothers and Priest Dhaumya, and said, 'These Brahmins wouldn't leave us. I feel bad that I won't be able to feed them ... take care of them. But I can't abandon them either. Dhaumya, tell me, what should I do?'

Dhaumya ran his fingers through his long white beard and thought for a while. Then he said, 'The sun is the source of nourishment for all living beings. I suggest you worship the Sun god and ask for his help.'

Yudhishthira sat down to worship the Sun god. Pleased with Yudhishthira's prayers, the Sun god appeared before him. He handed a copper pot to Yudhishthira and said, 'Take this pot. For the next twelve years, this pot will provide you with an endless supply of food. Whatever Draupadi cooks in this pot will not finish until she has eaten her meal.'

Yudhishthira gave the pot to Draupadi, who took it to the makeshift kitchen and cooked a meal for the Brahmins. The amount of food in the pot didn't seem enough to serve even a single person. But as they served from the pot, it kept refilling. The Brahmins ate to their heart's content and the pot remained full. Next, the younger Pandavas had their meal, followed by Yudhishthira, and then Draupadi. After she had partaken of her meal, the pot became empty.

Meanwhile in Hastinapur, Dhritarashtra was suffering from severe guilt and remorse. He knew what he had done to the Pandavas was not right. He knew that Duryodhan's actions would bring misfortune and misery to the Kuru dynasty. He paced up and down his royal chamber, but couldn't make up his mind as to which side he should take. He called his attendant and said, 'Go and get Vidura. Tell him I want to see him now.'

The moment Dhritarashtra heard Vidura's footsteps inside the room, he said, 'Vidura, I need your help. You have clarity of thought and you know the subtleties of ethics and law. You wish well for all Kuru descendants too. So tell me, what can I do that would benefit both the Kauravas and the Pandavas?'

Vidura knew that advising Dhritarashtra was futile. However, as his minister, it was his duty to provide him with due counsel whenever asked for. He walked up to Dhritarashtra and said, 'It is a king's duty to ensure that all his subjects are treated with fairness and dignity. But Shakuni and your sons crossed all bounds of decency. They robbed Yudhishthira of his kingdom in an unfair and rigged game of dice. I suggest you punish Shakuni and return the Pandavas their kingdom, just as you did after the first game. If you do so, you might be able to save your kingdom and your family. If Duryodhan agrees to share the kingdom with the Pandavas and live in peace, you'll have nothing to worry about. If he doesn't, punish Duryodhan and make Yudhishthira the king. Let Duryodhan, Shakuni and Karna pledge their allegiance to Yudhishthira. Make Dushasana apologize in public to Bheem and Draupadi. Only then would the Pandavas consider sparing your sons. That's all I can say.'

As Vidura spoke, Dhritarashtra's face flushed with anger. This was not what he wanted to hear. He only wished for words of sympathy and support for his actions. Fingers clenching the armrest of his throne, he said, 'Vidura, you are repeating what you said during the game. Your advice would only benefit the Pandavas. You expect me to abandon my sons for their sake, do you? Why don't you understand, Duryodhan is my flesh and blood!' He stopped to catch his breath and then, with a stern voice, he added, 'Vidura, I respect you. But I find your words mean and biased. I am sick and tired of your ill advise. You may leave or stay or do whatever you wish. I don't care for you any more.' Dhritarashtra stood up and left the room, fuming.

Vidura watched the blind king stagger towards the door. He felt pity for the old man, but there was nothing he could do to help. He walked out of the room and called his charioteer: 'Bring my chariot. I want to join the Pandavas in exile.'

The Pandavas had moved west to the Kamyaka Forest near the banks of River Saraswati. The gentle gurgle of the flowing river, the murmur of the leaves and the chirping of the birds acted as a soothing balm on their restless souls. This felt like the right place to heal their wounds. They built their huts and lived in this forest along with the Brahmins, ascetics and hermits. The days were spent listening to the chants and hymns of the priests, collecting fruits and vegetables, and on occasion, going hunting for meat. Yudhishthira felt this life of peace and tranquillity was much better than the busy life in a palace.

One day, sitting by the banks of the river, Yudhishthira was discussing the scriptures with his brothers when he saw a chariot coming their way. It was Vidura. Yudhishthira stood up and asked Bheem, 'Why is Uncle Vidura here? Has Duryodhan sent him to invite us for yet another game of dice? Does Shakuni want to win our weapons too?' Bheem didn't reply.

Yudhishthira walked up to the chariot and greeted Vidura by touching his feet. He then asked, 'Uncle Vidura, what brings you to this forest?'

Vidura sat down on a fallen tree trunk and said, 'King Dhritarashtra asked for my advice. But my words didn't please him. So the angry king banished me.'

The Pandavas were stunned. What had taken over old Uncle Dhritarashtra? How could he let go of his most trusted and the wisest minister?

Vidura smiled. 'Don't worry about me. Dhritarashtra may abandon me, but I have you. I'll share whatever I know with you. I know you don't need any preaching, but still, let me say this: one who waits for his time, always wins. One who shares his wealth with his followers, also enjoys their support during times of distress. Never speak unnecessary words. And never let your ego rule over you. Follow these principles and you'll prosper for sure.'

In Hastinapur, Dhritarashtra couldn't bear the absence of Vidura and cursed himself for uttering such harsh words. His conscience kept tormenting him. He called his trusted charioteer Sanjay and said, 'Bring back Vidura from wherever you can. He is my dearest brother and my most trusted advisor. I cannot live without him. Find him and tell him, if he doesn't come back, I will kill myself.'

Sanjay sent out his spies and soon found Vidura's whereabouts. He rushed to the Kamyaka Forest and pleaded to Vidura, 'I have come to take you back to Hastinapur. Our great King Dhritarashtra misses you and has fallen ill. Please return to the palace and save our king.'

Vidura said to the Pandavas: 'I must go back to Hastinapur. My brother needs me.'

The moment Dhritarashtra heard Vidura's familiar footsteps, he rose from his bed. With his arms outstretched, he wrapped Vidura in a warm hug. 'I am so glad you came back,' he said. 'I was afraid you'd never return after what I said to you. Please pardon me for my behaviour.'

Vidura held his hand and said, 'You are my elder brother, my guru. How can I abandon you? I treat your sons and Pandu's sons with equal affection. I spoke in favour of the Pandavas only because they are in distress.'

Vidura's return to Hastinapur was a cause of great concern to Duryodhan. When Dhritarashtra had banished Vidura, Duryodhan felt that for once his father has done something right. Why did he have to call him back? What was going on in his mind? Would he return everything to the Pandavas and dash his hopes and ambitions again? He called Shakuni, Karna and Dushasana to his room for an urgent meeting. When they arrived, Duryodhan went up and closed the door behind them. He turned to Shakuni and said, 'Uncle, let me tell you one thing. If I see the Pandavas return to Hastinapur, I'll either drink poison or step into a fire or hang myself to death.'

'Don't talk like a fool!' Shakuni scolded Duryodhan as he sat down in a plush chair and poured himself a drink. 'The Pandavas have promised to go into exile for twelve years. They live by their word. Nothing can make them break their promise; not even your father's request,' he said.

Karna held Duryodhan's hand and said, 'Why do you worry, my friend? Even if they come back, we'll challenge them to a game of dice once again and Uncle Shakuni will defeat them.'

This failed to lift Duryodhan's spirits. Breathing heavily, he turned away from Karna and sat down in a corner. Karna felt sorry for his dear friend. He pulled out his sword and said, 'Friends, for Duryodhan's sake, we have been sitting idle for so long. In King Dhritarashtra's kingdom, we don't have the freedom to do what we want. Like slaves, we have kept our mouths shut and our hands bound. This cannot go on any longer. Let's go to the forest and kill the Pandavas and get rid of this problem once and for all.'

Dushasana applauded Karna's call to action. He said, 'You are right. Let's not seek permission from anybody.' Shakuni finished his drink and stood up. He looked at Karna and said, 'Go ahead. I'll follow you. Make sure nobody gets to know of this plan. If this news reaches the Kuru elders, your dreams will be shattered earlier than you expect.'

But the news didn't stay a secret. Rishi Vyasa, with his divine powers, came to know the details of the plan. And with his powers, he appeared in Dhritarashtra's bedroom. The angry rishi upbraided Dhritarashtra: 'Your sons have tricked the Pandavas in the game and sent them into exile. And now they are planning to attack and kill them in the forest. Stop them, else you can be assured of their death.'

Dhritarashtra was scared. His mouth dried up. Palms joined, he said, 'O great rishi, believe me! I was not in favour of this game of dice. Neither were Gandhari, Bhishma, Drona or Vidura. Some divine powers forced it to happen, and I couldn't stop it.' Dhritarashtra sat down at Vyasa's feet and said, 'I am sorry. My blind love for

Duryodhan has prevented me from abandoning him. If you care for me, I request you—please talk to Duryodhan and give him some good advice. Maybe he'd listen to you.'

'No, I won't talk to Duryodhan. Rishi Maitreya will. After meeting the Pandavas, he will come to Hastinapur. He'd say whatever is necessary to Duryodhan.' Saying so, Vyasa disappeared.

Soon, Maitreya arrived in Hastinapur. He said to Dhritarashtra: 'The Pandavas told me everything. O King, you should be ashamed of yourself. After what happened in your assembly hall, you won't be able to show your face to the Brahmins and the ascetics. How could this happen despite Bhishma and you being present?' Dhritarashtra sat quiet, with his head down. Maitreya called the attendant at the door and said, 'Take me to your prince, Duryodhan.'

Duryodhan was loading up his chariot with weapons when Rishi Maitreya arrived. In a gentle voice, Maitreya said, 'Duryodhan, you are strong and powerful. Still, I'd advise you, don't fight the Pandavas. Not only are they the most skilled warriors in the world, they are also united in their purpose. They are the most powerful men alive. They have killed vicious rakshasas and demons like Hidimb and Bakasura. Just a few days ago, Bheem killed the ferocious demon Kirmir with a single blow of a tree trunk. Before the Rajasuya ceremony, he killed the undefeatable King Jarasandh of Magadh. Besides, Vasudeva Krishna is their cousin, Drupad their father-in-law and Dhrishtadyumna their brother-in-law. How could you hope to win in a fight against them? Listen to me, Duryodhan: control your anger and try to make peace with your cousins.'

Duryodhan didn't bother to answer the rishi. Duryodhan's arrogance enraged Maitreya. With bloodshot eyes, he touched his sacred thread and cursed Duryodhan: 'How dare you disrespect me? You'll pay for your arrogance, you mindless brute! In the great war,

Bheem will break that thigh of yours with a violent blow of his mace and you'll die the most horrible death.'

Dhritarashtra panicked. He fell on Rishi Maitreya's feet and begged for his mercy. The rishi took pity on the blind father and said, 'I cannot take back my curse. But this much I can promise you: if Duryodhan behaves, my curse won't come true. Else, I can assure you that a grim and bloody future awaits him.'

23

Draupadi's Rage

IT WAS A SULTRY SUMMER AFTERNOON. THE PANDAVAS HAD JUST TAKEN A DIP in the Saraswati to cool themselves when they saw a cloud of dust in the horizon, fast approaching them. The Pandavas walked up the bank to take a closer look. The rumbling of chariot wheels and the galloping of the horses cautioned the brothers. Arjun and Bheem picked up their weapons. As the chariots approached them, the fluttering flags on them made it clear that it was their friends from the Bhoja, Vrishni and Andhaka clans who were paying them a visit. The chariots stopped at a distance and, from the leading one, dismounted Krishna.

Krishna rushed towards the Pandavas and knelt in front of Yudhishthira, touching his feet to pay his respects. The rest of the visitors surrounded the Pandavas, whose poor and ragged look brought tears to the eyes of the onlookers. Krishna's eyes lit up in anger. In a thunderous voice, he said, 'The Kauravas will be destroyed for sure. The battlefield will be drenched in the blood of Duryodhan, Dushasana, Karna and Shakuni. We will kill them all, and once again establish Yudhishthira as the emperor. To destroy evil is our divine duty.' Krishna noticed Draupadi standing teary-eyed in a corner. He came up to her and said, 'Panchali, don't despair. I am with you.'

'Lord Vyasa says you're the god of the gods. You are the lord of all beings. But to me, you are my friend. How could that evil Dushasana dare to drag me by my hair to the assembly hall? The sons of Dhritarashtra laughed at my humiliation. They wanted me to serve as their slave. Shame on the Pandavas, shame on Bheem's strength, shame on Arjun's Gandiva. While their wife was being molested, they just sat and watched—as if it were a game. Even a weak husband protects his wife: that is the norm. My husbands didn't. The Pandavas would give their lives to protect their subjects, but they did not protect me. Why?' Draupadi broke down crying.

Krishna held her and tried to console her. 'Don't cry, my dear sister. We are with you.'

'No! I have nobody. I have no husband, no sons, no brother, no father, and not even you. Those filthy creatures violated me, insulted me, humiliated me. Still you take no action against them?' asked Draupadi

'Trust me, Panchali, Arjun's arrows will kill all those who insulted you. Please be assured, I will do whatever I can to help the Pandavas. Now stop crying and stand by your husbands. I promise you, fourteen years from now, you'll be the empress of the world once again. Nothing can change that fact,' Krishna said.

Arjun held Draupadi's arm and said, 'Don't cry. Krishna's words will come true. I promise you.' Draupadi finally calmed down a little.

Krishna then turned to Yudhishthira and said, 'O King, if only I was in Dwarka, things wouldn't have turned out like this. I would have gone to the Kuru assembly hall even if I wasn't invited, and somehow managed to stop this evil game of dice. If Dhritarashtra refused to listen to my reasoning, I would have forced him to stop.

I would have *killed* those evil gamblers if needed. The moment I returned to Dwarka, Satyaki told me of your misfortune, and I came running to see you. I am so sorry to see you suffer like this.'

'Krishna, where did you go? Why weren't you in Dwarka?' Yudhishthira asked.

Krishna sat down next to Yudhishthira and said, 'I had to destroy Sauvanagar—King Salwa's flying city—and kill Salwa. He was angry with me because I killed his friend, Shishupal. So he attacked Dwarka when I was at the Rajasuya ceremony. My son Pradyumna, however, gave him a good fight and Salwa fled the battle.'

Yudhishthira asked, 'Tell us, how did you slay Salwa?'

'When I reached Dwarka after attending your Rajasuya ceremony, I was shocked to see my beautiful city in ruins. I took my army and went to find Salwa, who was in his airship, hovering in the sky over the oceans. I shot a barrage of arrows at his ship, but they failed to reach him. Then I hurled my fiercest guided missiles to his ship. Hundreds of soldiers in the airship were killed as they dropped down into the ocean. Salwa then began his illusory warfare. I used my Pragyastra weapon to diffuse his illusions. But his illusion only became stronger. Just then, a messenger of King Ugrasena of Dwarka arrived and gave me the most horrible news. He said, "Salwa has killed your father, Vasudeva. King Urgasena has ordered you to stop fighting and asked you to return to Dwarka at once." The news shattered me, but I kept fighting. Suddenly, I saw my father fall from the Sauva airship. He was screaming and flailing his arms and legs as he crashed into the ocean below. It was such a horrible sight that I lost consciousness. When I regained my senses, the airship was gone. I knew it was all an illusion to trick me. I thought, enough is enough. I summoned my faithful but deadly weapon, the Sudarshan Chakra, and instructed it to destroy the Sauva airship and its inhabitants. The chakra rose to the sky like a second sun and hurled itself towards the airship. Just as a saw cuts through a piece of log, the Sudarshan Chakra cut the airship into pieces. Salwa tried to flee, but the chakra followed him and severed his head from his body.'

Krishna paused for a while. The Pandavas were left speechless by the awe-inspiring story of Krishna's battle with Salwa. Krishna stood up, held Yudhishthira's hand, and said, 'O King, now you know why I couldn't come for the game of dice. If I were there, I would have never let this happen to you.'

Later in the afternoon, Draupadi treated Krishna and his entourage to a delicious meal cooked in the magic pot gifted by the Sun god. After the meal, Krishna and his friends bade farewell to the Pandavas and left.

In the evening, when the sages and Brahmins began their evening prayers in front of the fire, Yudhishthira sat down and listened to the hymns. His face glowing in the light of the pyre, he pondered over Krishna's visit. Krishna's support and his reassuring words washed off the disturbing thoughts that had bothered him since the game of dice. He felt tranquil.

Draupadi stood by the door of her hut and noticed Yudhishthira sitting relaxed and listening to the Brahmins chanting. She couldn't comprehend how a man could stay so calm after what they all have been through. Doesn't he have a shred of anger in him? Even Krishna was furious to see the plight of the Pandavas.

She walked up to Yudhishthira and said, 'Tell me something, are you really a Kshatriya? They say that no Kshatriya can be devoid of anger. I see you are an exception. You, the emperor, who lived the life of luxury in a grand palace, now live like a pauper. Doesn't that make you angry? Bheemsen alone could have destroyed the Kauravas.

But he tolerated the humiliation only for you. Your brothers ... all of them are suffering because of those Kaurava scoundrels. And you still don't want to punish them. I, Draupadi, the only daughter of the great King Drupad, the daughter-in law of the great King Pandu and Queen Kunti, am leading the life of a forest dweller because of those heartless brutes. Doesn't that make your blood boil? How could you pardon those sinners? People are contemptuous of a Kshatriya who fails to display his power and valour when needed. You are the most learned of all. Don't you know what the great King Prahlad said to his grandson, Bali? When Bali asked, what is better—to pardon or to punish, Prahlad said, neither. Each has its time and place. One who pardons all the time, often suffers, and is disregarded even by servants and commoners. Again, one who never pardons suffers too. Hence, you must be tough when needed, and lenient when the circumstances dictate such action. Someone who has done good to you in the past should be pardoned even for his gravest mistake. One who unknowingly commits a crime is also pardonable. But one who commits a crime knowing very well what he is doing, and later feigns ignorance, should never be pardoned. Everybody deserves to be pardoned for their first crime, but not for their subsequent misbehaviours. The sons of Dhritarashtra have knowingly committed these terrible crimes, not once, not twice, but several times. You should never pardon them.'

Yudhishthira was baffled to hear Draupadi's long speech, and took some time before speaking. 'My dear Draupadi, you are a knowledgeable woman and well-versed in the scriptures. You should know that although anger can be beneficial at times, it can also cause great harm. Luck favours those who are able to control their anger. An angry person loses their head and can commit the most heinous crimes. Nothing can stop them. They can kill the innocent or worship the criminal. These thoughts help me control my anger. Remember, one who can control his anger with his knowledge and consciousness, is praised by all. The Pundits think of such men to be the most powerful of all. Only fools confuse anger with power. When Bhishma, Krishna, Drona, Vidura and Vyasa advise Uncle Dhritarashtra to pursue peace, I am sure he will return us our kingdom. But if he succumbs to his greed and refuses to give us our due, he will suffer the consequences.'

Yudhishthira's words did not please Draupadi. She looked up at the heavens said, 'I salute the Almighty who has plunged you into this delusion. That's why you have digressed from the path of your ancestors. Nobody can acquire wealth and power through kindness and righteousness. You have learnt many scriptures, acquired great knowledge, performed great sacrifices. You still lost your mind and played the game of dice to lose your kingdom, your wealth, your brothers and even me. Did you ever think why? I will tell you why. It is said that the Almighty decides the fate of mortals based on their karma from their past life. It is the Almighty who makes us do what we do at every moment. Like a marionette, he plays us by the strings and we obey his commands. Just like human beings use metal to cut through metal, God uses a human to kill a human. He does not treat us living beings as his children. Rather, he treats us as despicable wretches who deserve to be punished at every moment. Watching your plight and Duryodhan's success, I despise the Almighty who has created this situation. If a man suffers the consequences of his sins, then God is also a sinner. And if a sinner does not suffer for his sin, that's because he is powerful and strong. It's the weaklings I feel sorry for the most.' Draupadi was trembling with excitement as she paused to take her breath.

Draupadi's cruel words bore into Yudhishthira's heart like a spear. But he kept his calm and said, 'Yagnaseni, you speak well, but your logic is flawed like that of an atheist. I do what I am supposed to do and my actions are not dictated by what I will get in return. I donate for the sake of donation, I sacrifice for the sake of sacrifice, I pray for the sake of prayer. One who exploits religion to achieve one's goals can never achieve the benefits of religion and righteousness. Only atheists doubt the worth of righteous action. Draupadi, you are arguing beyond the limits of your knowledge. Do not doubt the power of truth and righteousness. And never ever condemn our lord, the almighty God.'

Draupadi realized that she has been too harsh. She said, 'I do not condemn the Almighty. I am sorry that I have been rude, but my words were caused by my severe pain. I want to say something more. Please listen to me with an open mind. O King, shake off your depression and act. One who relies on fate and accidents is foolish and misguided. The results one desires can be obtained either by God's grace, or by human will power. O King, we have suffered a great misfortune. Now get up and use your will to win back what is rightfully yours.'

The rest of the Pandava brothers were overhearing this conversation between Draupadi and Yudhishthira with great interest. Bheemsen was fuming in rage. When Draupadi stopped speaking, he stepped ahead and stood in front of Yudhishthira, who realized that the time had come for him to face his brothers. Unless he could convince them, there was no chance for him to regain his pride and his kingdom.

24

Bheem's Argument

DRAUPADI'S ARGUMENT STRUCK A CHORD IN BHEEM'S HEART. THE ANGRY Pandava looked straight into Yudhishthira's eyes and said, 'Brother Yudhishthira, tell me, why should *we* always have to sacrifice? Why do *we* have to suffer? Like a jackal who steals from a lion, Duryodhan stole our kingdom from us, and you, in the name of Dharma, accepted it as your destiny and agreed to this hardship. Tell me, what has this Dharma of yours given you? It has only made you a spineless coward. And we, your brothers, are following you like blind men. Our inaction has made our friends unhappy while our enemies are living in luxury. Shame on us!' Bheem was panting with excitement, but he continued.

'Brother, Dharma, wealth and desire—one should pursue them all in their life. Chasing only one of those should never be one's only goal. The scriptures say, one should fulfil their desires and enjoy the pleasures of life during their youth, pursue and accumulate wealth during their midlife, and practice religion and righteousness during their old age. And those who want to lead the life of an ascetic should give up all the three practices. So, you should either practice all three or give up everything. For a Kshatriya, their strength and energy is their religion. Shrug off your weakness and pick up your arms. Fight for what is yours, even if that requires you to give up your righteousness a little. Just as a farmer sows a small amount of seed to harvest a bountiful crop, you too must give up a little of your Dharma to achieve something greater. Let us join hands with Krishna and the other allies to attack the Kauravas and win back our kingdom.'

Yudhishthira was listening to Bheem patiently. His brother's accusations hurt him to the core. Yet, he was not angry. He turned away from Bheem as if to hide his pained expression. He looked at the distant stars and said, 'My brother, your words strike me like sharp arrows. But I can't blame you. You are right. It is because of my improper behaviour and action that you are suffering this horrible punishment. I had taken part in the game of dice with the desire to win Duryodhan's kingdom and wealth. Shakuni exploited my naivete and used unfair means to defeat me. Duryodhan made us his slaves. I must thank Draupadi for rescuing us from that humiliation. But I didn't learn my lesson and played the game again, and lost again. Now I cannot get out of my obligation as a loser. I must keep my promise to live in exile for thirteen years.'

Yudhishthira then turned back to Bheem and said, 'You wanted to burn my arms that played the unholy game. Arjun stopped you. You picked up your iron mace to strike, but you stopped again. Why? Why didn't you use it then? Why didn't you stop me from accepting the challenge the second time? You didn't act when it was needed. So what's the point in complaining now? Just as one plants a seed and waits for the tree to bear fruit, you too should wait for the happy days to return after thirteen years.'

Bheem was not pleased to hear this at all. 'My brother, too much practice of Dharma has robbed you of common sense. You have become soft and weak like a Brahmin. I am surprised, how you could be born a Kshatriya? Thirteen years is a long time. We will all die in this forest before that. As the scriptures permit, you must consider thirteen months as equivalent to thirteen years and reclaim your throne. If that doesn't seem satisfactory, just absolve yourself of your sin of breaking your promise by performing the penance ritual: feed a bull.'

Hearing this, Yudhishthira realized that words of righteousness and Dharma won't please a warrior like Bheem. He must speak the language of valour and warfare for Bheem to comprehend his strategy. He replied, 'Brother Bheem, one must use force only after proper planning and after accumulating adequate resources. Without a strategy, you are doomed to fail. Remember, Duryodhan and his brothers are valiant warriors and are skilled in the use of deadly weapons. The kings we conquered before the Rajasuya sacrifice are not happy with us either, and they'll join the Kauravas when asked to take sides. Bhishma, Drona and Kripa may be neutral in principle, but they are loyal to the throne of Hastinapur, and they would never hesitate to protect their provider, Dhritarashtra. The mighty warrior Karna is also against us. You cannot destroy Duryodhan unless you destroy these powerful men. And to do that, we need adequate preparation.'

This time, Yudhishthira's words hit home. Bheem, although saddened, realized that they cannot win back their kingdom overnight. He went back to his room and sat down to meditate and calm his mind.

Yudhishthira's mind was still disturbed. He thought, how could he gather the resources needed to win back the kingdom? Arjun's Gandiva alone couldn't fight the mighty Kauravas. They must acquire a huge arsenal of powerful weapons. And then they'd have to build alliances with powerful kings who'd join them to fight the Kauravas. He went to his hut and, with closed eyes, summoned Rishi Vyasa.

Within moments, Vyasa arrived. He smiled at Yudhishthira and said, 'I understand your predicament, my dear Yudhishthira. But don't worry. I will give you a special mantra called the Pratismriti. With this knowledge, Arjun should be able to acquire the deadliest weapons from the gods.'

Yudhishthira knew that Arjun would have to travel far to collect the weapons from the gods. It may take years before he could return. Without Arjun, they would be vulnerable to attacks from their enemies. Acquiring weapons was only half the job. One had to learn how to use them too. And for that, Arjun was the best person. Yudhishthira had no option but to take a chance.

He called Arjun and said, 'Brother, you know, to defeat the Kauravas and win back our kingdom, we need to acquire powerful weapons. And I want to entrust you with that job. A few days ago, Rishi Vyasa taught me this special mantra which I want to pass on to you. Learn it by heart and travel to the north. Use this knowledge to collect the most powerful weapons from the gods.' Arjun agreed.

Arjun's Journey

After completing the yagna, Arjun picked up his weapons to begin his long trek. Draupadi marked his forehead with the holy ashes from the extinguished fire. She said, 'Parth, our wellbeing, our happiness, our life, our kingdom and our wealth depends on you. May you succeed in your endeavour and come back victorious. May the gods protect you in your journey.'

Arjun travelled north and crossed the Himalayas. Then he passed by the Gandhamadan peak to reach the foothills of the Indrakeel Mountains. Suddenly he heard a voice ring out, 'Stop! Don't move.'

Arjun turned around and saw a frail-bodied, copper-toned ascetic sitting under a tree. The man was smeared in dirt and his head covered with matted hair. 'Who are you, my son? Why are you carrying those dreadful weapons? You don't need them in this peaceful hermitage. Abandon your weapons and enter these hallowed grounds in peace,' said the man.

Arjun didn't care to put down his weapons. He stood in defiance in front of the ascetic and tried to anticipate his next move. The ascetic laughed and said, 'You look worried. Relax, my son. I am your father, Indra. I was waiting for you. Tell me, what do you want?'

Arjun bowed in front of Indra: 'Father, I am in search of divine weapons. You possess some of the deadliest weapons on heaven and earth. Would you be kind enough to share some of them with me? I need them to win back our kingdom.'

'You must prove yourself worthy of such weapons. Worship Lord Shiva. If you are able to please him, I will give you the weapons.' Saying so, Indra disappeared.

Arjun walked farther down the valley till he reached a dense forest. There, he picked a spot under a huge banyan tree and sat down to worship Lord Shiva, using Vyasa's Pratismriti mantra. When Shiva came to know of Arjun's worship and his strict austerities, he took the guise of a tribal hunter—Kirat—and appeared in the forest with his bow and arrows. As Shiva walked towards the meditating Arjun, an eerie silence engulfed the forest. The rivers and waterfalls stopped their flow. The birds stopped chirping. The animals hid in their burrows, as if they knew something ominous was about to happen.

Just that moment, a demon named Mook, taking the form of a wild boar, ran towards Arjun to attack him. Hearing the charging boar, Arjun woke up from his meditation and engaged an arrow to his bow to shoot the animal. Before he could release the arrow, Shiva, disguised as Kirat, said, 'Leave the boar. I had desired to shoot that animal before you did.'

Arjun didn't bother to pay attention to a tribal hunter and shot his arrow at the boar. Kirat had also shot his arrow, and the two arrows struck the boar at the same instant. The boar returned to its dreadful demonic form and crashed to his death. His loud death cry ran shivers down the spine of the forest dwellers.

Angry Arjun looked at the Kirat and said, 'Who are you? Why did you shoot my target? You have violated the rules of hunting and insulted me. I will kill you for your insolent behaviour.'

Kirat laughed. 'Don't be scared. I won't harm you. I live in this forest. But who are you, and what are you doing in this godforsaken land?'

'How dare you ignore my question?' said Arjun. 'Apologize, else I will kill you right now.'

Kirat laughed again. Arjun raised his Gandiva bow and shot at the man. To his surprise, the arrow bounced off his body. Arjun continued shooting arrows at the hunter, but they all struck him and fell away like straws. Soon, his quiver ran out of arrows. Arjun couldn't believe what he saw. He was too angry to come to his senses and realize that this tribal man was not a normal human being. He raised his bow and struck a fierce blow to the Kirat's head. The Kirat laughed, snatched the bow from Arjun's hand and threw it aside. Arjun attacked him with his sword, but the blade bounced off the hunter's skin and shattered into pieces. Desperate, Arjun threw stones and branches of trees at the man, but they had no effect on him. Arjun then attacked the hunter with his bare hands. He threw punches at him and tried to wrestle the hunter down. The hunter grabbed him by his neck and cut off his air. Arjun gasped and fell unconscious.

When he came to, he saw the hunter sitting at a distance and smiling at him. Insulted and humiliated, Arjun prayed to Lord Shiva. He picked up a flower garland from his place of worship and offered it to the clay idol of Shiva he had built. To his amazement, he saw the garland fly and settle on the Kirat's neck. That is when Arjun realized that the hunter was none other than Lord Shiva himself. He knelt before him and sought his forgiveness.

Shiva took off his Kirat disguise and pulled Arjun to his chest in a warm embrace. He said, 'Parth, I am pleased with your worship and your valour. Tell me, what can I offer you?'

Arjun bowed in front of Shiva and said, 'Lord, you have the greatest and the most powerful weapon in heaven and earth—the Brahmashir Pashupat. I pray you give me the Pashupat to fight the Kauravas.'

Shiva agreed and gave Arjun the deadliest weapon of all, the Pashupat. He taught him how to release the weapon and how to retract it. He also warned Arjun of its disastrous effects and said, 'Use this weapon responsibly and only as a last resort.' Saying this, he disappeared.

Soon after, the gods Varuna, Kuber, Yama and Indra visited Arjun and gifted him their best weapons. Indra said, 'My son, you should visit the heavens, for a great task awaits you there. There, I will also give you several other divine weapons that will make you invincible. Wait here, I will send my chariot to take you to the heavens.' Saying this, Indra and the other gods took their leave.

25

Arjun's Journey

ARJUN SAT UNDER THE BANYAN TREE AND WAITED FOR THE CHARIOT TO arrive. He was curious about the heavens. He knew that a mortal being could go to the heavens only after his death. How could *he* visit the abode of the gods in flesh and blood? But Indra would surely not lie to him ...

Moments later, the skies lit up with a crimson-yellow glow. With a deep, sonorous sound, the divine chariot of Indra came piercing through the clouds and landed in front of Arjun. Arjun was awestruck by the beauty and complexity of this huge craft. The vehicle was powered by the strength of a thousand horses. Machines built with gears, chains and wheels ran on different parts of this fantastic craft and made a peculiar sound. The deck was loaded with various weapons, ranging from swords, bows, arrows, spears and missiles, to many others. The charioteer Matali held the door open for him and said, 'Arjun, I am here to take you to heaven. Please mount the chariot. Your father Indra and the other gods are waiting to meet you.'

Arjun bowed to him and said, 'I am honoured to have this opportunity to ride this divine chariot. Let the divine horses that power this craft calm down a little while I finish my prayers.'

Arjun came back to the banyan tree and worshipped his ancestors and asked for their blessings before embarking on his journey. Then he stepped into the chariot.

Matali closed the doors. With a deep growl, the craft powered up and lifted off the ground. To Arjun's amazement, the chariot climbed through the clouds above and raced towards the heavens at an incredible speed. Soon, the chariot left the visible world and entered a realm in space where there was no sun or moon. The stars which looked tiny from the earth, now seemed much larger. The charioteer Matali looked at Arjun and said, 'Parth, those great men whom you thought to be the stars, they live happy in their proper abodes in the heavens.'

Soon, the chariot landed in heaven. The gandharvas and the rishis arrived to welcome Arjun. As he got off the chariot, they placed garlands around his neck and sprinkled fragrant water on him while singing welcome songs and hymns. Indra welcomed his son too, and pulled him to his chest in a warm embrace when Arjun bowed to touch his feet and pay his respects.

'Welcome to Amaravati, dear Arjun. Your arrival has made us all happy,' Indra said. He escorted Arjun to his fantastic palace and said, 'Rest a little. We'll have a grand celebration in your honour in a little while.'

Later in the day, Arjun was escorted to the court of Indra. The magnificent hall, decorated with gold and precious jewels, dazzled him. It was a sight he had never experienced before. He looked around and saw the gods, the sages and rishis sitting around the hall. Arjun bowed to them to pay his respects. Indra was seated in an ornate throne in the centre of the hall. Celestial maidens fanned him with peacock feathers. Indra smiled and said, 'Come here, my son. Come and sit beside me.'

Arjun walked up to the throne and bowed to Indra, who held his hand and guided him to the throne next to him. 'We have a special performance, composed and choreographed in your honour by our gandharva musicians and our apsara dancers. I am sure you will like it.' He then raised his hand and said, 'Let the celebrations begin.'

The gandharva musicians began their musical performance. The sweet melody enchanted Arjun. As the music built up to a crescendo, the beautiful apsaras Ghritachi, Menaka, Rambha and Urvashi, dressed in fine golden fabric and precious jewellery, entered the floor and began their spectacular dance performance. The sensuous bodies of these celestial maidens undulated to the tunes and rhythms of the intoxicating music. The audience was in a trance. So was Arjun. He had never witnessed a performance like this in his life. His eyes were transfixed on Urvashi, whose beauty was beyond any description. He lost his sense of time and place. Even when the performance concluded, he sat still, staring at Urvashi as she walked away. Indra gave Arjun a gentle nudge and said, 'My son, the performance is over.'

Arjun blushed at Indra's comment. 'I am sorry, Father. The music and dance mesmerized me.'

'These performances happen every evening. You are welcome to attend anytime,' Indra said as they walked towards the dining hall.

During dinner, Indra said, 'Arjun, it seems you have a strong liking for music and dance. Why don't you take dance lessons from Chitrasena, the gandharva? He is the best instructor one can have.'

Arjun was a bit surprised at the proposal. He replied, 'Yes, I love music and dance. But I am a Kshatriya and my job is to fight battles, not dance.'

Indra smiled and said, 'I don't think it's forbidden for a Kshatriya to practise music and dance. These activities can help you relax and prepare for battle. They can also make you more creative in using your weaponry. I will instruct Chitrasena to teach you from tomorrow.'

Arjun was still hesitant. 'But, Father, I am here to learn about your divine weapons ...'

'Don't worry, you will learn how to use them. Learn the performing arts too. You never know when these skills will come in handy.'

The next day, as per Indra's advice, Arjun began his lessons in music and dance from the gandharva guru, Chitrasena. Arjun had natural talent and picked up the skills quite easily. When he dressed up as a woman and danced to the music of the gandharvas, nobody could tell that it was none other than the valiant Prince Arjun, the fiercest archer on earth. His skills impressed Chitrasena.

Along with his music lessons, Arjun also received training in using the divine weapons that Indra had offered him. Vested with terrible power, the weapons had to be used with much skill and precision. Arjun had to learn how to fire and even retract them when needed. Soon, he became an expert in using the weapons which, till then, were available only to the gods.

Every evening, he would attend the dance performance of the gorgeous apsara, Urvashi. When Urvashi danced, Arjun couldn't even blink his eyes. Every movement, every step, every stance of hers gave him immense pleasure and joy, and his face would light up in an ethereal glow, as if watching something magical.

Noticing Arjun's infatuation towards Urvashi, Indra called Chitrasena and said, 'It seems Arjun is in love with Urvashi. Go and tell her, she should not disappoint the great Kuru prince.'

So Chitrasena went to Urvashi and said, 'My dear, the great Kuru prince Arjun is attracted to you. Lord Indra has requested that you pay him a visit.'

The news didn't come as a surprise to Urvashi. She had noticed the way Arjun looked at her during her performances. Appreciative and lustful stares from men were not new to a celestial beauty like Urvashi. But Arjun was different. The human prince's graceful looks impressed Urvashi, and she felt a strange attraction towards him. Urvashi smiled and said, 'Chitrasena, please tell Lord Indra, it will be my pleasure to entertain Prince Arjun.'

As Chitrasena left the room, Urvashi began to prepare herself. She bathed in fragrant water, wore her most sensuous dress, adorned her long and graceful neck with pearl necklaces and her wrists with golden bracelets. She put on silver anklets that tinkled with each step. She chewed betel leaves that made her lips crimson coloured and her breath fragrant. And then, when the moon rose to adorn the night sky, she departed for Arjun's residence.

Arjun was in his room, going through the techniques he had learnt to use the divine weapons that day. He knew, the only way to perfect his skills was through rigorous practice. He was going through his notes again and again to make sure he missed nothing. Just then, he heard a knock on the door. Arjun opened the door and was struck by a thunderbolt. The beautiful Urvashi was standing at his door. She smiled and said, 'Prince Arjun, won't you ask me to come in? Or should I leave from your doorstep?'

Arjun was embarrassed. He held the door wide open and said, 'Oh, how rude of me. Please come in.' Urvashi stepped into the room. Arjun closed the door and, said with his palms joined: 'My lady, please accept my deepest regards. Tell me, what can I do for you? I am your most obedient servant.'

Urvashi laughed and said, 'My servant? No, my dear Arjun. Tonight, I am here to serve you.'

Arjun looked surprised. 'Serve me? I am sorry, I don't understand.'

Urvashi came close to Arjun and whispered, 'Really? Then let me help you. Your dance teacher Chitrasena says that you seem to be quite infatuated with me. At least that's what Lord Indra thinks. The way you look at me during my performances made him think that you have developed a strong liking for me.' Urvashi moved closer to Arjun and put her hand on his chest. 'To tell you the truth, I have developed a strong desire for you too, my handsome prince. So please accept me and let us fulfil our mutual desire.'

Arjun sprang away from Urvashi as bitten by a snake. He covered his ears with his hands and said, 'Please don't say those words and make me a sinner. I have never looked at you with lust and desire. You are like a mother to me, just like my mother, Kunti.'

'I am not your mother,' Urvashi said, affronted. 'I am an apsara and apsaras are nobody's mother.'

'But you gave birth to my ancestor, Ayu, the son of Pururaba. You are the great grandmother of Puru. You are greater than my mother. And that's why I looked at you with amazement: how could you be still so youthful, so beautiful and so graceful. Pardon me if my eyes carried the wrong message.' Arjun knelt in front of Urvashi's feet with his palms joined.

Urvashi was furious. No man had ever dared to refuse her. She said, 'I told you, I am a celestial maiden—an apsara. You should not treat me like a mere mortal. The laws of human relationships don't govern my actions. Many of your ancestors have had relationships with me and have fulfilled my desire with pleasure. You should not hesitate either. Come to me. Please me.' Urvashi held Arjun and tried to wrap him in her embrace. Arjun pulled himself out of her arms and dropped to her knees.

'I beg your pardon, my lady. Please don't lure me any more. I cannot think of you as a lover. The only image I have of you is as a mother figure.'

Urvashi was trembling with rage. 'Arjun, I came here at your father's behest and offered myself to you. I offered you the greatest pleasure a man could dream of. But like a eunuch, you rejected me and denied fulfilling my desire. For this, I curse you! You'll become a eunuch and live an unworthy life among women.' Saying this, Urvashi stormed out of the room, with Arjun lying helpless on the floor.

When Indra came to know of Urvashi's curse, he called Arjun and said, 'My son, today you have made Kunti a proud mother. Your self-control and resolve could put even a rishi to shame. Don't worry about your curse. It will come in handy during the thirteenth year of your exile, when you have to live in hiding. You'll spend the year disguised as a eunuch dancer, and regain your manhood at the end of the year.'

Relieved, Arjun spent five long years in the heavens with Indra and became an expert in divine weapons and a virtuoso in music and dance.

26

The Pilgrimage

WHILE ARJUN WAS SPENDING HIS DAYS IN HEAVEN, LEARNING MUSIC, dance and the use of Indra's weapons, the rest of the Pandava brothers were leading their austere life in the Kamyaka Forest. The hardship was taking its toll on their health and fortitude. Bheem would often become impatient and implore Yudhishthira to attack the Kauravas. Yudhishthira would patiently quell his anger and provide moral justification for his decision.

Arjun's absence was another cause for their grief. While they worried about his well-being, they also missed his presence, which always gave the brothers the confidence to deal with adversity. They didn't hear from him for years and wondered whether he was safe and sound.

One day, the great sage, Rishi Brihadaswa, visited the Pandavas in their hermitage. Yudhishthira greeted him with respect and offered him food and drink. The rishi noticed that Yudhishthira was not his usual self, and seemed rather morose and tired. He asked, 'My dear Yudhishthira, why do you look so sad? What's bothering you?'

Yudhishthira replied, 'O Rishi, I am the most unfortunate and ill-fated man this earth has ever seen. My actions have caused great suffering to those I love and care for. I failed to protect my people who depend on me. It pains me to see my brothers and Draupadi go through this hardship, only because of me. I sent my dear brother Arjun to the far northern lands to fetch weapons and haven't heard from him since. I don't know whether he is dead or alive. At times, I feel like I am the greatest loser and a disgrace to the Kuru dynasty.'

Rishi Brihadaswa held Yudhishthira's hand. 'Don't despair, my son. Have faith in yourself and your brothers. I am sure you will come out victorious one day. Haven't you heard of Nala, the king of Nishada? The handsome and virtuous king had to go through hell on earth because of Kali, the god of the Dark Age. Just like you, he lost all his wealth and kingdom in a game of dice to Pushkara. He went mad and deserted his beautiful wife, Damayanti. Alone and without any belongings, the poor king wandered naked in the forests. Still, he recovered from his misfortune and got back everything he lost. In comparison, I'd say you are much better off. You have the support of your valiant brothers and your wife Draupadi. You have powerful friends like Krishna and King Drupad. You should not feel sorry at all. Stay on the path of Dharma and you will emerge victorious.'

Rishi Brihadaswa's words calmed Yudhishthira. He bowed down to the Rishi's feet.

A few days later, a sage named Lomash arrived at the hermitage. He embraced Yudhishthira and said, 'I have great news for you. I met your brother Arjun at Indra's palace. He is doing fine. He requested me to tell you that Lord Shiva has gifted him the Pashupat weapon. He has also acquired several other powerful weapons from Indra.'

The brothers were ecstatic to hear the good news. Yudhishthira touched the great rishi's feet and said, 'O great sage, you have brought to us the most wonderful news. Tell us, when is our dear brother coming back?'

'Lord Indra has asked me to inform you that Arjun will return soon after he completes an important assignment. He suggests you use this time to visit the various places of pilgrimage around the country and learn the myths and legends about them. It will be an illuminating and inspirational experience for you. He asked me to accompany you on these pilgrimages,' the rishi said.

'That is a wonderful idea. We are tired of living in this forest without Arjun. A visit to the holy places will keep us engaged, and enrich our knowledge about this great land of ours.'

'Then let's prepare for the journey. I suggest you travel light, since the path is quite perilous. Only the toughest of the tough can make this journey,' came the reply.

Yudhishthira understood what the rishi meant. He went to the Brahmins and rishis who had accompanied them into the forest and said, 'Friends, we have lived together in this forest for very long and you've always stood by our side. Now we plan to embark upon a trip to visit several pilgrimages. Rishi Lomash will be our guide. However, he warns me that the journey won't be smooth. We may have to climb mountains, cross deserts and travel in extreme weather conditions. Food and drink are likely to be scarce. I cannot subject you to this hardship. I request you to go back to Hastinapur. I am sure King Dhritarashtra would welcome you with open arms. In case he doesn't, go to Panchal, and King Drupad would accept you for sure.'

The news saddened the Brahmins and most of them left for Hastinapur with a heavy heart. Few refused to go back. They said, 'O great Pandava, we don't care for the dangers or any hardship. We will accompany you on your journey. Please take us with you.' Yudhishthira couldn't turn them down.

Soon after, on an auspicious day, the Pandavas along with Draupadi, Dhaumya and the accompanying Brahmins began their journey, with Rishi Lomash leading them.

After visiting the pilgrimages of Naimisharanya, Prayag and others, the Pandava entourage arrived in Manimati, the hermitage of Rishi Agasthya. Curious about Agasthya, Yudhishthira asked, 'Rishi Lomash, I heard that Agasthya was a great sage. But I don't know why he is considered great and why his ashram is a place of pilgrimage.'

Lomash said, 'Sit down, and I will tell you the legend of Agasthya.

'Once, a demon clan named Kaleya, led by Brityasura, attacked the gods in the heavens. The tormented gods went to Brahma and asked for a way to destroy the demons. Brahma said that only a weapon made from Rishi Dadhich's bones could kill Brityasura. Lord Vishnu led the gods to Dadhich and asked for his bones. Dadhich was happy to oblige Lord Vishnu and gave up his life, following which the gods asked Vishwakarma to make a weapon using Dadhich's bones. Vishwakarma built a powerful thunderbolt, armed with which Indra and the gods attacked Brityasura. During the fight, Indra hurled the thunderbolt at Brityasura and killed the evil giant.

'The death of Brityasura scared the demon army and they all fled under the sea. However, they would emerge from the oceans in the night and kill the Brahmins and hermits living near the ocean. Indra and the gods went to Agasthya to seek help. Agasthya went to the seaside and, in one huge gulp, drank the waters of the ocean, leaving it bone dry. The demons were exposed and the gods killed them all. Indra then requested Agasthya to throw up the water he drank to fill the oceans back again.

'Agasthya replied, "I am sorry. The water has been digested. Please try some other option."

'The gods were in a fix. How could the oceans remain dry?

'Brahma said, "Don't worry. Many years from now, King Bhagirath would once again fill up the oceans with water."

'Here's another one: Agasthya was revered not only by humans, demons and gods, but also by the mountains, rivers and oceans. Once, the Vindhya Mountains called the Sun and said, "I want you to circle me, just like you circle the earth."

'The Sun replied, "I don't circle the earth of my own will. I do it as per the wish of the Almighty."

'This angered Vindhya. The mountain began to grow higher and higher to obstruct the path of the Sun. Vindhya's antics worried the gods. Again, they approached Agasthya to help resolve the crisis.

'Agasthya went to the foothills of the Vindhya Mountains and said, "Vindhya, I need to cross you and travel to the south to finish some urgent duties. I request you to not grow till I come back." Vindhya couldn't say no to the revered sage and stopped growing.

'Agasthya crossed the mountains and went south, but he never came back, halting Vindhya's growth forever.'

As he completed retelling the legendary stories of Rishi Agastya, Lomash asked the Pandavas to pay their respects to the great sage, for his blessings would help remove any obstacles that came in their path to victory.

27

The Story of Bhagiratha and Rishyasringa

YUDHISHTHIRA WAS INTRIGUED ABOUT THE UNFINISHED STORY OF THE dried-up ocean. He asked, 'Rishi Lomash, please tell us how the oceans filled with water once again.'

Lomash started narrating the story: 'Long ago, there lived a king named Sagar, belonging to the Ikshvaku dynasty. The king didn't have any sons. Advised by his spiritual gurus, King Sagar, along with his two queens, went to the Kailash Mountains to pray to lord Shiva for a child. With Shiva's blessings, the king had 60,000 sons from his first wife and one son from his second wife. When the sons grew up, Sagar decided to perform the horse sacrifice or the Ashvamedha Yagna. The sacrificial horse roamed around the country with the 60,000 princes on guard.

'One day, the horse wandered to the edge of the dry ocean and disappeared. Sagar's sons were worried. They searched every inch of the surrounding meadows, but couldn't find the horse. They dug into the ocean bed and killed any living being that came their way. At last, on the northeastern edge of the ocean floor, they found the horse grazing near the hermitage of Rishi Kapil. The princes thought that Kapil must have stolen the horse and attacked Kapil to punish him. But the moment the rishi's blazing eyes fell on them, the 60,000 princes burnt to ashes in an instant.

'King Sagar was heartbroken. He had banished his second wife's only son, Asamanja, for killing innocent young boys by throwing them into the river. Now the king was left with no son.

'Asamanja had a son named Anshuman. Sagar called Anshuman and said, "My dear grandson, you'll have to save me from this misfortune. Go to Rishi Kapil and get the sacrificial horse by any means."

'Anshuman went to Rishi Kapil's hermitage and begged for his forgiveness. Pleased with Anshuman's prayers, the rishi returned the horse to Anshuman and said, "Take the horse back to your grandfather and complete the sacrifice. However, your uncles' souls would go to heaven only when the waters of the Ganga touch their ashes. One day, your grandson would please Lord Shiva and bring the Ganga to rescue your uncles."

'Anshuman came back to his grandfather with the horse and the sacrifice was completed. After King Sagar died, Anshuman ascended the throne. He had a son named Dilip, who fathered a son named Bhagirath.

'When Bhagirath became the king, he handed over the duties of the kingdom to his ministers and left for the Himalayas. There, he began his worship of Ganga. After many years of arduous worship, Ganga appeared before Bhagirath.

'Bhagirath bowed to her and said, "O Mother, Rishi Kapil's curse has burnt 60,000 of my ancestors to ashes. I pray to you, please drench their ashes with your waters. Only then would they be able to achieve their salvation."

'Ganga blessed Bhagirath and said, "I will fulfil your wish. But when I fall from the heavens, nothing can withstand my force, except Lord Shiva. I suggest you worship Lord Shiva and request him to hold me in his head when I fall from the heavens."

'Bhagirath followed Ganga's advice and pleased Lord Shiva with his worship. Then the mighty Ganga plunged from the heavens, down into Lord Shiva's head. The matted hair on Shiva's head buffered the impact. From there, the waters of the Ganga flowed down to the earth. Bhagirath led the mighty river through the plains, down to the ocean. The waters of the Ganga flowed into the ocean bed and, once again, the oceans filled up with water. The ashes of King Sagar's sons were drenched by the holy waters and their salvaged souls departed for the heavens,' Lomash concluded his tale.

Yudhishthira said, 'O great sage, we are blessed to be able to listen to these wonderful stories from you. We feel energized and invigorated to travel and know more. Please lead us to our next destination.'

Lomash smiled and said, 'Next, we go to the Mahendra Mountains and meet the great sage Parashurama, the sixth incarnation of Lord Vishnu.'

28

The Story of Parashurama

THE PANDAVAS CONTINUED THEIR PILGRIMAGE AND AFTER A LONG TREK they arrived at the holy confluence of River Ganga with the ocean and then the Vaitarani River in the Kalinga province. When they arrived at the foothills of the Mahendra Mountains, Rishi Lomash stopped and said, 'Here, we will meet Lord Vishnu's avatar, the great sage Parashurama.'

Rishi Parashurama's disciple, Akritavrana, greeted the Pandavas and welcomed them to the ashram.

Yudhishthira asked, 'When can we have the privilege of meeting Lord Parashurama?'

Akritavrana replied, 'Lord Parashurama is aware of your visit. He meets visitors only on the eighth and the fourteenth day of the moon. You get some rest tonight, and tomorrow, which is the fourteenth day of the moon, you'll receive his blessings.'

Yudhishthira asked, 'Tell us about the glory of Lord Parashurama. We are eager to know.'

Akritavrana then narrated this story: 'Long ago, there lived a ferocious king named Kartavirya who had a thousand arms. He received a boon from Rishi Dattatreya that gave him immense power. However, instead of using his power for the good of others, Kartavirya abused the boon by torturing all living beings. The gods were fed up with his atrocities. They complained to Lord Vishnu about him and said that only Vishnu can kill him.

'Lord Vishnu smiled and said, "Don't worry, I will kill Kartavirya. But to do that, I need to appear on earth as a human being."'

'During that time, a king named Gadhi ruled the province of Kanyakubja. He had a beautiful daughter named Satyavati. Richik—a Brahmin sage and the son of the great sage Maharishi Bhrigu— fell in love with Satyavati. He went to King Gadhi and asked for his daughter's hand in marriage. Gadhi was not keen on marrying his only daughter to a poor Brahmin, but he couldn't refuse him either. To make things difficult for Richik, he said, "You can marry my daughter, but you must give me a handsome dowry. Get me a thousand white horses with black ears."

'Richik went out on a quest to find the horses. Soon, he acquired the horses from Varuna, the god of water, and gave them to King Gadhi as his dowry. The king had no option but to marry his daughter to Richik.

'A few months later, Maharishi Bhrigu and his wife came to visit their son Richik and their daughter-in law Satyavati. Pleased with Satyavati's hospitality, the rishi offered her a boon. Satyavati knew what she wanted: a son. But she was also pained by her father's ill fortune of not having a son as an heir to the throne. Satyavati knelt before Maharishi Bhrigu and said, "Father, if you permit, I would like to ask for two boons. Please bless me and my mother to have a son each."

'Bhrigu raised his hand and said, "So be it." He gave her a bowl of a sacred potion and said, "Ask your mother to drink this potion and she will have a son." Then he gave another bowl to Satyavati. "This is for you to drink. And you will give birth to a handsome and powerful son, worthy of being my grandson."

'Satyavati gave her mother, the queen of King Gadhi, the potion. The queen suspected that the maharishi must have prepared a special, more potent potion for his daughter-in law, and swapped the potions, drinking the one meant for her daughter. Satyavati drank the potion that was given for her mother.

'However, Satyavati's mother couldn't fool the wise and all-knowing Rishi Bhrigu. He called Satyavati and said, "Your mother has tricked you and swapped the potions. For this, your son will be born a Brahmin but he will be a Kshatriya by profession. And your mother's son will be born a Kshatriya but will be a Brahmin by vocation."

'Satyavati threw herself at Bhrigu's feet and said, "O father, please be kind to me. Do not penalize me for my mother's sin."

'Bhrigu remained firm: "I am sorry, Satyavati. I cannot do anything about it."

'"Please have pity on me. I can accept if my grandson becomes a Kshatriya, but not my son. Please!" she cried.

'Bhrigu said, "Alright, then. Your grandson will be a Kshatriya."

'In due course, Satyavati gave birth to a boy named Jamadagni, who grew up to be a learned and wise man, and a skilled warrior. He married Renuka, the beautiful daughter of King Prasenjit. Together, they had five sons. The youngest of them was Rama, or Parashurama. He was the wisest and the strongest of the brothers. But nobody knew that Parashurama was the incarnation of Lord Vishnu and he was born to fulfil a mission.

'One day, Rishi Jamadagni's wife Renuka went to the river to fetch water. There, she saw the handsome King Chitraratha swimming and playing in the water with his wives. A surge of desire overwhelmed her senses. She fought hard to control herself and ran back home in her wet clothes.

'As she entered her house, she found her husband waiting for her. Jamadagni asked, "I am thirsty. Where is my water?"

'Still trying to recover from her condition, Renuka couldn't answer. Jamadagni observed her flushed face and realized the reason. Furious, he said, "You unfaithful woman, you were overcome with desire for another man. You are a disgrace to this house, to this family. You have no right to live." He called his sons. All four sons, except Parashurama, came to the room. Jamadagni ordered them: "Kill this wretched woman. Now!"

'The brothers were shocked to hear this. How could their father ask them to kill their mother? They stood speechless. The furious rishi cursed the sons and they turned into mindless creatures.

'Parashurama had gone to the forest to collect firewood. When he returned home with a pile of wood and an axe in his hand, the angry rishi ordered him: "Rama, I order you to kill this unfaithful woman, right now!"

'Parashurama did not hesitate for a second. With a powerful blow of his axe, he beheaded his mother.

'Jamadagni's anger subsided. He called Parashurama to his side and said, "My son, you have obeyed my orders and carried out the most difficult task. Ask what you want, and I will fulfil your wishes."

'Parashurama replied, "Father, I wish for my mother to be alive again. I wish to forget this incident forever, and may I be pardoned for my terrible and sinful act. I also wish for my brothers to regain their usual self. Bless me with a long life and may I become the most powerful and undefeatable warrior in the world."

'Jamadagni granted him all his wishes.

'Parashurama's story does not end here. One day, while Jamadagni's sons were not home, King Kartavirya attacked and plundered their hermitage and stole Jamadagni's sacred cow. When Parashurama returned home and saw the destruction, he was mad with rage. He picked up his axe and ran after Kartavirya. A fierce battle ensued. Kartavirya was no match for Parashurama and was soon overpowered by him. Parashurama chopped off Kartavirya's thousand arms before decapitating him. Kartavirya's body crashed to the ground and the earth was rid of a tyrant. Thus, Lord Vishnu fulfilled his promise.

'The angry sons of Kartavirya decided to avenge their father's death and attacked Jamadagni's hermitage again. Jamadagni was busy with his daily prayers when Kartavirya's sons pounced on him with their weapons. Jamadagni, although a powerful warrior, refrained from defending himself since he was in a place of worship. He tried to call his son, "Rama! Rama!" Before he could say more, Kartavirya's sons killed him.

'Parashurama was devastated to find his father dead in his prayer room. With the fire of vengeance burning in him, he completed his father's funeral and last rites. Then he proceeded to destroy the sons of Kartavirya, killing each of them, as well as their followers, with his bare hands. This did not satisfy him and he vowed to cleanse the earth of all Kshatriyas. He travelled around the world and purged the earth of Kshatriyas twenty-one times. His grandfather Richik pleaded with him to stop going on a rampage against a whole clan. This finally calmed the angry sage. He stopped the killings and retired to the Mahendra Mountains.'

Akritavran's story left the listeners half eager and half afraid to meet the mercurial sage.

The next day, Lord Parashurama met the Pandavas and their entourage. He asked Yudhishthira to spend one more night with him in the Mahendra Mountains. Yudhishthira was happy to oblige.

Meeting with Krishna and Balram

The Pandavas visited the Godavari river basin, the Dravida province, and many other holy places of pilgrimage before arriving in Prabhasa, the land of the Vrishnis. When Krishna heard of their arrival, he and Balram came to pay them a visit. Krishna and Balram were heartbroken to see the toll taken on the health of the Pandavas by the long and arduous journey.

Balram embraced Yudhishthira and said, 'Following the path of Dharma does not ensure happiness; not following Dharma does not ensure unhappiness either.' He turned towards Krishna and the other Vrishnis and said, 'Look at Yudhishthira, look at our cousins, look at Draupadi. They wear tattered clothes, their hair knotted, their skin blistered. The rulers of Indraprastha are suffering in the jungles, while that evil Prince Duryodhan and his brothers enjoy the luxuries of the palace. Watching this, people would think it is better to avoid the path of truth and righteousness. Shame on Bhishma, Kripa, Drona and Dhritarashtra. How could they enjoy their life in the palace while making their relatives live a life of such hardship?'

Satyaki said, 'No point in lamenting now. We must do the right thing even if Yudhishthira doesn't want us to. Let us, the Vrishnis, the Bhojas and the Andhaka clans get together and attack Duryodhan and destroy him. Let Yudhishthira keep his promise and live in the forest for the remaining period. We would install Abhimanyu as the ruler of Hastinapur till he returns.'

Krishna said in a calm voice: 'Satyaki, we could have followed your advice. However, I don't think Yudhishthira would like to accept a kingdom that he didn't win with his own efforts. Yudhishthira, his brothers and Draupadi, none would give up their morality for the sake of worldly riches.'

Yudhishthira stood up and said, 'Truth is the only thing we need to protect, not the kingdom. Krishna knows me well, and I know him too. Satyaki, when Krishna feels the time has arrived to exercise our might, go and attack Duryodhan. Till then, let us follow our path of truth and struggle.'

29

The Story of Ushinara

AFTER VISITING RIVER SARASWATI, SINDHU, THE PLAINS OF KURUKSHETRA, the land of Kashmir, the Manas Lake and many other places, Yudhishthira and his team arrived near the banks of the rivers Jala and Upjala. Lomash said, 'Here the great King Ushinara performed his fire sacrifice and passed the test of Lord Indra and Lord Agni.'

'Tell us more,' said Yudhishthira as they gathered around Rishi Lomash, who began his story: 'Long ago, there lived a king named Ushinara. He was known to be the most kind and righteous king of the time. Once, while he was performing his fire sacrifice, Indra and Agni decided to test him. Agni took the form of a little dove and Indra that of a vicious hawk. The hawk chased the dove, which fled for its life and took shelter on King Ushinara's lap. Ushinara placed his arms around the dove to protect it from the diving hawk.

'The hawk perched on top of a flagpole and spoke out in a human voice: "O King, I am hungry. That dove is my food. Don't try to protect him for the sake of righteousness. It would be sinful to deprive me of my food."

'The king countered, "This scared little dove took refuge in me. I cannot abandon one to whom I granted shelter. That is against my duty and my religion."

'The hawk replied, "If you deprive me of my food, I'd die. And if I die, so would my family. You are destroying many lives for the sake of a single dove. Remember, a religion that counters another's way of life is not a religion to pursue. Your decision should be weighed by the value it offers to the most."

'"O great bird, you speak wisely. But why ask me to abandon a refugee? If you want to partake of meat, I can offer you any animal you want—cow, goat, deer, anything. Please spare this dove."

'"This dove is destined to be my food. I won't eat anything other than this bird."

'The adamant king replied, "I can give you my kingdom if you'd like, but not the dove."

'The hawk waited a while, and then said, "Well, if you are hell bent on being so kind to the dove, here's a deal: weigh the dove and give me as much flesh from your body."

'King Ushinara pondered over this and came to the conclusion that it shouldn't be difficult. After all, the tiny little dove weighed almost nothing. He asked his attendants to bring a scale balance, and placed the dove on one end. He then cut a piece of flesh from his thighs and placed it on the other pan of the scale. To his amazement, he found that the dove weighed more. He clenched his teeth to bear the pain as he cut another piece of flesh from his arm and placed it on the scale. The dove still weighed more. Again and again, the king cut off pieces of flesh from his body and placed them on the balance, but the dove seemed to get heavier and heavier. The hawk kept watching the scene as the king, covered in blood, continued hacking his body with his knife.

'When the king had no flesh left on his body, he himself mounted on the scale. At that moment, the hawk spoke out, "King Ushinara, I am Lord Indra, the king of the gods. That little dove is Agni, the god of fire. We came here to test your righteousness and resolve, and you have passed with flying colours. We are sorry for putting you through so much pain. But I can assure you, you will be known to the world as the most kind and righteous king who ever lived. This deed of yours will be remembered forever."

'Indra and Agni then took their original forms and returned to the heavens. Ushinara ruled his kingdom for many years and became famous for his illustrious deeds before he died and went to the heavens.'

30

The Story of Ashtavakra

AFTER TRAVELLING FOR DAYS, THE PILGRIMS ARRIVED AT THE BANKS OF River Samanga. Lomash pointed to a hermitage and said, 'Look, there is the ashram of Rishi Uddalak, the son of the great sage Swetaketu. During the Treta Yuga, Swetaketu and his nephew Ashtavakra were the best of the Vedic scholars, and their story is worth listening to.' The Pandavas once again gathered around to hear the story.

'Rishi Uddalak gave his daughter Sujata's hand in marriage to his student, the learned sage Kahore. One day, Rishi Kahore was chanting from the Vedas while his pregnant wife Sujata was busy with housework. Suddenly, the child spoke from his mother's womb, "Stop! Your chanting is incorrect."

'Kahore was surprised to hear this. "How dare you say such a thing. You are not born yet, and you judge my knowledge of the scriptures?"

'The child replied, "Listening to you and the others in the ashram, I have learnt the scriptures from inside my mother's womb. Trust me, you are wrong."

'Kahore felt insulted. He stood up and cursed his unborn child: "You have insulted and humiliated me. I curse you, you'll be born crooked in eight parts of your body."

'Sujata was shocked to hear this. She pleaded with Kahore to withdraw his curse, but Kahore didn't budge. During the final trimester, Sujata called Kahore and said, "We are penniless. How can I bring up my child? A father's duty is to provide for his child. You should try to earn some money for your family."

'Kahore went to meet the great King Janaka to request for a stipend. King Janaka greeted Kahore and said, "I can give you any stipend you want, but you must prove yourself worthy of my gift."

'Kahore asked, "How can I prove my worth to you?"

'King Janaka's court pundit Bandi stood up and said, "The same way the other Brahmins who came before you did. You must fight an intellectual debate with me. If you win, the king will shower you with riches that you can only dream of. If you lose, you will be drowned in the river next to the palace."

'Rishi Kahore was not aware that no Brahmin had ever been able to defeat Bandi in a debate and they all had to drown in the river. He accepted Bandi's challenge, but he too was no match for Bandi. So, Bandi and his men took him to the river and drowned him.

'When Uddalak came to know of Kahore's fate, he called his daughter and whispered into her ears, "Keep this a secret from your child. He should not know about his father's unfortunate death at the hands of Bandi."

'In a few months, Sujata gave birth to a deformed boy. Rishi Kahore's curse had come true. The boy was crooked in eight places. Hence, he was named Ashtavakra. During the same time, Uddalak also had a son, named Swetaketu.

'Ashtavakra and Swetaketu were growing up together in Uddalak's ashram. Ashtavakra had no knowledge about his father and thought Uddalak was his father and Swetaketu his brother.

'One day, when Ashtavakra was about twelve years old, he was sitting on his grandfather Uddalak's lap, studying the scriptures. Swetaketu grew jealous of his nephew. He held Ashtavakra's hand and pulled him off Uddalak's lap, saying, "Get off my father. I want to sit on his lap."

'Ashtavakra said, "Why should I get off? He is my father too."

'"No, he is not your father," asserted Swetaketu. "If you don't believe me, go and ask your mother."

'Ashtavakra went to Sujata and asked, "Mother, who is my father? Where is he?"

'Sujata told him about his father Kahore and the story of Bandi defeating him in the debate and drowning him in the river.

'When Ashtavakra heard the story, he planned how he could avenge his father's defeat. He called his uncle Swetaketu and said, "Let's go to King Janaka's court. There, we could listen to stimulating debates between the Brahmins and enjoy sumptuous meals." Swetaketu agreed.

'Soon, Ashtavakra and Swetaketu arrived in Janaka's court. Ashtavakra stepped up to Janaka and said, "O King, I understand you drown and kill the Brahmins who lose in debates with your court pundit, Bandi? Where is that arrogant man? Call him. I challenge him to debate with me."

'King Janaka laughed and said, "Young man, you don't know what you are talking about. Many learned rishis and Brahmins have tried to defeat Bandi, but they all failed and lost their lives. Go back to your mother. She must be worried."

'Ashtavakra replied, "Bandi is yet to face an opponent like me. Ask him to debate with me, and watch how I cut him down to size."

'The king could sense that Ashtavakra was no ordinary boy. Before he could subject him to the challenge, he wanted to check if the boy really was what he claimed to be. He asked Ashtavakra some difficult questions from the Vedas. The boy answered them with such clarity and eloquence that the king was impressed. He said, "Young man, you are indeed the most knowledgeable person I have ever met. You are the right person to debate with Bandi."

'Ashtavakra then sat across Bandi and engaged in a fierce battle of wits. After a prolonged exchange of questions and answers, Bandi was exhausted of his knowledge. He sat with his face down and admitted his defeat. The Brahmins and rishis in the court rejoiced at his humiliation. They thanked Ashtavakra and praised him for his intellectual prowess.

'Ashtavakra said, "This man has killed many Brahmins by drowning them in the river. Now let us drown him too."

'With his palms joined, Bandi said, "O Brahmins, I have a confession to make. I am the son of Varuna, the water god. Many years ago, my father began a fire sacrifice and wanted to invite learned Brahmins and rishis to witness the yagna. But nobody wanted to come to this ceremony that was to be held under the waters of the ocean. Therefore, I had to trick them. The Brahmins I drowned are not dead. They have been sent to witness my father's ceremony. The yagna is over and they are all on their way back home. Ashtavakra will soon meet his father Kahore. My work here is done. I too can return to my father's abode under the water." Saying this, Bandi bade goodbye, stepped into the river and disappeared below the surface.

'Ashtavakra then bade farewell to King Janaka and departed for their home along with his father Kahore and uncle Swetaketu.

'Looking at Ashtavakra's deformity, Kahore felt guilty for cursing him when he was in his mother's womb. He called Ashtavakra and said, "My son, go and take a dip in the river."

'As Ashtavakra took a dip in the river, Kahore closed his eyes and uttered a mantra. When Ashtavakra emerged from the water, he was a perfect and handsome man, free from any deformity. All his limbs and body parts were straight, with no crookedness. Since then, the river was known as Sama-Anga, or the straight body river.'

The Story of Narakasura and Varaha

After crossing the Mainaka Mountains, the Pandavas arrived near the river with seven streams or the Sapta-Dhara Ganga. Lomash said, 'Our next destination will be the Kailash Mountains, the land of Kuber, the king of the yakshas. There, we can meet your brother, Arjun. Try to get some rest now, for the path ahead is difficult and hazardous. The land is guarded by the fierce rakshasas, kinnaras and yakshas. We must take extra precaution and be prepared to fight those demons.'

On the way to the Kailasha, the Pandavas arrived in Pulinda. Subahu, the king of Pulinda, welcomed them to his palace. The Pandavas rested for the night and, at daybreak, they departed for Kailasha.

On the way, Lomash pointed at a huge pile of rocks, as high as the mountains, and said, 'That hill is not made of rocks. Those are the bones of the demon, Narakasura. Narakasura acquired immense power through the strict practice of austerities. Then he attacked the gods to take over the heavens. The gods went to Lord Vishnu who, with a mere touch of his hand, killed Narakasura. The giant crashed to the ground and his bones piled up to form this hill.'

The Pandavas hailed Lord Vishnu. Having whet his appetite for stories of Vishnu, Lomash then narrated the story of how Lord Vishnu saved the world by taking the form of a boar. He said, 'There was a time during Satya Yuga when creatures were born, but never died. Soon, the earth became overpopulated with humans, animals, birds and insects. The weight of the living creatures was too much for Mother Earth to bear, and its surface kept sinking. Soon, it came to a point that the earth was on the verge of collapse. Vishnu was called upon to avert the crisis. The Lord took the form of a huge and vicious sabre-toothed boar and dug deep into the earth. The boar hooked the Earth in its tooth and, with a mighty heave, lifted the surface by hundreds of miles. The immense force caused earthquakes and calamities of unprecedented nature. The gods went to Lord Brahma and asked him to intervene. Brahma assured them not to worry, and, at his request, Lord Vishnu unhooked the earth from his tooth and returned to his original form.'

The Pandavas continued their journey through the mountain pass. When they reached the Gandhamadan Mountain, a severe blizzard started blowing. The Pandavas ran for shelter. A little later, they found a cave and took refuge inside. When the blizzard calmed down, they came out of the cave to resume their trek. However, within a mile, Draupadi fainted and collapsed on the snow-covered ground. The Pandavas carried her back to the cave and tried their best to revive her. They covered her with deerskin and lit a small fire to warm her up. Yudhishthira held her hand and lamented: 'It is all my fault. It is because of my sin that she has to endure this suffering. How can I ever pardon myself?'

Bheem tried to console him: 'Don't worry, Brother. Draupadi will be fine. She is just tired. Let her take some rest and then we can continue our journey.'

'But how could she continue the journey through these perilous mountains?'

'Wait a moment, I have a plan.' Saying so, Bheem walked out of the cave and called his son Ghatotkach. As soon as Bheem thought of his son, Ghatotkach appeared and said, 'Father, you bade me to come and here I am. Tell me, what can I do for you?'

Bheem said, 'Your mother is tired and unwell. Carry her on your shoulders and travel with us to the Kailasha Mountain. Make sure she is comfortable.'

Ghatotkach lifted Draupadi in his arms and flew through the sky, following the Pandavas who were carried by Ghatotkach's rakshasa followers. Soon, they arrived in the beautiful hermitage, the Badrika Ashram of Nara-Narayana. Draupadi felt much better. The pleasant surroundings of the ashram rejuvenated the Pandavas as they waited for Arjun.

31

The Story of Bheem and Hanuman

THE PANDAVAS ENJOYED THEIR DAYS IN THE BADRIKA ASHRAM WHILE they waited for Arjun. The long overdue rest helped Draupadi recover from the strain of the arduous trek. One day, while she was relaxing in the gardens, a lotus flew in with the northeastern breeze. The beautiful flower with a thousand petals and a sweet fragrance, enchanted Draupadi. She picked it up and said to Bheem: 'Look at this pretty flower. I have never seen a more fragrant lotus in my life. I want to give this to Yudhishthira.'

Bheem was not a great admirer of flowers, but the sparkle in Draupadi's eyes made him happy. 'Yes, indeed. It is a magnificent flower. I wonder where it is from.'

Draupadi held the flower close to her heart and said, 'Bheem, if you love me, then go and get me as many of these lotuses as you can. I want to take them to our home in the Kamyaka Forest.'

'Draupadi, for you I can bring anything from anywhere. I will be back with the flowers in no time.' Bheem picked up his weapons and headed in the direction where the lotus came from.

Following the scent of the flower, Bheem arrived in the valley of the Gandhamadana Mountains. He walked through the dense forest for several hours, but couldn't find any trace of the enchanting lotus. Frustrated and angry, the mighty Pandava arrived in a beautiful garden of banana trees filled with ripe bananas. But he was in no mood to enjoy the fruit. He uprooted any tree that came in his path till he reached a lake with lotus blossoms of various kinds. Bheem jumped into the water to find the thousand-petaled lotus Draupadi wanted. He crisscrossed the lake several times, but couldn't find the lotus. The furious prince came out of the water and stomped the ground in such rage that it caused a minor earthquake.

The great primate Hanuman, an ardent devotee of Lord Rama, was spending his days in the banana garden. Hanuman and Bheem happened to be brothers since both were fathered by Pavan, the god of the winds. When Hanuman came to know that Bheem was in the vicinity, he decided to play a prank on him. He lay down on the narrow path through the banana trees and thrashed his tail on the ground. The sound of his tail falling to the ground reverberated through the mountains and startled Bheem. He followed the source of the noise and arrived at the spot where Hanuman lay on the ground, pretending to sleep.

Bheem was amazed to see a huge monkey blocking his path. He raised his hands and let out a huge roar to scare away the animal. The monkey didn't move at all. He opened his eyes a little and said in a sleepy voice, 'I am sick and tired. Please don't wake me up from my siesta.'

Bheem was taken aback to hear a monkey talk like a human. In these parts, he knew, strange things happened quite often. He stood his ground and said, 'I am not scared to hear you speak and I don't care for your siesta either. Get off my path.'

Hanuman still didn't get up. He said, 'I may be a mindless animal, but you are a knowledgeable human being. You should know better that all animals deserve kindness. Tell me, who are you? Where do you want to go? This path leads to the heavens, and human beings are forbidden from going there alive.'

'I am Bheem, the Pandava prince. You don't seem to be an ordinary monkey. Who are you?'

'I am just a poor little monkey ... nothing else. I suggest you give up your plans to travel this path, else you will die.'

'I am not scared of death. So, if you don't want to get hurt, get out of my way.'

Hanuman did not move. In a feeble voice, he said, 'I am too weak to move. If you must go, you may jump over me and continue your journey.'

'The Almighty lives in you. It would be disrespectful of me to ignore him and jump over you,' responded Bheem. 'Else, I could have jumped over you just as the great Lord Hanuman crossed the oceans.'

'Hanuman? Who is he?' asked Hanuman, enjoying this little game with his brother.

Bheem was not amused. 'You don't know who Hanuman is? Shame on you! He is the greatest monkey that ever lived. He is Lord Rama's supreme devotee and is the most powerful and most intelligent creature on earth, and he is my brother. Pavan, the god of the winds, is our father. Trust me, I am as powerful as my brother, and I can teach you a good lesson if you don't listen to me.'

Hanuman replied, 'I don't wish to fight you. I am old and weak, and I don't have the strength to get up. Why don't you do me a favour? Lift my tail and put it aside to make your way.'

Bheem felt insulted. He decided to grab the monkey by its tail and thrash him to death. He went behind Hanuman and grabbed his tail to move it. But the tail seemed as heavy as a mountain and

Bheem couldn't lift it even an inch off the ground. Bheem tried again and again—his muscles flexed to the extreme, his eyes bulged out of their sockets, his body drenched in sweat, but the tail stayed where it was. The great Bheem couldn't move it at all. He realized that this was no ordinary monkey. He knelt in front of Hanuman and with his palms joined, said, 'O great one, please pardon me for my insolent behaviour. Please tell me, who are you?'

Hanuman smiled. 'I am your brother, Hanuman. Lord Rama had given me this boon that as long as Lord Rama is remembered, I would live too. By the grace of Mother Janaki, I have everything I need to survive. I stopped you because this path leads to the heavens and is not open to mortal human beings. The lotus you seek is not far from this place. I will give you the directions.'

Bheem sat next to Hanuman and said, 'I am lucky to have met you. Your actions have always amazed me ... inspired me. How I longed to see you in the form you took when you leaped across the oceans to reach Lanka! Would you please grant your brother this little wish?'

Hanuman smiled and slowly stood up. With a huge roar, the great monkey began to grow. Soon, he was as large as the Vindhya Mountains. Bheem was thrilled to behold this spectacle. With his palms joined, he said, 'I am forever grateful to you for showing me this form of yours. I will never forget this sight. You may now get back to your normal form.'

Hanuman returned to his normal size and said, 'How could I refuse my brother this little request?'

Bheem said, 'With you by his side, why did Lord Rama had to fight the rakshasa king, Ravan? You alone could have destroyed the evil king and his army.'

Hanuman replied, 'You are right. Ravan was no match for me. But if I had destroyed him, I would have deprived Lord Rama of this noble deed.'

Hanuman then led Bheem to the edge of the banana plantation and said, 'This road will lead you to the thousand-petaled lotus you are looking for. The flowers bloom in a river that flows through Kuber's garden. Pick as many flowers as you want, but try to refrain from using force.'

Hanuman embraced his brother and Bheem felt like he had gained the strength of a thousand elephants. Hanuman added, 'If you want, I can kill the sons of Dhritarashtra and destroy Hastinapur at once.'

Bheem touched his feet and said, 'Thank you for your offer, Brother. However, with your blessings, we should be able to destroy the enemy ourselves.'

Hanuman was pleased to hear this. 'I will always be on your side. In the battlefield, when you yell to scare your enemies, my voice will join yours. I'll reside on the flag of Arjun's chariot and make such a huge roar that your enemies will freeze in fear and you'd be able to kill them at will. I pray to Lord Rama to always guide you to follow the right path.' Saying this, Hanuman took a giant leap and, in an instant, vanished from Bheem's sight.

After a short walk, Bheem arrived in the gardens of Kuber, the king of the yakshas. A river, adorned with thousands of the beautiful lotus blossoms, flowed through the garden. Bheem was overjoyed. He waded through the waters and prepared to collect the flowers. The garden and the river were guarded by ferocious demons and rakshasas. They came out and asked, 'Who are you? How dare you try to pick these flowers?'

'I am Bheem, son of the great King Pandu and brother of Emperor Yudhishthira. I am here to collect these flowers for our wife, Draupadi,' said Bheem.

'This is Kuber's playground; humans are not allowed here. If you are the brother of Yudhishthira, why do you steal these flowers? Anyone who comes here without our king's approval dies.'

Bheem didn't care to pay heed to their threats and warnings. He waded through the water and began to pluck the flowers. The rakshasa guards picked up their weapons and attacked Bheem. But they had no idea whom they were dealing with. Within minutes, hundreds of rakshasas died in Bheem's hands as he crushed them with powerful blows of his mace. Those who survived ran for their lives to Kuber's palace. When Kuber heard of Bheem, he said, 'I know him and I know he is collecting those flowers for the love of his life, Draupadi. Let him take as many lotuses he wants.'

Right then, in Badrika Ashram, a sand storm blew in from nowhere and covered the village in a thick coat of dust. Meteor showers lit up the sky and scared the residents. Yudhishthira was worried for his family. He asked his brothers: 'Where is Bheem?'

Draupadi replied, 'He has gone to collect lotuses for me.'

Yudhishthira was alarmed. 'He must be in trouble. We must immediately go and help him,' he said.

He summoned Ghatotkach and asked him to carry them to Bheem. Ghatotkach flew them to Kuber's garden on his shoulders. When they arrived at the riverbank, they found Bheem standing amidst a pile of dead rakshasas, with his mace on his shoulder.

Yudhishthira rushed to Bheem and said, 'Why did you do this? You didn't have to kill so many to collect a few flowers for Draupadi. This would make the gods very unhappy. Never do this again.' Yudhishthira consoled them and expressed his sorrow for their loss.

The Pandavas then spent a few more days in the enchanting garden of Kuber. Later, Yudhishthira summoned Ghatotkach once again to fly them back to Badrika Ashram.

32

Pandavas Reunited

O NE DAY, THE PANDAVAS SAW THE SKY LIGHT UP ABOVE THEM, AS A HUGE and gorgeous airship appeared from behind the clouds. With a thunderous roar, the airship glided through the air and slowly landed in the yard of the hermitage. Matali, the driver of the celestial chariot, opened the door and the Pandavas saw their brother Arjun jump out. He was wearing golden armour, glittering jewels and fine clothes. Arjun ran to his brothers, bowing down in front of Dhaumya, Yudhishthira and Bheem, and hugging Nakul and Sahadev. Matali helped Arjun unload the divine weapons and the precious gifts he had brought from the heavens.

Arjun took the gifts he had brought for Draupadi and went inside to meet her. Ecstatic to see him, Draupadi embraced Arjun. 'Thank the gods. You are back. I was so worried for you. The heavens are not for us mortals and I was always afraid something bad might happen to you.'

Arjun smiled. 'Don't you have faith in me? Nobody could ever stop me from coming back to you!' he said, handing her the presents he had brought for her. 'These are the jewellery and costumes that the apsaras and goddesses wear in the heavens. You'll wear them now.' Draupadi was delighted.

The next morning, Lord Indra visited the Pandavas in his flying chariot. He called Yudhishthira and said, 'You may now return to the Kamyaka Forest. Rest assured, you will once again rule the earth. Arjun has acquired the deadliest of weapons and the skills required to use them. He also paid me his dues by completing a difficult mission for me. I can tell you, armed with my weapons, he is undefeatable in any battle.'

After Indra's departure, Yudhishthira asked Arjun, 'Brother, tell us, what mission did you conduct for Lord Indra?'

Arjun said, 'After the completion of my training, Lord Indra said, "My son, now you must pay me my tutoring fees—my guru dakshina."

'I was eager to please him and told him that I would be happy to do anything for him.

'The lord smiled and said, "Deep in the ocean, in an impenetrable fortress, live thirty million of my most vicious enemies, the giant demons called the Nivatakavachas. Destroy them, and that will be my guru dakshina—my fee."

'I wore my armour, picked up my Gandiva and mounted Indra's chariot. Matali, the charioteer, took me deep into the oceans, to the fortress of the Nivatakavachas. As the demons noticed my arrival, they attacked me in hordes with spears, maces, swords and many other weapons. Using my Gandiva, I sprayed them with arrows, killing thousands at a time. The demons then invoked their magical powers and began to shower me with huge rocks, blasted me with strong winds and tried to burn me with firestorms. Soon, I was engulfed in darkness. I pulled out my magic-buster weapon and hurled it towards the demons, clearing up their illusions. The demons then began to hurl huge boulders at Matali and me. Soon, we were under a huge pile of rocks, which formed a cavern around us. Matali said, "Arjun, use the thunderbolt weapon Lord Indra gave you. That will destroy them all."

'I picked up the weapon and, as Lord Indra had instructed me, I set it up, uttered the mantra and hurled it at the demons. With a loud roar, the weapon blew away the rocks and landed amongst the demons with a huge explosion. The blast killed all the demons in an instant.

'Matali and I came out of the cave and walked into the fortress. It was indeed a spectacular city. I said, "Matali, this city looks better than Indra's city in the heavens. Why don't the gods live here?"

'Matali replied, "This city belonged to Indra. Empowered by Brahma's blessings, the Nivatakavacha demons drove out the gods and occupied this city. When Indra asked Brahma for help, he said that it is destined that Indra himself would destroy these demons, but in a different form. That is why Indra taught you, his son, the use of these weapons."

'On our way back, we saw a beautiful airborne city, lit with bright and colourful lights hovering in the sky. Matali told me, "This is Hiranyapura, the great city created by Brahma. Puloma and Kalaka, two demon women, worshiped Brahma for thousands of years. Pleased with their devotion, Lord Brahma granted them a boon: their sons Paulam and Kalkeya would be indestructible by the gods and demons, and they would live in this wonderful city. These demons are Lord Indra's sworn enemies. You must destroy them."

'I asked Matali to take me close to the city. When the demons saw us approaching, they recognized Indra's chariot and attacked us with a volley of deadly weapons. I launched my counterattack. My arrows killed thousands of demons. I hurled powerful missiles at the city, but the flying city dodged my attack by rising up, going down, or moving sideways. Hundreds and thousands of ferocious demons came in spectacular flying chariots and began to fight me. They surrounded me and stopped any weapon I threw at them. I began to panic and prayed to Lord Shiva for his permission to use the fierce Pashupat weapon named Raudra. The deadly weapon was my last resort, for it destroys anything that comes in its way. As I engaged the weapon, a strange man appeared before me. He had three faces, nine eyes and six arms. His matted hair glowed like a thousand suns, with fiery serpents surrounding them. It was Shiva himself. I sought his blessings and launched the Raudra. As soon as the weapon left my Gandiva, something fascinating happened. Thousands of fierce animals—elephants, lions, tigers and snakes—appeared from nowhere and attacked the demons. Thousands of armed soldiers—from the gods to the gandharvas, yakshas and rakshasas—appeared and pounced on my enemies. I was no longer alone. With Lord Shiva's blessings, I had a huge army fighting for me. I regained my confidence and began to kill the demons in hordes. Soon, the city of Hiranyapura was free of the evil demons.

'When we returned to the heavens, Lord Indra was overjoyed to hear about my conquest. He lauded me: "My son, you will be invincible in the battlefield. Bhishma, Drona, Kripa, Karna and all their allies taken together won't be a fraction of your strength and prowess."

'Then he gave me an indestructible armour, a golden garland, the celebrated conch shell named Devadatta, and many other heavenly costumes and jewellery. After spending five years with my father Indra, I asked for his permission to return to you.'

Listening to these glorious tales, Yudhishthira was overwhelmed with joy and asked Arjun to give his brothers a demonstration of the weapons he had acquired.

The next morning, while Arjun prepared to give a demonstration of his divine weapons, the air stood still, the oceans swelled, the sun didn't rise, and darkness covered the earth. Watching these ominous signs, Rishi Narada came to Arjun and said, 'Do not use the divine weapons without a proper cause. Misusing these weapons can result in grave consequences. Use them only when you fight your fiercest enemies and only when you have no other option.'

Yudhishthira then asked Arjun to retract his weapons, and things returned to normal once again.

Nahusha's Curse

After spending ten years of their exile period, Bheem called upon Yudhishthira and said, 'We are on our eleventh year of exile. As per our promise, we will have to go into hiding on our thirteenth year. I think it is high time to begin preparations for the battle ahead of us.'

Yudhishthira concurred.

The Pandavas left the Gandhamadana Mountains, arrived in the Vishakhayupa Forest near the source of River Yamuna, and decided to make it their home for the rest of the year.

One day, Bheem went into the forest to hunt. While strolling through the thick foliage looking for deer, a huge mountain snake pounced on him from the tree above and coiled around him in a tight embrace. The mighty prince tried hard to escape, but the snake constricted his body so tight that Bheem suffocated and was about to pass out. Surprised by the snake's tremendous strength, Bheem asked in a feeble voice: 'No ordinary snake can overpower me. Tell me, who are you?'

'I am King Nahusha, your ancestor. Cursed by Rishi Agasthya, I have become a snake. It's been a long time since I had anything to eat. Today I got lucky and found you, my prey. I will devour you and satisfy my hunger.' Saying this, the snake tightened its grip a little more to make sure Bheem was robbed of all his strength.

In the meantime, in the Vishakhayupa Ashram, Yudhishthira felt uneasy—as if something terrible were about to happen. He came out of his hut and saw Arjun, Nakul, Sahadev and Draupadi. But Bheem was missing. 'Where is Bheem?' he asked.

'He left to hunt a while ago. He should have been back by now,' Draupadi replied.

Yudhishthira knew Bheem must be in some sort of danger. He took priest Dhaumya along and walked into the forest looking for Bheem. Yudhishthira knew, wherever Bheem went, he'd leave a wide track of broken trees and uprooted shrubs. Following the trail, they soon arrived at the place where Bheem lay crushed inside the serpent Nahusha's deadly coil. Yudhishthira knelt before the snake and said, 'O great snake, spare my brother. I will provide you with whatever food you desire.'

Nahusha said, 'I caught this man as my prey and he will be my meal today. Nothing else would satisfy me. Leave now, else I will catch you and eat you tomorrow.'

Yudhishthira did not leave. 'King Nahusha, I cannot leave without my brother. Tell me, what can I do to make you spare my brother?'

'Alright, if you can answer my question, I will let go of your brother.'

'Ask me whatever you wish. I will answer to the best of my ability,' replied Yudhishthira.

'You seem to be a smart person. Tell me, who is a true Brahmin? What is the ultimate knowledge?'

'One who is kind, truthful, generous, nonviolent, good-natured and learned is a true Brahmin. The supreme Brahman who is beyond happiness or sorrow, the knowledge of whom frees us from grief, is the ultimate knowledge,' Yudhishthira answered.

The serpent said, 'But shudras, the men of the lowest caste, can also possess the traits you mention. And nothing is beyond happiness and sorrow.'

Yudhishthira replied, 'If a shudra possesses these traits, then he should be a Brahmin. And if a Brahmin doesn't exhibit these virtues, he is nothing but a shudra. You may say whatever you like, but I believe that the knowledge of the supreme Brahman frees us from all attachments.'

The snake countered, 'If virtues make a person a Brahmin, then one cannot belong to the Brahmin caste until he masters them all.'

Yudhishthira stood up and said, 'O great snake, I believe there exists no pure race or pure caste. The human race is a product of interracial unions. Hence, it is impossible to claim purity of race or caste.'

Nahusha was pleased with Yudhishthira's answers and he released Bheem from his grip. He then had a long discussion on philosophy and theology with Yudhishthira. Later, Yudhishthira asked him: 'You are learned and one of the most knowledgeable persons I have ever met. You lived in the heavens. Then why do you have to suffer this misfortune?'

Nahusha sighed: 'I was one of the most powerful kings of the heavens. I travelled on airships, and was revered by the gods, gandharvas and the rishis. They paid me taxes. A thousand Brahmin rishis pulled my carriage. One day, when Rishi Agasthya was carrying me, my feet touched his head. He felt insulted and cursed me. I turned into a snake and fell from the heavens to the earth. I cried and prayed for mercy. Agasthya took pity on me and said, one day the great King Yudhishthira, the son of Dharma, would free you of your curse. Today is the day. Thank you for relieving me of my burden.' Saying so, Nahusha shed off his snake body and departed for the heavens. Yudhishthira, Bheem and Dhaumya returned to their ashram to join the rest of the Pandavas.

33

Rishi Markandeya's Visit

AFTER SPENDING THE MONSOON AND AUTUMN IN THE VISHAKHAYUPA
Forest, the Pandavas moved back to the Kamyaka Forest to pass
the rest of their exile period. One day, Krishna, along with his wife
Satyabhama, came to visit the Pandavas. Draupadi ran to Krishna as
soon as she spotted him and asked, breathlessly, about the well-being
of her sons, whom they had left in Krishna's care: 'Krishna, tell me
how are my sons doing? Do they miss me?'

Krishna smiled. 'Don't worry, Panchali, your sons are doing fine
and growing up to be worthy descendants of the Kuru dynasty. They
are mastering the skills of archery and warfare. Your father King
Drupad and your brother Dhrishtadyumna have invited them several
times to stay with them in Panchal, but they prefer to stay with us in
Dwarka. Subhadra is caring for them just as you did, and is trying
her best to fill your place in their hearts. They receive lessons in horse
riding and chariot driving from my son Pradyumna and my nephew
Abhimanyu.'

Krishna went to meet Yudhishthira and said, 'O King, the Yadava Army is at your disposal. If you want, you may attack Hastinapur and destroy Duryodhan and his brothers any time you want. Or, if you wish, you can continue your exile while the Yadavas conquer Hastinapur and wait for you to return.'

Yudhishthira bowed in front of Krishna and said, 'You are our friend, philosopher and guide. I know we would get your help whenever we ask. We have almost completed the twelve years of our exile and have only one more year to spend ... in hiding. We shall seek your help after that. Till then, let us continue our journey.'

Krishna decided to spend some more time with the Pandavas and his best friend, Arjun. One day, the great rishi, Markandeya, arrived in the ashram. Markandeya was more than a thousand years old, but he looked like a handsome young man of no more than twenty-five. The Pandavas received him with due respect. After having a good meal, he sat under a tree while the Pandavas gathered around him.

Yudhishthira said, 'O great rishi, you have experienced a lot in your life. We wish to hear from you about the mysteries of our world. Please enlighten us.'

And so, Markandeya narrated the story of Manu, the son of King Bibaswan: 'After inheriting the kingdom from his father Bibaswan, Manu went to Badrika Ashram and engaged in a strict penance for a thousand years on the riverbank. One day, a small fish swam close to Manu and said, "Please save me from the big fish in the river. They'll eat me if they catch me."

'Manu felt pity for the fish. He picked it up gently and released it into a pot of water, naming the fish "Matsya". Matsya began to grow larger and larger, and soon outgrew the pot. Manu then released it into a lake. The fish continued growing, until one day the lake was too small for him. Manu then released it into the Ganga. Soon, Matsya became so large that the river too ran out of space for him. Matsya said to Manu: "Lord, I have become so large, I cannot move in this river. Take me to the ocean and release me there." Manu arranged to drag the mighty fish through the Ganga towards the oceans. After a long journey, they arrived at the estuary of the river. Freed from the bounds of the river, the happy fish Matsya swam into the open seas.

'As Manu was about to leave, the giant fish swam back to Manu and said, "You have protected me all my life. It is my turn to pay you back now. Listen to me carefully. A great flood will soon engulf the earth and submerge all land. Nothing can escape this impending disaster. Build a sturdy boat and a long, strong rope. Carry with you the seeds of life needed to repopulate the earth. Then, with the seven rishis, board the ship and wait for me. When the time comes, I will come to save you." The fish bade goodbye to Manu and dived into the deep ocean.

'Manu knew that Matsya was no ordinary animal, and took the advice with all due seriousness. He built a huge and strong boat, and wove a long and strong rope. Then, along with the seven rishis, he boarded the boat and waited for the great flood to strike.

'Manu didn't have to wait for long. Matsya was right. A huge flood engulfed the earth and submerged everything in sight. The waves carried Manu's boat as it tossed and turned in the tumultuous waters. Manu panicked. He called the fish, "Matsya, where are you? Save us from our impending death."

'Soon, the huge fish surfaced in front of the boat. Matsya had grown a long horn on its head. Manu tied one end of the rope to the horn and the other end to the hull of the boat. The giant fish pulled the boat and took it out to the open sea. The entire earth was submerged and all land animals had perished. Only Manu and the seven rishis survived.

'After floating in the oceans for several years, the waters began to subside. Matsya took them near the Himalaya Mountains, where some of the peaks were now visible above the water. As per Matsya's instructions, Manu tied the boat to one of the peaks. The fish then said, "Manu, I am Brahma, the creator. I have taken the form of a fish to save you from the flood. Now, it is your duty to repopulate the earth." Saying this, the fish disappeared.

'Manu and the rishis then began the arduous task of rebuilding and repopulating the earth from the seeds they carried. After many years of strict austerities and with Brahma's blessings, they succeeded. The earth was again filled with humans and other living creatures.'

Markandeya then told Yudhishthira about the system of the celestial calendar. One celestial year equals 360 earth years. The Satya Yuga or the age of Satya runs for 4,000 celestial years, followed by the Treta Yuga, which runs for 3,000 years. Next comes the Dwapar Yuga, which runs for 2,000 years. The final age is the Kali Yuga, which takes 1,000 years. Taking the transition period between the yugas into account, one cycle of the four yugas takes twelve thousand celestial years to complete. And a 1,000 yuga cycles constitute one day for Brahma. Then comes the night, the period of annihilation. During this time, no life exists, and the universe stays submerged in a primordial fluid.

Markandeya said, 'Once, during this period of universal destruction, while I was alone floating in the eternal ocean, I had this wonderful vision. I saw at a distance a young, divine-looking boy sitting under a banyan tree. The boy's skin was blue, and his eyes were like lotus petals. He called me and said, "Dear Markandeya, you are tired. Live in my body and get some rest." He opened his mouth. I entered his body through his mouth and inside I found a whole new world, full of people, animals, birds, rivers, mountains, meadows, cities and forests. For more than a hundred years, I roamed inside his body but couldn't reach its end. I cried for help, and suddenly I was thrown out of his body through his mouth. I found the divine boy sitting on a tree branch. He smiled at me and said, "Markandeya, I hope you had a pleasant stay in my body."

'I held my head to his feet and said, "Lord, whoever you are, I pray to you—please reveal yourself to me."

'The divine boy said, "In the ancient days, I named water as Nara. During the period of destruction, the same water became my abode or my Ayana. That is why I am Narayana. Several times have I appeared before you as Brahma, for half of my self is Brahma. Brahma is asleep and while he sleeps, I'd live here as a boy. When this dark period ends and Brahma awakes, I would merge with him and begin to recreate the universe—the sky, the earth, the planets ... everything. Till then, you rest in peace." Saying this, he disappeared.'

Markandeya paused for a moment and then said, 'Yudhishthira, the divine boy whom I had met during the time of universal destruction is none other than the man sitting next to you, your cousin, Lord Krishna. With his boon, I have an indestructible memory and I have the power to live as long as I wish. Take refuge in him and he will protect you forever.' Hearing Markandeya, the Pandavas bowed down to Krishna and paid him their respects.

Yudhishthira asked Markandeya: 'Lord, tell us, how did King Kubalashwa of the Ikshvaku dynasty come to be known as Dhundhumar?'

Markandeya replied, 'During the time of the great destruction, when the universe was only a great ocean of primordial fluid, Lord Vishnu lay in a deep slumber on the floating body of the great serpent Ananta Naga. From his navel grew a divine lotus. And on the lotus, Lord Brahma came to being. Lord Brahma sat on the lotus and was in a deep meditation when the two fierce demons Madhu and Kaitabha attacked him. Scared of the demons, Brahma shook the lotus stem to wake up the lord. Vishnu opened his eyes and with a smile he welcomed the demons, who laughed at him and said, "We are in a good mood today. Ask anything you want and we will fulfil your wish."

'Vishnu said, "To protect my devotees, I wish to kill you. Please grant me my wish."

'The demons replied, "Lord, we have always been virtuous. We never lie and we have always been generous to the weak. We will grant your wish. But we have a request. Kill us in a place that is uncovered. In return, we wish to be your sons in our next life."

'"So be it. I grant your wish."

'Lord Vishnu searched the heaven and earth for an uncovered place, but he couldn't find any. He then removed the clothing off his thigh. Then, with his Sudarshana Chakra, he beheaded Madhu and Kaitabha right on his exposed thigh.

'Madhu and Kaitabha's son Dhundhu had pleased Lord Brahma with his worship and been granted a special power that made him indestructible by the gods, demons, yakhsas and rakshasas. Dhundhu stayed hidden under the desert sand and slept for most of the time. Once a year, when the huge demon blew his nose from under the desert sand, it would cause earthquakes for weeks. The burst of dust and sand would cover the Sun, and the earth would plunge into darkness. And when he woke up from his slumber, he would plunder the nearby hermitage of Rishi Utanka, killing his family members and disciples. Rishi Utanka prayed to Lord Vishnu for help. Many years ago, pleased with Utanka's worship, Lord Vishnu wanted to give him a gift. Utanka refused to accept any, saying that he was happy to see his lord. No other gift was necessary. Lord Vishnu then promised to help him whenever needed. So, bound by his word, Vishnu said, "Utanka, I will help you destroy your enemy."

'Vishnu then entered the body of King Kubalashwa without his knowledge and summoned one thousand of his sons and marched to the desert to kill the ferocious demon, Dhundhu. After digging the desert floor for more than a week, they found Dhundhu's body. The noise of the army woke up the giant. The angry demon let out a huge roar and hurled fireballs from his mouth at Kubalashwa's sons. The fire scorched the thousand sons and killed them instantly. Kubalashwa used his yogic powers and extinguished Dhundhu's fire. He then pulled out his divine weapon, the Brahmastra, and fired it at Dhundhu. The weapon struck the giant and blew up his body into a huge ball of fire. The world was freed of Dhundhu's terror and Utanka was relieved. Since then, King Kubalashwa came to be known as Dhundhumar—the slayer of Dhundhu.'

34

The Virtuous Butcher

MARKANDEYA THEN PROCEEDED TO TELL THE STORY OF A VIRTUOUS butcher to the Pandavas.

'Let me tell you a story. In the olden days, there lived a rishi named Kaushik. One day, while he was studying the scriptures, a crane flew over him and defecated on the rishi's head. The angry Rishi looked up at the bird, and his glowing eyes killed the crane instantly. The bird dropped from the sky and fell at the hermit's feet. Looking at the dead bird, Kaushik felt bad—he ought to have controlled his anger, he thought.

'A few days later, Rishi Kaushik went to beg for alms in a village. He stood in front of a house and prayed for alms. The lady of the house asked him to wait and went inside to get some rice and vegetables for the rishi. In the meantime, her husband returned from work and the woman got busy taking care of him. She forgot about the beggar waiting at the door. Later, when she remembered, she rushed to the door to serve the rishi. She said, "Pardon my delay. I was busy serving my husband."

'The rishi was furious. "How dare you keep me waiting? Don't you know a Brahmin's rage can destroy the world?" he said.

'The woman said, "Control your anger, sir. I am not a bird that you can kill with your looks. I am sorry for the inconvenience, but for me, my husband is my priority. He came home tired, and I had to take care of him first. That is my duty."

'Kaushik was surprised. How did this woman know about the incident when he had burnt the bird to cinders?

'The woman said, "Your anger killed a poor little bird and I know all about it because of my special powers. I acquired this power due to my devotion to my husband. O great Rishi, if you cannot conquer anger, lust and desire, you cannot claim to be a Brahmin. You may be well-versed in the scriptures, but you need to learn the basics of human virtue. Go to Mithila and meet the virtuous butcher. He will teach you the ways of life better than any Brahmin or rishi."

'Kaushik was curious. How could a butcher be as virtuous as a Brahmin? He went to Mithila looking for the virtuous butcher. The Brahmins directed him to a meat shop where he found the butcher selling deer and buffalo meat to his customers. Kaushik felt a surge of nausea when he saw the way the butcher chopped meat and handled the blood and viscera of the dead animals. Kaushik controlled his feelings and introduced himself to the butcher: "I am Kaushik. I come from far to ..."

'The butcher stopped him and said, "I know who you are, and I know that the virtuous lady has asked you to come to me. But this is not the right place to have a conversation. Come with me to my home."

'The butcher took Kaushik to his house. The baffled Rishi asked, "I don't understand. The woman told me that you are as virtuous and as wise as a Brahmin. Then how could you conduct this filthy business? This is not what a virtuous man should do."

'The butcher replied, "Selling meat is my family business and I have no qualms about it. I conduct my duties according to the norms of a virtuous human being. I serve my parents, I speak the truth, I don't envy others. I donate as much as I can, and I eat only what is left after serving my guests and servants. I do not eat meat, I do not kill any animal, ard I sell the meat that I get from other hunters. Meat serves the hungry. Hence, there is no sin in killing animals for food. The learned say that rice, vegetables, fruits, medicinal plants, animals and birds—all are edible by human beings. The kitchen of King Rantideva cooked two thousand cows every day and the meat was served to all the king's guests. The food chain connects all living beings, and we can only survive by eating another. We cannot avoid killing. When a man walks, he kills thousands on the ground without his knowledge. Nobody in this world can avoid killing some living being or the other."

'The virtuous butcher then gave Kaushik a long lecture on Dharma, philosophy and spirituality. Later he said, "Come with me. Let me show you how I practise my way of life, my Dharma."

'He took Kaushik to a beautiful house. Inside, he saw the butcher's parents taking rest after partaking of their meal. The butcher touched their feet to pay his respects. Then he turned to Rishi Kaushik and said, "My parents are my gods. I worship them and serve them instead of worshipping those in the heavens. Rishi Kaushik, you have ignored your parents. Instead of taking care of them in their old age, you abandoned them. You left home to study the scriptures, leaving your parents alone. They have gone blind crying for you ever since you left. You should go back to your parents. That is your duty."

'The rishi felt ashamed. He touched the feet of the butcher and said, "You have saved me from a terrible sin. I will go back to my village and take care of my parents as long as they are alive."

'The butcher held him and pulled him up to his chest.

'Kaushik asked, "You cannot be a shudra. Tell me, what misfortune has caused you to adopt this profession?"

'The butcher said, "In my past life, I was a learned Brahmin and a dear friend of our king. One day, I went hunting with the king and mistook a rishi wearing a deerskin to be a deer and shot him with my bow and arrow. When I heard his cry, I was shocked. I ran to him, pulled out the arrow from his body and took him to his ashram. Fortunately, the rishi survived. The angry sage cursed me that in my next life, I'd be born a shudra butcher. I begged for mercy. The rishi took pity on me and said that although I'd be born a Shudra, I'd be as learned and wise as a Brahmin. I'd also remember everything about my past life. He said that if I led a life of righteousness and took care of my parents like gods, then in the following life, I'd be born a Brahmin."

'Kaushik took the butcher's lesson to heart and went back to his village to care for his parents.'

35

The Pandavas Rescue the Kauravas

AFTER MARKANDEYA AND HIS FOLLOWERS LEFT THE PANDAVA HERMITAGE, Krishna and Satyabhama also bade goodbye to them and departed for Dwarka. Yudhishthira felt that it was time for them to leave the Kamyaka Forest. This time, they selected the beautiful forest of Dvaitavana as their home. They built their huts next to a blue lake and began to spend the rest of their days in exile.

Meanwhile, in Hastinapur, Duryodhan was growing impatient. He knew that the Pandavas' exile would be over soon, and they would go into hiding for a year. In order to send them into exile for twelve more years, they had to be dug out from their hiding place in the thirteenth year. Duryodhan knew his spies were the best and, with help from his uncle Shakuni, the Pandavas would be exposed for sure. But what if his spies failed? What if the Pandavas used some magic trick and stayed untraceable for the whole year? They had the gods as their friends and if the gods helped them, it would be impossible to find the Pandava brothers.

While Duryodhan was brooding over his thoughts, Karna and Shakuni entered the chamber. Karna said, 'My dear friend, you are thinking about the Pandavas, right?'

Duryodhan rose from his seat and said, 'Twelve years are almost over, and we have only one more year to go. Shouldn't we be concerned?'

Karna laughed. 'Don't worry, we will find them in the thirteenth year. Meanwhile, enjoy the kingdom as much as you can. I suggest you go visit the Pandavas and see how they are suffering in the forest. Watch them, just as the mountain dwellers watch the tiny people down in the plains, or the rich and prosperous watch the poor and wretched. Trust me, there is nothing more satisfying than watching your enemy suffer.'

Duryodhan replied, 'Karna you have spoken my mind. Oh, how I wish to witness the misery of the Pandavas. But that won't be possible. The old king would never allow me.' Sighing, Duryodhan sat down again.

Shakuni stood listening to this conversation with a crooked smile on his face. He said, 'My dear nephew, as far as my knowledge goes, the Pandavas now live in the forest of Dvaitavana. And close to Dvaitavana is your cattle ranch. It is the time of the year when the representatives of Hastinapur visit the ranch to account for the cattle. If you were to tell your father that you'd like to supervise the counting in person, he wouldn't stop you.'

Duryodhan's eyes lit up. Moments later, Duryodhan, Shakuni and Karna were in the royal chamber.

Shakuni said, 'O King, it is time to count the cattle in your ranch and account for the livestock you own. The cowherds and caretakers are waiting for our visit. I suggest you send Duryodhan to perform this duty and spend a few days hunting in the forest.'

The blind king realized that the request was not as innocent as it sounded. He sat down on his throne and said, 'I am pleased that Duryodhan is volunteering to visit our cattle ranch. A hunting trip would be nice too. But the mighty Pandavas live close by and that is a cause for concern. I am not worried about Yudhishthira. He is kind and virtuous. But Bheem may not remain calm if he sees Duryodhan. I also hear Arjun is back from the heavens with a huge arsenal of divine weapons. I am afraid, when he sees them, my son would do some mischief to belittle the Pandavas and their wrath would destroy him.' Turning to Duryodhan, he said, 'I cannot let you do this to yourself. Don't worry about the ranch, I'll send someone else to take care of the cattle.'

Shakuni stepped close to the king and said, 'I understand your concern. I can promise you, we will not go anywhere near the Pandavas. We will only go to account for the cattle and have some fun, nothing more.' The reluctant king had no choice but to agree.

With a huge entourage, Duryodhan departed for the cattle ranch near Dvaitavana. Dushasana, Shakuni and Karna accompanied him along with their wives and consorts. Thousands of elephants, horses and chariots carried the Kauravas, their provisions and their weapons. A huge battalion of soldiers accompanied the princes. Brahmins, entertainers, storytellers and dancers joined the team to keep the travellers engaged during their time of rest. Soon, they arrived at the ranch. The ranch keepers were delighted to have their prince amongst them. They got busy trying to entertain the prince and his guests, while Duryodhan got busy counting the cows and calves.

Duryodhan called his servants and soldiers and said, 'Go to the forest of Dvaitavana and build houses for me and my friends. I wish to relax there for a few days.' The servants left for Dvaitavana along with several artisans.

During that time, the gandharva king Chitrasen was visiting the Dvaitavana Forest along with his entourage. When the Kaurava artisans and soldiers arrived, the gandharva soldiers stopped them. 'Leave these grounds right now,' they said. 'King Chitrasen is resting here. Do not disturb his peace.'

The artisans didn't dare to challenge the fierce gandharva soldiers. They went back and reported the incident to Duryodhan, who grew furious. He called some of his bravest soldiers and said, 'How dare the gandharvas stop me? Go and teach them a lesson.' But the gandharvas were too powerful and defeated Duryodhan's soldiers in a matter of hours.

Duryodhan called his entire army and, along with Karna and Dushasana, he attacked the gandharvas. Chitrasen was not happy to have his peaceful vacation being disrupted by the arrogant Kaurava prince. He ordered his army: 'Destroy these people. Let nobody escape.'

The fierce Gandharva Army pounced upon the Kauravas. Duryodhan never realized how well-equipped the gandharvas were. Soon, his army was in disarray. His brothers gave up the fight and began to retreat. Karna, however, did not give in so easily. He fought hard and used his superior skills to destroy hundreds of gandharvas. Duryodhan joined him. Chitrasen knew he had to change his strategy. Being a gandharva, he was a master of illusions. With magic, he rendered his army invisible to the human eye. Armed with the magical power, the gandharvas began to wreak havoc among the Kaurava army. They destroyed Karna's chariot and, just as they were about to kill him, Karna jumped into Vikarna's chariot and fled the battlefield. Duryodhan's army panicked and began to flee. Duryodhan was adamant and continued fighting. Soon, his chariot was destroyed and he plunged into the ground. The gandharvas captured Duryodhan, Dushasana and their wives, and took them to a secret place.

The Kauravas who remained uncaptured were at a loss. They didn't know what to do. Somebody suggested: 'The Pandavas live nearby. Let's seek their help.'

When they approached the Pandavas, Bheem laughed and said, 'I'm glad the gandharvas did our job. Duryodhan must have planned to humiliate us. Now he's been taught a lesson by our gandharva friends, without us even lifting a finger.'

Yudhishthira chided his brother: 'This is not the time to be cruel to our cousins, Bheem. These men have come to us to seek help and we cannot refuse them. By capturing the men and women of the Kuru dynasty, Chitrasen has committed a grievous crime. We must stand by our family during this time of distress. Bheem, think about it, Duryodhan is helpless and is asking for our help. What can be more glorious? Go, pick up your weapons and rescue our cousins. Request Chitrasen politely to release them, but do not hesitate to use force if he refuses to listen.'

Bheem, Arjun, Nakul and Sahadev wore their armours, picked up their weapons and mounted their chariots to meet the gandharvas. Arjun went up to the gandharva chieftain and said, 'We ask you to release our brother Duryodhan and his family.'

The gandharva army chief laughed. 'How dare you order us? We only take orders from Indra; nobody else.'

Arjun reiterated his request: 'We don't wish to fight you. But if you do not oblige, we'd be left with no other option.'

The gandharvas were amused. 'You humans want to fight us? Don't you know what we've done to your Kaurava brothers?'

Bheem couldn't take it any more. He pounced upon the Gandharva Army with his mace, and a fierce battle broke out. Arjun attacked the gandharvas with his Gandiva. His arrows killed thousands of gandharva soldiers. Chitrasen himself picked up his mace and appeared in the battlefield to defend his people. Arjun's sharp arrows shredded his mace into bits. Chitrasen resorted to his magic powers. He became invisible and attacked the Pandavas. Arjun was too smart to be tricked by this simple trick. He pulled out his sound-guided weapon and engaged it on his Gandiva for a final blow to destroy Chitrasen. Chitrasen gave up and appeared in front of Arjun with his palms joined. 'I surrender, O great Pandava prince. Please consider me your friend.'

Arjun retracted his weapon and said, 'Alright, I will spare you. But why did you abduct Duryodhan and his family?'

'Duryodhan and his entourage came here wanting to humiliate you. When Indra heard of their plan, he asked me to capture Duryodhan and his family and take them to the heavens. I was only obeying his orders.'

Arjun said, 'Come with me. Yudhishthira would like to talk to you.'

The Pandava brothers took Chitrasen to their hermitage in the Dvaitavana Forest. Chitrasen met Yudhishthira and paid him his respects.

Yudhishthira said, 'Chitrasen, you are brave and strong. Duryodhan and his brothers have disturbed your peace and have learnt their lesson. I am glad that you didn't kill them. I request you to release them and save the honour of our family.'

Chitrasen said, 'O Emperor Yudhishthira, you are my friend now, and it will be my pleasure to honour your request.' He ordered his soldiers to release Duryodhan and his family. The gandharvas brought the cages where Duryodhan and the others were held, and opened the doors.

Duryodhan stepped out of his cage and walked towards Yudhishthira with his head held low in shame and disgrace.

Yudhishthira said, 'Dear brother, never ever try such a misadventure. You are lucky that we were nearby and were able to help in time. Else these gandharvas would have killed you. Now go back to Hastinapur is peace.'

Duryodhan bowed down to Yudhishthira to express his gratitude. In his heart, he was burning in humiliation. Disgraced and ashamed, the Kaurava prince began his journey back to Hastinapur while the cheerful Pandavas bade them farewell.

36

Duryodhan's Dream and the Vaishnava Yagna

AS THE ROYAL CONVOY TRUDGED TOWARDS HASTINAPUR, DURYODHAN sat still in his chariot with his head hung low. He could have tolerated the crushing defeat at the hands of the gandharvas, but being forced to accept the pity of the Pandavas was worse than death. Bheem and Arjun must have been snickering when Yudhishthira asked Chitrasen to release him. Duryodhan felt that the generosity of the Pandavas was laced with pride and arrogance. It would have been better if the gandharvas had killed him, thought Duryodhan. He could hear the men and women who had accompanied him on this journey praising the Pandavas. He couldn't take it anymore and called out to his charioteer to stop the caravan.

The convoy stopped, and the surprised members of the caravan watched Duryodhan step out of his chariot and walk away. They were at a loss and didn't know what to do. Shakuni, Dushasana and his brothers got off their chariots. They too were disheartened, but now they were worried about Duryodhan, who was now sitting gloomily.

Karna had joined the caravan some time ago. He was too ashamed to show his face to Duryodhan. He felt guilty for deserting his friend in the battlefield and couldn't gather the courage to face him. Dushasana came up to him and said, 'Karna, go and talk to him. I'm afraid Duryodhan might do something terrible.'

Karna was reluctant, but he felt he had to do something to relieve the tension. He sat next to Duryodhan and said, 'Dear friend, we are both lucky to have survived those mystical gandharva soldiers, and we are lucky to meet again. Those dreadful creatures chased me and almost killed me with their poisoned arrows, and I was forced to flee the battlefield. Trust me, I was planning to come back with a larger army and rescue you from those devils. But I was late. I am happy to see that you and your brothers have won the battle and returned safely.'

Duryodhan looked up at Karna. His eyes were red, and tears were rolling down his chin. With a hoarse voice, he said, 'Karna, you know nothing of what happened. We were defeated and captured by the gandharvas. We were bound in chains and shoved into iron cages like animals. And you know who saved us? The Pandavas. When Chitrasen told Yudhishthira that we had come to enjoy the misery of the Pandavas, I wanted to die. It was so humiliating, so disgraceful. I should have killed myself right then. But enough is enough. I cannot bear this any more. I won't go back to Hastinapur. I don't want to be the king any longer. Dushasana, you go back and become the ruler of Hastinapur. I shall sit here and fast until death.'

Dushasana dropped at Duryodhan's feet and said, 'No, you cannot do this. I won't let you die. You must come back with us.'

Karna cajoled his friend: 'Why do you feel so bad? Occasionally, even a general in the army gets cornered and captured by the enemy, only to be rescued by his men. The Pandavas are your subjects, your servants. To rescue you was their duty. You should not feel ashamed about that.' His words, however, failed to console Duryodhan. He turned away and looked the other way.

Shakuni turned his nephew's chin towards himself: 'You fool, look at me. I have made you the ruler of Hastinapur, made you the wealthiest and the most prosperous king in the world. Now you want to give it up and die? Well, an easier way would be to make it up with your cousins. Give the Pandavas their kingdom and their wealth and make peace with them. That should make you and your people happy, right?'

Duryodhan was in no mood to appreciate Shakuni's sarcasm. He was hell-bent on ending his life, and asked his brothers to leave him alone. Then, after saying his prayers, he lay down on a straw mat to fast unto death.

That night, Duryodhan had a strange dream. He saw a ferocious looking creature grab him and drag him into the deep underground. There, the demons gathered around him and said, 'O great king Duryodhan, it is a sin to commit suicide. You'd have to spend an eternity in hell. Your dynasty would be disgraced. You have been created by the grace of Lord Shiva, hence you are not a mere human being—you are a super human. We, the evil spirits and demons of the dark, are here to help you. During the war, we would possess the bodies of Bhishma, Drona and Kripa, and make them abandon their compassion for the Pandavas. They would become merciless and kill your enemies like flies. The spirit of the evil Narakasura would possess the body of Karna and fight Krishna and Arjun on your behalf. We would deploy thousands of ferocious demons and rakshasas as the Samsaptak army to fight on your behalf. Soon you will be free of all enemies and rule the world as an emperor. Now shrug off your malaise, go back to your kingdom, and prepare for the war.'

Duryodhan woke up with renewed vigour. The dream made him regain his confidence. He was sure he would soon prevail over the Pandavas. He went back to the convoy and said, 'Let's return to Hastinapur.'

Karna, Dushasana and the others were ecstatic with joy. Karna said, 'I am glad you have got back to your senses. My dear friend, death cannot solve your problems. Stay alive and you'd be victorious. I promise, I'll kill Arjun and take your revenge.' Duryodhan smiled and mounted his chariot and the procession once again rolled towards Hastinapur.

When Duryodhan and his entourage arrived in Hastinapur, Bhishma received them. Duryodhan bowed to touch his feet. Bhishma pulled him up and said, 'Duryodhan, I had advised you not to go to the Dvaitavana Forest. You ignored my advice and paid the price. Your friend, the mighty Karna, abandoned you and fled the battlefield. If it weren't for the Pandavas, you'd have been dead by now. They rescued you and restored your honour. Do you finally see who your well-wishers are? There's still time. Abandon your evil friends and make peace with the Pandavas.' Duryodhan and Shakuni scoffed and went inside the palace, ignoring the old man. Bhishma sighed at their ignorance and muttered in a low voice, 'You fool, you'll never learn.'

After settling down in Hastinapur, Duryodhan called his trusted comrades Karna, Shakuni and Dushasana, and said, 'Friends, I've decided: just like Yudhishthira, I would also perform the Rajasuya fire sacrifice and declare myself the emperor. What do you think about that?'

Karna was delighted to hear this. 'My friend, you are the most deserving king to perform the Rajasuya. I will always be by your side and destroy any king who defies your claim to the emperorship,' he said.

Shakuni was more practical: 'Well, the Rajasuya Yagna is no simple task. You remember, the Pandavas had to cross many hurdles to conduct the ceremony. You must consult your priests and advisors.'

Dushasana fetched the chief priest of the palace. Duryodhan asked, 'I wish to perform the Rajasuya. Tell me, what do I need to do?'

The old priest was not sure how to respond to his prince. Shakuni noticed his hesitation and said, 'Priest, you don't have to fear anything. Please advise the prince if he can perform the yagna.'

The priest looked up and said, 'O prince Duryodhan, with your father and Yudhishthira still alive, you cannot perform the Rajasuya sacrifice. But...'

'But what?' asked Dushasana.

'There is another great fire sacrifice—the Vaishnava Yagna—which is as fruitful. I suggest you perform that. The kings and rulers who accept you as their emperor will have to pay you their taxes in gold. With the collected gold, you'd have to build a plough, which would be used to till the land where you intend to perform the yagna. Perform this yagna and all your wishes and dreams would be fulfilled.'

Duryodhan stood up and announced, 'I'll perform the Vaishnava Yagna! Dushasana, Karna, go ahead and make the necessary arrangements.'

Dhritarashtra was happy with Duryodhan's decision to conduct the sacrifice. He ordered the exchequer to spend generously for the grand ceremony and to not spare any expense. With great enthusiasm, the Kauravas began their preparation for the Vaishnava Yagna. Messengers were sent to all the kings and Brahmins to invite them to the Hastinapur palace to take part in the proceedings. Dushasana called a messenger and said, 'Go to the forest of Dvaitavana and invite the Pandavas and the Brahmins accompanying them. Tell them,

Duryodhan is conducting the Vaishnava fire sacrifice which is as glorious as the Rajasuya.'

As the messenger conveyed the message, Yudhishthira said, 'Duryodhan is lucky to perform the great Vaishnava sacrifice. His ancestors would be pleased with this great deed. We will also go to him, but not now. We'll see him after we complete our year of exile.'

Bheem was not as generous. 'Tell your prince, after the thirteenth year, Yudhishthira will set foot in Hastinapur only after our weapons ignite the flames of the great war and Duryodhan has been sacrificed in that blaze. I'd enter the palace only when all the descendants of Dhritarashtra have burnt to a cinder in the great fire of our rage.'

Duryodhan's fire sacrifice was uneventful. But the yagna was not without its critics. Some fastidious kings and Brahmins compared it with Yudhishthira's Rajasuya and found it wanting.

Duryodhan's friends tried to please their prince, saying, 'This fire sacrifice of yours has surpassed all. We have seen nothing like this. You have shown the world that you are the best.'

However, Duryodhan was not happy. He knew, his Vaishnava Yagna was only a poor substitute for the Rajasuya and, with Dhritarashtra and Yudhishthira alive, he could never achieve this feather on his crown.

Karna could feel his friend's frustration. He held Duryodhan's arm and said, 'My friend, do not despair. When we destroy the Pandavas in the war, you will get your opportunity to conduct the Rajasuya sacrifice. Till then, have patience.' But to Duryodhan, Karna's words sounded as hollow and meaningless as those of the sycophant Brahmins. He freed his arm from Karna's grip and turned away. Karna was hurt. Blocking Duryodhan's path he said, 'Listen, my friend, today, I make this vow in your presence. Until I kill Arjun in the battlefield, I won't wash my feet, I won't eat meat, I won't drink wine or any other intoxicating drink, and I won't turn back anybody who asks something of me.'

A smile lit up Duryodhan's face. Karna sighed in relief.

37

The Story of Rishi Mudgal

ONE NIGHT, YUDHISHTHIRA HAD A STRANGE DREAM. HE SAW HIMSELF standing amidst a herd of deer. The deer were crying and praying to him. They said, 'O King, we are the last few surviving deer of this Dvaitavana Forest. Your mighty brothers have killed most of us for food. We pray to you to spare us and let our tribe grow.'

Yudhishthira felt pity for the deer. Since the Pandavas arrived, they had been hunting deer for their meat, not realizing that the deer population was dwindling and on the verge of extinction, thanks to their protracted stay there. He called his brothers and told them about his dream. He said, 'We have one year and eight more months to live in the forest, and deer meat is what we need to survive. So I have decided to leave Dvaitavana and spare the deer of this forest. We'll return to Kamyaka Forest and spend the rest of our exile there. It has a large deer population and should be enough to sustain us.'

The Pandavas moved back to the Kamyaka Forest and built their hermitage there. After the completion of their eleventh year, one day, the great Rishi Vyasa visited them. After the customary greetings, the Pandavas gathered around him to listen to his words of wisdom.

Vyasa narrated the story of Rishi Mudgal: 'In Kurukshetra lived a sage named Mudgal. He followed a severe path of penance and asceticism, and wouldn't consume anything that wasn't necessary for the minimal sustenance of himself and his family. Just like a bird, he would collect and eat the grains left in the fields after harvesting; that too only once every fifteen days. On full-moon and new-moon days, he would perform the fire sacrifice while his wife cooked the grains in a magic pot. He would then feed his guests first, and refuse nobody who came for a meal. He had no shortage of food for his guests, for the remaining food in his magic pot would increase whenever a new guest arrived. After the guests had had their fill, Mudgal would eat whatever was left in the pot.

'One day, when Mudgal was preparing his fortnightly meal, the great sage Durvasa arrived. Durvasa was known for his ill-temper and his tendency to curse anyone who displeased him. People tried to avoid him at any cost. Durvasa, his head shaven and no clothes on, arrived, shouting and yelling like a mad man. He hurled nasty insults at whoever crossed his path. He stood in front of Mudgal and said, "I am hungry. Where is my food?"

'Mudgal served Durvasa everything he had in the pot. Durvasa ate everything and when he was full, he scraped off the remaining food from the pot, smeared it on his body, and left, leaving nothing for Mudgal and his family.

'After fifteen days, Durvasa visited again, and did the same thing. Mudgal went hungry again. For six consecutive full moons and new moons, Durvasa tortured Mudgal by leaving no food for him to eat. Mudgal didn't complain. Durvasa was astounded by Mudgal's patience and virtue. He said, "Mudgal, you have proved yourself to be a selfless man and a true giver. I am impressed with your sacrifice. Words of praise about your patience and generosity have reached the heavens. You have earned the privilege of going to the heavens alive."

'Soon, a fantastic airship arrived at Mudgal's hermitage. A devadoot, messenger from heaven, stepped off the ship and said, "O great sage, I have come to take you to the heavens. Please step into this chariot and I will take you there."

'However, Mudgal was not keen on boarding the craft. He asked, "I am glad that the gods have been kind enough to invite me to the heavens. Before I board your ship, tell me, what are the advantages and disadvantages of going to the heavens?"

'The messenger was taken aback. He had never heard a question like this before. It was rare for a mortal human to go to the heavens alive. Who would ask about its advantages and disadvantages? He answered, "Only those who are virtuous and selfless donors, who have mastered their senses and their desires, and those killed in wars, can go to the heavens. In heaven, there is no pain—only happiness exists. Once there, you won't have any feelings of sorrow and greed. You won't experience jealousy or hatred. You won't feel tired and your heart will always be filled with joy. You will live in eternal peace. But it has disadvantages too. In the heavens, you can enjoy the fruit of your good karma, but you won't gain any new karma. So, for example, if the riches and facilities of some other inhabitants cause negative feelings in you, you might lose your karma. Losing your karma can cause you to fall from the heavens back to earth."

'With his joined palms, he said, "Please accept my apologies. I do not want the pleasures of the heavens. I seek that state of existence where men are not only free from pain and sorrow, but they also don't have to fear about coming back to this wretched human life."

'After the messenger left for the heavens, Mudgal began his search through the practise of knowledge. After many years of arduous meditation, he attained moksha, the state of ultimate freedom from the cycle of birth and death.'

Durvasa's Visit

While the Pandavas were spending their penultimate year of exile in the Kamyaka Forest, Rishi Durvasa landed in Hastinapur with 10,000 of his disciples. He went to Duryodhan and said, 'My son, I want to be a guest in your palace. I hope you have no problem with that.'

Duryodhan was aware of Durvasa's temper and knew that if he said or did anything to displease him, Durvasa would punish him with some horrible curse. On the other hand, if he could please the powerful rishi, he might give him a boon. He welcomed the rishi and said, 'O great Rishi, we are honoured to have you as our guest. Please feel at home and let us know how we can serve you.'

Durvasa and his disciples settled down in the palace. Duryodhan instructed the servants and staff to ensure that the rishi had nothing to complain about. Durvasa and his disciples exploited Duryodhan's hospitality to the fullest. Sometimes he would say, 'I am hungry. I must get my lunch as soon as I return from my bath in the river.' He would then leave the palace while the servants and cooks scurried about to prepare his meal. But then he would not return till late in the evening and go to bed. Sometimes he would say, 'I am not hungry, so don't arrange for my meal.' Then, moments later, he'd declare that he was starving and would ask to be served his food. Sometimes, he would wake up in the middle of the night and ask for his meals. Duryodhan and his staff were tired of Durvasa's whims and demands. Still, Duryodhan and his staff served him without losing their patience.

A few days later, the sage called Duryodhan and said, 'My son, it is time for me to leave. I am pleased with your hospitality and would like to grant you a wish. Ask what you want.'

Duryodhan was expecting such an offer and had planned for this moment with his partners in crime Karna, Dushasana and Shakuni. He said, 'O great rishi, if you'd like to grant me a wish, please go to the Kamyaka Forest and enjoy the hospitality of my brother Yudhishthira. I would also request you to arrive at their hermitage in the late afternoon, after Draupadi has finished her meal.' Durvasa agreed.

Soon, Durvasa with his 10,000 disciples arrived in the forest and knocked on Yudhishthira's door. The brothers were enjoying their afternoon siesta after a heavy meal. Yudhishthira woke up and opened the door. Durvasa said, 'Dear Yudhishthira, we are here to stay with you as your guests for a few days, and would like to rest and recuperate here. Do you mind?'

Yudhishthira was flabbergasted. He replied, 'O great rishi, we consider ourselves fortunate to have you as our guest. It is a great honour. Please come in and let me know how I can serve you.'

Durvasa replied, 'We are hungry. Please arrange for our meals while we take a dip in the river.' The sage then left with his disciples to bathe.

Yudhishthira went to Draupadi and informed her about their revered guest. Draupadi was dismayed. It was only a few moments ago that she had finished her meal. The magic pot given by the Sun god was now empty. She couldn't cook anything in that pot that day. How would she serve her guests? What would she serve? She knew that if the ill-tempered rishi didn't find a hot meal ready for him when he returned, he would be mad with rage and would punish them with a terrible curse. Left with no option, Draupadi prayed to Krishna, 'O Lord, please save us from this awful crisis. You saved me once from that brute Dushasana, now save me from Durvasa.'

Within moments, Draupadi found Krishna standing next to her. He smiled at her and said, 'Draupadi, here I am. Before you say anything, give me some food. I am starving.'

Draupadi was in tears. She said, 'I am sorry, Krishna, I have nothing to offer you. The divine pot contains food as long as I don't eat. After my meal, the pot becomes empty. I have finished my meal and the pot doesn't have a single grain left in it.'

Krishna said, 'You must be kidding. I don't believe you. Bring me the pot.'

Draupadi went to the kitchen and brought back the pot. Krishna looked inside and, after a thorough search, he picked up something from a corner of the pot. 'Here is a grain!' he exclaimed. 'It has a little bit of vegetable with it too.' He put the grain in his mouth and chewed it with great pleasure before swallowing it. 'Ah, I am full. I feel much better now.'

Krishna said to Sahadev: 'Go and fetch the rishis for their meal.' Though puzzled, Sahadev didn't question Krishna's intentions and left to call the rishis.

In the meantime, Durvasa and his clan were taking a bath in the river. Suddenly, they felt bloated and full, as if they had just eaten a huge meal. They turned to each other in surprise as they let out loud burps.

One of the disciples said, 'Sir, we feel as if we've already had a big meal. How can we go back to Yudhishthira's ashram and eat?'

Durvasa massaged his belly and said, 'We committed a grave mistake by asking Yudhishthira to prepare a meal for us for no reason. Now if we go back to him and refuse to eat, they'd be offended, and the son of Dharma could curse us. I suggest we leave the forest.'

When Sahadev reached the riverbank, the rishis were gone. The Pandavas couldn't relax, for they worried that Rishi Durvasa might return in the middle of the night and ask for food. Krishna assured them, 'Don't worry about Durvasa. He has left for good and would never come back to bother you.'

The five brothers and Draupadi bowed to Krishna and said, 'O Lord, just as a raft saves a drowning man, you rescued us from this unforeseen crisis. How can we ever thank you?'

Krishna smiled and said, 'I am your friend. Call me whenever you need me.' Saying so, he disappeared.

38

The Abduction of Draupadi

I T WAS A BRIGHT SPRING MORNING IN THE KAMYAKA FOREST. THE PANDAVAS woke up early and after completing their prayers, they sat down for breakfast. Draupadi served them milk and fruit gathered from the forest. While the brothers enjoyed their meal, Draupadi said, 'We are out of meat. If you'd like to have meat, I suggest you go hunting.'

Bheem smiled, 'That should not be a problem. Give me an hour and I will get enough meat for all of us.'

'I won't let you go alone,' said Draupadi. 'Remember the time when the serpent Nahusha almost killed you?'

Bheem laughed again. 'That was an exception. Nahusha was no ordinary serpent.'

Yudhishthira finished his meal and stood up to wash his hands. 'Don't worry, we will all go hunting right now. Priest Dhaumya will stay here with Draupadi and her maid.'

The Pandavas picked up their spears, maces, bows and arrows, and left the hermitage to look for wild boar, deer and buffalo. As they walked out of the hermitage, Yudhishthira had a strange feeling.

Something was not right, but he couldn't figure out what. He turned to Draupadi and said, 'Panchali, be careful. Do not leave the hermitage. Stay alert.'

Draupadi smiled. 'I will be fine. Nobody would dare to harm the wife of the mighty Pandavas.'

Once the Pandavas left, Draupadi called her maid and said, 'Let's go to the river and fetch some water.'

King Jayadrath, husband of Duryodhan's sister Dushala, was travelling through the forest to join the swayamvara of the princess of Salwa. He was accompanied by hundreds of horsemen, charioteers and foot soldiers. As the entourage passed the riverbank, Jayadrath noticed Draupadi bathing in the river. Her beauty struck him like a thunderbolt. He had never seen a woman more beautiful in his life. From his moving chariot, he kept staring at Draupadi as she stepped out of the river and walked towards the hermitage with her pail of water. When she disappeared from view, Jayadrath came to his senses. He called his trusted friend Katikasya and said, 'Did you see that gorgeous woman? I want her.'

Katikasya said, 'She is pretty. But, Jayadrath, why do you want this forest dweller? Soon, you will have the princess of Salwa as your wife.'

'If I get this woman, I don't care for the Salwa princess,' said Jayadrath. 'Go, follow that woman. Find out who she is. Ask her if she would be mine.'

Katikasya left the caravan and followed Draupadi to the hermitage. There, he asked Draupadi, 'Who are you, pretty lady? What are you doing in this god-forsaken forest?'

Draupadi felt amused by this funny looking man. 'Before I answer you, tell me, who are you? What are you doing here?' she asked.

Katikasya was relieved that the woman wasn't angry with him. He came closer and said, 'I am Katikasya, the son of King Surath. I am here with King Jayadrath and his army. I am here at his behest ...'

Before he could finish his sentence, Jayadrath arrived at the hermitage in his chariot. Draupadi was surprised that Jayadrath did not know who she was. After all, he was her brother-in law. Maybe they never had a chance to meet before. Draupadi looked at Katikasya and with a raised voice, she said, 'I am Krishnaa, daughter of King Drupad. The mighty Pandavas, the rulers of Indraprastha, are my husbands. They went hunting and would come back soon. Please ask Prince Jayadrath to come to the hermitage and give me the chance to extend my hospitality. King Yudhishthira would be pleased to welcome you.'

Captivated by Draupadi's beauty, Jayadrath lost his sense of time and place. He stepped off his chariot and entered the hermitage with six of his attendants. He faced Draupadi and, with a big smile on his face, he said, 'Thank you for your offer. But you'd serve me better if you came with me. Your poor homeless husbands can't take care of a beauty like you. They don't deserve you. You don't have to suffer anymore. Come with me. I will make you the queen of my kingdom of Sindhu-Saubir. Come, step into my chariot.'

Draupadi was furious. 'Hold your tongue, Jayadrath,' she hissed. 'How dare you insult my husbands? Do you want to herald in your death?'

Jayadrath laughed. 'The Pandavas don't scare me, my darling. Get into my chariot or cry and plead for mercy.'

'Never! Who do you think I am? A weak and helpless woman? I warn you, leave these grounds. Else, you will curse yourself when you die a painful death at the hands of my husbands.'

Mad with lust, Jayadrath grabbed Draupadi's arm. Draupadi pulled away and with a powerful blow threw him to the ground. She cried out, 'Dhaumya, where are you? Help me!'

Dhaumya, the priest, was deep in meditation and Draupadi's cries didn't reach him. Draupadi's maid came out of her hut and saw Draupadi trembling with rage, Jayadrath splayed on the ground. She ran to Draupadi and stood in front of her to guard her from Jayadrath's assault. Jayadrath stood up and shook off the dust from his body. He grabbed the maid and threw her aside. The girl hit her head on a tree stump and lost consciousness. With a quick move, Jayadrath lifted Draupadi off her feet and ran to his chariot. Draupadi screamed, 'Dhaumya! Dhaumya! Help ... help me!'

Her cries finally reached Dhaumya's ears. He woke up from his meditation, ran out of his hut and saw Jayadrath pin down Draupadi on the chariot seat and order the charioteer to leave.

Dhaumya ran after the vehicle. 'Stop! Stop, Jayadrath. If you want to live, stop now.'

Jayadrath didn't pay heed to Dhaumya's cries. His chariot and his friends, along with his horsemen and soldiers, raced as fast as they could through the forest. Dhaumya merged with the foot soldiers and followed Jayadrath.

Deep in the forest, Yudhishthira was aiming his arrow at a deer. Such a wonderful creature, he thought. Yet, he must kill this animal to provide for his family. It was his duty. He aimed again, but suddenly he felt his heart leap, and a chill run down his spine. He saw the deer raise its head, as if it had heard something. Before Yudhishthira could release his arrow, the deer jumped and ran away. Yudhishthira put down his bow and looked above. The birds in the forest sounded restless. He heard the animals running away to avert some unknown danger. Yudhishthira felt uneasy.

Bheem stepped out of the forest with two huge wild boars on his shoulder.

'Crushed their skulls with a stone,' he said. 'These would be tasty.'

Arjun brought with him two deer carcasses. Nakul and Sahadev brought their share of meat with them. The moment Arjun laid his eyes on Yudhishthira, he knew something was wrong. 'What is it?' he asked.

Yudhishthira said, 'We must go back to the ashram now. I feel something dreadful has happened.' The Pandavas mounted their chariots and raced towards the hermitage.

As they entered the hermitage, they found the maid sitting on the ground, crying. Yudhishthira picked her up. 'What happened? Where is Draupadi?'

'King Jayadrath was here. He took the queen in his chariot by force. Priest Dhaumya is following them. You must catch him before he goes too far.'

Bheem stomped the ground and said, 'Jayadrath! How dare he touch Panchali? I will crush his bones to dust.'

Yudhishthira said, 'We should not wait. He can't move fast in this forest. We should be able to catch him.'

Soon enough, the Pandavas could see the cloud of dust from Jayadrath's horses. Dhaumya saw the Pandavas and screamed, 'Bheem, Arjun, come quick. Draupadi is in Jayadrath's chariot in the front.'

Yudhishthira said, 'Don't worry. We will free Draupadi from Jayadrath's clutches.'

Jayadrath saw the Pandavas chasing him. Scared, he called out his accompanying kings and guards and said, 'Stop the Pandavas. We out number them many times over. They can't beat us.' The kings turned around to fight the Pandavas while Jayadrath ordered his charioteer to speed up.

The Pandavas fell upon Jayadrath's army like a tornado. A single blow from Bheem's mace killed Katikasya. Arjun's arrows decimated Jayadrath's army. Those who survived the initial blow ran for their lives. Jayadrath panicked. He pushed Draupadi off his chariot and sped away.

Yudhishthira picked her up on his chariot. Bheem said to Yudhishthira, 'You go back to the ashram with Draupadi, Nakul and Sahadev. Arjun and I will chase Jayadrath and send him to his death.'

Yudhishthira said, 'No, Bheem, don't kill him. He is our cousin Dushala's husband.'

Angry Draupadi spat out, 'If you care for me, you must kill that evil scoundrel. An enemy that steals one's kingdom or wife should not be spared.'

Arjun and Bheem left to catch Jayadrath, while Yudhishthira went back to their hermitage. The brothers' fast chariots soon caught up with Jayadrath. Arjun's arrows killed his horses and his chariot came to a crashing halt. Jayadrath jumped off and ran for his life. Chasing him, Arjun shouted, 'Jayadrath, why are you running away? It is with this courage that you went to steal other men's wife. Stop running if you want to live.' But Jayadrath kept running.

Bheem ran up to Jayadrath, grabbed him by his hair, and thrashed him to the ground. The king screamed in pain as Bheem crushed his head with his knee and beat him to a pulp. Arjun said, 'Brother Bheem, please stop. Yudhishthira instructed us to not kill him.'

Angry Bheem released Jayadrath. 'This devil dared to insult Krishnaa,' he said. 'He does not deserve to live. Our kind brother always prevents me from doing the right thing.' He pulled out a sharp, half-moon arrow and shaved off Jayadrath's head. Grabbing him by his neck, he said, 'You fool, if you'd like to live, say that you are our slave.'

Jayadrath winced in pain and said, 'I am your slave.'

Bheem shook him and said, 'Promise, you'd say this to everybody.'

'I promise.'

Bheem dragged Jayadrath to his chariot and took him to their ashram. He threw Jayadrath at Yudhishthira's feet and said, 'Jayadrath has agreed to be our slave.'

Yudhishthira took one look at Jayadrath and said, 'Bheem, let him go.'

Incredulous, Bheem turned to Draupadi and asked, 'What do you want me to do with him?'

Draupadi shot Jayadrath a sharp look filled with disgust and said, 'You have shaved his head and made him a slave. He has been humiliated enough. Let him go.'

Jayadrath touched Yudhishthira's feet and thanked him for his generosity. Yudhishthira said, 'I release you from slavery. Never try to do anything like this ever.'

With his head held low, Jayadrath left the ashram. He was burning with anger. He must have his revenge, he thought. He went to the mountains and sat down to worship Lord Shiva. Impressed by his strict penance, Lord Shiva appeared before him and offered a boon. Jayadrath said, 'Give me the power to defeat the Pandavas.'

'That is impossible,' said Shiva. 'But this much I can grant you— during the Great War, you'd be able to stall them for one day.'

Jayadrath returned to his kingdom with the certainty that at least for one day, he'd be able to avenge his humiliation.

39

The Story of Savitri and Satyavan

HEARING ABOUT THE UNFORTUNATE INCIDENT OF DRAUPADI'S ATTEMPTED abduction, Rishi Markandeya came to visit the Pandavas. Yudhishthira narrated the incident to him and said, 'I feel sorry for Draupadi. She has sacrificed a lot for our sake and saved us from slavery after I lost the game of dice with Duryodhan. She has been looking after us during our long exile. And now she had to suffer this humiliation from Jayadrath. Is there any other woman who has done so much for her husband?'

Markandeya asked, 'Have you heard the story of Savitri?' The Pandavas gathered around Markandeya to listen to Savitri's story.

'In the olden days,' Markandeya began, 'there lived a pious king named Aswapati in the kingdom of Madra. With Lord Brahma's blessings, Aswapati's queen gave birth to a beautiful girl named Savitri. Savitri grew up to be a learned woman, well-versed in the scriptures. Her strong and powerful personality made her parents proud, but made it difficult for her to find suitors. Men were too scared to approach her. Her worried father called Savitri and said,

"My dear, it is my duty to give your hand in marriage to a suitable man. Unfortunately, nobody is willing to accept you as their wife. You are wise and learned. I believe, if you look yourself, you should be able to find the man you deserve." Savitri agreed. With a team of advisors, she mounted a chariot and left the palace looking for a husband.

'A few months later, while Aswapati was busy talking to Rishi Narada, Savitri returned to the palace. Narada asked, "Where is your daughter returning from? She has grown up and you should arrange for her marriage."

'Telling Narada the reason behind Savitri's trip, the king asked his daughter if she had been successful in her mission.

'"Dyumatsena, the king of Salwa, lost his eyesight due to some unfortunate event. His kingdom was taken over by his enemies. He fled to the forest with his young boy and has been living there as a hermit ever since. The boy has grown up to be a handsome young man. His name is Satyavan. I have chosen him as my husband," smiled Savitri.

'Narada nodded: "My dear Savitri, you are making a mistake in selecting your husband. Satyavan is indeed suitable for you in all aspects. But his life is short. One year from now, he will breathe his last."

'King Aswapati knew Narada's prediction could never go wrong. He held Savitri's hand and urged her, "My dear daughter, you must find someone else."

'Without batting an eyelid, she replied, "I cannot go back on my word. His life may be short, but Satyavan will be my husband for life."

'Aswapati had no option but to hand over Savitri to Satyavan as his wife.

'After the wedding, Savitri carried out all her duties as Satyavan's wife. But the thought of his impending death never left her mind.

'Four days before the predicted date of Satyavan's death, Savitri announced that she'd go on a fast for the next three days. Her father-in-law, Dyumatsena, tried to dissuade her. But Savitri was firm.

'On the predicted day of Satyavan's death, Savitri finished all her chores and rituals before noon. Her parents-in-law asked her to break her fast. She offered to break it after sunset.

'In the afternoon, Satyavan picked up his axe and was about to leave the hermitage to fetch some firewood. Savitri insisted that she wanted to go with him.

'Surprised, Satyavan said, "You've never been to the forest. The path is difficult and perilous. Besides, you are tired from fasting. You won't be able to bear the strain."

'Savitri insisted, "I am not tired; you cannot stop me from going with you."

'Satyavan gave up and they went to fetch wood. After walking for hours, they arrived deep inside the forest. Along the way, Savitri did not take her eyes off her husband for a moment. She was worried: if the prediction was correct, Satyavan would drop dead any moment.

'Satyavan stopped in front of a huge tree, raised his axe and began to chop it. Soon, his body began to sweat. He grabbed his forehead, dropped down on his knees and said, "Savitri I am not feeling well. I feel my head is about to burst in pain."

'As they sat down, Satyavan rested his head on Savitri's lap, motionless. Savitri knew that Narada's prediction had come true.

'Moments later, Savitri saw a huge, dark man standing next to them. Dressed in crimson clothes, gold jewellery and carrying a trap in hand, he looked at Satyavan with bloodshot eyes. Savitri gently put Satyavan's head to the ground and stood up. Palms joined respectfully, she said, "Your appearance suggests that you must be a god. Please be kind and introduce yourself."

'"I am Yama, the god of death. Your husband is dead, and I have come to fetch his soul."

'The soul left Satyavan's body and entered the trap. Yama shut the trap, put it back on his belt and began to walk away. Savitri didn't cry, neither did she stay with the body. Instead, she started following Yama.

'Yama stopped and turned towards Savitri: "Why are you following me? You should go back and arrange for your husband's funeral and last rites."

'"It is my duty to follow my husband wherever he goes ... or wherever he is taken. That's what the scriptures say."

'Yama was taken aback by her answer. Smiling awkwardly, he said, "You are right, but mortals cannot accompany me. You must stop. Let me grant you a wish. Ask anything you want, except Satyavan's life."

'Savitri said, "Lord, return the eyesight of my father-in-law."

'"Your wish is granted. Now go back. You look tired."

'"Why would I be tired?" retorted Savitri. "I never tire of my husband's companionship. Wherever he goes, I go. Lord, you are the wisest of the wise, and it is said, the companionship of the wise should always be pursued."

'"You speak well," said Yama. "Ask for another boon—anything except your husband's life."

'"Let my father-in law get his kingdom back."

'"So be it. Now stop following me." Yama resumed walking.

'Continuing her pursuit, Savitri said, "Lord, you maintain the balance of life on earth. You take souls away when their time comes, not because you wish to, but as per their Karma. That is your duty. You know, people on earth are weak, mortal. They have no control over their destiny. Wise men are kind to those who surrender, even if they are not a friend."

'"Your words come from the bottom of your heart and are a pleasure to listen to. Ask another boon, anything but Satyavan's life. And then you leave me alone." Yama was getting impatient.

'"I wish to bear a handsome son from Satyavan," said Savitri without batting an eyelid.

'"So be it. You will have a handsome son. Now go back." Yama increased his pace.

'Savitri persisted. She ran after Yama and said, "Wise men always follow the path of Dharma. They don't repent after giving a gift. Their generosity is never wasted. Prayers and wishes to them don't go unfulfilled. They are our saviours."

'"You are right. Go ahead, ask for another boon—my last and final boon." Yama waited for Savitri to speak.

"Savitri paused for a while and then spoke. "Lord, you have rewarded me with your boons because you felt I deserve them. Now I ask for my final reward. Please give me back my husband's life. Without him, I cannot enjoy any gift you give me. You granted me Satyavan's son. Without Satyavan, that wish won't be fulfilled either. Grant me my wish and your reward will not go in vain."

'Yama realized he was ensnared. He smiled and said, "You got me. Well, so be it. I will release Satyavan and he will live again. Enjoy your long life with your husband." Yama released Satyavan's life force from his trap and walked away.

'Savitri went back to Satyavan and took his head back on her lap. She gently rocked him and said, "Wake up, my love. It is getting dark. We must return to our hermitage."

'Satyavan woke up and said, "How long have I been sleeping? Yes, we should go back. Father must be worried."'

Contented, Markandeya paused to take a breath. Then he continued, 'The next morning, Dyumatsena got back his eyesight. Messengers from his lost kingdom came and informed him that the people of Salwa had overthrown the evil ruler, and that they wanted Dyumatsena back on the throne. So you see, Yudhishthira, a powerful and pious woman who loves her husband can work miracles. Draupadi is as powerful and wise as Savitri. She can do wonders for you.'

Yudhishthira and his brothers knelt before Markandeya to pay their respects. Draupadi stood nearby, a faint smile playing on her face.

40

Karna's Gift

I T WAS A PLEASANT DAY IN THE HEAVENS. INDRA WAS ENJOYING AN enchanting performance by the apsaras. As he watched the beautiful jewellery and costumes of the dancers, he remembered a promise he had made to Arjun. When Arjun was visiting the heavens to collect divine weapons from Indra, he had expressed his concern about Karna. Arjun had said, 'Karna's skills with his weapons don't bother me. What worries me is his body armour, the one he was born with. It is impenetrable to any weapon. My arrows would bounce off his chest like bamboo sticks.'

Indra knew Arjun's concern to be valid. With his armour and earrings, it would be impossible to kill Karna. He had promised Arjun that he'll strip the armour from Karna's body before Arjun's exile ended.

The Pandavas were now in their twelfth year of exile and to keep his promise, he had to act fast. He knew that Karna had earned the reputation of a great philanthropist who never refused anybody who asked for a gift. Indra decided to disguise himself as a Brahmin beggar and ask for Karna's armour as alms.

The plan, however, didn't stay a secret. Karna's father, the Sun god, came to know of Indra's plot. He appeared before Karna in his dream and said, 'My son, Indra wants to steal your armour to help the Pandavas. He knows that you would never refuse alms to a beggar. He plans to visit you as a Brahmin beggar and ask for your armour. Do not oblige him.'

Karna asked, 'Who are you? Why are you telling me this?'

'I am your father, the Sun god. I am here to warn you. If you give Indra your armour, you will make yourself vulnerable to the Pandavas.'

'The world knows, if a poor Brahmin asks for something from me—even my life—I wouldn't turn him down. I know that if I give away my armour, it will help the Pandavas. Still, if Indra begs for it, I will grant him his wish. The king of the gods may not care for his honour, but I do.'

The Sun god tried his best to dissuade his son, but Karna remained adamant. In his sleep, Karna said, 'Lord, please do not worry about me. I have been trained by the great Parashurama, and I won't let it go in vain. Even if Arjun thinks himself to be as powerful as Kartaviry Arjuna, I will defeat him.'

The Sun god knew it was futile to try further. He said, 'Well, then at least listen to this advice. In return for your armour, ask Indra to give you the deadliest, most infallible weapon that'd destroy any target on whom it is aimed.' Karna agreed.

The next day, Karna arrived at the banks of the river for his daily worship. First, he would bathe in the river and then, standing in the cool waters, he would pray. During this time, Brahmins from far and near would gather to ask him for help. Some asked for money, some would request for land, some demanded cattle and some hoped to get food. Karna would grant all their wishes and they would return happy, singing his praises.

As always, Karna stepped into the river and took three dips in the water. As he rose from the water and shook his head, little streams of water ran down his chest. As he wiped off the water from his chest, he felt the steel-like armour inside his skin. He remembered the dream and his father's warning. A faint smile appeared on his lips. He closed his eyes and with palms joined, he prayed to the Sun.

Then, Karna waded through the water and walked towards the bank where the Brahmins waited. Any other day, there would have been a long line of favour seekers. But that day, only one Brahmin stood waiting. Karna smiled and asked, 'O Brahmin, tell me, what can I offer you?'

The Brahmin, with an apprehensive look, said, 'They say, you are the greatest giver and you grant any wish someone asks of you. Is that true?'

A tinge of pride flashed in Karna's eyes but he controlled himself and said, 'Yes, I took a vow not to turn back anyone who asks for something from me. Tell me, Brahmin, what do you want?'

'Karna, you are a great warrior and a great king. But what I want might be a tall order even for you. Think twice before you commit.'

Karna felt insulted. 'There is nothing in the world I cannot give you. Ask.'

'If you insist! ... I want the armour and the earrings that adorn your body since your birth. Cut them out and give them to me.'

So the Sun god's warning was not a mere dream. Karna took a second to regain his composure. In a calm voice, he said, 'Brahmin, I can give you money, jewellery, cattle, land, even my kingdom. But how can I give you my armour? They are a part of my body, and they make me invincible. Ask for anything else, and I won't disappoint you.'

'I told you to think twice before you committed. I want nothing else. If you can't give me what I ask for, I will go back. So, Karna is not the great giver he claims to be.' The Brahmin turned around to walk away.

'Stop, Lord Indra,' said Karna. 'You may shed off your disguise. I knew who you were the moment you asked for my armour. I will give you what you want. But, isn't it strange of you, the king of the gods, to pray for a gift from a mere mortal like me? Rather, you should be granting me a boon. That is the appropriate thing to do.'

Indra smiled and said, 'The Sun god must have warned you. I should have known better. Alright, I will grant you a boon. Ask for anything except my thunderbolt.'

Karna said, 'I will give you my armour and earrings. In exchange, you give me a weapon guaranteed to destroy any enemy it is hurled upon.'

Indra thought for a while and said, 'I can give you such a weapon. But it would kill only one person, and then the weapon would come back to me.'

'That should be enough. I desire to kill only one person,' replied Karna. 'The man whom I fear the most.'

'The man whom you want to kill is protected by the one whom the entire world worships as the supreme lord—Krishna. Under Krishna's protection, your enemy is indestructible.'

Karna's face flushed as anger surged within him. He clenched his fist and said, 'I don't care who protects him. You needn't care for that either. You give me the weapon that'd kill the mightiest of the mighty, and I will give you my armour.'

'So be it.'

And so, Karna pulled out his knife and raised it to cut open his chest. Before the knife touched his skin, he stopped and said, 'Lord Indra, I will cut open my chest and give you my armour. I will cut off

the earrings from my ears. But you must ensure that my body doesn't get deformed.'

'I assure you, there will be no wound in your body,' Indra assured him.

Karna plunged the knife inside his chest and in a slow but firm move, he cut open the skin and pulled out the armour. Next, he held his left earring with one hand and cut it out with the other. He did the same for his right earring. Blood gushed out of his wounds, but Karna didn't even wince. He picked up the armour and earrings, and handed them to Indra. As soon as Indra took the blood-soaked armour and earrings, Karna's wounds disappeared from his body, as if nothing had happened.

Indra raised his hand to the sky, and the deadly Ekaghni weapon appeared in his fist. Indra handed over the weapon to Karna and said, 'Karna, here is the Ekaghni you asked for. Remember, you can use it only once. However, if you use it when you have other weapons at your disposal and your life is not in danger, the weapon will turn back on you and destroy you.'

Karna picked up the weapon and said, 'Don't worry. I will use it only when all my other weapons have failed, and I have no other option to defend myself.'

Indra took the armour and earrings with him and left. Karna walked to his chariot, gently placed the Ekaghni in his quiver and said, 'Arjun, you cannot escape me now. Your father has handed me your death warrant. Enjoy the limited time you have on earth.' He mounted his chariot and sped towards Hastinapur to give Duryodhan the good news.

41

Yudhishthira and the Crane

IT WAS A FINE MORNING IN KAMYAKA FOREST. YUDHISHTHIRA WAS SITTING under a peepal tree with his brothers, discussing their strategy for the thirteenth year, when a Brahmin came and stood before them. Yudhishthira said, 'O Brahmin, what brings you here? Is there something we can do for you?'

The Brahmin replied, 'O King Yudhishthira, I have a serious problem. I had left my bow-drill hanging on the branch of a tree. A deer came to eat the leaves and somehow the bow got stuck in his antlers. Scared, it ran away with the bow-drill. We tried to catch the deer but failed. Please help us get back our bow-drill. Without it, I won't be able to light the fire for my evening worship.'

The Brahmins used bow-drills to light fires and missing the evening fire worship would amount to a serious lapse.

Yudhishthira stood up and said, 'Don't worry. We will find the deer and get your bow-drill before your evening worship.'

The Pandavas picked up their weapons and walked into the forest, looking for the deer. A little later, they found the deer with a bow-drill stuck in its antlers. Nakul raised his bow and aimed, but before he could release the arrow, the deer jumped and ran away. The brothers chased the deer, but failed to catch it. They were drawn deeper and deeper into the forest.

The exhausted and frustrated brothers sat down in the shade of a banyan tree to cool off. Nakul said, 'What are we going to say to the Brahmin? We have never disappointed anyone who asked for our help. We have never deviated from the path of Dharma. Why did we fail today?'

Yudhishthira wiped off the sweat from his brow and said, 'Troubles and defeats can come in different forms. It isn't always possible to pinpoint the reasons. Only Dharma determines the consequences of our karma.'

Bheem said, 'I know the reason. We did not punish Dushasana for insulting Draupadi. It is for that sin that we are facing such a humiliating defeat.'

Arjun said in a bitter voice, 'I tolerated those insults from Karna and that's why we have failed today.'

Sahadev said, 'I didn't kill that evil Shakuni when he defeated us in that rigged game of dice. That's the reason for our failure.'

The heat and exhaustion made them thirsty. Yudhishthira said to Nakul: 'Climb up this tree and see if you can find a lake nearby.'

Nakul made his way to the top of the tree and looked around. At a distance, he saw some trees and vegetation that grow near water bodies. He also heard the cries of cranes and waterfowls. Climbing down, he said, 'There must be a lake nearby. Let me take this quiver and fetch some water.'

Nakul ran through the forest towards the place. Soon, he arrived at a beautiful lake surrounded by palm trees. Waterfowls, cranes and swans played in the crystal-clear waters. Nakul's mouth was parched. He knelt by the water to have a drink when a voice rang out from above: 'Stop! This lake belongs to me. Before you drink this water, you must answer my questions.'

Nakul looked around but couldn't see anybody. He was too thirsty to play games. He ignored the voice, cupped his hands, and dipped them into the lake to scoop up some water. But before the water could touch his lips, Nakul's heart stopped and he collapsed to the ground, dead.

Yudhishthira and the other brothers were waiting for Nakul. It shouldn't take so long to fetch water, thought Yudhishthira. He called Sahadev and said, 'Go, find Nakul and bring some water for us.'

Sahadev followed Nakul's tracks and arrived at the lake. He was delighted to see the clear water of the lake. He was so excited that he didn't even notice Nakul's dead body lying on the lakeshore. As he was about to take a drink, the voice rang out again. Sahadev ignored the voice and he too fell dead beside the lake.

Yudhishthira then sent Arjun, followed by Bheem. Both experienced the same sequence of events and suffered the same fate as Nakul and Sahadev. Realizing that things might have gone seriously wrong, Yudhishthira picked up his weapon and followed the path of his brothers. Soon, he too arrived at the lake, the beauty of which enchanted him. The gentle sound of water lapping on the lakeshore enhanced his thirst. He walked towards the water and what he saw was the worst sight of his life—his siblings lying dead with their weapons scattered all around. Yudhishthira was shocked. Engulfed in pain and trembling like a leaf, he dropped on his knees next to his brothers. He felt like crying out loud, but no sound emerged from his parched throat. How could such gallant warriors die such an unceremonious death? Who could have killed them? Could it be some assassin employed by Duryodhan and Shakuni? He couldn't find any wounds on his brothers' bodies, nor any footmarks on the ground. He stood up and looked around. He stepped into the water and, as the cold water touched his feet, thirst gripped his throat again. He dipped his cupped hands into the water to have a drink when the voice rang out again, 'Stop, Yudhishthira. Look at me. I am the crane sitting on the tree above you. I own this lake. You cannot drink this water without answering my questions. Your brothers ignored me, and I have sent them to their end. You too will die if you don't obey me.'

Yudhishthira looked up and saw a huge crane sitting on top of a tree next to him. Yudhishthira knew this couldn't be an ordinary crane. He looked up and, with his hands joined, said, 'No ordinary being could kill my valiant brothers. You must be a god or some celestial being. I bow to you. Please be kind and identify yourself.'

The huge crane came down from the treetop and stood before Yudhishthira on one foot. The bird was as tall as the palm tree. Its eyes glowed like the sun. In a thunderous voice, the bird said, 'I am Yaksha. I warned your brothers several times, but they defied me and tried to drink the water. So I killed them. You must answer my questions before you can drink the water from this lake.'

Yudhishthira replied, 'I do not intend to drink the water without your permission. Ask your questions and I will try to answer them to the best of my knowledge.'

'Tell me, Yudhishthira, who holds the Sun up in the sky? Who orbits around the Sun? Who sends the Sun to its rest? What is he established on?'

Yudhishthira answered, 'Brahman holds the Sun up in the sky, the gods orbit around the Sun. Dharma sends him to his rest, and it is the truth that establishes him.'

'What gives a Brahmin his divine attribute? What makes him a saint? What makes him human? What makes him evil?'

'Study of the Vedas and scriptures gives a Brahmin his divineness. Practice of penance and worship makes him a saint.

He is mortal, and that makes him a human. Speaking ill of others makes him evil.'

'What gives a Kshatriya his god-like qualities? Which practices make him a saint, a human and an evil being?'

'Acquiring skills with weapons gives him his god-like qualities. The practice of sacrifice and yagna makes him a saint. Fear makes him human. And to abandon someone who seeks refuge in him makes him evil.'

'Who is heavier than the earth? Who is taller than the sky? Who is faster than the wind? Who is more abundant than grass?'

'Mother is heavier than the earth. Father is taller than the sky. Our mind can race faster than the wind, and our thoughts are more abundant than grass.'

'Who doesn't close their eyes during sleep? Who doesn't move after birth? Who doesn't have a heart? Who grows with speed?'

'Fish don't close their eyes when they sleep. An egg doesn't move after birth. A rock doesn't have a heart. A river grows with speed.'

'Who is a friend of an expatriate, of a family person and of a sick person?'

'An expatriate's friend is his companion, a family person's friend is his spouse, and a sick person's friend is his doctor.'

'Giving up what makes a person popular? Quitting what rids a person of his grief? Forsaking what makes a man rich? Abandoning what makes a man happy?'

'Giving up ego makes a person popular. Quitting anger rids him of his grief. Forsaking desire makes a person rich. Abandoning greed makes him happy.'

'What is the most important message? What is strange? What is the best path? Who is happy? Answer these four questions and you can drink the water.'

Yudhishthira thought for a while and replied, 'Humans and animals are constantly being cooked with this illusory world as its pot, the sun as its fire, and the months and seasons as its utensils. This is the most important message. Animals are dying every moment, every day. Still they try to live and strive to become immortal. What can be stranger? The scriptures are many, so is knowledge. No two wise men agree on a single path of knowledge. Hence, the path taken by the majority of the wise is the path to follow. One who is free from debt, doesn't live abroad, and can afford a simple meal of vegetables a day, is the happiest person.'

Yaksha said, 'You have answered all my questions to my satisfaction. So I offer to revive one of your brothers. Tell me whom you'd like to see alive.'

Yudhishthira responded, 'If you so wish, please revive Nakul. I want him to be alive.'

Yaksha was curious. He asked, 'That is strange. I know Bheem is your favourite and Arjun is your strength. Instead of saving them, why would you want to save your stepbrother Nakul?'

Yudhishthira replied, 'Kunti and Madri are both our mothers. I want at least one son of each to live.'

Yaksha was satisfied with Yudhishthira's answer. He said, 'O King Yudhishthira, you are indeed the living embodiment of Dharma. Instead of wealth and might, you prefer the path of non-violence. I will grant life to all your brothers.'

With Yaksha's blessings, Bheem, Arjun, Nakul and Sahadev woke up from their death sleep. The brothers drank from the lake and felt refreshed and invigorated. Yudhishthira bowed to Yaksha and said, 'Lord, you stand in the lake on one foot in the form of a crane. I am sure you are not a Yaksha, because a Yaksha cannot kill my brothers. You must be a god. Please reveal yourself to us.'

The Yaksha shed the form of a crane and said, 'My son, I am your father—Dharma. I am pleased with you. I would like to give you a gift. Tell me what you want.'

Yudhishthira replied, 'We were searching for the bow-drill of the Brahmin. Please make sure that he is not deprived of his duty of performing the fire sacrifice.'

Dharma smiled: 'It was I who took the form of a deer and stole the bow-drill in order to test you.' Saying this, he returned the bow-drill to Yudhishthira. 'Ask for something else.'

Yudhishthira said, 'We have spent our twelve years in exile. Now we go into hiding for one year. Bless us such that nobody can recognize us in our thirteenth year.'

Dharma said, 'Don't worry. I bless you, even if you stay the way you are, nobody would be able to recognize you. Spend your thirteenth year in the kingdom of Virat. You would be able to live there in whatever way you wish.'

The Pandavas thanked Dharma and went back to the hermitage and returned the bow-drill to the Brahmin. The Brahmin thanked them and left happy, to perform his evening ritual of fire sacrifice.

42

The Pandavas Go Incognito

THE TWELVE YEARS OF EXILE WERE OVER. THE PANDAVAS HAD TO GO INTO hiding now.

Yudhishthira sat down with his brothers and Draupadi, and said, 'As per Lord Dharma's advice, we should spend the thirteenth year in Matsya, the kingdom of Virat, serving the king. I will take the guise of a dice player and propose that King Virat accept me as his court dice player. I will play with him, advise him and entertain him. Bheem, what would you do?'

'It's easy. I will serve as a cook in Virat's kitchen. I can also entertain him by fighting with elephants and bulls.'

'Arjun, what about you?' asked Yudhishthira.

'I will take the guise of a eunuch, dress as a woman, and teach music and dance to the ladies of the palace. It is a destiny that I must fulfil.'

Nakul chimed in, 'I am an expert with horses. I know all about them and can treat their illnesses. I will take refuge in King Virat's stables as his horse keeper.'

Sahadev added, 'I will be the caretaker of King Virat's cattle. I know how to take care of cows and I can serve him well.'

Yudhishthira then looked at Draupadi and said, 'Panchali, you are a princess and a queen. I wonder how you would handle the life of a servant.'

Draupadi smiled and said, 'A woman who agrees to serve as a maid of her own will is known as a sairindhri. I will serve Sudeshna, the queen of Virat, as her personal hairdresser and maid. I am sure she will treat me well.'

Yudhishthira was satisfied with the plan. 'Well, then. Let's prepare for our life in Virat. Let's see what fortune awaits us there.'

Yudhishthira summoned the men and women who had been accompanying them during their exile and said, 'Friends, as per our agreement with Duryodhan, we must now spend a year in hiding. You have supported us and cared for us all these years. Now, we must part ways. I request you to go back to Panchal and wait for us. If anybody asks, say you don't know anything about us.'

Dhaumya, the Pandava priest, held Yudhishthira's hand and said, 'Yudhishthira, you have always been a king and never have you served a king as his employee. You may be aware of the norms and rules of a commoner, but let me give you some advice on how to be a royal servant. You may be the king's favourite; still, never ride his chariot or sit on his throne. If not asked, do not offer the king any advice. Do not try to be friends with the queen or the ladies of the palace. Do not do the smallest of tasks without the knowledge of the king. While expressing an opinion, try to say what the king likes and what is good for him, but prefer that which is beneficial to him. Do not sit in front of the king, always sit to his right or left. Do not try to correct the king if he tells a lie. Do not show off your knowledge or prowess. Do not touch your mouth, shake your legs, or speak loudly in front of the king. If you see or hear something funny in the court, do not laugh like a maniac. One who tolerates both insults and appreciation with nonchalance, one who doesn't feel perturbed about doing any job that is asked of him, only he deserves to live in the palace and earn the king's trust. Use the costumes and jewellery given to you by the king, and you will be his favourite. Yudhishthira, follow these rules for a year and you will emerge from your exile a winner.'

Dhaumya blessed the Pandavas, mounted his chariot and headed towards Panchal.

The Pandavas began their trek on foot down the banks of the Yamuna towards the Matsya kingdom. Walking through perilous paths, crossing mountains and forests, they arrived at the outskirts of the state of Matsya. The long journey made them frail and weak. The sun had tanned their skin, the harsh weather had rendered their clothes tattered. Long hair and beard covered their faces. It was hard to recognize them as the rulers of Indraprastha.

Before entering the capital city of Virat, Yudhishthira said, 'If we enter the city with our weapons, people would be worried and doubt our intentions. Most warriors know Arjun's Gandiva bow. They'd recognize us the moment they see it.'

Arjun agreed, 'You are right. We cannot carry our weapons into the city. I saw a huge Sami tree on a hill near the cremation ground. Let's hide our weapons in it.'

The Pandavas went to the Sami tree and put down their weapons. They unstrung their bows and tied the weapons together to make a tight bundle. Nakul climbed up the tree and fastened the bundle to a strong branch near the top, such that it was well protected from the elements from above as well as the curious eyes from below. Then he pulled a half-burnt dead body from the cremation ground and tied it to the tree. The stench from the decomposing body would help keep people away.

A few shepherds who were roaming nearby got curious. Nakul said, 'She is our deceased mother. She was more than eighty years old. We tie our dead to trees. That is our funeral ritual.' The shepherds went away.

The Pandavas then shaved, took a bath, wore new clothes and entered the city of Virat.

King Virat was enjoying his day in court when a tall and handsome young man walked in and bowed to him. The majestic man startled the men in the court. His regal appearance, his royal demeanour drew everybody's attention.

The enchanted King Virat asked, 'Who are you? Tell me, what can I do for you?'

In a gentle and deep voice, the man said, 'My name is Kanka. I am a Brahmin. I have lost everything and have come to you to find a job. I used to be King Yudhishthira's friend. I am a skilled player of dice and I used to play with Yudhishthira.'

Virat said, 'I will give you whatever you ask for. You are suitable to be a king. If you so desire, you can rule my kingdom on my behalf.'

'No, my king. I do not wish to rule your kingdom. If you'd be kind enough to employ me as your personal dice player, I'd be grateful.'

Happy with Kanka's humility, Virat said, 'My dear Kanka, I love to play dice. From today, you will be my friend and personal dice player.' He addressed the men in the court and said, 'From today, treat Kanka with the same respect you treat me with. Kanka is my friend, and he is no different from me. Kanka, you can stay in my palace for as long as you wish. You can go anywhere you want. No doors are closed for you. If anybody shows any disrespect, let me know and I will take the most severe action.'

Kanka bowed to Virat. 'Thank you, my king. You are most kind.'

Virat held Kanka's hand and asked him to sit on a throne next to him. Thus, Yudhishthira found his place in the court of Virat as Kanka, the dice player.

The next day, Bheem arrived in the court. He wore black garments and carried a bunch of cooking utensils in his hand. Bheem bowed to the king and said, 'O King, I am Ballav the cook. I can prepare delicious meals. I used to cook for King Yudhishthira, who loved my dishes. I am also skilled in wrestling and hand-to-hand combat. I can feed you well with my cooking skills and entertain you as a fighter.'

Virat was moved by Bheem's physique and poise. 'From today, I employ you as the head chef of my kitchen,' he announced.

Draupadi, her hair tied in a knot and wearing a dark costume, was roaming around the quarters of the queen of Virat. Sudeshna, the queen, spotted her from her rooftop and was struck by Draupadi's beauty. She asked her maid to bring Draupadi to her room.

When Draupadi stepped into the room, the women stared at her in amazement. They had never seen a more beautiful and charming woman in their life. Sudeshna noticed their appreciation and, turning to Draupadi, she asked, 'Who are you? Why were you roaming outside my palace?'

Draupadi bowed to pay her respects. With her palms joined, she said, 'O Queen, I am Sairindhri, the hairdresser. I wish to serve you.'

Sudeshna stood up and walked around Draupadi to take a closer look. 'You have a perfect body and you are as pretty as a goddess. It is hard for me to accept you as a hairdresser.'

'Trust me, I am indeed a hairdresser,' said Draupadi. 'I am skilled in make-up, beauty treatments and hair styling. I used to serve Krishna's wife Satyabhama. I also served Panchali, the Pandava queen. They treated me well. Queen Satyabhama called me Malini.'

Sudeshna was still sceptical. 'I can retain you as my hairdresser, but I am afraid my husband, King Virat, would not be able to control himself if he lays his eyes on you. And why not? Your beauty has cast a spell on the women of my palace too, I can only imagine how the men would react. I am quite certain, once my husband sees your divine beauty, he'd forget me. It would be stupid of me to bring you into the palace.'

Draupadi turned around and, with a stern voice, said, 'No man, not even King Virat can touch me. I have five powerful gandharva husbands, and they always protect me. I am serving as a maid only to complete a penance. If a man lusts for me, he'd die a painful death in the hands of my husbands the same night.'

Sudeshna held Draupadi's arm and said, 'Sairindhri, I will retain you as my hairdresser, and ensure you are treated with respect. Welcome to my palace.'

Next came Sahadev to Virat's court. 'I am Tantipal. I know all about cows and take good care of them. I used to tend to the Pandavas's cattle, but I don't know where they are now. I'd be obliged if you'd be kind enough to employ me in your cattle ranch,' he said.

Virat gave him a warm welcome. 'Welcome to my kingdom, Tantipal. From today, I give you the responsibility of my cattle. I have millions of them and they are cared for by thousands of cowherds. You will be their master.'

The following day, the men in Virat's court saw a tall, dark person enter the hall. Although the person looked like a man, he wore fine women's costume and gold jewellery. His long hair cascaded down his shoulders and he walked with feminine grace. It was Arjun guised as a eunuch. The surprised king took one look at him and enquired, 'Who are you? You have the stature of a handsome man, but you behave like a woman. I can imagine you as a warrior, but not a woman.'

Arjun bowed to Virat and said, 'O King, I am neither a man, nor a woman. Fate has made me a eunuch and maybe some day I will tell you my story. My name is Brihannala, and you may treat me as your son or your daughter. I am a virtuoso musician and dancer. Please allow me to teach your daughter, princess Uttara, the skills of music and dance.'

Virat readily agreed.

Next arrived Nakul. He bowed to Virat and said, 'Hail O King Virat. I am Granthik. I am an expert with horses. I used to be the head of the keepers of the Pandava stable. I can take care of your horses if you'd like.'

Virat welcomed Nakul and said, 'I'd consider myself fortunate to have you as my stable keeper. From today, you are in charge of my horses, my stables and their staff.'

And so, the Pandavas who once ruled the earth, began to serve their time in hiding as servants of King Virat.

Ten months passed without any untoward incident and the brothers were looking forward to their freedom in two months. Just when everything was looking good, things took an unpleasant turn. Once again, Draupadi's beauty posed a major challenge and threatened to reveal their identity to the world.

43

Bheem Kills Keechak

QUEEN SUDESHNA HAD A STRONG AND POWERFUL BROTHER NAMED Keechak. At Sudeshna's behest, King Virat had appointed him the general of his army. With the army by his side, Keechak possessed significant power and influence in the running of the kingdom, and Virat could hardly control him.

One day, Keechak came to visit Sudeshna. As he stepped into the room, he spied Draupadi massaging Sudeshna's scalp with fragrant oil. Keechak stood frozen at the door. Draupadi's beauty left him dumbfounded. He forgot why he was visiting his sister.

With Keechak gawking at her, Draupadi felt embarrassed. She excused herself and left the room. However, Keechak's lustful eyes followed her. Sudeshna noticed her brother's reaction and ribbed him, 'You seem to like my maid, Sairindhri.'

Keechak turned back and said, 'Liked? I am in love, Sister. Who is she? Where is she from? A beauty like her doesn't deserve to be your maid. I want to make her my queen.' Keechak stormed out of the room looking for Draupadi.

Draupadi was waiting outside the room for the visitor to leave.
Keechak was glad to find her there. With a silly grin on his face,
Keechak said, 'My darling, you are wasting your beauty here in
Sudeshna's quarters. Come with me. I will get rid of my wives and
make you my queen.'

Her eyes glued to the floor, Draupadi said, 'Please leave me alone.
I am a maid from an inferior caste. Royalty like you do not deserve
me. Besides, I am married and, if my gandharva husbands know of
your indecent proposal, they'd kill you.' Draupadi left before Keechak
could respond.

Rejected by Draupadi, the frustrated general went to Sudeshna
and said, 'My dear sister, you must do something. I cannot live
without Sairindhri. By hook or by crook, make her come to me.'

Sudeshna thought for a while. Draupadi's beauty always made her
uneasy and she feared that one day her husband would fall for her. If
Keechak could entice Sairindhri and marry her, she wouldn't have
to worry about Virat any more. She leaned conspiratorially towards
Keechak said, 'I have a plan. You invite me to a feast at your place.
Prepare delicious meals and arrange for exotic wines. I will feign
sickness and ask Sairindhri to go to your house and fetch me some
food and wine. And when she arrives, you can seduce her with your
charm.' Keechak agreed.

Two days later, Keechak invited Sudeshna to a grand feast in his
palace. Sudeshna called Draupadi and said, 'Sairindhri, my brother
has invited me to dinner at his place. He has arranged for some of
my favourite drinks. But I don't feel too well. Would you please go to
Keechak's house and bring me the food and drink?'

Draupadi was reluctant. 'My lady, please don't ask me to go to
Keechak's house. He is a brute and he lusts after me. If I go, he would
force himself on me. You have many maids. Please send one of them
to fetch your food and drink. Spare me.'

Sudeshna held Draupadi's hand and said, 'Don't worry, my dear. Keechak wouldn't dare harm someone whom I send. Go and get my drink. I am dying of thirst.'

Draupadi couldn't stall her any further. With a golden flask in hand, she proceeded towards Keechak's house.

Keechak was overjoyed to see Draupadi. He held the door wide open for her and said, 'Welcome to my humble abode, my darling. I knew you'd come. My soft white bed is eagerly waiting for your lovely body. I have delicious wine, bought specially for you. Come and enjoy with me.'

Draupadi's face flushed with rage. Her voice trembling, she said, 'The queen sent me to fetch some wine for her.'

Keechak held Draupadi's hand and said, 'Don't worry about the wine. My maids will take care of that. You come with me.' Keechak pulled Draupadi to his chest. Draupadi pushed him away to free herself and ran towards the door. Keechak laughed and grabbed her from behind.

'Where are you going, my darling?' mocked Keechak. 'You cannot leave without fulfilling my desire.' He dragged Draupadi towards his bedroom. Indignant, Draupadi summoned all her strength and, with her elbow, struck a powerful blow to Keechak's chest and freed herself from his grip. The blow left Keechak out of breath and he stumbled to the ground. Scared and humiliated, Draupadi ran towards King Virat's court. With a loud cry, the furious general chased Draupadi. The moment she entered the court, Keechak caught up with her, grabbed her hair and kicked her to the ground.

King Virat was shocked. He rose from his throne and said, 'Keechak! What are you doing?'

The general didn't care to respond. He glared at Draupadi lying on the floor, spat on the ground and left the court. Bheem and Yudhishthira were also present in the court. Bheem's face turned red with rage. He jumped up from his seat and was about to pounce on Keechak, but Yudhishthira held his arm and stopped him.

Draupadi noticed Yudhishthira's actions as she crawled up to Virat. Her eyes glowing with hatred, voice cracked , she said, 'O King, your brother-in-law kicked me in your court, humiliated me in front of you and your ministers. Still, you let him go. Is this how a king is supposed to treat his people? Can't I expect any justice from my king? Where are my powerful husbands, my saviours? How could they stay calm after this?'

Virat was in trouble. Keechak was not only his brother-in law, but also the commander-in chief of his army. He couldn't risk offending Keechak. He said to Draupadi, 'Sairindhri, you blame me for no reason. I don't know what happened between you two. How can I judge without hearing from both the parties?'

Streams of sweat flowed down angry Yudhishthira's brows. He said, 'Sairindhri, stop crying and go back to Queen Sudeshna. I believe your gandharva husbands don't think this is the appropriate time to demonstrate their rage. Else, they would have arrived to avenge you and uphold your honour.'

Draupadi was miffed by Yudhishthira's words. She refrained from arguing further and went back to Sudeshna's quarters. Draupadi's tears pained Sudeshna. She held Draupadi's hand and said, 'Sairindhri, it was for me that you went to Keechak's house. If you so desire, I will have him executed for insulting you.'

Draupadi wiped her tears and said, 'You don't have to do anything. Keechak will be punished. Tonight will be his last night on earth.' Draupadi went to her room and took a long bath to cool her body and calm her mind. Bheem was the only person who could avenge her insult.

That night, when the palace went to sleep, Draupadi surreptitiously stepped into Bheem's room. Draupadi embraced her sleeping husband

and said, 'Wake up, Bheem. Keechak has insulted your wife, kicked her in front of a court full of people. How could you sleep?'

Bheem woke up and held Draupadi in his arms. 'Why did you come here? What would happen if somebody saw you here? Our thirteen years of hardship would go in vain. Tell me what you have to say and go back to your room.'

Draupadi couldn't control herself any longer. She broke into sobs and said, 'A woman who has Yudhishthira for her husband is bound to be insulted and humiliated. It was because of Yudhishthira that evil Dushasana dared to insult me, Jayadrath attempted to kidnap me, and today Keechak had the gall to kick me. It is thanks to his poor judgment that we had to go through such hardship. Shame on me that I am still alive. I should have died long ago.'

Bheem's voice was choked when he spoke next: 'Shame on me that you had to go through such distress. Believe me, if not for Yudhishthira, I'd have killed Keechak in the court, right in front of the king.'

'I don't want to listen to any excuses. If you don't kill Keechak by tomorrow morning, I would drink poison and kill myself.' Saying this, Draupadi started crying.

Bheem held Draupadi in his arms and said, 'I promise, I will kill Keechak tomorrow. Ask him to wait for you in the dance hall at night. There is a nice bed in the room. He'll meet his death right on that bed.'

The next day, Keechak arrived at Sudeshna's quarters. He pulled Draupadi to a corner and said, 'I hope you realize how much power I wield in this kingdom. I kicked you in the court and nobody dared raise his voice, not even the king. Virat is only a showpiece of a king. The truth is, I rule this kingdom. Be my lover and I will adorn you with gold. Hundreds of maids and servants will serve you. You will be the queen of Matsya.'

Draupadi looked around to check if anybody was listening. She came close to Keechak and, with a naughty smile, whispered, 'Promise me, you'll keep our relationship a secret? Promise you won't tell anybody—not even your friends or your siblings—about our love? I am afraid of my gandharva husbands. If they come to know ...'

Keechak was ecstatic to hear this. He held Draupadi's hands and said, 'Don't worry, nobody will know.'

A smile flashed on Draupadi's lips. 'Come to the dance hall tonight. There is a beautiful bed there. I'll wait for you.' She then quickly picked up flowers and oils for Sudeshna and disappeared from Keechak's view, leaving him giddy with joy.

That evening, when darkness enveloped the kingdom and torches lit up the palace corridors, Keechak walked towards the dance hall. He had dressed in flashy clothes and jewellery, splashed the most exotic perfumes on his muscular body and wrapped a lotus garland around his neck. As he stepped inside the dance hall, he could see, in the faint light, a body lying under the sheets in the bed that lay in the corner of the room.

Tonight, my dream will come true. My love, my Sairindhri, is waiting for me in bed, thought Keechak. He shut the door behind him and tiptoed to the bed. Trembling with excitement, he sat on the bed and gently touched the reclining body. 'Darling, I am here. Look at me. Women say they have never seen a more handsome man. Get up and embrace me.'

A voice from under the covers said, 'I am lucky to meet a self-proclaimed handsome man like you. Your touch gives me the shivers.' The next instant, the covers blew away and Bheem sat up on the bed, laughing like a mad man. With his strong arms, he held Keechak and said, 'Now you'll get to feel my touch.' Bheem lifted him and threw him on the marble floor.

'You evil man, how dare you lay your eyes on Sairindhri? I will kill you.' Bheem pulled up Keechak and dealt a powerful blow to his belly, slamming him against the wall. A fierce fight broke out between the two giants. Keechak was no match for Bheem and he was soon pinned to the ground. Bheem hammered him with powerful blows. Each and every bone in Keechak's body was crushed to a pulp. Bheem caught Keechak's neck in his strong hands and cut off his air. Keechak struggled and thrashed around, but Bheem didn't let go. Soon, he stopped moving and his body lay still. But Bheem was not done with Keechak. He kept thrashing Keechak's dead body until it turned into an unrecognizable, bloody pile of flesh and bones.

Bheem opened the door and found Draupadi waiting. He said, 'Look what I have done to Keechak. This is how I, Bheemsen, deal with someone who lays an evil eye on you. Call the guards and let them know.'

Bheem went back to the palace kitchen. Draupadi was stupefied. It took few moments for her to get back to her senses. She called the guards and said, 'Come, see what my gandharva husbands have done to your evil general Keechak for insulting me.' The guards rushed to the dancing hall and stood shocked to see the ghastly scene. They looked around for Keechak's head and other body parts, but found nothing but a huge ball of flesh.

Keechak's brothers, friends, followers were devastated to see their hero die such a gruesome death. As they were carrying Keechak's body to the crematorium, they saw Draupadi standing by the palace corridor. 'There she is—the evil Sairindhri,' yelled one of the carriers. 'We should throw her into the fire with Keechak.'

King Virat didn't have the courage to protest. Keechak's followers grabbed Draupadi and dragged her to the crematorium to burn her alive. When the news reached Bheem, he burst out in rage. He changed into a disguise, uprooted a tree and ran after Keechak's friends. The moment they saw Bheem running towards them with a tree tucked under his arm, they left Draupadi and ran for their lives. Bheem caught up and killed them all.

The gruesome death of Keechak and his friends frightened King Virat and his ministers. Virat called Sudeshna and said, 'Ask Sairindhri to leave my kingdom. Tell her, the people of this land are scared of her husbands and they don't want to get into trouble.' Sudeshna, still in shock after her brother's death, conveyed the message to Draupadi.

Draupadi shot an imperial look at Sudeshna and said in a calm voice: 'My queen, thirteen days from now, my gandharva husbands will return from their assignment and take me with them. Till then, I wish to stay here.'

Draupadi's confidence and the command in her voice left Sudeshna with no choice but to agree. Draupadi sat behind Sudeshna to tend to her hair with flowers and fragrant oils.

44

The End of Exile

WHILE THE PANDAVAS WERE LOOKING FORWARD TO THEIR FINAL DAYS in hiding in the kingdom of Virat, Duryodhan was growing increasingly anxious. His spies had fanned out far and wide to find the Pandavas, but they returned with bad news.

'We searched everywhere—cities, villages, forests and mountains. We didn't find any trace of them,' the chief spy told him. 'Their charioteers and servants took refuge in Dwarka, but the Pandavas are not there. They seem to have vanished from the face of the earth. We think the Pandavas didn't survive the hardship in the forest.'

The Kauravas rejoiced at the news. But Duryodhan was not convinced. He said, 'It's not easy to kill the Pandavas. They are smart and enjoy the favour of the gods. We tried several times to destroy them, but they always survived. What if they return to Hastinapur after completing their exile and demand the kingdom back? We can't let that happen.'

The spy chief knew that his prince was not pleased with their performance. He noticed King Susharma of the Trigarta kingdom sitting next to Duryodhan. He bowed to Duryodhan and said, 'I am sorry I couldn't give you better news. However, you will be happy to hear that Keechak, the general of King Virat who defeated and humiliated the Trigarta Army several times, has died. The gandharvas killed him. They also killed Keechak's brothers and all his friends.'

Susharma was delighted to hear this news. He sprang up and said, 'That is excellent news! It was because of Keechak that King Virat attacked my kingdom and harassed me several times. I am glad that evil Keechak is dead. Virat is weak and now is the right time to avenge our defeat. Let us attack the Matsya kingdom and win Virat's riches and his cattle. We can defeat him and win his allegiance. Virat's support will strengthen the Kauravas.'

Karna agreed to Susharma's proposal. He knew Duryodhan needed some distraction, and the war would help keep his mind off the Pandavas for a while. He said, 'King Susharma is right. Why bother about the Pandavas? Let them go to hell. Let us attack the Matsya kingdom and loot Virat's cattle. I suggest we split our army and attack Matsya from different directions. That will bewilder his weakened army and we will win with ease.'

Duryodhan agreed.

On the seventh day of the month, Susharma gathered his huge army at the southeastern border of the Matsya kingdom. The following day, Duryodhan, along with Bhishma, Drona, Karna and his huge Kaurava Army arrived at the northern border of Matsya.

On the day that the Pandavas completed their year of exile, Susharma attacked Virat's kingdom and raided his cattle farm. One of the cowherds fled and ran to the capital. He arrived in Virat's court and said, 'O King, the Trigarta Army has attacked your farm. They looted hundreds of thousands of your cows and are herding them away.'

Virat was furious. He called his brother Satanik and his son Sankha and said, 'Put on your armour and get ready to defend the kingdom. Take my entire army with you. We must teach Susharma a lesson that he won't forget.'

'Susharma's army is huge, and he has several fierce warriors with him. It was because of Keechak and his brothers that we had kept him at bay. I am afraid Sankha and Satanik won't be able to counter the Trigarta might,' intervened one of Virat's ministers.

Virat knew his minister was right. It was Keechak who took care of the wars and battles. His sons and brothers were not experienced in warfare. Seeing Virat in trouble, Yudhishthira stood up and said, 'O King Virat, maybe I can be of some assistance to you in your time of distress. I have some experience with weapons and wars. If you permit, I can help you defend your kingdom. Your chef Ballav can also help.'

Virat's eyes lit up. He said, 'Yes, of course. I think Tantipal and Granthik can also help. Sankha, provide them armours and weapons. They'll join you to fight the Trigarta Army. With Kanka by my side, I will join too.' Yudhishthira, Bheem, Nakul and Sahadev wore the armours, mounted their chariots, and marched along with Virat's army.

That afternoon, the armies clashed and a fierce battle ensued. Virat attacked Susharma on his chariot. However, the old king was no match for Susharma and he was soon defeated. Susharma captured Virat, tied him up, shoved him into his chariot and drove away from the battlefield. Virat's army panicked and ran for their lives.

Yudhishthira realized he had to do something. He called Bheem and said, 'Go after Susharma and rescue Virat. We've lived in his palace for very long and he deserves our support.'

Bheem uprooted a tree and chased Susharma's chariot. Yudhishthira yelled at him, 'Stop, Bheem. If you attack with that tree, they would recognize you. Drop it and use conventional weapons like bows, swords, maces or spears.'

Yudhishthira, along with Nakul and Sahadev then launched a fierce attack on Susharma's army, killing hundreds of soldiers. Inspired by the Pandavas, Virat's soldiers turned back and joined the fight. Bheem dropped the tree, picked up a spear and raced his chariot to catch up with Susharma. Soon, Susharma's chariot was in sight and Bheem launched his spears, killing his horses, his charioteer and his guards. Virat freed himself and leapt to the ground. Susharma tried to run away, but Virat grabbed him, snatched the mace from his hand and struck him repeatedly. The old king seemed to have regained his youth. Bheem grabbed Susharma's hair, threw him to the ground and kicked his head. Susharma lost consciousness. The shocked Trigarta Army scattered and ran for their lives.

The Pandava brothers recovered the cattle from their enemy and gathered around Virat. Bheem threw Susharma at Virat's feet and said, 'This evil man does not deserve to live. Tell me, what should I do with him?'

Yudhishthira saw Susharma writhing in pain and took pity on him. He said, 'O King Virat, I pray you pardon this man.' He then turned to Susharma and said, 'Pledge your allegiance to King Virat if you'd like to be pardoned.'

In great pain, Susharma knelt in front of the king. Virat said, 'It is because of Kanka that you are alive today. Go away and never come back.' Susharma, left the battleground, his head held low.

Virat turned to Yudhishthira, Bheem, Nakul and Sahadev, and said, 'My friends, how could I ever pay you back? It is because of you that I am alive today. Tell me what you want. I can give you anything, even my kingdom.'

Yudhishthira bowed and said, 'Thank you for your offer. Your kind acknowledgement means a lot to us. We don't want anything.

I suggest you send a messenger to your capital with the news of your success and ask them to prepare for your reception.'

While Virat was busy fighting the Trigarta Army, Duryodhan, along with Bhishma, Drona, Karna and others attacked the northern border and looted thousands of cattle. A messenger came running to Uttar—Virat's youngest son—and gave him the bad news. 'O prince Uttar, please come and stop the Kauravas. King Virat has left you to defend the kingdom.'

Uttar had no real experience in fighting a war. However, he was smart enough to not expose his weakness. He said, 'My charioteer died during my last fight. If I had a good charioteer, I could have taught the Kauravas a good lesson. Alone, I could have destroyed the Kaurava greats. My fury and prowess would have reminded them of Arjun. They would have fled the battlefield thinking Arjun had attacked them. If only I had a good charioteer ...'

Draupadi had been listening to Uttar's ranting for some time and she couldn't take it anymore, especially the comparison with Arjun. She called the prince and said, 'Prince, let me give you a tip. I know Brihannala used to serve Arjun as his charioteer and received weapons training from him. Your sister Uttara is Brihannala's student. Why don't you ask her to request Brihannala to be your charioteer? Brihannala would never refuse Uttara's request.'

Uttar had no option but to ask Uttara. Uttara was amazed to discover this new side of Brihannala. She went to the dance hall and found Brihannala teaching music to the girls. Holding Brihannala's arm, she said, 'The Kauravas have attacked our kingdom and are looting our cattle. Uttar needs your help to defend the kingdom. He wants you as his charioteer. I beg you to help him during this hour of crisis.'

Arjun, disguised as Brihannala, feigned surprise. 'Me, a charioteer? That too in a battle with the Kauravas? My princess, you

must be out of your mind. I am a dancer and a musician. I know
nothing but dance and music.'

Uttar, who had followed Uttara to the dance hall, said in a stern
voice, 'I don't care if you are a dancer or a musician. Come with me
and drive my chariot. It is an order.'

Arjun tried several amusing antics to justify his disguise as a
transgender. He feigned ignorance and tried to wear the armour
upside down. He fell trying to lift a sword and held the bow in the
opposite direction. Uttara and the girls hooted with laughter. Uttar,
however, was not amused. He held Arjun and helped him put on the
armour properly. As they were about to leave, Uttara called Arjun and
said, 'Brihannala, promise me something. Defeat the Kauravas and
bring me their fine costumes. We'll make dresses for our dolls.'

Arjun smiled and said, 'If Uttar wins, I promise, I will bring their
beautiful costumes and fabrics for you.'

Uttar left to defend his kingdom with Arjun as his charioteer.
Arjun sped the chariot like the wind, and Uttar realized Draupadi was
right. Within hours, their chariot arrived near the cremation ground
where the Pandavas had hidden their weapons. From a distance, Uttar
could see the Kaurava Army assembled in a formation, like a huge,
dark forest. Their combined war cries sounded like the ocean waves
crashing on rocks. In the horizon, he could see the great Kaurava
warriors like Bhishma, Drona and Karna leading the formation on
their gorgeous chariots. Butterflies fluttered in Uttar's belly. His
knees trembled in fear. It had been foolish of him to make such tall
claims. How could he ever dare to fight the mighty Kauravas? He
asked Arjun to stop the chariot.

'Brihannala, take me back to the palace,' he said. 'I won't fight the
Kauravas. Even the gods can't defeat those mighty Kaurava warriors.
Who am I to fight them? I have no army with me, and I am only a

boy. I have no battle experience. How can I fight them? Turn around. I want to go back.'

Arjun stopped the chariot and said, 'Prince, you made huge promises and boasted about your prowess to the men and women of your palace. Why do you want to retreat now? If you return without your cattle, they'd ridicule you, taunt you. And how can I return empty-handed? I cannot disregard Sairindhri's praise, nor can I break Uttara's heart.'

'I don't care for their ridicule. The Kauravas outnumber me a million times over. They are more powerful than anybody on earth. Let them loot our cattle. I'm in no mood to commit suicide.' Saying this, Uttar jumped off the chariot and ran away from the battleground.

Arjun chased after Uttar and soon caught hold of him. The young prince cried and pleaded with Arjun. 'My dear Brihannala, please let go of me. I want to live, for a dead man is of no use to society. Listen to me. Take me back to the safety of my palace and I will shower you with riches. I will give you a thousand gold coins, precious stones and jewellery. I will gift you a brand-new, gold-adorned chariot with powerful horses. I will give you ten strong bull elephants. Anything you ask, I will give you. Please let me go.'

Arjun laughed. He pulled Uttar to the chariot and said, 'Well, if you can't fight, then let me do your job, and you do mine.' Arjun placed the reins in Uttar's hand, pointed his finger towards the Sami tree near the cremation ground, and said, 'Take me to that Sami tree. I must pick up a few things before I start my fight.' Bedazzled, Uttar turned the chariot around and drove towards the Sami tree.

45

The Battle for the Cattle

WHEN UTTAR'S CHARIOT ARRIVED AT THE SAMI TREE, ARJUN POINTED to the top of the tree and said, 'Uttar, do you see something hanging from the branches up there?'

Uttar looked up and said, 'Looks like someone hung a dead body there.'

Arjun laughed. 'It isn't a dead body. It's a package,' he said. 'Climb up the tree and bring it down.'

'Are you sure?' Uttar was sceptical. 'Don't forget that I am a prince. I don't want to touch a filthy decomposed body. It is beneath my dignity.'

'Trust me. I wouldn't ask you to do anything inappropriate. If you want to defeat the Kauravas, do as I say.'

Uttar couldn't defy Arjun's commanding tone. He climbed up the tree and brought down the heavy bundle.

'Now, open it.'

Uttar untied the ropes and unpacked the bundle. As he removed the cover, he was astounded to see the contents inside. Ornate bows, strange-looking arrows, heavy maces, swords, armours, spears, and many other lethal weapons dazzled his eyes. Brihannala picked up a gem-studded bow decorated with a thousand golden lizards and said, 'This is the famous Gandiva bow belonging to Arjun. He received this as a gift from Varuna, the god of the waters, during the burning of the Khandava Forest.' He then pointed to the other weapons and said, 'The one with the golden handle is Bheem's. The one decorated with red and black dots is Yudhishthira's. Nakul uses this bow with the emblem of the golden sun carved on it. And the one specked with golden insects belongs to Sahadev.'

Prince Uttar stood there, dumbfounded. Brihannala smiled and said, 'You don't look like you believe me.'

'How do you expect me to believe you? Why would the Pandavas leave their weapons hanging in this tree? If these are their weapons, where are the mighty Pandavas themselves? Where is their wife Draupadi?'

Brihannala held Uttar's arm and said, 'It is time to reveal the truth to you. I am Arjun. Kanka, your father's friend, is none other than Emperor Yudhishthira. Chef Ballav, who cooks your delicious meals, is my brother Bheem. The chief of your stables is my younger brother Nakul, and the person in charge of your cattle is Sahadev. Sairindhri, your mother, Queen Sudeshna's personal maid, is our wife Draupadi. She is the cause of your uncle Keechak's death.'

Uttar bowed to Arjun and said, 'Pardon me, Sir, for my arrogance. I have been rude to you. I bragged in front of you. I am ashamed of my behaviour. Punish me in whatever way you wish.'

Arjun laughed and pulled up Uttar. 'Prince Uttar, it wasn't your fault. Whatever you did was because of your ignorance. Now get up and drive my chariot. I will fight the Kauravas and win back your cattle.'

Uttar mounted the chariot and held the reins. Arjun strung his Gandiva and pulled the string, which let out a loud twang. The sound reverberated through the valley and made shivers run down the spines of the Kaurava Army. The resonance of the mighty Gandiva was well-known to them and they feared Arjun was closer than they would have liked him to be. Drona called Duryodhan and said, 'Look at your soldiers. The sound of Arjun's Gandiva has drained the blood off their face. They know Arjun's arrows will slaughter them. If you want to survive, take the cows and go back to Hastinapur. We'll wait for Arjun.'

Duryodhan laughed and said, 'If this is Arjun, then I'd be the happiest person on earth. The Pandavas are yet to finish their thirteen years in exile, and now that Arjun has exposed himself, they would have to go into exile for twelve more years.'

Drona said, 'The Pandavas are not fools. They wouldn't make their identity known unless the thirteen years are over. Arjun will arrive any moment. Flee, or else, say your final prayers.'

Drona's caustic remarks didn't please Duryodhan. 'I am sure grandfather Bhishma can tell us whether the thirteen years are over or not. But what makes you so sure this is Arjun? It could be King Virat's men or perhaps Virat himself. Let me tell you, whoever it is, I am not afraid to fight. It is your habit to scare us and sing Arjun's praises.' Duryodhan turned to his generals and said, 'It was my mistake to bring these oldies with me. They know only to blabber and find fault in others. Send them behind the army column and get ready to fight.'

Karna said, 'Be it Arjun or Virat, today, he'll get a taste of my arrows. I have my teacher, Guru Parashurama's blessings—nobody can beat me in a battle. I alone can defeat Arjun. Watch me as I destroy his chariot and bring him down to his knees, to Duryodhan's feet, and then kill him in front of you all.'

Kripacharya couldn't take it any more. He addressed Karna sternly: 'Karna, you think of war as if it is the only means to resolve any dispute or problem. Wise men have said that, of all means to resolve a dispute, war is the worst and the most sinful. It is justified only when all other means of reconciliation fail. It would be foolish of you to fight Arjun. After thirteen years of exile, he is as ferocious as a hungry lion. Do you think he'd let you go free?'

Karna laughed. He moved close to Kripa's chariot and said, 'You think Arjun is the only archer in this world who can shoot an arrow? Old man, who do you think I am? An idiot? I know why you try to scare us. You want to protect your favourite student—that's all. You want to make sure that he doesn't become a laughing stock in front of the Kaurava Army.'

Drona's son Aswathama was furious. He looked Karna in the eye and said, 'Karna how dare you insult my uncle? A teacher treats his students like his sons. It is natural for uncle Kripacharya to speak in Arjun's favour. And what he said is true. Karna, you always boast about your prowess. But have you ever succeeded in defeating any of the Pandavas? You and your friend Duryodhan always used sly means to humiliate and defeat them, but you've always failed in combat. Remember, Arjun's Gandiva doesn't shoot dice, it shoots sharp and lethal arrows. So, get ready to fight. Let your "advisor" Shakuni fight. If my father Drona wants to fight Arjun, he may. But I won't.'

Bhishma sensed a rising dissent amongst the Kaurava generals and tried to calm things down. He called Aswathama and said, 'Karna is only trying to inspire you to fight. He didn't mean to insult anybody.'

Duryodhan came to Drona with his palms joined and said, 'Gurudev, I apologize to you on behalf of my friend. Please pardon us and lead us in this battle.'

Duryodhan's apology and Bhishma's words calmed Drona. He asked Bhishma: 'Well, then, tell us, have the Pandavas completed their thirteen years of exile?'

Bhishma nodded. 'As per my calculations, they have. Arjun would never reveal himself unless he has kept his part of the bargain. Now, Duryodhan, you decide what you want to do. Give back their kingdom or prepare to fight.'

'Giving back their kingdom is not an option at all,' said Duryodhan. 'Let's get ready to fight.'

Bhishma sighed and said, 'Well, then, allow me to suggest a strategy. Duryodhan, you return to Hastinapur along with a quarter of the army to protect you. Let another quarter of the soldiers take Virat's cows to your ranch. The rest stay here with us and fight Arjun.'

Duryodhan agreed. He left the battlefield with a fourth of the army guarding his chariot. Another team left with the stolen cows. The rest of the soldiers stood in a Diamond formation with Drona in front, Aswathama to the right, Kripa on the left and Karna guarding the rear. Bhishma stood on his chariot in the centre of the formation.

Soon, the Kauravas sighted the banner atop Arjun's chariot. The rumbling of his chariot wheels and the reverberation of his conch sent shivers down the spines of the Kauravas. Arjun raised his bow and shot two arrows in the air. They came flying and fell in front of Drona's feet. Drona smiled and said, 'This is how my student Arjun pays his respects.'

Arjun asked Uttar to take the chariot around the formation. He was looking for Duryodhan, but couldn't find him. He said to Uttar: 'Duryodhan must have left with the cows. Let's leave these soldiers and try to catch up to Duryodhan and rescue your cattle. That is our main objective.'

As Arjun's chariot veered away from the formation, Drona knew what his student was up to. He yelled, 'Arjun is going after

Duryodhan. We must stop him.' The Kaurava Army turned around and, with a huge roar, chased Arjun's chariot.

Arjun said to Uttar: 'Keep driving till you find your cows. In the meantime, let me deal with the Kauravas.' Arjun turned around and sprayed the Kaurava Army with arrows. The continuous boom of the Gandiva, the rumbling of the chariot wheels and the death cry of the Kaurava soldiers reverberated throughout the battlefield. Soon, Arjun's chariot reached the herd of cows. His arrows scattered the soldiers chasing the cows, and Uttar's chariot veered the cattle towards the Matsya kingdom.

Once the cows were rescued, Arjun asked Uttar to take the chariot to Karna. Arjun's barrage of arrows took Karna by surprise. Overwhelmed, he called for help. Duryodhan's brother Vikarna and other Kaurava warriors rushed in to defend him. But Arjun's rapid-fire arrows were too much for them to handle. They ran for their lives. Karna's brother Sangramjit sacrificed his life to let Karna escape Arjun's wrath.

Uttar then took the chariot to Kripa and a fierce battle broke out. Arjun's arrows killed Kripa's horses and threw him to the ground. Arjun allowed Kripa to get up and gather his weapons. Kripa took advantage of the respite and struck Arjun with ten arrows. Arjun smiled and, with a few quick shots, shattered his armour and his bow. A group of Kaurava warriors rushed in to save Kripa, and taking him on their chariot, fled the battleground.

Arjun then faced his teacher, Drona. He bowed to Drona and said, 'We completed our exile and have come to take our revenge on our enemy. But I don't want to fight you unless you strike first.'

Drona smiled, lifted his bow, and shot a volley of arrows at Arjun. Arjun retaliated and an intense battle ensued between the teacher and student. Arjun's arrows engulfed Drona and the old man had a tough time countering them. His armour shattered and his body was covered with blood. Aswathama came from behind to defend his father. Arjun moved away to engage with Aswathama, allowing a bruised Drona to escape the battle. Soon, Aswathama ran out of arrows and was left with no option but to flee. Arjun didn't bother to chase Aswathama. Rather, he wanted to face his arch-rival Karna once again.

Karna had recovered from his earlier wounds and returned to the battlefield to settle his score with Arjun. Once again, the titans clashed. But it was Arjun's day. He was indomitable and soon Karna had multiple arrows stuck in his chest. Crying in pain, Karna once again fled the battlefield.

Arjun turned to Uttar and said, 'Now take me to that golden chariot in the centre of the field. Grandfather Bhishma is waiting for me.'

Uttar was exhausted. The violence of war and the death and destruction all around was too much for him. With a trembling voice, he said, 'Arjun, I can't take it any more. We have completed our mission. We got back our cows. Can we please go back now?'

Arjun soothed him: 'Don't be afraid. You are doing fine. Hang on a little longer and take me to Bhishma. You will have the privilege of witnessing what great warriors can do in a battlefield.'

Uttar took the chariot to the centre field and faced Bhishma.

Arjun bowed to Bhishma and said, 'Grandfather, I seek your blessings.' Bhishma didn't answer. He lifted his bow and hurled a deadly weapon at Arjun. Within a split second, Arjun's arrows shot it down. The two great warriors then engaged in the fiercest of battles one can imagine. The Agni weapon lit up a huge blaze, only to be countered by torrential rains from the Varuna weapon. The rains were then blown away by strong winds from the Vayu weapon. Arjun's deadly and unending assault was too much even for Bhishma to withstand. He felt dizzy and sat down on his chariot. Arjun stopped for a moment and Bhishma's charioteer took the opportunity to flee the battlefield.

In the meantime, Duryodhan recovered from his injuries and returned to the battlefield to attack Arjun. This time, he did not come alone. Drona, Kripa, Aswathama, Karna and Bhishma accompanied him. They circled around Arjun and attacked him from all directions. Arjun kept fighting with his conventional weapons, but realized he was being overpowered. He pulled out the famous hypnosis weapon he had acquired from Indra and hurled it at the Kauravas. The weapon exploded with a huge blast and the great Kaurava warriors lost consciousness and dropped to the ground like flies. Uttar was stunned to see the power of the weapon. Arjun said, 'Uttar, we must keep our promise to your sister Uttara. Go and get the white clothes off Drona and Kripa. Get the yellow scarf from Karna, and the blue costumes from Aswathama and Duryodhan. Fetch Bhishma's clothes, but be careful: he is stunned but he can wake up any moment. He knows the antidote to this weapon.'

Uttar went to each of the gallant warriors and took off their clothes. Then he mounted the chariot and turned around to leave the battlefield. Bhishma woke up and when he saw Arjun leaving, he attacked him. Arjun turned around and, with a few quick blows, killed Bhishma's horses.

Duryodhan woke up and cried out, 'Grandfather, strike him. Don't let him escape.'

Bhishma laughed and said, 'Why are you screaming now? Where was your valour a few moments ago when Uttar took off your clothes? Consider yourself lucky to be alive. It was Arjun's magnanimity that he didn't kill you while you were unconscious. Now go back to your kingdom and let Arjun return to Matsya with the cows.'

Duryodhan sighed and ordered the Kauravas to retreat to Hastinapur. Arjun watched them from a distance and smiled. He said to his charioteer: 'Uttar, you have accomplished your mission. You got back your cows. Let's go back to the palace now.'

Uttar smiled and drove the chariot towards the palace of King Virat.

46

The Pandavas Reveal Themselves

AFTER DEFEATING THE KAURAVAS, ARJUN AND UTTAR TOOK THEIR chariot back to the Sami tree. Once again, Arjun tied up his weapons in a bundle and hung them from one of the top branches of the tree.

Before entering the city, Arjun said, 'Uttar, your horses are tired. Let them drink water and rest a while. We will arrive at the palace by sunset. In the meantime, send a messenger to let your father know of your victory. He must prepare for a grand welcome.' Uttar agreed.

Arjun changed back to his disguise as Brihannala and said, 'Prince, when we return to the palace, do not let your father know of our identity. The shock may be too much for him to bear. For now, tell him that you defeated the Kauravas on your own.'

Uttar knelt in front of Arjun and said, 'O great warrior, no other person on earth could defeat the mighty Kauravas except you. However, your wish is my command. I won't reveal to the king the truth of this battle.'

When King Virat returned from the battlefield after defeating the Trigarta Army, he was given the news that his son Uttar had gone to fight the Kauravas alone, with Brihannala as his charioteer. Shocked and scared, Virat called his army generals and said, 'Go and find out if my son is still alive. With that eunuch Brihannala driving his chariot, Uttar has no chance of surviving the might of the Kauravas.'

Yudhishthira smiled and said, 'King Virat, don't worry about your son. With Brihannala as his charioteer, rest assured, Uttar would defeat the Kauravas and bring back your cattle.'

Virat was not convinced. 'Never mind what Kanka says. Go to the battlefield and help Uttar—if he is still alive.'

However, before the generals could leave the court, the messengers arrived and delivered the good news. King Virat jumped up from his throne in joy. He called his men and said, 'Did you hear the news? My son Uttar has defeated the mighty Kauravas! The indomitable Bhishma, Karna, Drona, Kripa, all failed in front of my son's arrows. Arrange for a grand welcome.' He then turned to Yudhishthira and said, 'Kanka, I am so happy. Let's celebrate by playing a round of dice.'

'King Virat, it is said that an excited person should avoid playing dice. The excitement can blur one's judgment and result in a disaster. You know how Yudhishthira lost everything in a game of dice. However, if you insist, I will play with you.' Yudhishthira cautioned him.

'Don't worry, Kanka. I am excited but I am still in my senses. Let's play while we wait for my victorious son's arrival.'

Yudhishthira fetched the board and set it up to play the game. While playing, Virat said, 'Kanka, I still can't believe that my boy Uttar has defeated the Kaurava giants.'

Yudhishthira set the dice pieces and said, 'I don't find it hard to believe. After all, Brihannala was his charioteer.'

Virat wasn't pleased with Yudhishthira's reply. With a big frown, he said, 'How dare you compare my son with a eunuch? You think Brihannala could fight a great warrior like Bhishma? You insult me with such a despicable comparison. Since you are my friend, I pardon you. But never say such a horrible thing to me again.'

Yudhishthira gently rolled the dice on the board and said, 'O King, please don't be upset. Trust me, Brihannala is the best person to fight the indomitable Kaurava warriors. No other living being could defeat them. Not even the gods.'

Virat was furious. 'I warn you one more time: stop praising Brihannala. Else you'll be punished for your insolent behaviour.'

Yudhishthira smiled and said, 'I have only uttered the truth.'

Virat couldn't take it any more. He picked up the dice pieces and threw them at Yudhishthira. The hard ivory pieces hit Yudhishthira's face and his nose began to bleed. Yudhishthira covered his nose with his palm and turned to Draupadi., who ran inside, brought a bowl of water and held it under Yudhishthira's face. Just then, the guard announced the arrival of Prince Uttar.

Arjun had once vowed that if anybody dared to spill Yudhishthira's blood anywhere other than in a battlefield, he'd kill the assailant immediately. Yudhishthira knew that if Arjun saw his bloody nose, Virat would be dead in no time. He called the guard and said, 'Don't allow Brihannala to come to the court. Bring only Prince Uttar.'

Uttar entered the court and was flabbergasted to see Yudhishthira on the floor with his bloody nose and Draupadi tending to his wound. Anxious, he asked, 'Father who did this horrible thing to Kanka?'

Virat wasn't happy to see his son's concern for Kanka. His voice full of scorn, he said, 'I punished him for disobeying my orders. He is lucky that I didn't execute him for insulting me in my court. When I was praising your gallant victory, this audacious man kept praising the eunuch.'

Uttar was shocked. He knew his father had insulted the great Pandava Yudhishthira. He said with much urgency in his voice:

'Father, you have committed a grave sin. Kneel before this Brahmin and ask for his forgiveness, else his wrath will destroy us all.'

Uttar's plea scared Virat. Joining his palms, he said, 'Kanka, I don't know what came upon me. I lost my temper. Please forgive me for my barbaric behaviour.'

By then, Yudhishthira's nosebleed was under control. He lifted his head and said with a faint smile: 'I am not angry with you, my friend. I have already pardoned you. Else, if my blood had touched the ground, you and your kingdom would have been destroyed. I'd like to request you to welcome Prince Uttar's charioteer Brihannala to the court.'

Arjun entered the court disguised as Brihannala and paid his respects to the king and Yudhishthira. Virat called Uttar to his side and said, 'My son, I am proud to be your father. I am amazed how you defeated the mighty Kauravas and won back our cattle. Tell us, how did you conquer Bhishma, Drona, Karna, Kripa and the others?'

Uttar felt embarrassed to be praised in front of Arjun and the other Pandavas. Arjun looked at him and, with a gentle nod, reminded Uttar of his promise. Uttar couldn't accept the undue glory either. He turned to the court and said, 'To tell you the truth, I didn't defeat the Kauravas. Neither did I win back our cattle. Rather, I was scared and was about to flee the battlefield. Suddenly, a man appeared from heaven. The dark and handsome man was carrying a strange bow and several other weapons. He mounted my chariot and asked me to head back towards the Kauravas. And then this amazing man fought the Kaurava giants like a fierce lion. Bhishma, Drona, Karna, Kripa ... nobody could counter his brutal attack. They all fell to the ground unconscious. He then asked me to go and collect their costumes for Uttara.'

The excited king Virat asked, 'Where is this gallant warrior? I'd like to meet him and express my gratitude.'

Uttar glanced at Arjun and said, 'Unfortunately, soon after the battle, the man disappeared. However, he promised he'd come back soon. May be in a day or two.'

Three days later, the Pandavas woke up early, bathed in the river, said their prayers and arrived in the court, dressed in white silk. It was early in the morning and King Virat was yet to appear in his court. Bheem and Arjun led Yudhishthira to the throne. Yudhishthira sat down on Virat's throne while Bheem, Arjun, Nakul, Sahadev and Draupadi sat next to him. When Virat arrived and saw Yudhishthira on his thrown, he was furious. 'Kanka, how dare you sit on my throne? Did you forget that you are only a servant?' he thundered.

Arjun laughed and said, 'King Virat, this man, whom you know as your friend Kanka, deserves to sit on Lord Indra's throne. He is Dharma reincarnated. He is regarded as the ascetic emperor of the world, and he always speaks the truth. He is the ruler of the earth, the great Pandava, Yudhishthira. Don't you think he deserves to sit on your throne?'

Virat couldn't believe his ears. He countered, 'That is impossible. I heard the Pandavas have vanished after their defeat in the game of dice. We assumed they are dead. If Kanka is Yudhishthira, then where are the other Pandava brothers? Where is their wife, Queen Draupadi?'

Arjun replied, 'We are the Pandavas and we have been hiding in your palace to fulfil our obligation to Duryodhan. I have already introduced you to Yudhishthira. The giant sitting next to Yudhishthira, whom you know as Ballav the cook, is none other than Bheemsen. Next to him is Nakul, who looked after your horses as Granthik. And the man next to him is not Tantipal, but the fifth Pandava, Sahadev. The lady whom you know as Sairindhri is our wife, Draupadi. And I am Arjun. I disguised myself as Brihannala, the eunuch dancer.'

Virat was stunned to hear this. Uttar came up to his father and said, 'Father, the divine man who defeated the Kaurava greats was none other than Arjun. He is the person who won back our cattle and restored our glory. It was because of the Pandavas that we could defeat Susharma and his Trigarta Army. We should be ever grateful to these mighty men.'

Virat, palms joined gratefully and tears welling in his eyes, said, 'Yudhishthira, pardon me for my behaviour. Several times have I been rude to you and treated you like an ordinary servant. But you have always been kind to me, helped me during my time of distress. How can I make up for my ill behaviour? My kingdom, my wealth, my army—everything is yours.'

Yudhishthira said, 'King Virat, you provided us shelter and protection when we needed them the most. We are thankful to you.'

Virat then turned to Arjun and said, 'Arjun, I don't know how to thank you. You have saved us from the wrath of the mighty Kauravas. It is because of you that my son lives today. I wish to offer you my daughter Uttara's hand in marriage. Please accept her as your bride.'

Arjun replied, 'King Virat, I am honoured that you consider me worthy of being your son-in-law. However, I cannot accept Uttara as my bride.'

'Why not? Don't you think Uttara is worthy?'

'Quite the contrary,' laughed Arjun. 'Uttara has been my student for the past year. I have taught her music and dance. I cannot marry my student. She is like a daughter to me. If you agree, I'd like to accept her as a daughter-in-law, as my son Abhimanyu's bride. Abhimanyu has grown up to be a fine young man and he is a skilled warrior. He'd be the perfect husband for Uttara.'

Virat had no reason to decline the proposal. He asked his men to prepare for the grand wedding. The Pandavas moved to the city of Upaplavya and sent out invitations to their family members.

Krishna, along with Balram, Satyaki and Subhadra arrived to attend the wedding. From Panchal came King Drupad and the five sons of Draupadi, along with Shikhandi and Dhrishtadyumna.

King Virat arranged Uttara and Abhimanyu's wedding to be held with great pomp and grandeur. Sumptuous meals of meat, vegetables and sweets were served to the guests, along with a variety of wine and other drinks. Musicians and performers entertained the guests. Krishna himself supervised the ceremony.

As the festivities continued, Yudhishthira was in deep thought. The time had come to claim the throne of Indraprastha. He knew, Duryodhan wouldn't give in easily. His recent defeat at Arjun's hands must have made him mad with anger. Yudhishthira watched Krishna bless the newlywed couple and realized he would be the best person to resolve the issue. He would seek Krishna's advice as soon as possible. At that moment, Krishna turned to him and smiled. Krishna's reassuring smile melted away Yudhishthira's anxiety. He was at peace.

47

Preparations for the Confrontation

THE DAY AFTER THE WEDDING, THE PANDAVAS, ALONG WITH THEIR friends and relatives, assembled at King Virat's palace. Krishna, Balram, Satyaki, Drupad, Pradyumna and many other stalwarts graced the court. The servants and courtesans served them fresh fruit and drinks. The musicians played festive music. They all looked happy and contented after the long festivities. However, the Pandavas knew that the peace and joy won't last long. They must make plans and prepare to get back their kingdom from Duryodhan. While the others had a great time, Yudhishthira glanced at Krishna, who noticed the anxiety in his friend's eyes. He stood up and raised his hand, and the music stopped. The guests stopped talking and turned their attention to Krishna.

Krishna said, 'Dear friends, after twelve long years in exile, followed by one year in hiding, the Pandavas have honoured their promise. Duryodhan defeated Yudhishthira in a rigged game of dice. Still, Yudhishthira and his brothers accepted their loss and did whatever they had agreed to do. Now it is Duryodhan's turn to return the Pandavas their kingdom. Knowing Duryodhan, it is unlikely that he'd do the right thing. The Pandavas have the might to crush the Kauravas if they want. I am sure, if needed, you won't hesitate to join them in this righteous battle either. However, before resorting to violence and war, I suggest we send a messenger to Hastinapur with the request that they peacefully return the Pandavas's half of the kingdom.'

Balram, who taught Duryodhan the finer points of fighting with a mace, felt that his disciple was being treated unfairly by Krishna and his followers. He stood up and said, 'I agree with Krishna's proposal of sending a messenger of peace to Duryodhan. But the messenger and his message should not antagonize him. He is not weak and has friends. And his friends do not think Yudhishthira was defeated in a rigged game. It was Yudhishthira's fault that he accepted the challenge when he knew he had limited skill in the game. Shakuni is an expert player and he defeated Yudhishthira, fair and square. I don't understand why Duryodhan is always blamed for Yudhishthira's folly!'

Satyaki didn't like the way Balram defended his disciple. 'How could you say the game was fair? A game is always played between equals. Duryodhan knew Yudhishthira was an inexperienced player and he was never a match for Shakuni. Still, Yudhishthira accepted the defeat with grace and fulfilled his promise. Now, it is their turn. Why should the Pandavas beg for what they rightfully deserve?'

Drupad, the king of Panchal and the father-in-law of the Pandavas, stood up to address the gathering. Supporting Satyaki's views, he said, 'You are right. A vile person like Duryodhan would never return their kingdom to the Pandavas without a fight. The Kuru elders wouldn't be of any help either. Dhritarashtra would only follow his sons. Bhishma and Drona are tied by their obligation to the throne. Hence, I strongly recommend that we prepare for war while keeping the peace negotiations on. We must arrange to send emissaries to all the kings and kingdoms, and ask them to join us as our allies. I am sure Duryodhan would do the same. Remember, the kings would support those from whom they receive the request first. That is the norm.'

Krishna bowed to Drupad and said, 'You are the oldest and the wisest amongst us. Please do whatever you think is best for the Pandavas. Arrange to send a qualified messenger to Hastinapur with the message of peace and reconciliation. If Duryodhan doesn't budge, then arrange to pursue allies for the Pandavas.'

The meeting ended on that note.

Krishna went back to Dwarka along with his contingent. Drupad, Virat and Yudhishthira began their long meetings to strategize. They felt it would be foolish to wait for a response from Duryodhan and begin the war preparations only after the inevitable came into being. They decided to dispatch messengers to their friendly kings, requesting their support in case a war was afoot.

Drupad called one of his senior ministers and said, 'You know the history of the Pandavas and the Kauravas. I entrust you with the job of delivering the message of peace to the Kuru King Dhritarashtra and humbly requesting him to return to the Pandavas their half of the kingdom. If you can convince Dhritarashtra, there is a possibility Duryodhan might change his mind. Vidura would support you and so would Bhishma and Drona. If you can convince enough of the advisors and ministers that they should refrain from war, then it would be difficult for Duryodhan to get them back in line. We could use that time to increase our strength and gain more allies. Do you understand?'

The minister smiled. 'Don't worry, my king. I will do my best.' Saying so, he prepared to depart for Hastinapur.

The news of the Pandavas's attempt to seek allies did not remain a secret for long. The spies informed Duryodhan that the Pandava messengers were crisscrossing the land, going from one kingdom to the other, convincing their kings to join their ranks. Duryodhan jumped into action. He immediately sent out his emissaries to gain allies and bolster his military might. He knew, the most prized ally would be their common cousin, Krishna. He knew Krishna favoured the Pandavas. But if he could reach him in person before the Pandavas did, then, as per the norm, Krishna would have to join him. The moment this thought came to his mind, Duryodhan left for Dwarka on his fastest chariot.

When he arrived in Dwarka, he was relieved to discover that the Pandavas hadn't beaten him in the race. Duryodhan was told that Krishna was asleep. If he wanted, he could wait in his bedroom until he woke up. Duryodhan stepped into the room and found Krishna sleeping soundly in his bed. He tiptoed into the room and sat down on a chair near Krishna's head.

A few moments later, Arjun walked into the room. He was disappointed to find Duryodhan already there. However, he didn't leave. Arjun sat down on the bed near Krishna's feet.

A little later, Krishna woke up and saw Arjun seated near his feet. Then he turned around and saw Duryodhan on the chair next to his head. Both Duryodhan and Arjun stood up and bowed to Krishna to show their respect. Krishna welcomed them and said, 'It is great to see you cousins together after a long time. What brings you here?'

Duryodhan said, 'Krishna, you must be aware of the possibility of a war between us and the Pandavas. I pray it doesn't really happen and that we resolve our dispute without any bloodshed. However, if war happens, I request you to support us. You are our cousin and I know you treat us both with equal compassion. I was here first, and as per the norms, you should join me.'

Krishna smiled and said, 'Duryodhan, you may have come here first, but I saw Arjun before I spotted you.'

Duryodhan's face turned red with humiliation. Anger licked at his inside him as he glared at Arjun and said, 'I should have guessed.'

Krishna laughed and said, 'But don't worry, Duryodhan. I want to support both of you. I have two choices to offer. You can either opt for me or take one hundred million of my fierce Narayani warriors. Each Narayani warrior is as powerful and strong as I am. If you opt for me, I'll join you only as an advisor and not as a warrior. I will not pick up a weapon and will not fight. Now you decide what do you want. Since Arjun is younger and I saw him first, I'd like to ask him first. Arjun, what would you opt for?'

Arjun knelt in front of Krishna and, with palms joined reverentially, he said, 'Krishna, I choose you.'

'Are you sure? Remember, I won't fight. The Narayani warriors are the most dreaded in the world and any army would be fortunate to have them.'

Arjun didn't budge. 'I want you by my side, nothing else.'

Krishna held Arjun and said, 'Well, then, you'll have me.' Then he addressed Duryodhan: 'Duryodhan, you can have my one hundred million Narayani soldiers. I hope you are happy.'

Duryodhan was indeed happy. How could Krishna help if he didn't fight? He bowed to Krishna and said, 'I humbly accept your offer. Thank you, cousin.'

After Duryodhan left the room, Krishna asked Arjun: 'Why did you pick me? How could I be of help to you in a war?'

Arjun smiled and said, 'I have always wished to have you as my charioteer. With you as my charioteer, I can conquer the world.'

Krishna embraced Arjun and said, 'So be it. I shall be your charioteer and fulfil your wish.'

After leaving Krishna's quarters, Duryodhan went to visit his guru, Balram. After paying his respects, Duryodhan asked Balram for his support. Balram said, 'My dear Duryodhan, I tried to defend you at the meeting we had in Virat's court. Krishna didn't listen to me. Trust me, I am not at all happy about the way they treat you. But I can't leave my brother Krishna either. Hence, I have decided that I won't support either of the parties.'

Although he didn't get Balram's support, Duryodhan left Dwarka feeling good about his trip. With a neutral Balram and an unarmed Krishna, he had already won half the battle. The hundred million Narayani warriors would do the rest.

Shalya, the king of Madra, was one of the most powerful kings, whose support was sought by both the sides. The Pandavas were his nephews, since the late queen Madri, mother of Nakul and Sahadev, was his sister. Shalya longed to see his nephews and was on his way to the city of Upaplavya. When Duryodhan came to know of this, he hatched a plan. He instructed his men to build several rest camps on the way to the Pandava retreat. The camps were beautifully decorated and loaded with delicious food and drinks. Musicians and acrobats were hired to entertain the tired travellers. Duryodhan's men invited the king and his entourage to the rest camps whenever he passed them. Shalya and his men couldn't avoid their invitation and they were treated like gods. Pleased with the hospitality, Shalya asked, 'Who built these wonderful rest camps? I wish to reward him.'

Duryodhan was but waiting for this opportunity. He stepped out and bowed to Shalya. 'Uncle Shalya, I am glad you liked my humble arrangements. It has been an honour to serve you,' he said.

Shalya embraced Duryodhan and said, 'I am really pleased. Ask me for anything and I will give it to you.'

Palms joined, Duryodhan said, 'O King, if you wish to reward me, I have a humble request. Please take charge of our army and lead us in the forthcoming battle.'

Shalya was taken aback. He had always intended to support the Pandavas, his nephews. But now he couldn't take back his word. He said, 'So be it. I will fulfil your wish and join your team in the battle.'

Duryodhan was ecstatic. He said, 'Well, then, after you visit the Pandavas, please come to Hastinapur. I look forward to your advice and guidance.'

Shalya reached the Pandava camp and narrated the incident to them.

Yudhishthira said, 'Uncle, I would never ask you to take back your word. But I would like to request you to do us one favour: when Arjun fights Karna, I am sure you'd be Karna's charioteer. And when this happens, I'd ask you to demoralize Karna and make him weak by whatever means possible. You must do this for us.'

Shalya reassured his nephew, saying, 'Don't worry. I will serve the evil Karna as his charioteer. During the battle, I will pour such vile words into his ears that he would lose his concentration and his will to fight. He would lose his powers and Arjun will kill him easily.'

The Pandavas and the Kauravas continued their efforts to augment their strength. Hundreds of kings from far and near joined the Pandava side and promised to support them with their military might. Soon, the Pandavas amassed an army of seven akshauhinis. An akshauhini comprised 21,870 chariots; 21,870 elephants; 65,610 cavalry and 109,350 infantry.

The Kauravas were also able to build a huge army with support from the kings all around. Finally, the strength of their army rose to eleven akshauhinis—four more than the Pandavas. Duryodhan felt confident that the Pandavas had no chance against him when the war happened. However, the Kuru seniors were not so sure. They wanted to give diplomacy a chance before an all-out war broke out between the cousins, for they knew such a war would have devastating consequences and would wipe out a huge number of men from the land of Bharata.

48

The Diplomacy Continues

WHILE THE PANDAVAS AND THE KAURAVAS REINFORCED THEIR MILITARY strength, the diplomatic process remained underway, but with little success.

Drupad's priest tried to convince the Kaurava seniors to give the Pandavas what was due and avoid a war. 'The Pandavas have the strength to wipe out the Kauravas whenever they want and, if forced, they won't hesitate to do so,' said the priest. 'But things don't have to turn out that way. Return the Pandavas their kingdom and they'd be happy.'

Bhishma agreed. 'Your words may sound harsh to Kaurava ears, but they are true. The Pandavas have suffered a lot of distress and they deserve to get their kingdom back. Their might is well known. Arjun alone can destroy the Kauravas,' he said, his eye pointing meaningfully at Karna.

This infuriated Karna. He addressed the priest: 'Why do you keep repeating the same thing over and over? The Pandavas have failed to keep their promise. They came out of their hiding before the end of their term. Tell Yudhishthira to go back into exile for twelve more years, followed by a year in hiding. Lord Duryodhan might consider giving back their kingdom after that.'

Dhritarashtra intervened. 'Let's not discuss this now. Brahmin, please go back to the Pandavas and tell them, I will think the issue over and send Sanjay with our response.'

A few days later Dhritarashtra called his trusted charioteer and friend Sanjay, and said, 'Please go to Yudhishthira and tell him, all I want is peace. You are smart and well-versed in politics. You know our situation. Do whatever you can to prevent a war.'

Sanjay arrived at the Pandava camp and said, 'You know very well, Duryodhan is surrounded by evil advisors. King Dhritarashtra doesn't approve of war, but he is held hostage by his love for his son. And this dilemma is causing him immense pain. You and your brothers are invincible. But the Kauravas are no cowards either. They have on their side giants like Bhishma, Drona, Kripa and many others. A war would mean unthinkable destruction on both sides. Yudhishthira, you are the most knowledgeable, the most righteous person on earth. You figure out a way to ensure peace.'

'We don't want war either. But isn't it unfair to expect peace by depriving us of our rightful property? Dhritarashtra is suffering because he is indulging his evil sons and his evil friends. Tell him to give us back our Indraprastha and there will be no war.'

'I would think, even if you don't get back your kingdom, you should avoid war. What would you gain by killing your relatives? Would you enjoy your life in the palace without them? It is better to forgive and forget than to get into a bloody war. I don't know who is instigating you to fight a war. It will only make you stray from the path of Dharma.'

Yudhishthira was offended by Sanjay's words. In a firm voice, he said, 'Sanjay, I always try to stay on the path of Dharma. Situations like this create doubts as to what is right and what is wrong. Krishna is here. Let him say if I have strayed from Dharma.'

'Sanjay, you speak of peace now, but have you forgotten the atrocities inflicted upon the Pandavas by Duryodhan and his followers?' Krishna asked. 'Time and again, Yudhishthira has demonstrated his preference for peace, else a war would have happened a long time ago. Now, if Yudhishthira must fight to get back his kingdom, it would be justified as his Kshatriya right. I want peace and, if needed, I would love to broker a peace agreement. But would the Kauravas listen to me? I doubt it. Please go and tell your king that the Pandavas would love to resolve the dispute peacefully. But if the situation demands, they are prepared to fight.'

Yudhishthira further reasoned and said, 'Pay my respects to Bhishma and tell him to do whatever possible to ensure that his grandsons stay alive and happy. Tell Duryodhan to give us one small province from his vast kingdom and there will be no war. If a province is too much for him, ask him to give us five brothers five small villages—Kusasthal, Vrikasthal, Makandi, Varanavat, and one more. That'll be enough to make us happy and avoid a bloody war. Otherwise, a war is inevitable.'

Sanjay went back to Hastinapur and delivered the message to Dhritarashtra's court. Bhishma stood up and said, 'The Pandavas have made a modest request. It would be foolish of Duryodhan to let go of this opportunity and avoid utter destruction.'

Duryodhan didn't care to answer. He turned away from Bhishma in a rude display of defiance. Bhishma shrugged off the insult and added, 'Duryodhan, you lost your sense of honour a long time ago and I know you don't care for my advice. Still, I insist: stop listening to your evil trio of advisors—Karna, the son of a charioteer who was cursed by his guru Parashurama; the vicious Shakuni who is bent upon destroying you; and your stupid brother Dushasana. Or else, you'll be responsible for the death of thousands.'

Karna was furious and jumped up from his seat. 'Why do you speak ill of me? I have always stayed on the path of Dharma. Yet, you despise me for no reason at all. O King Dhritarashtra, stop worrying. I will destroy the Pandavas alone. Once an enemy, always an enemy. It is futile to think of peace negotiations with them.'

Bhishma chuckled and said, 'You'll kill the Pandavas? Where were you when Arjun killed your brother in the battlefield of Virat? What happened to you when he defeated us all and took off with your clothes? Why did you flee when the gandharvas thrashed your friend Duryodhan? And now you thump your chest like a wild ape?'

Before Karna could answer, Drona interjected, 'O King, listen to what Bhishma says. We all know, we cannot beat the Pandavas in a war. So, it is better to negotiate a peace deal before it is too late.'

Dhritarashtra did not pay attention to Bhishma or Drona. He kept probing Sanjay about the strengths and motives of the Pandavas, as if trying to find a hint of weakness that could be used to tear them apart. Sanjay's responses were not encouraging at all.

'I fear Bheem the most,' said Dhritarashtra. 'He is a monster. He never forgives, never forgets his enemies. He alone can kill my sons. Yes, I know Bhishma and Drona are with us and they would serve the throne of Hastinapur till the end, but they have become old. I am not sure how long they can stand up to Arjun's onslaught. Karna is good, but he is forgiving and often careless. I can't rely on him. To tell you the truth, I feel we are no match for the might of the Pandavas and I don't think it is advisable to fight a war against them. If you all agree, I am willing to negotiate a truce with them.'

Duryodhan stood up and said, 'Father, don't be afraid. When we sent out the Pandavas to their exile, I was afraid they would defy our orders, turn back and attack us. It was the best time for them. Public opinion was also against us. At that time, Bhishma, Drona and the other Kuru seniors assured me, the Pandavas could never beat us. I wonder what has changed between then and now! There is no reason to believe that Bhishma, Drona, Kripa and others have lost their valour in these thirteen years. Rather, the hardship of the forest has weakened the Pandavas. In these thirteen years, we have conquered the world and all the powerful kings are on our side. Let me tell you, they have asked for five villages not because of their generosity of heart. Rather, they scaled down their demand because our military strength has scared them. And don't fear Bheem. Everybody knows that I am the best mace fighter. I can kill him with one blow of my mace. How could Arjun survive against Karna, who has Indra's Ekaghni weapon? Besides, we have an army of eleven akshauhinis, while the Pandavas have only seven. They are no match for our strength.'

Dhritarashtra was not convinced. 'My son has gone mad,' he said. 'He can never defeat Yudhishthira. Bhishma is aware of their strength. That's why he is reluctant to fight. Duryodhan, give up your war ambitions. Half the kingdom is enough for your survival. Give the other half to the Pandavas and live in peace. I don't want war.'

Duryodhan couldn't take it any more and blew his top. 'I never depended on you or Bhishma or Drona,' he blurted out. 'Karna, Dushasana and I can fight the Pandavas and we don't need your help. I amassed our army on my own and I will fight my own battle. I can never stay together with the Pandavas. Listen to me once and for all: I won't give the Pandavas even a tiny spec of land that one can hold on the tip of a needle.'

Hiding his face in his palms, Dhritarashtra said, 'Listen, everybody, from this moment, I disown my son Duryodhan, for he is headed towards a horrible death. I pity all who follow him. The gods will protect their sons, the Pandavas. All who challenge the Pandavas would have to face the wrath of the gods.'

Duryodhan ran to his father's feet and knelt before him. 'The gods have denounced earthly love, and that's why they are gods. They don't have the human feelings of love a father has for his son. Father, trust me, the Pandavas can't defeat us. I have all the powers the Pandavas have. I can do whatever they can.'

Supporting Duryodhan's claims, Karna said, 'My guru Parashurama gave me the fiercest of weapons. The Pandavas don't stand a chance against them.'

'Why don't you tell us about your guru's curse too?' Bhishma interrupted Karna. 'Or would you not say the truth?'

'I don't lie and I am never ashamed of my guru,' replied Karna. 'My guru, the great Parashurama vowed never to teach a Kshatriya. But I was desperate to learn from him. So, I introduced myself as a Brahmin to take my lessons in archery and weaponry. Pleased with my dedication and performance, Lord Parashurama granted me the most powerful weapons available to humans. After the completion of my training, one day, my guru felt tired and wanted to take a nap. I sat on the ground and offered him my lap as a pillow. He put his head on my lap and went to sleep. A little later, a venomous insect crawled up my thigh. The insect bit my skin and then burrowed into my flesh. The incredible pain caused by the insect and its venom was unbearable. I clenched my jaws and kept still, without flinching a single muscle. I was afraid any movement would disturb my guru's nap. When my guru woke up and saw my bleeding thigh, he said that I cannot be a Brahmin, for no Brahmin could tolerate such excruciating pain. He understood that I was a Kshatriya and cursed me in anger. He said that when my final hour arrives, I will forget the weapons he gave me. I fell on his feet and asked for his forgiveness. Later, he calmed down, but he couldn't take back his curse. But look, I am still alive and I still remember my weapons. Let the old men—

Bhishma, Drona, Kripa—stay with you. With my guru's blessings, I will destroy the Pandavas myself.'

Bhishma laughed at Karna's confidence. 'Keep dreaming, Karna. You have no idea about the strength of your opponent. Your weapons will be shred to smithereens by Krishna's Sudarshan Chakra. Arjun's arrows would shatter your divine weapons mid-air. You'll die a horrendous death at Arjun's hands.'

Karna couldn't take it any more. He got off his seat and hollered, 'Stop! I've had enough of your caustic remarks. I can't take it any more. From today, I lay down my weapons. You won't see me fight in the war, neither would you see me in this court. I will take up my arms only after Bhishma's death. Only then would the world be able to witness my prowess.' Karna stormed out of the court. Duryodhan was stunned to hear this and ran after Karna along with Dushasana to stop him.

Bhishma laughed and said, 'Come back. Karna's promise is nothing but empty words. This evil man lost all his credibility the day he lied to his guru, Parashurama. Now his words mean nothing.' Bhishma walked away in disgust.

A strange silence engulfed the court. The ministers and kings lost their words. Helpless, they looked at each other. The blind king Dhritarashtra stared at the ceiling and waited to hear something from his son Duryodhan ... a few words of hope and encouragement. But nobody uttered a word. Slowly, they rose from their seats and left the court. The king sat alone on the throne with only his trusted friend Sanjay by his side.

49

Krishna, the Emissary

AFTER SANJAY LEFT FOR HASTINAPUR, THE PANDAVAS WENT TO Krishna. Yudhishthira said, 'It seems you are the only person who can save us from this debacle. Dhritarashtra wants peace, but he is not willing to give us back our kingdom. I have powerful friends like you. Still, for the sake of peace, I asked for just five villages. I know Duryodhan won't agree to that either. A war only kills the good people—the ones who are wise and peace-loving. The evil ones always survive. We all know, violence begets more violence. I don't want destruction, I don't want war, but I don't want to give up what is rightfully ours either. We must try all means to achieve truce. We should fight a war only if we fail and we run out of all other options.'

Krishna kept quiet for a few moments. Then he said to his visitors: 'For your sake, my dear cousins, I will go to Hastinapur and pray to Dhritarashtra for peace. If I can get you your kingdom without a war, I'd be the happiest person.'

'What if Duryodhan disregards you?' asked Yudhishthira. 'What if he insults you? What if he and his brothers harm you? I can't let that happen.'

Krishna smiled, 'Well, even if I am unable to broker a peace agreement, at least people won't blame us as war hawks. They would realize we did all we could to avoid a bloody war.'

Yudhishthira sighed. 'Krishna, do whatever you think is right. You know best.'

'I will try to present your case to the best of my ability,' said Krishna. 'However, knowing Duryodhan, you should be prepared to fight the war. Whether we win or lose, there is nothing more glorious for a Kshatriya than to fight a war for the right cause. Weakness doesn't suit him.'

Bheem was sitting in a corner of the room, his head held low. Slowly, he raised his head and said to Krishna: 'When you go to Hastinapur, don't try to intimidate the Kauravas. Duryodhan is impatient and doesn't understand what's good for him. Be kind to him when you speak. Don't say anything to enrage him. We'd rather accept defeat, but we don't want the total annihilation of the Bharata dynasty. Yudhishthira, Arjun, I ... we all prefer peace to war.'

Krishna was taken aback by Bheem's response. He laughed: 'How strange of you to utter these words! You have always been eager to destroy the Kauravas. You promised to kill Duryodhan with your mace. You promised to tear apart Dushasana's chest. And now you speak of peace? What's come over you? Are you afraid of the war? Dear cousin, shake off your malaise and prepare to fight. A Kshatriya doesn't accept anything that he doesn't acquire with his might.'

Bheem jumped up from his seat. His face was red with rage. In a thunderous voice, he said, 'How could you say such harsh words to me? You either don't understand me, or you have taken me for granted. Listen: I am no coward, and I am not afraid of war. When the time comes, you'll see how I crush the enemy under my feet. Krishna, when the war happens, you'll know what I am made of.'

Krishna stood up and embraced Bheem. 'Don't be angry, my dear cousin. I had no intention of insulting you. I was only trying to boost your spirits.'

Arjun said, 'Krishna, we will do whatever you advise. If you think war is the only way out, so be it. Give us the order and we will fight without hesitation.'

Nakul chimed in too. 'Krishna, we trust you'll do whatever is best. It is natural for men to change their minds. Listening to you, the Kauravas might have a change of heart too.'

Sahadev, however, had a different view. 'I don't know why my brothers are insisting on peace. I want you to ensure the war happens. Even if the Kauravas have a change of heart and they want a truce, you must make the war happen. After what they did to Draupadi, I can never have peace without seeing the dead body of Duryodhan. Tell that fool Duryodhan, we'd either win back Hastinapur or go back to the forest.'

Draupadi had been listening to the entire conversation quietly. Krishna saw her standing and weeping in a corner of the room. He asked, 'Panchali, don't you have anything to say?'

Draupadi looked up and said, 'Krishna, I was born of the yagna, the fire sacrifice, and that is why people call me Yagnaseni. Despite all my valiant husbands being alive, despite having you as a dear friend, I had to suffer the worst humiliation any woman could ever imagine. Shame on Arjun's weapons, shame on Bheemsen's strength, that Duryodhan is still alive.' She held her hair and swung it in front of Krishna. 'When you speak to the Kauravas, remember this hair of mine that was pulled by Dushasana when he dragged me to the dice game. How can I rest in peace without seeing those hands severed from his evil body? If Bheem and Arjun want peace, let them step aside. My old father, my gallant brothers, my five sons and Abhimanyu will fight the Kauravas. They will kill Dushasana and let me have my revenge.'

Krishna placed his hand on Draupadi's head to console her. 'My dear sister, rest assured, those who humiliated you, tortured you, will die a horrible death. If the sons of Dhritarashtra don't listen to my advice, their dead bodies would be devoured by rats and dogs in the battlefield. Stop crying. Soon, your husbands would kill their enemy and regain their fortune and glory.'

A few days later, on an autumn morning, Krishna mounted his chariot to travel to Hastinapur. Satyaki accompanied him. On the way, Krishna met Vyasa, Narada, Parashurama, and many other sages who were all travelling to Hastinapur. Parashurama said, 'We are going to the Kaurava court to listen to you make your case for peace. Go ahead, we'll see you in Hastinapur.'

When Dhritarashtra heard that Krishna himself is coming to Hastinapur as an ambassador of peace, he called Duryodhan and said, 'Make gala arrangements to welcome Krishna to the city. Make sure he is treated with respect and dignity.' Then he turned to Vidura and said, 'I wish to offer expensive gifts to Krishna. How about sixteen golden chariots driven by powerful horses, eight elephants, one hundred servants and one hundred maids? I am sure that'll make him happy.'

Vidura laughed, 'I understand your motives. You are reluctant to give the Pandavas five small villages, but you want to bribe Krishna with these expensive gifts. I know, Krishna won't accept any of your gifts. Rather, the greatest gift you could offer him would be to accept his proposal and bring peace to the Kaurava dynasty.'

Duryodhan agreed. 'For once, Vidura is right. Krishna won't be pleased with our gifts, for he is on the Pandava side. If we offer him expensive gifts, he'd think we are scared and are trying to appease him. Father, I've told you several times: sharing the kingdom with the Pandavas is out of the question, so don't even think about it. Now listen to my plan. When Krishna arrives in our palace, I will capture him and throw him to the dungeon. If we can neutralize Krishna, the world will be ours.'

Hearing Duryodhan's plan, the blind king shuddered in fear. 'Don't even think of capturing Krishna,' he said. 'He is not only the emissary of the Pandavas, he is also our revered relative. He should be treated with respect.'

Bhishma, who was trying to ignore Duryodhan for some time, couldn't stay quiet any longer. Addressing Dhritarashtra, he grunted, 'Stop your son from trying such a foolish act. Or else, Krishna's rage will destroy him instantly.'

The next day, Krishna arrived in Hastinapur. Dhritarashtra, Bhishma and Drona welcomed him with open arms. Duryodhan walked up to him and said: 'Krishna, you must be tired from your long journey. We can have our formal talks tomorrow. For now, please come inside and rest a while. Our cooks have prepared delicious meals for you.'

Krishna bowed to Dhritarashtra and the other Kuru seniors to pay his respect. Then he turned to Duryodhan and said, 'I am sorry, Duryodhan. As an emissary of the Pandavas, I cannot accept a meal from you until my mission is accomplished.'

'We have no animosity with you. Why wouldn't you accept our hospitality?'

'The Pandavas are my friends. An enemy of the Pandavas is my enemy too. Now, I'd like to visit Kunti and have my meals at Vidura's place, where I also intend to spend the night. Tomorrow morning, I'll come to your court and offer my proposal.'

Kunti was overwhelmed with emotion when she saw Krishna. Embracing him, she said, 'I am so glad to see you. Tell me, how are my boys? What an unfortunate mother I am. My sons, who would have been the rulers of the world, had to suffer thirteen years as beggars in the forest.'

Krishna held Kunti and said, 'Dear Aunt, please don't blame yourself. The bad times will pass soon, and your sons would once again rule the world.'

After spending some time with Kunti, Krishna went to Vidura's house. Vidura was overjoyed to have Krishna as his guest. He served him with whatever meagre food he had in his kitchen. 'I am sorry, I couldn't offer you anything better,' he said. 'You should have had your dinner at the palace.'

Krishna said, 'A meal served with love is more delicious than from any royal kitchen in the world.'

After the meal, Krishna reclined on a straw mat to take rest. Vidura sat near his head and said, 'You shouldn't have come to Hastinapur. The Kauravas won't listen to you. That arrogant Duryodhan thinks he can do whatever he wants. Now, with his eleven akshauhini armies and the loyal service of Bhishma, Drona, Kripa and Karna, he thinks he is invincible. I am afraid, tomorrow Duryodhan would lose his temper and try to do something horrible to you. I suggest you go back.'

Krishna smiled. 'Come what may, tomorrow I will do whatever I can to stop this deadly family feud. Otherwise, history would blame me for not trying. If Duryodhan doesn't listen, he will have to suffer the consequences.'

'Well, so be it. Let's hope for the best. Maybe tomorrow will herald a new chapter in the saga of the Bharata dynasty.'

50

The Diplomacy Fails

KRISHNA WOKE UP EARLY THE NEXT MORNING. AFTER COMPLETING HIS morning ablutions, he mounted his chariot and arrived in the court of Dhritarashtra. Vidura and Satyaki held him by his hand and escorted him into the great hall. Dhritarashtra stood up and greeted him. The men in the court hailed Krishna. The court musicians played welcome songs in his honour. A special golden seat had been designated for Krishna. He took the seat graciously after bowing to the seniors in the court. Great sages like Narada, Parashurama and many others flocked to the court. Krishna bowed to them and took his seat.

Krishna said to Dhritarashtra, 'O King, I am here today to pray for peace. It is my humble request that you prevent the impending war between the Kauravas and the Pandavas, and bring about peace in the family. The Kuru dynasty is the greatest in the world, and it is up to you to ensure that its glory isn't tarnished. You know, your son Duryodhan and his brothers, with their arrogance and evil motives, are bent upon destroying this family. But you can still stop this devastation and bring back the Pandavas under your guardianship. Think about it, if the Pandavas join the Kauravas, even Indra won't dare to challenge you, and you'd be the undefeatable emperor of the world. I pray you don't let go of this opportunity. Losing your sons or the Pandavas in this bloody battle won't give you any peace of mind. Thousands of good men on both sides will perish unless you do something about it. Please listen to this message the Pandavas asked me to deliver to you. They said, "O King Dhritarashtra, we obeyed your orders and spent twelve years of our life in exile, followed by a year in hiding. During this period, we endured enormous pain and suffering, but we didn't break our promise. You are like our father. We pray to you, please keep your promise and return to us our share of the kingdom. We all have made mistakes and we request you, who is the closest we have to a guardian, to forgive us and bring us back on the path of truth."'

Krishna then addressed the assembled kings and ministers: 'My dear friends, do you think this request is unjustified? Is Yudhishthira's demand devoid of merit?' He turned back to Dhritarashtra and said, 'O King, time and again, Yudhishthira has demonstrated his preference for peace. He and his brothers have been ill-treated several times by your sons. Their wife Draupadi was humiliated in front of a court full of men. Still, he always yielded to you to avoid unpleasantness in the family. The Pandavas are willing to serve you once again if you let them. Otherwise, they have the might to win back what is rightfully theirs. It is up to you to decide their course of action.'

The men in the court remained silent. They liked what they heard, but didn't have the courage to speak up. Duryodhan, Dushasana and the other Kaurava brothers watched everybody and darted threatening looks at everyone. Finally, Parashurama spoke, 'It is foolish to fight an army that is led by Arjun and Krishna. They are the reincarnations of Nara and Narayana, and nobody can defeat them.'

Duryodhan laughed.

Rishi Kanwa said, 'Duryodhan, if you want to stay alive, don't fight the Pandavas. Krishna is Lord Vishnu himself. Surrender to him and give up your desire to fight.'

Duryodhan laughed again.

Rishi Narada spoke up, 'Arrogance and temper was the reason for Yayati falling from the heavens. My advice to you, give up your arrogance and make truce with the Pandavas.'

Duryodhan ignored him.

Dhritarashtra was listening to the rishis' comments. He said, 'Krishna, I agree with each and every word you say. But I am helpless. Duryodhan doesn't listen to me. Why don't you try to convince him?'

Duryodhan was sulking in his seat, looking away from Krishna. Krishna smiled and said in a soft voice: 'My dear Duryodhan, you are a learned man. You belong to a great family and you have a responsibility to uphold its glory. Most of your family members, your friends, your advisors, they all want truce with the Pandavas. It is your sacred duty to honour their wish. Remember, one who doesn't follow the advice of his well-wishers, soon finds himself in deep trouble. All your life, you have been cruel to the Pandavas, but they pardoned you. Don't consider it a weakness on their part. Trust me, even with the help of your mighty lieutenants like Bhishma, Drona, Karna and others, you won't be able to defeat Arjun, for he humbled the gods in the Khandava Forest and impressed Lord Shiva in combat. Can any mortal defeat him? Remember how he thrashed you during your little adventure in Virat? Prince Duryodhan, don't become the cause for the destruction of your family. People would curse you for that. History would never pardon you for your poor judgment. Make a truce with the Pandavas and they will accept Dhritarashtra as their king and you as the crown prince. Give them their share of the kingdom and rule yours in peace.'

Duryodhan looked at Krishna with hatred glowing in his eyes. 'You are biased in favour of the Pandavas and blame me for no reason,' he seethed. 'My father, you, Vidura, Bhishma, Drona, you always find fault with me and not with the Pandavas. I thought about all my actions you blame me for—even the tiniest one—but couldn't find anything wrong with them. Yudhishthira is addicted to the game of dice and he agreed to play of his own will. And then Shakuni defeated him and won their kingdom. Not me. Was that my fault? We obeyed our father's order and returned their kingdom. But they were foolish enough to play again and lose again and had to go into exile. Why am I to blame for their stupidity? I don't understand why you are bent upon destroying us. Remember, we fear nobody and we bow to nobody. Forget the Pandavas, even the gods can't beat Bhishma, Drona and Karna. I'd prefer a glorious death in the battlefield than a humiliating surrender. Krishna, listen to me for one last time. Forget the kingdom, without waging war, I won't give the Pandavas even a spec of dirt you can hold on to the tip of a needle.'

Krishna laughed. 'Glorious or not, you'll meet your death on the battlefield. You are an idiot and that's why you don't see any fault in your actions. Rest assured, soon, you would fall and lose everything to the Pandavas.'

Duryodhan was left fuming. Dushasana came to him and said, 'Brother, look at Bhishma and Drona. They are boiling in anger. I think they are hatching a plan. I won't be surprised if they capture us and hand us over to the Pandavas. I think we should leave.' A startled Duryodhan jumped up from his seat and left the court with his followers.

Bhishma sighed in disgust. 'A man who succumbs to anger and strays from the path of Dharma becomes a loser and a laughing stock.'

Krishna wasn't amused. He said sternly: 'The Kuru elders are to blame for this. You have given a fool the powers of a king, and then failed to control him. My uncle, the evil Kansa, took over his father Ugrasen's kingdom while he was still alive. The Yadavas, the Vrishnis and the Andhakas were terrified by his atrocities. So I had to kill him and restore Ugrasen to the throne to save my family and my tribe. I suggest you do the same. Capture Duryodhan and hand him over to the Pandavas. It is said, give up the evil member to save the family, give up the family to save the village, give up the village to save the country and give up the earth to save yourself.'

Dhritarashtra knew he had to do something, but he was out of options. He called Vidura and said, 'Go, bring Queen Gandhari. She might be able to control Duryodhan.'

Soon, Gandhari, with her blindfold, was escorted into the court. Dhritarashtra briefed her about the situation. She said, 'You are the culprit. You have handed over the reins of your kingdom to an arrogant and undisciplined rogue. Now you must suffer the consequences.'

Dhritarashtra asked Vidura to bring Duryodhan back into the court. Hearing Duryodhan's footsteps, Gandhari turned to face him.

'My son, listen to your father, listen to Bhishma and Drona,' she said. 'To rule a kingdom requires wisdom and virtue. Evil men want to rule, but they can't do it for long. It's not too late to change course. Join hands with the Pandavas and the world will be yours. Surrender to Krishna and he will guide both the parties in the right direction. War has no glory. War cannot bring peace. You have tortured the Pandavas for thirteen years; let go of your jealousy now and make amends. You are banking on Bhishma, Drona and Kripa to win the war for you. But if you think they would give their best while fighting against the Pandavas, you are a fool. They are loyal to the throne and they'd give their lives for you, but they could never treat Yudhishthira and his brothers as their enemies. Listen to me. Let go of your anger and greed. Make friends with the Pandavas.'

Gandhari's words, however, had no effect on Duryodhan. He left the court and huddled with his confidantes to devise a plan: 'Krishna is the main problem. If we can neutralize him, we will win for sure. He wants Bhishma and Drona to capture me and hand me over to the Pandavas as a prisoner. But I won't allow him the pleasure. Here is my plan: we go inside and, with a sudden move, attack Krishna and tie him up in chains. Father won't like it, Bhishma might try to stop us, but I don't care for any of them. Capture Krishna and we win the war.'

Satyaki overheard the conversations and ran out to Kritavarma and said, 'Gather the soldiers and ask them to wait in a formation at the gate.' He then ran into the court and announced, 'Duryodhan is about to attack Krishna and capture him. The fool doesn't know what he is getting into.'

Dhritarashtra panicked.

Krishna consoled him and said, 'O King, if your sons want to capture me, please let them try. If I want, I can destroy them in an instant. That'd resolve all problems. But I won't do such a thing, especially not in front of you. Duryodhan has my permission. He can do whatever he wants.'

Just then, Duryodhan and his brothers burst into the hall with fierce weapons in their hands. Dushasana carried a long iron chain to tie Krishna. Duryodhan yelled, 'Dushasana, wrap the chain around Krishna. Don't let go of him.'

Dhritarashtra cried out, 'What are you doing, my son? Have you gone crazy? Just like your hands can't hold the winds, your head can't hold the earth, Krishna cannot be held by any mortal being. Stop this idiocy right now.'

Duryodhan didn't care to listen to his father. He and his brothers surrounded Krishna like a pack of wolves ready to pounce on their prey.

Krishna laughed and said, 'Duryodhan, you think you can catch me? If you think I am unarmed and helpless, you are wrong. Look at me—the Pandavas, the Vrishnis, the Andhakas and all my friends are with me.' All of a sudden, Krishna seemed to grow double in size and from his forehead appeared Lord Brahma. Lord Shiva appeared from his chest, and Agni the god of fire appeared from his mouth. Indra and other gods, along with the gandharvas appeared from his limbs. The Pandava brothers, Krishna's brother Balram, the Vrishni, and the Andhaka warriors appeared from nowhere with divine weapons in their hands. Krishna stood in the middle like a huge tower. He seemed to have thousands of eyes, thousands of arms, thousands of legs. His terrifying stature scared the men in the court. The bright rays emanating from Krishna's body blinded them. They closed their eyes. Only Bhishma, Drona, Vidura, Sanjay and the rishis could watch the wonderful sight. The gods, the gandharvas and the sages bowed to the Almighty and said, 'Lord, please have mercy on us. Control your fury and spare your creation from imminent destruction.'

The heartfelt appeals calmed Krishna down and he slowly regain his original form. The deities who had appeared to protect Krishna also disappeared into thin air. The men in the court sighed in relief while Duryodhan and his brothers lay on the ground, unconscious. Krishna held Vidura's and Satyaki's hands and left the hall.

As Krishna was about to mount his chariot, Dhritarashtra came to him and said, 'Krishna, you saw how little influence I have on my sons. You heard how I tried to stop Duryodhan. Everybody knows I am for peace and how I keep trying to prevent war.'

Krishna turned to Vidura and Satyaki: 'You saw what happened today. You witnessed how Duryodhan tried to imprison me. And Dhritarashtra admits he has no control over his sons or his kingdom. I tried my best to bring peace, but I failed. Now let us all wait for the inevitable.' Saying so, Krishna mounted his chariot and left the palace grounds to meet Kunti.

51

Krishna and Karna

AᴘᴘFRUSTRATED AND DISAPPOINTED Kʀɪsʜɴᴀ ARRIVED AT Kᴜɴᴛɪ's ᴘʟᴀᴄᴇ. He paid his respects to her and narrated the disastrous events that had transpired in the palace. Kunti was outraged. 'It is futile to make further attempts for peace. Ask Yudhishthira to shed all thoughts of peace and prepare to use his might to win back his throne. His attitude is more like a Brahmin's than a Kshatriya's. He thinks more than he acts. Tell him, Lord Brahma created the Kshatriya from the muscle of his arms. That's why a Kshatriya should always use the power of his muscles to resolve a dispute. Tell him, a weak and non-violent king can never control his subjects. Follow the path of your gallant ancestors and use all your strength to win over your enemy. That's what a true Kshatriya should do. How shameful it is that I, being the mother of the great king Yudhishthira, must depend on the pity of others for my survival. Shame on such a son.' Kunti couldn't hold back her tears any longer.

Krishna tried to console her: 'My dear Aunt, don't worry, your days of misery are over. Yours sons will soon rule Hastinapur and you'll be the queen mother. Now, please let me take your leave. I have to complete a task before I head back.'

Krishna left Kunti's house and asked his charioteer Satyaki to head towards Karna's house. Karna was flabbergasted to see Krishna arrive at his doorstep. He welcomed Krishna into his house. 'Krishna, I am honoured to have you as a guest at my humble abode. Please have a seat. Tell me, what can I offer you?'

Krishna sat down on an ornate throne and said, 'My dear Karna, I am here with a proposal. If you accept, I will have whatever you offer me. But first listen to what I have to say.'

'Fair enough,' said Karna as he sat next to Krishna.

Krishna paused for a moment and then said, 'Karna, you are well-read and well-versed in the scriptures. You must be aware of the intricate rules and laws prescribed by the learned pundits. One such law says that if an unmarried woman gets pregnant, the child born can either be kaneen, or sahodha. A kaneen child is one who is born before the woman is married, and a sahodha child is the one born after marriage. The man who marries such a woman is regarded as the legal father of both the kaneen and sahodha children.' Krishna stopped to take a breath.

Karna was impatient. 'Yes, I know. But why are you telling me this?'

'Karna, you are the kaneen son of Kunti. And Pandu is your legal father.'

Karna was shocked. He stood up and said, 'What are you talking about? Are you out of your mind?'

'Please hear me out before reaching a conclusion. Your mother Kunti, when she was only a teenager, received a boon from Rishi Durvasa—a mantra that gave her the power to summon any god and have a child from him. Curious and unaware of the consequences, Kunti summoned the Sun God and conceived a child—you. But a child out of wedlock would have been a disaster. So, when you were born, Kunti put you in a basket and set it afloat in the Ganga. Fortunately, Adhirath the charioteer saw the basket downstream and took you home to his wife Radha. Adhirath and Radha brought you up as their own son.'

Karna's head was spinning. His eyes were bloodshot with rage. He said, 'If I had heard this from someone other than you, I would have killed him that very instant for uttering such an outrageous lie.'

'You think I am lying to you?' Krishna smiled.

'That's the problem. But I can't believe my ears either.'

'Trust me. Every word I say is true. You are the first son of King Pandu. And you deserve to be the ruler of Hastinapur—not Yudhishthira, nor Duryodhan.'

'You tell me I am the senior-most Pandava brother? Yudhishthira, Bheem, Arjun, Nakul, Sahadev are my brothers? I have the right to the throne?' Karna's voice trembled as he uttered these words.

Krishna went close to Karna and held his arm. 'Come with me, Karna. Come and join the Pandavas. When your brothers come to know of your true identity, they'll be overwhelmed with joy. They will surrender at your feet. All the kings and rulers who support the Pandavas will yield to you. Draupadi will accept you as her sixth husband. We will make you the king. Yudhishthira will be the crown prince and stand by your side. Bheem will hold the shades over your head. Arjun will drive your chariot. Nakul, Sahadev, the five sons of Draupadi, the Panchals, the Vrishnis—they will all follow you. O son of Kunti, join your brothers and rule the world.'

Karna walked away from Krishna and gazed out of the window. Krishna stood next to him and said, 'Karna, join the Pandavas and this war will not happen. Duryodhan would lose his will to fight and surrender to you. Millions of lives will be saved.'

Karna turned to Krishna and said, 'Krishna, I know what you say is true. Yes, as per the scriptures, I am the first son of Pandu, and that makes me a claimant to the Kuru throne. But I can't forget the fact that my mother Kunti abandoned me without caring for my life. It was the poor charioteer Adhirath and his wife Radha who rescued me and brought me up. Adhirath considers me as his son, and I know him as my father. He sent me to the best teachers for my education and my arms training. I am what I am only because of my parents' blessings. There is nothing in this world that can make me disown them. And I cannot abandon my friend Duryodhan either. It is because of him that I am respected as a king and not as a mere charioteer. Duryodhan depends on me. He embarked upon this war only because he knows I'll always be on his side. He expects me to fight Arjun and defeat him. No amount of riches can make me break his trust.'

Krishna sighed. 'Think again. My proposal would benefit both sides.'

A faint smile surfaced on Karna's lips. He said, 'I know, what you say is for the good of mankind. But I am sorry. I cannot give up my principles to become the king of the Kuru kingdom.' Karna paused a moment and then said, 'One more thing. Please keep this discussion a secret, especially from Yudhishthira. If he knows that I am his elder brother, he will never accept the throne. He'd hand it over to me. And if I get the throne, I would hand it over to Duryodhan. So, let Yudhishthira be the king, you his advisor and Arjun his protector. I pray to you, bless those who die in this war of Kurukshetra so that they attain heavenly abode.'

Krishna stood up and said, 'Karna, I offered you the kingdom of the world, but you refused to accept it. The Pandavas will win for sure. Nobody can defeat them. Please tell the Kuru seniors to prepare for war. This autumn is the best time for battle. The weather is mild, crops are abundant, and the fields are dry. A week from now, on the day of the new moon, let the war begin. Tell the kings and warriors on your side, their wishes will be fulfilled. They will all die and go to heaven.'

Krishna turned around to leave. Karna stopped him and said, 'Krishna, before you leave, let me ask you a question. Why are you doing this? Why this acting, this show? You know very well that nobody can prevent this bloody war. Duryodhan, Dushasana, Shakuni or I—we are mere excuses for the inevitable. I have had horrible nightmares. I saw you holding a blood-drenched earth in your hands. You toss it over to Yudhishthira who, while sitting on a pile of skeletons, grabs the earth and devours it.'

Looking serious, Krishna replied, 'My words had no effect on you. Hence, destruction is inevitable.'

Karna laughed and replied, 'So be it. Give me a hug before you leave. Who knows if we'd get this chance again.'

Karna moved up to Krishna and wrapped his arms around him in a warm embrace. Moments later, Krishna stepped out of Karna's home and mounted his chariot. 'Let's go, Satyaki,' he said. 'We have no time to lose.'

Krishna's chariot sped away to the city of Upaplavya, where the Pandavas were waiting eagerly to know about the outcome of his meeting.

52

Karna's Promise

AFTER KRISHNA LEFT, VIDURA WENT TO SEE KUNTI, WHO WAS EAGERLY waiting to hear about the peace talks. Vidura stood before Kunti and nodded in frustration. 'You know, I tried my best to stop the war. Not once or twice, I tried several times. Duryodhan didn't listen. Old King Dhritarashtra's misguided affection for his son is not helping either. Today, Krishna also failed to bring them to their senses. Now, a devastating war is inevitable. It is because of this foolish and stubborn attitude of the Kauravas that thousands will lose their lives.'

Kunti felt a sudden fear deep in her heart. She knew her sons, the Pandavas, were indomitable. But the Kauravas had Bhishma, Drona and Karna on their side, and these great warriors had the capability of destroying the Pandavas. Perhaps Drona would be kind to his students and not be his fierce self against her sons. Maybe Bhishma too would go easy on his favourite grandchildren. Karna has no such affection for the Pandavas. He was desperate to kill them. He could do anything to please Duryodhan. If only ...

Kunti thought for a while and decided to meet Karna. The time was ripe to reveal the truth.

The next morning, Kunti went to the banks of the Ganga, where Karna performed his daily worship of the Sun God. Karna was standing knee deep in the water, facing the rising sun. With his eyes closed and palms joined together, he prayed to his lord. Kunti asked her charioteer to stop at a distance and walked towards Karna. Deeply engrossed in his prayers, he couldn't hear her footsteps. Kunti stood behind him and waited.

Karna was taking unusually long to finish his prayers. The impending war and the sudden revelation of his identity by Krishna was causing a storm in his mind. He wanted to calm his tormented soul. Maybe his father, the Sun God, would show him his right path, he thought. At around noon, when the Sun was high up in the sky, Karna concluded his prayers and opened his eyes. As he turned around, he saw Kunti standing right behind him. Karna felt a lump in his throat. A sudden surge of emotion overpowered him. With great effort, he controlled himself and walked up to the bank and bowed to Kunti.

'O great queen, I am Karna, the son of Adhirath and Radha. Please tell me, what can I do for you?' Karna stood with his palms joined.

Kunti's eyes were moist. With a trembling voice, she said, 'No, Karna, you are wrong. Adhirath is not your father. You weren't born of Radha either.' Kunti paused for a moment to gather strength. 'Today, I come here to tell you the truth about your birth. Karna, you are my son. It was I who gave you birth when I was a mere child—a foolish unmarried girl. The Sun God is your father. You were born in my father Kunti Bhoja's palace—a beautiful baby with a natural armour on your chest and divine rings in your ears.'

Karna didn't look surprised. He wrapped a scarf around his chest and said, 'Why are you telling me this now?'

'I want you to know who you are,' replied Kunti. 'You are not the charioteer's son people think you to be. You have royal blood in your veins. You deserve to be the king.'

'I know who I am.' Karna was getting impatient now. He wanted to run away from this lady who claimed to be his mother. 'Is there anything else I can do for you? I am late and I need to be back in the palace soon.'

'Listen to me, my son. Join hands with your brothers, the Pandavas,' Kunti reached out to touch Karna, who moved away. 'You are the older brother of Yudhishthira, Bheem, Arjun, Nakul and Sahadev. You six have the same blood in your veins—my blood. You shouldn't side with Duryodhan and fight against your brothers. Leave the Kauravas and, along with your brothers, win back what is rightfully yours—the throne of Hastinapur.'

Karna was speechless. Millions of thoughts raced through his mind. Here was Kunti, the queen mother of Yudhishthira, begging him to join the Pandavas. The other day, Krishna—Lord Vishnu incarnate—was promising him the throne of Hastinapur. Why was all this happening now? All these years, he had been worshipping the Sun God, for he felt an inexplainable attraction towards the lord of the skies. He heard the voice of his lord, the Sun God, speak to him: 'Kunti speaks the truth. She is your mother, and I am your father. Listen to her, for she means well. Leave Duryodhan and join the Pandavas, for that is the only way to bring about peace.'

Kunti was anxious. She asked, 'My son, are you listening to me? Trust me, if you fulfil my request, you'll be treated with respect, just as a Kshatriya king ought to be. Nobody would dare to humiliate you as the son a charioteer.'

Kunti's final words sparked a fire in Karna's heart. He opened his eyes and said, 'My dear queen mother, I am not ashamed of my charioteer heritage. Adhirath and Radha gave me life. They brought me up, while you abandoned me to die in the river. How could you expect me to leave them and join you? You deprived me of my Kshatriya heritage, and now you come to give me back my rights? You have done to me the worst crime one could ever commit to their offspring. How could you be so cruel? And now you beg me to join your sons only to save them?'

Kunti was in tears. 'My son, trust me, I had no other option. It was foolish of me to use the mantra without thinking of its consequences. I was only a child. Can't you forgive me for my sin?'

Karna felt his heart melting. He felt like throwing himself at Kunti's feet and seeking her blessings. He stood quiet for few moments and then said, 'I hold no grudge against you. But try to understand, I cannot join the Pandavas.'

'Why not?'

'Nobody knows I am a brother of the Pandavas,' replied Karna. 'If I join them now, people will think I am a coward. They'll think I fear Arjun and am trying to save face. The sons of Dhritarashtra have always been kind to me. They respect me. I cannot abandon them when they need me the most. They have embarked upon this war only because I am on their side. I know, what you say is for my good. But I am sorry. I cannot desert my friends. It's against my principle. Like any other soldier, I will give your sons a good fight.' Karna paused and gazed into Kunti's disappointed eyes. As she slowly bowed her head and prepared to leave, Karna said, 'You know, nobody returns from me empty-handed. This is what I promise you: although I can kill all your sons, I will not do so. I will only fight Arjun to death. In this battle, either he will survive or I will. So, whoever dies, you'll still be the mother of five sons—your five Pandavas.'

Kunti was astounded to hear this. With trembling arms, she embraced Karna and said, 'So be it. Let our fate decide what lies in our future.' Karna stood stiff as he tried hard to control his emotions. Kunti released him from her embrace and, as she was about to leave, she turned around and said, 'My son, please remember your promise. You would leave my sons unhurt, except Arjun.' Saying this, Kunti turned around and walked away.

Karna kept watching her as long as she was visible. Then he mounted his chariot and sped towards the Hastinapur palace.

In the meantime, in Upaplavya, Krishna sat with the Pandavas and gave them the news of his failure to broker a peace deal. 'I am afraid, we have no other option but to fight this war.'

Yudhishthira sighed. 'Well, so be it. Let us then prepare for war. First, we must appoint a commander-in-chief of our army. Who do you think is the best person to lead us in battle?'

Sahadev suggested King Virat. 'He is a good friend and experienced in warfare.'

Nakul suggested Drupad. 'Our father-in law has been our guardian since we left the palace. He is trained by the great Rishi Bharadwaj, and can counter Bhishma and Drona with equal might.'

Arjun opined, 'I think the gallant warrior Dhrishtadyumna is best suited for this job. He was born of the sacrificial fire to destroy Drona and the Kauravas.'

'I understand Shikhandi is destined to kill Bhishma. Let us make him the commander,' suggested Bheem.

Yudhishthira then turned to Krishna and asked, 'You are our chief advisor. Whom would you suggest?'

Krishna responded, 'All the names you suggest are capable of leading your army. But if you want my advice, I'd go with Arjun's choice—Dhrishtadyumna. I think he is the best choice.'

'Your advice is my command,' said Yudhishthira. 'Tomorrow, after finishing our prayers, we will march to Kurukshetra and set up our camp.'

The next day, the Pandava Army marched towards the Kurukshetra battlefield. The rumble of the chariot wheels, the galloping of the horses, the trumpet of the elephants and the war cries of the soldiers sent shivers down the spines of the villagers along the way. Thousands of cooks, servants, healers and workers accompanied the army. Draupadi and the other ladies stayed back in Upaplavya.

Arriving in Kurukshetra, Yudhishthira searched for an appropriate place to set up his camp. Finally, he selected the plains next to River Hiranvati that had enough trees, grass, wood and provided easy access to supplies. He ordered his architects and workers to build camps equipped with armaments, food, drink, firewood and other supplies. Separate camps were built for the accompanying kings, warriors and healers. The Pandavas gradually settled down in their camps and developed their war strategies.

Krishna's brother Balram arrived in the Pandava camp. Yudhishthira and his brothers greeted him and sat around him. Balram said to Krishna, who was sitting next to Yudhishthira: 'I know you have tried your best to prevent this war. I pray that all of you survive unscathed. Yudhishthira, I told Krishna, both the Kauravas and Pandavas are our relatives. He should not side only with you. He must also help the Kauravas. His love for Arjun made him support you with all his might. But this is unfair. And I can't support Duryodhan and go against Krishna either. Duryodhan and Bheem are my students and I love both of them. So, I've decided not to support anybody and recuse myself from this war.' With this, Balram stood up and left the camp.

53

The Story of Shikhandi

As the Pandavas set up camp, Duryodhan wasn't sitting idle either. He moved his huge army of eleven akshauhinis to Kurukshetra and built his camp on the banks of River Hiranwati, not far from where the Pandavas were.

It was time for him to pick his commander-in-chief. He went to Bhishma and said, 'Grandfather, one cannot win a war without a commander-in-chief. We are lucky to have so many spirited and experienced warriors on our side, but we need to stay united and follow one commander. I don't think there is anybody better than you to lead us in this war. Grandfather, please accept my offer and become the commander-in-chief of the Kaurava Army. The kings and warriors will be honoured to serve under your leadership.'

Bhishma was sardonic: 'Why me? Your friend Karna claims he can destroy the Pandavas in an instant. You should make him the commander-in-chief.'

Karna wasn't pleased with Bhishma's sarcasm. He stood up and said, 'Duryodhan, you know I promised not to touch my weapons as long as Bhishma is alive. You leave me out of this war until Bhishma falls.'

Duryodhan knelt before Bhishma and said, 'Grandfather, please don't turn me down. Only you can be the Kaurava commander. I beg you, lead us to victory.'

Bhishma gestured to Duryodhan to rise. 'To me, the Pandavas and the Kauravas are the same and I hate to harm anybody from either side. Still, I am obliged to serve the throne of Hastinapur. So, I will fight on your behalf in whatever role you ask me to serve. However, before I accept your offer, I must tell you one thing: I won't kill any of the Pandavas. But I promise you, each day of the war, I will kill ten thousand soldiers of the Pandava Army.'

Duryodhan was relieved. 'Don't worry about the Pandava brothers. We'll take care of them.'

Putting a stop to Duryodhan's premature elation, Bhishma said, 'One more thing I ought to mention: I will not fight Drupad's son, Shikhandi. I will not hurl a single arrow at him, even if he attacks me with full force.'

'But why?' asked a surprised Duryodhan. 'You said you'd destroy Drupad and his family. Then why wouldn't you fight Shikhandi?'

'Because I don't fight women,' replied Bhishma. 'Shikhandi was born a woman and later transformed into a man.'

Duryodhan was curious. 'Shikhandi was a woman? He is regarded as one of the bravest and fiercest warriors in the Pandava camp!'

'Let me tell you the story of Shikhandi,' Bhishma began narrating the story of Amba and her vow to kill Bhishma. '... After she was abandoned by everybody who mattered to her, Amba took refuge in a hermitage. A few days later, her uncle Hotrabahan visited the hermitage. Amba spilled her misery to him and told him how I was the cause for her misfortune. Hotrabahan asked her to stay in his palace and assured her that he would ask his friend Lord

Parashurama to punish Bhishma for humiliating her. A few days later, Parashurama came to visit Hotrabahan and heard the story. He felt sorry for Amba and said, "My dear, I will ask Bhishma to marry you. He is my student, and he won't refuse me. If he does, I'll destroy him." A few days later, Guru Parashurama called me to Kurukshetra. I met him and offered my respects. He asked, "Why did you turn down Amba? You brought her from her father's palace against her will. You are responsible for her misfortune. Marry her and make her your wife. That's an order." I knelt before my guru and said, "Lord, I am sorry. You know I have vowed never to marry in my life. Please don't ask me to break my promise." Parashurama was furious. "How dare you disobey my orders? You'll pay for your impudent behaviour." He raised his bow and thundered, "Defend yourself if you can. I'll kill you and leave your body to be devoured by the vultures." I had no option but to counter his attack. The fight soon turned into a raging battle. My mother Ganga appeared and prayed to Parashurama to stop. But he didn't listen. He kept spraying arrows at me. The battle continued for days. The gods and sages arrived and said, "Lay down your weapons. Neither of you can defeat the other." The gods appeared before me and said, "Bhishma, stop the war. Go and bow to your guru." I obeyed. Parashurama placed his hands on my head and said, "My son, you fought well. You are the greatest Kshatriya warrior alive, and nobody can defeat you." He called Amba and said, "I am sorry, my dear. I tried my best but couldn't defeat Bhishma."

'Frustrated but desperate, Amba then went to a hermitage next to the Yamuna River and began an arduous penance. The sages tried to dissuade her, but she was adamant. "I don't worship to attain the heavens," she said. "I want lord Shiva to grant me the power to kill Bhishma." Shiva was pleased with Amba's perseverance. He appeared before Amba and said, "You cannot kill Bhishma in your present life. But your wish will be fulfilled in your next life." Amba was impatient and couldn't wait for death to come to her. She killed herself in a funeral pyre with the hope of being reborn soon.

'During that time, King Drupad was worshipping Lord Shiva to have a son. He spent huge sums of money in yagnas and sacrifices with the hope that the lord would bless him with a son and an heir to his throne. Pleased with Drupad's worship, Shiva assured Drupad that he'd soon have a son. However, when the time came, Drupad's wife gave birth to a baby girl. The queen thought that the news of a girl child might upset her husband. Besides, Lord Shiva's words couldn't go wrong. She hoped that a miracle would transform the girl into a boy some day. So she announced to the king that a boy was born to him. King Drupad was happy to hear the news and named the child Shikhandi.

'The queen raised Shikhandi as a boy. Shikhandi wore boys' clothes, played and took lessons in warfare with the boys. When Shikhandi attained her youth, Drupad decided to get his "son" married. The queen was worried, but didn't dare to reveal the truth and enrage the king. With great fanfare, Shikhandi was married to the daughter of Hiranyavarma, the king of Darshan. On the wedding night, however, the princess got a rude shock when she discovered that her husband wasn't a man. Disappointed and feeling cheated, the princess sent her maids to her father with the unfortunate news.

'Hiranyavarma was furious. He sent a harsh message to Drupad. "My daughter's maids tell me that your son Shikhandi is not a man," his message said. "I am sending a team of courtesans to check your son's masculinity. If what I hear is true, I'll punish you severely for cheating my daughter. I will attack you with my full force and burn down your kingdom to ashes."

'A shocked king Drupad rushed to his wife and asked if the accusations were true. The queen admitted that she had been concealing Shikhandi's identity to please the king. "I thought, one day a miracle would transform Shikhandi into a man, for Lord Shiva's boon cannot go unfulfilled," she pleaded. Drupad was in a fix. He knew, Hiranyavarma was a powerful king and could cause significant damage to him and his kingdom. He had no option but to fight a deadly war with Hiranyavarma.

'Shikhandi was saddened to hear the plight of her parents. She had been the cause of their troubles, she thought. And it would be humiliating to subject herself to the scrutiny of the courtesans. So she decided to run away from the palace, never to return.

'Shikhandi fled the kingdom and took refuge in a cave in a distant forest. She spent many days in the cave without food and drink, and was on the verge of death. The cave was home to a yaksha named Sthunakarna. When Sthunakarna saw Shikhandi is such a pitiful state, he appeared before her and asked, "What's troubling you, my dear? Why are you bent upon killing yourself? Tell me, and maybe I could help you." Shikhandi told him her story and asked, "Can you make me a man? That's what I want most. If I become a man and satisfy Hiranyavarma's courtesans, I'd save my father and his kingdom from imminent destruction.'

'Sthunakarna felt sorry for Shikhandi. He said, "This is what I can do for you: I have the power to trade my masculinity with your femininity. You'll become a man, and I a woman—but only for a limited time. Once your job is done, come back to me and we'll trade back our genders. Do you promise to do that?"

'Shikhandi was ecstatic to hear this. She agreed to Sthunakarna's proposal. Sthunakarna then exercised his special powers and soon Shikhandi transformed into a man and Sthunakarna into a woman. An overjoyed Shikhandi thanked Sthunakarna and went back to her father's palace.

'Drupad and his queen were relieved to see Shikhandi return as a man. When Hiranyavarma's courtesans came to test Shikhandi, they were more than satisfied with her manhood. Hiranyavarma apologized to Drupad and scolded his daughter for her misjudgement.

'In the meantime, Kuber, the king of the yakshas, visited Sthunakarna. Sthunakarna was nowhere to be seen. Kuber's attendants searched for him inside the cave and came out with a woman. They said, "Lord Kuber, this is Sthunakarna. He was ashamed to come to you. He exchanged his manhood with Shikhandi, the princess of Panchal, and turned into a woman." Kuber was angry. He said to Sthunakarna, "You fool, you've abused your power and humiliated the yakshas. I take back your powers. You won't be able to get back your manhood. Stay a woman all your life." Sthunakarna begged for forgiveness, but Kuber refused and left him lying on the ground in tears.

'As promised, Shikhandi came back to Sthunakarna and offered to exchange their gender once again. Sthunakarna told him about Kuber's curse and said, "This was your destiny. There must be some divine reason for this to happen. Go back to your palace and live your life as a man."

'Shikhandi returned to Panchal and began to train under Dronacharya to become the great warrior he is. Shikhandi is none other than Amba, reborn as Drupad's daughter Shikhandini.'

Duryodhan was thoughtful, 'How do you know all this?'

Bhishma smiled: 'I have always kept track of my nemesis Amba through my spies. They kept me informed about her activities during her previous life as well as her current life as Shikhandi. And, as I said, I promised not to fight a woman, or a man who has been a woman, or dressed as a woman, or claims to be a woman. If you agree to my conditions, I accept the offer to be your commander-in-chief.' Saying this, Bhishma stood up and retired to his quarters.

54

Kurukshetra: The Final Preparations

IT WAS EARLY MORNING. THE SUN WAS YET TO SURFACE ON THE HORIZON. While the rest of the land was still asleep, the grounds around Kurukshetra woke up to the clamour of armours and weapons, the cry of elephants, the neigh of horses and the excited voices of the soldiers.

Duryodhan held a meeting in Bhishma's tent with his generals. He asked, 'O great warriors, tell me, how long will it take for us to annihilate the Pandava Army?'

Bhishma said while putting on his armour: 'I told you, I will kill ten thousand foot-soldiers and a thousand charioteers a day. At this rate, the Pandava Army would be eliminated in a month.'

Drona said, 'I am old and don't have the vigour of my youth. Still, just like Bhishma, I can destroy the Pandava Army in a month.'

Kripa said, 'I would take two months.'

Young Aswathama, the valiant son of Drona, said, 'Give me ten days and the Pandava Army would vanish from the face of the earth.'

Karna smirked, 'I'd need only five days to finish them off.'

Bhishma laughed. 'Karna, you haven't yet met the Krishna-Arjun duo and that's why you make such outrageous claims. When Arjun is led by Krishna as his charioteer, nothing in this universe can stop them. They will be indestructible. But you have the right to your opinion.'

When Yudhishthira heard of the Kaurava claims from his spies, he felt uncomfortable. He called his brothers and shared the news. 'What do you think? Can the Kauravas really destroy us so quickly? Can Aswathama kill all our men in ten days, and Karna in five?'

Bheem laughed, 'These are nothing but empty claims. They want to scare us, and that's why they spoke in the presence of our spies.'

Arjun didn't take it so lightly, though. 'The Kaurava greats have spoken the truth,' he said. 'They do possess the might and skills to destroy our army in the time they claim. However, you needn't be concerned. With Krishna's guidance, I can destroy the Kauravas in an instant. Remember, I have the Pashupat weapon from Lord Shiva. But I think it is unfair to use such a powerful weapon on the enemy, for it would annihilate them without giving them a chance to defend themselves. I would fight them using conventional weapons. With help from our allies, I am sure we would prevail over the Kauravas soon.'

As the day progressed, the armies assembled on the battlefield. The Pandavas took the western side of the field, facing the east; while the Kauravas took the opposite end. The soldiers wore colourful uniforms to differentiate themselves. Flags and banners marked each general and their armies. The army bands played trumpets and drums to motivate the soldiers. The healers and their assistants waited in the flanks with medicine and ointments to care for the wounded. Men with supplies of weapons to replenish the warriors stood at strategic points with their stock. The horses, the elephants, the infantry stood in attention and waited for the signal to pounce upon the enemies.

Before the battle began, the ministers from both sides met to decide on the rules of engagement. After a short deliberation, a senior minister stood up and announced the rules: The battle will be fought from dawn till dusk. After sunset, both parties will cease fighting and maintain a cordial relationship, as they did before the war. During the battle, a charioteer would fight a charioteer, a horseman another horseman, an elephant another elephant, and an infantry another infantry. If a man chooses to fight with words, the other party should also use only words to counter and no other weapon. If a soldier leaves his battalion to take shelter or rest, he should not be attacked. One must first let his opponent know his intent to fight; they may engage only if the opponent agrees. One who is reluctant to fight should not be forced to. A wounded or helpless, unarmed man should not be attacked. Healers, band members and those who carry supplies should not be attacked either.

While the preparations were in progress, Dhritarashtra sat alone in his chamber in the palace of Hastinapur. Remorse engulfed him. He wanted to avoid the war, but Duryodhan wouldn't listen. It would be difficult to defeat the Pandavas, he thought. With Krishna as his charioteer and advisor, Arjun would be indomitable in the battlefield. Arjun had acquired divine weapons from the gods and was well prepared to counter Bhishma, Drona, Karna and the other Kuru generals. He would spare nobody. Bheemsen was extremely dangerous too, and never liked Duryodhan and his brothers. Dhritarashtra remembered the day when Dushasana humiliated Draupadi during the dice game, Bheem had promised to tear apart Dushasana's chest and drink his blood. He had vowed to kill Duryodhan by shattering his thighs with his mace. Dhritarashtra shuddered at the thought of such a horrible end to his dearest son. If only Bhishma, Drona, Karna and Kripa rose up to the occasion and showed their true prowess ... nobody would be able to touch Duryodhan. And why not? Bhishma was obligated to serve the throne of Hastinapur. So was Drona. It was their duty to protect their king. Besides, Karna was no less than Arjun. If Karna could control his arrogance, then he alone could destroy the Pandava Army. These thoughts made Dhritarashtra feel a little better. Just then, he heard his trusted friend Sanjay's footsteps entering his room.

'Come, Sanjay,' Dhritarashtra called. 'Tell me, is there any news from the battlefield? Has the war begun? Who's winning?'

Sanjay bowed to Dhritarashtra and said, 'O King, our messengers haven't yet arrived with updates. The battle begins today. Bhishma is leading the Kaurava Army, while Dhrishtadyumna leads the Pandavas.'

Dhritarashtra sighed, 'How unfortunate I am that I have to live so far away from the battlefield. My sons, my loved ones, my men, are fighting for my throne, and I sit here helpless and wait for the bad news to arrive.'

As soon as Dhritarashtra uttered these words, the great Rishi Vyasa appeared in the chamber. He touched Dhritarashtra's head and said, 'My son, stop lamenting your fate. You know very well that it is time for your sons to pay for their misdeeds. They'll all be killed in this epic battle. A war like this happens once in eons to cleanse the earth of evil. If you wish, I can give you special vision so that you can witness the battle sitting here in your room.'

Dhritarashtra shook his head: 'No, Father, I don't want special vision. I have been blind all my life, and now I don't wish to watch the horrible bloodshed involving my sons.' He paused for moment and said, 'I have my hearing. So, if you can, give me the power to listen to a detailed description and commentary of the war as and when it happens.'

Vyasa looked at his son with pity. 'Alright, then,' he said. 'I will give Sanjay special powers that will enable him to watch the battle as it happens. Sitting next to you, he can watch the battle and narrate to you every detail, as if he were standing right in the battlefield. Don't worry about your sons, for this war would open the gates of heaven to them. Remember, those who follow the path of Dharma would be the ultimate winner.' Saying this, Vyasa disappeared.

'Sanjay, do you have your special vision?' asked Dhritarashtra. 'What do you see?'

'I see the Kurukshetra battlefield,' said Sanjay. 'O King, I see it all, and I will narrate to you each and every detail I see.'

In the Kurukshetra battlefield, the Kaurava and the Pandava armies were getting restless. Donning a white helmet and a white armour, Bhishma mounted his chariot. He looked around at the kings and generals and said, 'It is a curse for a Kshatriya to die of old age and sickness. To be killed in battle is the highest honour a Kshatriya can wish for. Don't be afraid to fight, for this battle would lead you to the heavens.' The audience hailed Bhishma as he led the huge Kaurava Army towards the battlefield. Aswathama, Dronacharya, Bhurishrava, Duryodhan, Shalya, Kripacharya, Jayadrath, Bhagadatta and the other generals followed Bhishma with their respective armies. At Bhishma's orders, the generals arranged the army in a multifaceted formation, with cavalry guarding the sides, the elephants in the centre, and the valiant kings in their chariots leading in the front. The huge army moved slowly in formation and took their position on the battlefield.

On the other side, Yudhishthira called Arjun and said, 'Brother, you see the Kaurava formation? War strategists advise that if your army is smaller than your enemy's, create the needle formation. What do you suggest?'

Arjun replied, 'Don't worry. I am creating the Vajra formation that Lord Indra taught me.' Dhrishtadyumna helped Arjun create the formation and, soon, the Pandava Army began to move. Bheem led the formation with his mace in hand. Dhrishtadyumna, Nakul, Sahadev and King Virat followed Bheem. Shikhandi, Abhimanyu and the five sons of Draupadi went next. Satyaki followed Arjun as his cover. Yudhishthira moved with the formation with his chariot in the centre. Yudhishthira turned to Arjun and said, 'I still don't understand how we can fight an army led by our valiant grandfather Bhishma. His formation looks indomitable, and I am really concerned that we can ever beat him.'

Arjun smiled: 'Righteousness, truthfulness and patience lead to victory more often than mere physical strength. You have always followed the path of truth. Nobody can defeat you. Besides, we have Krishna on our side, and he will lead us to our victory.'

On the Kaurava side, Duryodhan asked his charioteer to take him to Dronacharya. Standing next to Drona, he said, 'Sir, look at the huge army of the Pandavas. Your disciple Dhrishtadyumna built their formation. They have the support of great warriors like Satyaki, Virat, Dhrishtaketu, Chetikan, Abhimanyu and many others. It won't be easy to defeat them. But we have you, Karna, Kripacharya, your son Aswathama and many other gallant warriors fighting for us. I request you to rise to the occasion and lend your full support to our leader Bhishma. Fight for the throne of Hastinapur. Fight for King Dhritarashtra.'

Bhishma blew his conch shell and the sound reverberated through the battlefield. The army band began beating their huge drums and blowing their trumpets. On the Pandava side, Krishna blew his mighty Panchajanya conch and Arjun blew his Devadatta conch. Yudhishthira and the other Pandava warriors blew theirs. The deep and ominous sound from the shells made shivers run down the spines of the soldiers waiting to pounce into the battlefield.

Arjun said to Krishna: 'Please take me to the centre of the battlefield between the two armies. I wish to see whom I'd be fighting.'

Krishna said, 'Are you sure you want to do this?'

Arjun was surprised. 'Yes, I do,' he said. 'I want to look at the faces of my enemies before I kill them.'

'So be it,' said Krishna. He tugged the reins and the chariot broke away from the formation as it slowly rolled towards the Kaurava Army.

55

The Bhagavad Gita

KRISHNA DROVE ARJUN'S CHARIOT TO THE CENTRE OF THE BATTLEFIELD, between the two armies. Pointing towards the Kaurava Army, he said, 'Arjun, can you see your enemy clear enough? There stands the huge Kaurava Army, eleven akshauhini strong. Valiant kings and warriors wait for orders from their chief, Bhishma.'

Arjun scanned the Kaurava Army and saw his grandfather, his teachers, his cousins and many others with whom he had grown up. They were standing right in front, ready to fight him. These people were his enemies and he was supposed to kill them. Suddenly, Arjun felt a strange shiver run down his spine. A deep sense of despair and panic made him numb. His head was spinning, and he felt nauseated. His feet trembled and his entire body shook like a leaf. He grabbed the side of the chariot to keep his balance. Sounding choked, he said, 'I see my dear relatives standing on the other side. They are eagerly waiting to fight me. Krishna, I feel sick. My body is trembling, my mouth is dry and my skin burns. I feel weak and my bow is slipping away from my hand. My legs have become weak and I am unable to stand.'

Krishna was surprised to hear this. He turned to Arjun and asked, 'But why? Moments ago, you were fine.'

Arjun was perspiring as his heart raced. He tried to loosen his armour to get some air. In a laboured voice, he said, 'I can't kill my family, Krishna. How can I kill my grandfather Bhishma on whose lap I grew up? How can I kill Dronacharya who taught me to shoot an arrow? I know, Duryodhan, Dushasana and his brothers are greedy and evil. Still, they are our cousins. We played together, shared meals and studied together. How can I kill them just for the sake of a kingdom? What pleasure would that give me? What happiness would I achieve by killing my cousins and relatives? It is a grave sin to kill your own folks. Killing them would result in the destruction of our family and of family values. I can't let that happen. I would rather let the Kauravas kill me.' Arjun threw down his bow, took off his armour and sat on the floor of the chariot.

Krishna was shocked to hear this. In a serious voice, he said, 'What has come over you, Arjun? Now, at this critical juncture, when both the armies are prepared to fight this decisive battle, how can you talk of giving up your arms and desert the battlefield? Come on, get up, pick up your arms and fight.'

Arjun didn't move. Sweat dripped from his forehead as he tried to lift his head. He wiped his brows and said, 'I am sorry, Krishna. It is impossible for me to kill Bhishma and Drona. I love them and respect them like my own father. I can never hurt them, let alone kill them in the battlefield. I'd rather live my life as a beggar than commit such a heinous crime. This war is a huge mistake. I am not sure if it is better to be conquered or to conquer. What pleasure would I get by winning a kingdom void of Bhishma, Drona and my other loved ones?' Arjun looked up at Krishna, his eyes welling up with tears. He looked back at the Pandava Army and saw his brothers eagerly waiting for him to come back and join them. He looked again at the Kaurava Army and saw Bhishma prepared to launch an attack. Palms joined, Arjun said to Krishna, 'I am confused, my friend. My mind is numb and I cannot think clearly. Tell me, what should I do? Be my guide and tell me, how can I overcome this weakness? Give me the knowledge that would help me see my path bright and clear.'

Krishna smiled: 'You speak sincerely, but your sorrow and weakness have no basis. A wise man does not lament the living or the dead. He knows, there never was a time when you, I and the kings and warriors gathered here have not existed. Nor will there be a time when we'll cease to exist. Just like a person grows from childhood to youth, on to his old age, at death, he just moves on to another body—another physical state. Your current physical existence is merely a transient experience. Understand this: the body is mortal but the inner Self that lives within the body is immortal, indestructible. Just as one abandons worn out clothes and wears a new one, when a body is worn out, the inner Self puts on a new body to experience another cycle of life. And this Self cannot be slain or destroyed by any weapon. One might think he is the slayer, and his victim might think he is slain. Both are wrong, because you are never born, and you'll never die. Once you know this, you realize that you could neither slay nor cause another to be slayed. Even if you believe the Self is subject to birth and death, you should know that death is inevitable for the living, and birth inevitable for the dead. Hence, you should not grieve. So, Arjun, get up and fight.'

Arjun, however, was not inspired by Krishna's spirited words. He was still morose and did not utter a single word. Krishna said, 'Arjun, try to understand. You are a Kshatriya and it is your duty to fight against evil. Upholding righteousness and protecting the innocent is your Dharma. This is your path to salvation. At this critical moment, if you drop your weapons and abandon the battlefield, you'd not only incur a grave sin, but you'd also lose your dignity and honour amongst your fellow Kshatriyas. Your enemies would ridicule you and say mean things about you. Won't that be more painful? Get up and fight. You have nothing to lose. If you get killed in the battle, you would ascend to the heavens. If you win, you would enjoy a kingdom. Rise above the earthly feelings of joy and sorrow, success and failure, victory and defeat, and engage in this righteous battle, and you will incur no sin.'

Arjun still didn't feel any better. He mulled over Krishna's advice but failed to derive strength from his words. Krishna noticed his helpless look and continued, 'I understand, you need more explanation than the Sankhya theories that I have been talking about. Let me tell you the principles of Yoga—the path in which no effort goes to waste. Arjun, ignorant people who follow the Vedas to the letter are full of desires and all their actions and prayers are only to achieve earthly pleasure or a good reincarnation. The Vedic scriptures are of little use to one who seeks the ultimate truth—the Brahman. You must rise above—and detach yourself from—the duality of pain and pleasure, joy and sadness. Remember, Arjun, you only have the right to your work and not to its consequence or reward. You should not be motivated by the profits of your action. Renounce any attachment to the rewards of action and become indifferent to success and failure. Only then can you free your mind and attain the state of deep Samadhi. Such a person can free himself from the laws of karma and from the necessity to be born again. When you transcend the charm of the Vedas and your mind attains the bliss of self-realization, only then can you achieve divine consciousness.'

Arjun looked up at Krishna as his eyes glittered with hope. He asked, 'O Krishna, tell me, how does a man, who has achieved this wisdom and realized the divine consciousness, behave? How does such a person talk, walk, sit?'

Krishna replied, 'A person who has renounced all sensual cravings and finds satisfaction in the Self alone, is always established in divine consciousness. Such a person's mind is unperturbed in misery, pain, pleasure, fear and anger. Just as a tortoise withdraws its limbs into its shell, a person can withdraw his senses from earthly objects. Remember, Arjun, attachment to sense objects breeds desire. Desire breeds anger, which clouds your judgment and you fail to differentiate between right and wrong. Those who can renounce all selfish desires and break away from the bondage of ego—the feeling of "I", "me", "mine"—they are the persons who are forever free. Only once you do this can you unite with the Lord. Attain this state and you'll pass from death to immortality.'

'Krishna, you say the path of knowledge is superior to the path of action. Then why do you ask me to follow the path of action? I am confused. Tell me, how can I attain eternal bliss?'

'Yes, indeed, there are multiple paths to attain bliss. The path of knowledge and the path of action are the two major paths. But the path of selfless action is the preferred one. No being can survive without action—even breathing is an action. There is nothing in this universe that I am required to do. Yet, I am always engaged in action, else the universe would have been destroyed. Arjun, perform your duties selflessly, in the spirit of sacrifice, without expectation of any reward, and you will attain the Supreme. Let me control all actions while you fight—not for the throne, but to serve your duty, for which you are chosen.'

Krishna's response intrigued Arjun. He was curious to know more. He asked, 'What makes a person do evil things? It seems they are impelled by some unknown force to do the things they aren't supposed to.'

'Selfish desire and anger are the primary causes of all sins,' answered Krishna. 'Selfish desire is your greatest enemy. It takes over your senses and intellect, and buries your knowledge and understanding. You must fight to control your senses, and then only will you conquer your enemy. Let your Atman rule your ego, for Atman lies above your intellect, your mind, your senses and your body.'

Krishna paused a moment and said, 'I taught this eternal Yoga, this secret, to Vivaswat. Vivaswat taught this to Manu, and Manu to Ikshvaku. Over the ages, this knowledge spread through the kings and sages. But, over time, people began to forget the practice of this Yoga and, now, it is almost forgotten. You are my friend; so I shall deliver these secret teachings for your benefit.'

Arjun was confused again. 'How is that possible? Bibaswan lived long ago, long before you were born. How could you teach him?'

Krishna laughed. 'You and I have been born many times and had many lives. You don't remember them, but I do,' he said. 'Listen to me, Arjun. I am the Lord, the eternal who dwells in every creature in this earth. Over the ages, whenever righteousness is in peril, I appear on earth to protect the good, destroy the evil and restore dharma. I am the cause of all action and their consequences, but I am changeless and beyond all action. Actions do not cling to me because I am not attached to their results. People make offerings of material and service to reach the Supreme Lord. Arjun, offerings of wisdom are better than any material offering.'

Arjun asked, 'You talk of the path of renunciation, and about the path of selfless action. Which is better?'

Krishna answered, 'Both the paths lead to the supreme goal. However, the path of action is better than the path of renunciation. Remember, Arjun, the Lord does not partake in the good and evil deeds of any person. When a person's wisdom is clouded by ignorance, he loses his sense of judgment. Only the light of knowledge of the inner Self can lift this cloud of ignorance. Those who gain this knowledge have equal regard for all. They see the same Self in all beings—a hermit, an outcaste, an elephant, a cow or a dog. To realize the Self, one needs to master his senses, his mind and his intellect through meditation. Only a focused and peaceful mind can connect with the inner Self—the Supreme.'

Arjun was not satisfied. Doubts and confusion raged in his mind. He asked, 'How can I control the mind? It is restless, turbulent and wild. Trying to control it is like controlling the wind.'

'Yes, the mind is restless and is difficult to control. But with regular practice and detachment, it can be conquered.'

'What if a man has faith, but lacks self-control and wanders from the path? Won't he ever be able to attain salvation?'

'No person does good work will ever fall from grace. Through multiple births, he continues his advancement on the path to perfection.'

Krishna noticed that Arjun was still not inspired. He could sense the doubts in his mind. He touched Arjun's shoulder and said, 'Listen to me, Parth. I will now reveal to you the knowledge that will clear all your doubts and which will enable you to know the essence of me.' He paused for a moment and then said, 'Arjun, I am the source of the universe and there is nothing superior to me. Everything begins from me and ends in me. Like a string of pearls, everything is threaded on me. Arjun, I am the taste of water, and the glow of the moon and the light of the sun. I am the fragrance of the earth and the warmth of fire. I am the life of the living, the consciousness of all those who have developed consciousness. I am the splendour of all things beautiful. I know everything about the past, the present and the future. But no one knows me completely. Those who take refuge in me with an urge to liberate themselves from old age and death, come to know the Brahman—the Self, and the nature of all action. Those who worship me and meditate on me, thinking about nothing else, I fulfil all their needs. I treat all creatures equally, none are less dear and none more. Those who worship me with love and devotion, they live in me. And

I come to life in them. Even sinners become purified when they take refuge in me. Remember, one who surrenders to me will never come to any harm. Arjun, give me all your love. Seek me in your self, and you will unite with me.'

Arjun knelt in front of Krishna and with joined palms, he said, 'Tell me more about you. I want to know more.'

Krishna said, 'How much do you want to listen to, Arjun, for there is no end to my attributes. Since you want to know, I will tell you some. I am the true self in the heart of every creature, and the beginning, middle and the end of their existence. Among the gods, I am Vishnu. Of the lights, I am the sun; and in the night sky, I am the moon. Of all the sciences, I am the science of Self-knowledge. I am the all-devouring death, as well as the source of all birth. Of the feminine qualities, I am fame, beauty, speech, memory, intelligence, loyalty and forgiveness. There is no end to my divine powers. Wherever you find strength, beauty, might and knowledge, rest assured that they have sprung from me.' Krishna paused and smiled at Arjun who was awestruck to hear these words. Then he continued, 'Arjun, what use is this detailed knowledge to you? Just remember, I pervade everywhere, and I support the entire cosmos with only a fraction of my being.'

Sitting at the feet of Krishna, Arjun said, 'You have taught me the mystery of the Self. You enlightened me with the knowledge to attain salvation. Your words have clarified all my doubts. I have one more request, and I pray you fulfil my wish. Just as you described your infinite glory, please reveal your true self to me. I want to witness with my mortal eyes the creator of the universe.'

'You can't see me with your physical eyes of flesh and blood,' said Krishna. 'But I will fulfil your wish. I grant you divine vision that will enable you to perceive my celestial being.'

Saying so, Krishna revealed his true form. Arjun saw Krishna standing in front of him as huge as the Himalayas. Brighter than a thousand suns, he seemed to look in all directions, with millions of faces and eyes. Within the body of the celestial being, Arjun saw the entire universe in all its glorious manifolds. Palms joined, Arjun said, 'O Lord, I see in you all the gods and every living creature. I see Brahma seated on a lotus. I see the ancient sages singing your praise. I see you everywhere, I see your infinite mouths, arms and eyes. You are the Supreme, the refuge of all creation, the everlasting spirit, and the eternal guardian of Dharma. O Lord, I tremble in fear to look at you. Your fierce mouth seems to engulf everything. I see the sons of Dhritarashtra, I see Bhishma, Drona, Karna—I see the warriors and kings who have assembled here to fight. With millions of other creatures, they all are being sucked into your wide-open jaws to their ultimate destruction. You swallow the entire universe in your fiery mouth as your entire creation bursts into flames. O Lord, I bow before you. Please have mercy on me and tell me who you are.'

'Know me, Arjun. I am time, the destroyer of all,' replied Krishna. 'I have come to devour the world. Whether you fight or not, all the warriors assembled here will die. Don't worry about killing your loved ones, for I have already killed them. Bhishma, Drona, Jayadrath, Karna, Dushasana, Duryodhan, I have killed them all. You are only my instrument. So, do not hesitate. Rise and fight, Arjun. Conquer your enemies.'

Arjun bowed to Krishna. 'O Krishna, you are the Lord of every being, you are the creator and protector of the universe. I am fortunate to have you as my guide. I have treated you as my friend, and at times I might have made careless and foolish remarks about you. Please forgive me if I sounded disrespectful. I was ignorant and did not know your true self. Now I see you in this splendid form and feel enthralled and scared at the same time. Please, O Lord, retract my divine vision and let me see you as the Krishna I know.'

'Arjun, no mortal has ever seen me in the form you witnessed today. Fear not, for I am your friend.' Krishna then assumed his human form and smiled at Arjun. 'I have given you the knowledge and wisdom to help you make your decision. If you understand what I said, you should not have any further confusion. Follow the paths I recommend, and you will attain Moksha for sure.' Krishna paused for a moment and then said, 'Arjun, you are my dearest friend, so let me tell you these final words: surrender to me with complete devotion, and you won't need to practice any of the Yogas I mentioned earlier. Abandon everything and come to me. Leave all your worries, anxieties and doubts to me and I promise, I will protect you, cleanse you of all sins and embrace you.'

Hands joined reverentially, Arjun said, 'You have cleared my mind of all doubts and delusions. Through your grace, I understand what my duties are and what path I should follow. My faith is stronger and I promise to do your will.'

Arjun bent down and picked up his Gandiva bow. Looking once again at the Kaurava Army, he said, 'Krishna, take me to my position. We have a battle to win.'

Krishna smiled and gently tugged at the reins, and the chariot rolled back to the head of the Pandava formation.

56

Day One of the War

YUDHISHTHIRA STOOD UP ON HIS CHARIOT AND SURVEYED THE battlefield in front of him. He saw the huge armies of the Kauravas and the Pandavas waiting in anticipation. With every moment, the soldiers were getting impatient and could hardly wait to pounce upon their enemy. It seemed the great war would begin any moment now. Suddenly, he put down his weapon on the chariot floor and took off his armour. He then dismounted his chariot and, with joined hands, began to walk towards the Kaurava Army. His brothers were puzzled, to say the least.

Bheem asked, 'Brother, what are you doing? Why are you walking towards the enemy unarmed? What is it you are trying to achieve? Please tell us.'

Yudhishthira didn't answer and kept walking. Bheem, Arjun, Nakul and Sahadev alighted from their chariots and followed their elder brother. The generals and soldiers of the Pandava Army were confused and looked askance at Krishna. He smiled and raised his arm to assure them.

The Kaurava Army was confused too. Some opined that Yudhishthira was scared and wanted to surrender. Others doubted this, for he had his gallant brothers by his side. Yet others felt that the Pandavas were no match for great warriors like Bhishma—whom even the gods feared—and Drona and Karna. Others doubted the Pandavas could even be real Kshatriyas, for no Kshatriya would surrender before the war had even begun.

The Kauravas began to wave their flags in joy as if they had already won the war.

Yudhishthira stepped up to Bhishma's chariot and touched his feet. 'O great Grandfather, it is an honour to fight an indomitable warrior like you. Please give us your permission to engage with you in battle, and bless us such that we can win this war.'

Bhishma smiled and touched Yudhishthira's head. 'O King, if you hadn't come to me like this, I would have been disappointed and would have cursed you for defeat. Your humility pleases me. You have my blessing to be the winner of this Great War, and to achieve all that you wish for. It is my misfortune that I must fight on behalf of the Kauravas. I am duty-bound to the throne of Hastinapur and I cannot turn my back to it. Like a coward, I must admit, I do not have the guts to defy the Kauravas and fight for you. Except for that, you may ask me whatever you want.'

'Sir, I don't ask you to fight for us. All I ask is for your advice.'

'I am your enemy. What advise do you want from me?' asked Bhishma.

Yudhishthira touched Bhishma's feet again and said, 'Grandfather, everybody knows you are undefeatable. Still, you bless us to win the war. How can we win the war while you are alive? If you really want us to win the war, tell me, how can we defeat you?'

Bhishma smiled. 'You are right. I don't know of any man who can defeat me. Besides, I don't intend to die now. Come back later and I might tell you how to defeat me.'

Yudhishthira knew the great old Kaurava wouldn't give up so easily. However, Bhishma's concluding statement gave him hope.

'Thank you, Grandfather, for your blessing. I will come to you again for help.' Yudhishthira bowed to Bhishma and walked away.

Walking up to Drona's chariot, hands joined, Yudhishthira circled around Drona and then touched his feet. 'O Lord, you are our teacher, our guru. On behalf of the Pandavas, I come here to seek your blessings and your permission to engage in battle with you. Please advise us how we can destroy our enemy.'

Drona smiled and raised his hand to bless Yudhishthira. 'I am glad you came to me before the war began. If you hadn't come, I'd have cursed you and ensured your defeat. You know how much I love you and your brothers. It is unfortunate that I cannot join you in this battle. The Kauravas are my masters and I can't be disloyal to them. Still, I wish you victory. Krishna is on your side—nobody can defeat you.'

'O great Drona, nobody can defeat you in the battlefield. As long as you fight this war, I don't know how we can defeat the Kauravas and emerge victorious.'

Drona said, 'You are right. When I have my weapons in hand, nobody in this world can kill me. However, if somebody whom I trust delivers me really bad news that breaks my heart—a news that would rob me of my desire to live—I would drop my weapons, give up fighting and await my death. That is the only way someone might be able to kill me.'

Yudhishthira then went to meet his other teacher, Kripacharya. 'O great Kripacharya, you are indomitable in battle. I don't know how we can win this war when you fight for the Kauravas. I ask for your blessing.'

Kripa blessed Yudhishthira and said, 'My dear Yudhishthira, you know my loyalty binds me to the throne of Hastinapur. You are right—nobody can kill me in battle. But every morning, when I wake up, I will pray for your victory.'

Yudhishthira then went to his uncle Shalya, bowed and touched his feet and asked for his blessings. Shalya said, 'I am happy to see you. It is unfortunate that I couldn't join your side. Tell me, how else can I help you?'

'Dear Uncle, you had once promised that, during the war, you'd make all efforts to demoralize Karna. I pray that you keep your promise.'

Shalya blessed Yudhishthira and said, 'Don't worry, Yudhishthira. I will fulfil my promise. I will speak so mean of Karna that he'll lose his concentration and his will to fight.'

Yudhishthira then walked back to his army. Just before mounting his chariot, he turned back to the Kauravas and shouted, 'Dear warriors of the Kaurava Army, we are about to engage in a great war. We have chosen our sides due to various reasons. Some of you might not have had any choice but to stick to the side you were asked to join. However, it is still not too late. If any of you would like to join us, join the side of Dharma, please reveal yourself. We will accept you with open arms.'

For a while, there was silence on both sides. Nobody expected Yudhishthira to make such a proposal. Suddenly, a man walked out of the Kaurava Army. It was Jujutsu, one of the hundred brothers of Duryodhan. Jujutsu stepped up and said, 'Yudhishthira, I am sick and tired of serving my evil brother Duryodhan. He never listens to reason. If you'd be kind enough to accept me, I'd like to join you and fight for you.'

Yudhishthira walked up to Jujutsu and embraced him. 'Welcome, my brother. You have made the right decision. Let's join hands and fight those stupid brothers of yours. At least you'll live to perform the last rites of your father Dhritarashtra.'

In the meantime, Krishna stepped aside to meet Karna who was waiting on the sidelines of the battlefield. Krishna went to him and said, 'I hear you have decided not to fight as long as Bhishma is alive. I have a proposal for you: while Bhishma is alive, why don't you fight on behalf of the Pandavas? After Bhishma's demise, if you so wish, you may return to the Kauravas and fight on their behalf.'

Karna gave Krishna a disgusted look and said, 'Krishna, it seems you haven't quite understood me as yet. Listen to this one last time: I will never do anything to harm my dear friend Duryodhan. I am his well-wisher and I am willing to sacrifice my life for his sake.' Krishna nodded and walked back to Arjun's chariot.

Yudhishthira mounted his chariot and put on his armour. The other Pandava brothers mounted their chariots too. The war drums began to beat. Trumpets and bugles rang out around the battlefield. The horses neighed, the elephants roared. The generals blew their conch shells as their chariots began to roll. The two armies moved towards each other. The great battle began.

Duryodhan and Dushasana, along with their twelve brothers, guarded Bhishma as he moved towards the Pandava Army. Abhimanyu, along with Draupadi's five sons, Nakul, Sahadev and Dhrishtadyumna attacked Duryodhan with a volley of arrows. Bhishma swung away his chariot and engaged Arjun in one-on-one combat. Deadly arrows left the bows of each warrior but failed to hit the target because the opponent's arrows struck and destroyed them mid-air. Watching their fierce battle, the other warriors got excited, and they pounced upon their enemies with full vigour. Satyaki fought with Kritavarma, Abhimanyu with the Koshal King Brihadbal, Bheem with Duryodhan, Nakul with Dushasana, Sahadev with Durmukh, and Yudhishthira with Shalya. Soon, there was utter mayhem and violence on the battlefield as all decency and rules of engagement were forgotten.

The warriors didn't care for past relations and friendships. The only relationship they cared about was whether the opponent was on their side or part of the enemy's camp.

Abhimanyu, the teenaged son of Arjun, attacked Bhishma. He sprayed Bhishma with his arrows, but the great grandsire didn't pay much attention to the young man and kept fighting the other Pandava soldiers. Abhimanyu was adamant. He fired a couple of powerful weapons at Bhishma and broke the mast of his chariot. Bhishma couldn't ignore him any longer. He asked his charioteer to turn towards Abhimanyu and began to spray the lad with arrows. The rapidity with which Bhishma shot his arrows was too overwhelming for Abhimanyu, who struggled to defend himself by dodging the arrows and countering them with his own. Watching Abhimanyu's distress, Bheem and Satyaki came to help. They attacked Bhishma with their arrows to relieve Abhimanyu from Bhishma's rage. Still, they were no match to Bhishma's skills. Alone, Bhishma fought all of them without any sign of weakness.

On the other side of the battlefield, Uttar, the son of King Virat, mounted a huge elephant and attacked Shalya. The elephant trampled Shalya's chariot and broke it to thousand pieces. Shalya jumped out of the chariot to save himself. Sitting on top of the elephant, Uttar shouted in joy: 'Take your last breath, Shalya. Today I will kill you and offer your body to King Yudhishthira.' He commanded his elephant to crush Shalya. Poor Uttar was not aware of Shalya's power. As the elephant rushed to trample him, Shalya picked up a deadly serpent-like weapon and hurled it at Uttar. The weapon cut through the air like a thunderbolt, struck Uttar on his chest and killed him before he could utter another word. Uttar's body rolled off the elephant's back and lay motionless at Shalya's feet.

When the news of Uttar's death reached his brother Sweta, he was furious with rage. 'How dare Shalya kill my brother?' he yelled.

'I promise to kill Shalya before the battle ends today.' Saying this, he turned his chariot and drove as fast as he could to attack Shalya. The Kaurava soldiers tried to stop him. Sweta killed them all and raced towards Shalya who, in the meantime, had mounted Kritavarma's chariot. Expecting retaliation from the Pandavas for Uttar's death, six Kaurava warriors, including Shalya's son Rukmarath and Brihadbal, surrounded Shalya to protect him.

A messenger went to Bhishma and said, 'O Sire, Sweta, the son of King Virat, is on a rampage. He is killing hundreds of Kaurava soldiers by the minute. Please stop him.' Bhishma called his charioteer and said, 'Take me to Sweta. It seems King Virat will lose his second son today.' When Sweta saw Bhishma approaching him, he shouted, 'Bhishma, get out of my way. I will avenge my brother's death, and nobody can stop me, not even you.' He picked up a heavy spear and hurled it at Bhishma with all his might. Bhishma shot an arrow and cut the spear to pieces. Enraged, Sweta began to shoot the deadliest of arrows at Bhishma. None could touch Bhishma's body. Bhishma then picked up a fierce weapon and hurled it at Sweta's chariot. The weapon hit the target with a huge explosion and killed Sweta's horses and his charioteer. Sweta jumped off his chariot, picked up his Shakti weapon and hurled it at Bhishma. The Shakti weapon was so powerful that any other man would have been killed by it in an instant. Bhishma was no ordinary man. He raised his bow and, with one shot of his arrow, he shattered the Shakti, rendering it harmless. Sweta was furious. He picked up his mace and attacked Bhishma. With powerful blows, he killed Bhishma's charioteer and his horses. Bhishma was left with no option but to strike the ultimate blow. He picked up a divine weapon, uttered the codes to activate it, and shot it at Sweta. The weapon escaped his bow with a huge roar and, before Sweta could understand anything, it pierced his armour and his chest, and entered the earth behind him. Sweta fell to the ground with a loud thud and lay dead.

Hearing the news of Sweta's death, the Kauravas began to dance in joy. The fall of a gallant warrior like Sweta was an enormous achievement.

As the sun began to set, the conch shells rang out to notify the end of battle for the day. The Kauravas and the Pandavas ceased their fight and retreated to their camps. The Pandavas were dejected after losing two great warriors, Uttar and Sweta. The Kauravas were jubilant and were confident that as long as Bhishma was with them, nobody could snatch away their victory.

57

Day Two of the War

THE FIRST DAY OF THE BATTLE DIDN'T GO WELL FOR THE PANDAVAS. THE generals and leaders assembled in Yudhishthira's tent as he sat on a wooden throne while the medics tended to his wounds. He looked morose and devoid of hope. As Krishna stepped into the tent, Yudhishthira looked up and said, 'Krishna, what took you so long? I have been looking for you all evening.'

Krishna sat next to Yudhishthira and said, 'I am here now. Tell me, how can I help you?'

Yudhishthira held Krishna's hand and said, 'Keshav, I think this war was a huge mistake. Bhishma is indomitable and I should have never dared to fight a war against him. Just as the summer fire burns down the grasslands, Bhishma is wiping out our army. We might be able to defeat the gods, but it is impossible to defeat Bhishma. I cannot subject my generals and my soldiers to his wrath. Facing Bhishma in battle is no different than facing death. Arjun has disappointed me. He seems to be distracted and is hardly exerting himself. Bheem is the only one trying his best and who seems to have inflicted the most damage upon the Kaurava Army. But, truth be told, with his naive strategy and simple man-to-man combat, we cannot destroy the huge Kaurava Army even in a thousand years. I feel hopeless. Maybe I should surrender to Duryodhan and take refuge in the forests. Keshav, tell me, what should I do?'

Arjun stood with his head held low. Bheem, Nakul and Sahadev didn't say a single word. Krishna knew, the loss of Uttar and Sweta on the first day had sapped the Pandava brothers of their will to win the war. He looked into Yudhishthira's eyes and said, 'Stop lamenting, Yudhishthira. Don't give up so soon. Today was only the first day of the war. We still have a long way to go, and we are all with you. Shikhandi is on your side, and I know he will be the cause of Bhishma's death. And our commander-in-chief, Dhrishtadyumna, is destined to kill Drona. There's no need to feel hopeless at all.'

Dhrishtadyumna knelt in front of Yudhishthira and said, 'O King, I promise, tomorrow will be our day. I will create such a difficult formation that it will be impossible for Bhishma to inflict any serious damage to our army.'

The next morning, the two armies stood facing each other once again for the second day's battle. Bhishma attacked the Pandava Army with renewed energy. He targeted the soldiers from Chedi and Matsya, and began to slay them indiscriminately. The continuous stream of arrows from his bow hit the Pandava soldiers like tsunami waves and wiped them off the battleground. The great Pandava warriors—Abhimanyu, Bheem, Satyaki and Dhrishtadyumna—tried their best to stop him and failed miserably. The violent barrage of arrows from Bhishma was too much for them to counter. They had to give up and run for their lives. The Pandava Army panicked. They broke formation and began to flee the battlefield.

When Arjun heard the news, he called upon Krishna and said, 'Take me to Bhishma. We must stop him.' Krishna turned his chariot and sped towards Bhishma. The mighty chariot—decorated with colourful flags and drawn by four powerful white horses—tore through the battlefield with a loud roar, while Arjun's Gandiva spewed an endless stream of arrows that killed every Kaurava soldier who crossed their path.

Duryodhan ran to Bhishma and said, 'Grandfather, how could Arjun kill all my soldiers when you and Drona are alive? It is because of you that my gallant friend Karna withdrew from the battle and is sitting out the war. Had he been present in the battlefield, I wouldn't have begged you. I am helpless and have no option but to plead to you to do something to stop Arjun. Instead of showing your affection towards the sons of Pandu, you should demonstrate your loyalty to Hastinapur at this time of distress.'

Duryodhan's insult struck Bhishma like a lightning bolt. He shot Duryodhan a look of pure disgust and said, 'I hate this job! I hate being a Kshatriya!' He turned his chariot and drove towards Arjun.

Soon, Arjun and Bhishma faced each other and a spectacular battle ensued. The warriors stopped fighting and watched their amazing warfare. The gods from the heavens watched the battle and said, 'Both of them are undefeatable. This war will continue till eternity.'

On the other end of the battlefield, Dhrishtadyumna was busy fighting a tough battle with Drona. Dhrishtadyumna knew he was born to kill Drona. But the way Drona was fighting today, it seemed like an impossible dream. The speed and agility with which the old Brahmin shot his arrows, and hurled his spears and maces, he seemed like a man in his prime.

The merciless Kalinga soldiers of the Kauravas were thrashing the Chedi soldiers of the Pandavas in a different sector of Kurukshetra. Bheem came to their rescue. Arrows rained from his bow, killing hundreds of Kalinga warriors. The Kalinga king Srutayu and his son Sukradev tried to stop Bheem, who picked up a huge mace and hurled it at Srutayu. The mace crushed Srutayu's skull like a coconut shell and killed him instantly. Sukradev tried to run, but Bheem hurled a spear at him, which tore him apart. Bheem jumped in his chariot and shouted in joy while hurling spears with both hands. The Kalinga soldiers were scared to see this dreadful side of Bheem and began to flee in hordes.

The news of Bheem's devastation of the Kalinga Army reached Bhishma, who realized he had to stop Bheem. He stopped fighting with Arjun and asked his charioteer to take him to Bheem. The moment he saw Bheem's chariot, Bhishma began to shoot arrows at him. Bhishma's arrows killed Bheem's horses. Enraged, Bheem jumped off his chariot and threw a mace at Bhishma. The mace hit Bhishma's charioteer and killed him. The scared horses jumped up and ran away at a frantic pace, chariot and Bhishma in tow. Bheem thumped his chest and yelled in joy.

Arjun's son Abhimanyu was engaged in a fierce battle with Duryodhan's son. Arjun came forward to help. Duryodhan too joined the fight to help his son, but failed to slow the rate at which Arjun kept destroying his army. In the meantime, Bhishma found a charioteer and rejoined the battle. Halfway into the battlefield, he found Drona trying to persuade the Kaurava soldiers from fleeing Arjun's wrath. Bhishma stopped beside Drona and said, 'I don't think we can stop Arjun today. He is fighting like a possessed man. Our soldiers are tired and scared. Let them go. The sun will set soon, and the battle will end. We'll start afresh tomorrow.'

As the sun began to set on the western horizon, the trumpets and conch shells blew to notify the end of the day's battle. The Kaurava soldiers sighed in relief while the Pandavas rejoiced as the day had certainly gone in their favour.

58

Day Three of the War

THE THIRD DAY'S BATTLE BEGAN WITH A HUGE MISFORTUNE FOR THE
Kauravas. Bheem and Duryodhan were engaged in a fierce
battle. Duryodhan was no weakling and was in fact regarded as one
of the greatest warriors. But Bheemsen's brutal attacks overwhelmed
him. The incessant flow of arrows, spears and maces from Bheem was
too much for Duryodhan to counter. Bheem picked up a powerful
weapon and hurled it at Duryodhan. The weapon hit Duryodhan's
armour with a huge blow and knocked him out. Duryodhan's
charioteer didn't wait any longer. He turned his chariot around and
fled the battlefield as fast as he could, with Duryodhan lying half
dead on the floor. The Kaurava soldiers were scared, and they too ran
for their lives.

Hearing this grave news, Bhishma was deeply concerned. If
Duryodhan fell, it might mean the end of this war. He asked his
charioteer to take him to Duryodhan's tent.

Duryodhan's injury wasn't fatal. By the time Bhishma arrived,
Duryodhan had already regained consciousness and was trying to

sit up straight, while the medics tried to treat his wounds. When Duryodhan saw Bhishma enter, he couldn't hold back his anger. Ignoring his pain, he stood up and lashed out at Bhishma: 'Tell me, Grandfather, who are you fighting for? It can't be for us for sure. The way you fight makes me think you are helping your favourites, the Pandavas. How is it possible that with you, Drona and Kripa on our side, our soldiers are panicking and deserting the battlefield? This would never have happened if you had demonstrated your true self. If you love the Pandavas so much, you should have told me earlier that you don't want to fight for us. If I knew your true intentions, I would have never considered you as my general, and Karna and I would have devised a different strategy.' Duryodhan winced in pain as one of the medics put some strong balm on his wound. As the pain subsided, he continued, 'Now tell me, Grandfather, are you with us or against us? If you are still with us, then go, fight and wipe the Pandavas off the face of the earth. I don't expect anything less from you.'

Duryodhan's insults entered Bhishma's ears like molten lava. He was furious with rage. Eyes bloodshot, he said to Duryodhan: 'King Duryodhan, I told you several times, the Pandavas are undefeatable. Even the gods cannot beat them. You expect too much from an old man like me. Still, I will return to the battlefield and defend the Kauravas from the wrath of the Pandavas. Alone. You will see how much devastation I can cause even at this age.' Saying this, Bhishma stepped out of the tent and mounted his chariot.

That afternoon, Bhishma unleashed his fury on the Pandava Army like never before. He was unstoppable. Bhishma and his warriors killed thousands of Pandava soldiers. Arjun and the other Pandava brothers tried their best to defend their army, but Bhishma couldn't be tamed by any means. It was as if their doom had arrived in the form of Bhishma and the Pandava Army began to flee the battlefield.

Arjun was amazed to behold Bhishma's fantastic warfare. All his life, he had seen his grandfather as a loving old man and never experienced his prowess as a devastating warrior. Engrossed, Arjun watched Bhishma tear apart his army with deadly precision.

Krishna turned to Arjun and said, 'My dear friend, wake up from your stupor. The time has come for you to show your true gallantry. Shake off your weakness and hit Bhishma hard with your deadliest weapons.'

Krishna's harsh words brought Arjun back to his senses. 'Yes, Keshav, take me to Bhishma. I will fight him.'

Krishna veered the chariot towards Bhishma. When Bhishma saw Arjun approaching, he raised his arms and said, 'Come, Arjun. It will be a pleasure to fight you. Come, strike me and show me what you've got.'

Soon, a fierce battle ensued between Bhishma and Arjun. However, Arjun seemed to be far less effective against Bhishma's attack. Bhishma's relentless arrows kept Arjun busy defending himself and he could hardly find a window to mount a counterattack. Krishna used his superior skills as a charioteer and drove his chariot in curves and circles around Bhishma, forcing him to change his direction of attack every moment. Still, Arjun failed to make any dent in Bhishma's armour. Krishna felt that Arjun was too enamoured with Bhishma's gallantry and was not exerting himself enough. He knew that this weakness could cost Yudhishthira his kingdom, for Bhishma was tearing into the Pandava Army with abandon. Not wanting to let that happen, Krishna decided to kill Bhishma himself.

In the meantime, Satyaki arrived and was shocked to find Arjun struggling to defend himself against the Kaurava warriors who had him completely surrounded, with Bhishma leading the attack. Scared to find Arjun is such dire straits, the Pandava soldiers broke formation and began to flee the battle. Satyaki called out to the soldiers: 'Don't flee, my friends. It isn't appropriate for a Kshatriya to run away from battle. Fight with honour and serve your duty as a warrior.'

Krishna called Satyaki and said, 'You don't have to persuade them. Let them go wherever they want. Today, I alone will kill Bhishma and the rest of the Kaurava soldiers. None will escape my wrath.'

Glowing with anger, Krishna raised his arm and, in an instant, the deadly Sudarshan Chakra appeared whirling on his index finger. Krishna jumped off the chariot and, with the terrible Sudarshan Chakra spinning on his finger and spitting fire in all directions, he ran towards Bhishma. The sight struck fear in all and they cried in fear of total annihilation. Only Bhishma wasn't scared. He put down his bow on the chariot floor and with joined palms, he bowed to Krishna and said, 'O Krishna, I bow to you. I feel honoured that you consider me worthy of killing with your own hand. You are the lord of all beings, and nothing can be better than to die in your hands. Please come, use your Sudarshan Chakra and relieve me from this life.' He knelt down on the chariot floor and waited for the chakra to sever his head.

Watching this dreadful sight, Arjun came back to his senses. What a terrible thing he was about to witness! Krishna had promised not to fight in this war. And now, because of his incompetence, he had had to pick up arms against Bhishma. A terrible shame overcame him. He jumped off the chariot, ran after Krishna and grabbed his hands from behind. Krishna dragged him through the dirt while Arjun dug his feet to stop him.

'Krishna, stop! Please stop and calm down,' croaked Arjun. He dropped down and grabbed Krishna's feet with both hands. 'Forgive me, my friend. I was about to make you break your promise. Trust me, from this moment onwards, I will shake off all my weakness and fight with all my might. I will show mercy to nobody, and I promise to kill anyone who comes to fight me.'

Krishna turned away from Arjun and said, 'Arjun, I tried several times to persuade you to do your Kshatriya duties. It seems your attachment to your enemy is strong enough to ensure it cannot cause them any serious damage. With this attitude, you can't defeat the Kauravas. I can't let that happen. I want to see Yudhishthira on the throne of Hastinapur. If you can't help with that, I will make it happen myself.'

Arjun held Krishna's feet in a tight grip and said, 'Lord, please trust me. My mind is clear of all doubts. I will fight and keep my promise. You guide me and I will destroy the Kauravas.'

'Well, then, I give you another chance,' said Krishna. 'I hope you don't disappoint me again. Now let's go back to the chariot and you show us how dangerous you can be with your Gandiva.'

Krishna and Arjun mounted their chariot and Krishna blew his Panchajanya conch shell. The sound reverberated through the battlefield and struck fear in the hearts of the Kaurava soldiers. Arjun placed the deadly Mahendra weapon on the Gandiva bow and shot at the Kaurava Army. The mighty weapon struck in the middle of the battlefield and instantly vaporized thousands of Kaurava warriors, their chariots, elephants and horses. But that was not enough. Arjun's chariot ploughed through the Kaurava Army and they experienced how devastating Arjun's wrath could be when he exerted himself. The fury with which Arjun attacked the enemy, it seemed he'd destroy the Kauravas before the day ended. Fortunately for them, the sun set behind the western horizon soon, marking the end of the third day's battle.

The Kauravas went back to their camp and when they sat down to account for the day's damage, they realized that Arjun alone had killed 10,000 charioteers, 700 elephants, and the entire armies of the Prachya, Soubir, Khudrak and Malab provinces. Bhishma, Drona, Kripa and all the other Kaurava generals had failed to check his fury. Concerned about their fate the next day, they went to bed and tried to get some rest before the fourth day's war began at sunrise.

59

Day Four of the War

IT WAS THE FOURTH DAY OF THE WAR. AFTER A DISASTROUS THIRD DAY'S battle, the Kauravas were determined to strike back with full fury. Bhishma asked his charioteer to take him to Arjun. He knew that only he could check Arjun's onslaught and prevent further losses to the Kaurava side.

On the other end of the battlefield, Aswathama, Chitrasen, Bhurishrava, Shalya and his son attacked young Abhimanyu, the gallant son of Arjun. Although Abhimanyu was only a teenaged boy, the Kaurava greats could hardly manage to control his wrath. Dhrishtadyumna saw Abhimanyu being attacked by the five Kauravas and veered his chariot to help the boy. Shalya's son tried to stop him. Dhrishtadyumna picked up his mace and hurled it at Shalya's son. The huge mace hit his head and shattered his skull, killing Shalya's son instantly. Shalya was furious. He turned and attacked Dhrishtadyumna and called Duryodhan to help him avenge his son's death. Duryodhan, along with his brothers Dushasana and Vikarna, joined Shalya to fight Dhrishtadyumna. Duryodhan knew, even if Bhishma managed to stop Arjun from destroying his army, Bheemsen alone could cause significant damage, especially when the rest of the Kaurava top brass were engaged in fighting Abhimanyu and Dhrishtadyumna. He ordered one of his generals to dispatch 10,000 elephant-mounted warriors to stop Bheem. When Bheem saw the wave of huge elephants coming towards him, he stood on his chariot and yelled, 'Duryodhan, you coward! You think you can scare me with your elephants? Watch how I destroy them.'

Bheem jumped off his chariot, swirled his mace above his head and embarked upon a killing spree that nobody could ever imagine. He jumped high in the air and struck his mace on the elephants' head and the huge beasts fell dead along with their warrior on their backs. Sometimes he would strike an elephant's leg and when the animal tumbled, he'd crush its skull with a second blow of his mace. Soon, thousands of elephants lay dead along with their warriors in the battlefield, with Bheem in the centre, thumping his chest and dancing in glee. Those who managed to survive Bheem's wrath, turned around and fled the battlefield as fast as they could.

Duryodhan had to do something to stop his army from deserting the battlefield. He called Senapati, Jalasandha, Sushen, Beerbahu, Bheemrath and fourteen of his brothers and said, 'Go, stop Bheem at any cost. Make sure he doesn't live to see the sunset today.' The eighteen valiant warriors turned their chariots and raced towards Bheem. Soon, Bheem was surrounded by Duryodhan's lieutenants. Bheem looked around, licked his lips, and hurled a spear at Senapati. The spear hit Senapati's shoulder and decapitated him instantly. And then in quick succession, Jalasandha, Sushen, Beerbahu and Bheemrath lay dead in the battlefield. Duryodhan's fourteen brothers turned their chariots and ran to save themselves from imminent death.

Duryodhan panicked. He ran to Bhishma and said, 'Grandfather, Bheem is killing us all. If we don't stop him, he alone will win this war for the Pandavas.'

Bhishma was busy fighting Dhrishtadyumna. He glanced at Duryodhan and said, 'Ask Bhagadatta to deal with Bheem. Only a warrior like Bhagadatta can stop him now.'

Upon Bhishma's orders, Bhagadatta mounted a huge elephant and attacked Bheem, who roared and attacked Bhagadatta with his mace. Bhagadatta stood atop his elephant, pulled out his most powerful weapon and hurled it at Bheem. The weapon struck Bheem's chest and knocked him out. He rolled down his chariot and lay unconscious. Bhagadatta commanded his elephant to trample Bheem and finish him for good.

Ghatotkach—the demon son of Bheem and Hidimba—was fighting nearby. When he saw his father lying unconscious and about to be stamped to death by Bhagadatta's elephant, the shape-shifter demon transformed himself into a huge giant. He then mounted Airavat the elephant, which was twice the size of Bhagadatta's elephant, and attacked Bhagadatta. His companion demon warriors climbed on giant elephants and joined Ghatotkach to defend Bheem. Seeing the huge demon elephants of Ghatotkach blowing their trumpets and hurtling down the battlefield to attack, Bhagadatta's elephant panicked and ran for its life, with Bhagadatta on its back.

Bhishma, Drona, Duryodhan and the other Kaurava warriors joined forces to help Bhagadatta and stop Ghatotkach. Yudhishthira called his generals and said, 'Go, help Ghatotkach. Stop Duryodhan and Drona from reaching him.'

Ghatotkach showed no signs of slowing down. He kept chasing Bhagadatta and killed whoever came in his way. His huge, grotesque appearance and ear-piercing cries struck terror in the hearts of the Kaurava soldiers. They began to flee in hordes.

Bhishma knew it would be impossible to stop Ghatotkach today. He would do anything to avenge his father's defeat in the hands of Bhagadatta. Bhishma watched the sun hanging over the western horizon and thought it would be better to call off the day's battle to prevent further damage. He called Duryodhan and said, 'I don't intend to fight Ghatotkach today. Our men are tired, and the sun will set any moment now. Let's announce the end of the day's battle and return to our camps.' He blew his conch shell, announcing cease-fire for the day and the Kaurava soldiers sighed in relief.

That evening, when Bhishma was about to retire, Duryodhan stepped into his tent. Bhishma enquired, 'What brings you here at this time of the night?'

Duryodhan sat down at Bhishma's feet and said, 'Grandfather, I hate to repeat myself, but it seems the war is slipping out of our hands. I could never imagine, with great warriors like you, Dronacharya, Shalya, Kripacharya, Aswathama, Bhagadatta and Bhurishrava on our side, we would have to suffer such enormous losses in the hands of the Pandavas. I simply don't understand how this is possible. What is it that we are doing wrong?'

Bhishma sighed: 'You really don't know? Well, that's not surprising either. I told you several times, but you chose to ignore me. Listen to me now. The Pandavas are blessed by the presence of Lord Krishna on their side. Even when he is not fighting, Krishna's mere company makes them invincible. I suggest you give up the dream of conquering them. It's still not late to make peace with the Pandavas and there is no dishonour in surrendering to Lord Krishna. That's the only way to save yourself, your brothers, and thousands of your soldiers. Or else, prepare to face total annihilation. Now, please leave my tent. I need some rest before tomorrow's battle.'

60

Day Five and Day Six of the War

O N THE FIFTH DAY, BHISHMA ARRANGED HIS ARMY IN THE MAKARA OR the Water Demon formation, while the Pandavas created the Eagle formation. Just as the conch shells rang out to mark the beginning of the battle, the two armies pounced upon each other. Emboldened by the previous day's gains, the Pandavas attacked their enemy with renewed vigour. The Kaurava Army had no option but to retreat. Duryodhan ran to Drona and said, 'Sir, please do something. I know, if you want, you can defeat the gods. Now, please rise to the occasion and help us.'

Duryodhan's words, however, did not please Drona. With a scornful look, he said, 'You are a fool and that's why you fail to see the reality. Nobody can defeat the Pandavas, not even me. Now get out of my way and let me do my job.'

Bhishma, on the other end, was engaged in a violent battle with Arjun. Unlike the previous days, Arjun showed no signs of weakness or reverence towards Bhishma. Bhishma too didn't seem to cut him any slack. Duryodhan, after being scolded by his teacher

Dronacharya, faced Bheem in battle. Their maces struck with loud bangs that ran shivers down the spines of the soldiers. Yudhishthira battled Shalya, while Drona fought Satyaki. Arrows, spears, maces, and other deadly weapons whizzed past in all directions and heads fell off the shoulders of the slain solders like a hail storm. Satyaki's ten sons surrounded Bhurishrava and rained arrows at him. Bhurishrava pulled out his lance and, in one big sweep, killed all the ten brothers. When Satyaki heard the news, he stormed through the battlefield and attacked Bhurishrava.

'You killed my sons. Now, I will kill you. Defend yourself if you can,' yelled Satyaki as he hurled his mace at Bhurishrava. Bhurishrava ducked, but the mace shattered the mast of his chariot. In no time, both Bhurishrava and Satyaki lost their chariots and horses. With machetes and shields in their arms, they faced each other on the ground. When they struck each other, sparks flew from their weapons. Their loud cries and roars rang through the battlefield, and everybody stopped fighting to watch the two giants clash against each other. Suddenly, Bheem ran in and pulled Satyaki into his chariot. At the other end, Duryodhan picked up Bhurishrava. Neither party wanted to lose their prized warriors towards the end of the fifth day. Soon, the sun went down and Bhishma blew his conch shell to call it a day.

On the sixth day, the Pandava chief Dhrishtadyumna directed his army to create the Makara formation, while Bhishma arranged his army in the Crane formation. Bhishma and Drona engaged in a tremendous battle against Bheem and Arjun. The relentless stream of arrows from both sides killed thousands. Soldiers from both sides ran to save themselves from impending death.

In the palace of Hastinapur, listening to Sanjay's narration of the battle, the blind king Dhritarashtra said, 'How is this possible, Sanjay? My soldiers are strong and powerful. We carefully picked the best soldiers who are well-trained in using all kinds of weapons and we pay them good money for their service. We engaged experienced and skilled warriors to lead them. Yet, I find them losing miserably to the Pandavas. Why is this happening? Maybe the gods have joined the Pandavas and have been killing our soldiers mercilessly. My son is a fool. Vidura gave him the right advice, but Duryodhan chose to ignore it. Now we all must suffer the consequences. This is our destiny.'

Sanjay addressed the morose king, 'O King, it was your fault that you let the evil game of dice happen. Your destiny was sealed at that moment.' Dhritarashtra sighed and waved his hand and Sanjay continued his narration.

In the battlefield, Bheem called his charioteer and said, 'Stop. Wait here. I want to destroy the Kauravas with my mace.' Bheem jumped off the chariot with his huge mace and stormed into the Kaurava formation with a huge roar. His mace struck whoever came in front of him—elephants, horses, soldiers. With each blow, Bheem killed dozens of enemy soldiers. The Kaurava charioteers tried to stop him and riddled Bheem with arrows from all directions. But the giant of a man couldn't be stopped. He continued his rampage like a man possessed.

When Dhrishtadyumna saw Bheem's empty chariot, he was worried. The charioteer pointed him in the direction where Bheem had gone. Dhrishtadyumna reached the scene and saw Bheem roaring like a lion and crushing the Kaurava soldiers' skulls with his mace. His body was riddled with arrows, blood gushing from his wounds. Dhrishtadyumna yelled at Bheem: 'Get into my chariot. Your wounds need to be treated.' Bheem didn't listen and continued with his killing spree. Dhrishtadyumna jumped off his chariot, held Bheem by his hand and dragged him to his chariot. Quickly, he pulled out the arrows from Bheem's body and asked his charioteer to take them to a clearing.

Duryodhan saw this from a distance and knew that this was the opportunity he was waiting for. Bheem was weak and tired and being treated by Dhrishtadyumna. This was the right moment to strike and kill his arch rival. He drove towards Dhrishtadyumna and called his brothers to back him up.

Dhrishtadyumna didn't have any time to fight Duryodhan. He picked up his Pramohan or hypnosis weapon and hurled it at Duryodhan. The weapon exploded and, in the next instant, Duryodhan and his brothers lay unconscious on their chariot floors. Dhrishtadyumna washed Bheem's wounds and gave him water to drink. On Dhrishtadyumna's advice, Bheem rested a little, and soon he was ready to fight again.

When Bhishma heard about Duryodhan, he realized it was the effect of the hypnosis weapon. He rushed to help the Kauravas and exploded his Pragyastra, the consciousness weapon, which woke up Duryodhan and his brothers.

Yudhishthira called upon Abhimanyu and Dhrishtaketu to take their armies and help Bheem and Dhrishtadyumna. They arranged their army in a needle-shaped formation and pierced into the Kaurava Army. A fierce battle broke out.

As the sun hung down towards the western horizon, Bheem yelled at Duryodhan, 'This is the moment I have been waiting for all my life. If you don't stop fighting, I will kill you today and avenge the humiliation of my mother Kunti and my darling Draupadi. Come forward and let me free you of your sins forever.'

Bheem's arrows shattered Duryodhan's bow and killed his horses. The relentless arrows struck him so hard, Duryodhan fell down unconscious once again. Kripacharya, who was fighting nearby, swung his chariot and picked up Duryodhan to save him.

That afternoon, Abhimanyu and the other Pandava sons killed Vikarna, Durmukh, Jayatsen and Dushkarna, four of Duryodhan's siblings. The battle continued till after dark, as both Bhishma and Dhrishtadyumna were too busy fighting and failed to notice the sun set. When it was too dark to fight, Bhishma came to his senses and blew his conch shell to announce the end of the day's battle. The soldiers sighed in relief and dragged their tired bodies to their camps.

61

Day Seven of the War

BHISHMA ENTERED HIS TENT AND SAT DOWN. HE FELT WEARY. IT WASN'T the battle. Fighting never made him tired. Fighting against his heart drained him of his energy. He detested the thought of waking up the next morning and taking up weapons against his beloved Pandavas. He sighed and called his attendants to help him take off his armour.

As the attendants helped him with his armour and cleaned his blood-stained body, Duryodhan entered, visibly distressed. Blood gushed from his wounds but he didn't seem to care. He grunted: 'You saw what happened today. The Pandavas tore apart your Crane formation and pounded us mercilessly. Bheem almost killed me. Every day I am losing hope. I don't know how we can win this war.'

Bhishma stood up and said, 'Duryodhan, you are wounded. Sit down and let my men treat your wounds.'

The medics cleaned Duryodhan's wounds and treated him with Vishalyakarani. The soothing balms calmed Duryodhan's pain and helped him relax. Bhishma said to him: 'My dear Duryodhan, you know I don't mince my words. I want to make you a winner and want to see you happy with all my heart. The Pandavas are strong and powerful and, with Vasudeva on their side, they are invincible. Even the gods don't stand a chance against them. Still, I will keep my promise and fight for you until my death. Either I will defeat the Pandavas, or they'll defeat me. Now go to your tent and get some rest.'

The next morning, Bhishma arranged his army in the Mandala formation. With the blowing of conch shells, the battle erupted. Right from the word go, Bhishma attacked Arjun with full force. Arjun fought back with equal vigour. His Gandiva spewed endless streams of arrows with the occasional volley of fiery missiles. Bhishma struggled to counter Arjun's onslaught. Duryodhan drove his chariot towards his generals and said, 'Go, lend your support to Bhishma. The old man is fighting without caring for his life. Help him and he'll lead us to victory.' The generals turned their chariots and rushed to support Bhishma.

Drona and Virat engaged in a fierce battle in another part of the battlefield. Virat was trying his best to fight Drona. Drona, however, was too powerful for Virat to handle. His arrows killed Virat's charioteer and horses. Virat's son Sankha came to rescue his father. No sooner had Sankha pulled Virat to his chariot than Drona shot a fierce weapon at him. The weapon pierced Sankha's chest and killed him instantly. Virat didn't wait any longer to face the might of Drona. He turned and fled the battlefield with his son's dead body on the chariot floor.

Dhrishtadyumna, the valiant son of Drupad, now made Duryodhan his target. His chariot circled around Duryodhan in a zigzag pattern and confused Duryodhan. One by one, Dhrishtadyumna killed Duryodhan's horses and then his charioteer. Duryodhan stood helpless on his stranded chariot and tried to deflect Dhrishtadyumna's arrows with his shield. Shakuni saw his nephew in distress and stormed in to provide him cover. As soon as he came near, Duryodhan scrambled into Shakuni's chariot and the next moment Shakuni drove his chariot away, leaving a frustrated Dhrishtadyumna behind.

Iraban, son of Arjun and Ulupi, was fighting Vinda and Anuvinda, the princes of Avanti. Iraban killed the four horses of Anuvinda's chariot. Anuvinda jumped off and got into his brother's chariot. Iraban then killed Vinda's charioteer. The scared horses jumped up and raced away in uncontrolled frenzy.

In another part of the battlefield, Shalya was enjoying his fight with his beloved nephews, Nakul and Sahadev.

Nakul yelled at him, 'Uncle Shalya, you better surrender now. Otherwise, our arrows won't spare you for being our uncle.' The brothers shot a volley of arrows at Shalya.

Shalya laughed and said, 'Well, then, my arrows shouldn't bestow any favours upon you either.' With a few rapid shots, Shalya broke Nakul's chariot flag post, tore apart his bow, and killed his horses and his charioteer. Sahadev, however, was not amused. He picked a fierce arrow from his quiver and shot at Shalya. It pierced Shalya's armour and he fell unconscious on his chariot floor. Shalya's charioteer turned away and fled the scene as fast as possible.

Chetikan and Kripacharya were busy in a hand-to-hand combat with machetes. With their chariots destroyed, they had no other option but to fight on foot. Swinging their weapons, they pounced on each other with a huge roar. The impact knocked both of them out and they lay unconscious on the ground. Karakarya, the young son of Shishupal, picked Chetikan on his chariot while Shakuni picked Kripacharya on his.

To relieve Arjun, Shikhandi tried to distract Bhishma. Bhishma, without paying much attention, casually shot an arrow at Shikhandi and broke his bow into pieces. Shikhandi stood helpless. As he was about to leave the battlefield, Yudhishthira came to his side and said, 'Shikhandi, didn't you promise your father that you would kill Bhishma? Why are you standing idle, then? Go and fulfil your promise. Bhishma has only cut your bow. You have many bows left in your chariot. Pick up one and shoot at Bhishma.'

Shikhandi was embarrassed. He turned back and attacked Bhishma again. This time, Bhishma noticed his attacker and remembered who Shikhandi really was—a woman in a man's body. Bhishma would never fight a woman. He turned away and chose to ignore Shikhandi.

As the sun settled behind the western horizon, the day's battle came to an end. The soldiers went back to their camps and tended to their wounds. The musicians and dancers entertained them with uplifting performances. Tonight, nobody spoke of the war and everybody went to bed happy and peaceful.

62

Day Eight of the War

O N THE EIGHTH DAY, BHISHMA BEGAN TO POUND THE PANDAVA ARMY
with renewed vigour. He seemed determined to prove to
Duryodhan that he was a man of his word who would perform
his duty as the commander-in-chief of the Kaurava Army. On the
Pandava side, Bheem's ruthless destruction of the Kauravas continued
unabated. He killed eight of Duryodhan's brothers and danced on the
battlefield like a madman. Duryodhan was devastated. He went to
Bhishma and said, 'Bheem is killing all my brothers. Why are we not
able to stop him? Grandfather, there must be some way to destroy
him. Tell me, what should I do?'

Bhishma was busy killing the Pandava soldiers. Listening to
Duryodhan's plea, he paused for a moment. 'Why do you make me
repeat the same words, Duryodhan? I warned you several times; so
did Drona, Vidura, Gandhari and many others that this war will
result in the total annihilation of Kauravas. Bheem will kill any son
of Dhritarashtra who crosses his path. Nothing can stop him. So, I

would advise you to stay calm and keep fighting until the doors of heaven open for you.'

During his exile, when Arjun was travelling across the country, he met Ulupi, the princess of the serpents or the Nagas, and fathered a son. Ulupi named the son Iravan, who grew up amongst the Nagas and never met his father, Arjun. When Arjun was training in the heavens with Indra's weapons, Iravan met him and introduced himself. Arjun was impressed to see his handsome and powerful son. Iravan offered to accompany Arjun and help him in any way possible. Arjun replied, 'For now, go back and take care of your mother and your subjects. When the war breaks out with the Kauravas, join me with your serpent army.' Iravan kept his promise and, along with his huge army, he launched a vicious attack on the Kauravas. Gaja, Gabakshya, Brishak, Charmavan, Arjak and Suk, the six brothers of Shakuni, joined hands to fight Iravan. Iravan was skilled in illusory warfare and would confuse his enemies with the power of hypnosis. Shakuni's soldiers stood no chance against him and his army, and were soon decimated. Iravan applied his magic on Shakuni's brothers and killed all six of them. Angry Duryodhan called the demon, the rakshasa Alambush, and said, 'This sorcerer Iravan is causing severe damage. You know magic too. Go, fight Iravan and kill him if you can.'

Alambush took a huge army with him and attacked Iravan. Soon, a strange warfare ensued. Iravan used his sorcery and took the form of a huge serpent to scare Alambush. His serpent army surrounded him to protect him. Alambush had some tricks up his sleeve too. He took the form of a giant eagle and devoured the serpents. Almabush's spell cast a dense fog around Iravan, who felt groggy and couldn't think clearly. As he stumbled around in the haze, Alambush struck with a huge sword and decapitated Iravan. As Iravan's dead body fell to the ground, the fog cleared, and the Pandava Army saw their valiant prince lying lifeless in a pool of blood.

When Ghatotkach heard the news of Iravan's death, he was furious. 'I will destroy the Kauravas today. None will escape my wrath,' he yelled. His thunderous voice shook the Kaurava soldiers to their bones. Ghatotkach enlarged himself into a giant and trod upon the Kaurava soldiers, trampling them under his feet. With each swing of his mace, hundreds of Kaurava soldiers lost their lives. Duryodhan knew he had to do something to stop Ghatotkach from destroying his army. He asked his charioteer to drive him towards Ghatotkach. At his command, the king of Banga followed him with 10,000 elephants. Ghatotkach, from his high vantage point, showered Duryodhan with arrows and forced his charioteer to retreat. With a single blow of his mace, Ghatotkach killed the huge elephant of the king of Banga. Drona tried to stop him but Ghatotkach shattered Drona' bow, forcing him to take shelter. Balhik and Chitrasen suffered severe injuries from Ghatotkach's weapons and had to flee the battlefield. Ghatotkach's javelin pierced Brihadbal's heart and killed him instantly.

Seeing his father's plight, Aswathama and his soldiers rushed in to fight Ghatotkach. Aswathama was a skilled and powerful warrior, and his weapons began to trouble Ghatotkach who then took recourse to his special powers of illusion and hypnosis. He cast a spell on the Kauravas, and they saw their King Duryodhan, along with his generals like Shalya, Drona, Aswathama and others, lying on the battlefield in pools of blood, screaming in agony. They saw thousands of Kaurava soldiers lying dead, hundreds of thousands of body parts of men, horses and elephants scattered all around them. The horrific sight set off panic amongst the soldiers. With the loss of Duryodhan and the other mighty generals, the Kauravas had suffered the worst defeat, they thought, and began to flee in hordes.

Bhishma turned his chariot towards the fleeing soldiers and yelled, 'Stop! Don't desert the battlefield. What you see is nothing but an illusion created by the shrewd demon Ghatotkach. Your king Duryodhan is alive and well. So are Drona, Aswathama and Shalya. This illusion won't last for long. Come back and fight for your king.' But his words failed to inspire the soldiers. They ran away as fast as they could.

Duryodhan came to Bhishma and said, 'Grandfather, it seems today is the last day of the battle. Our soldiers are deserting us. We are doomed. It's not Bheem or Arjun, we have lost the battle to this rakshasa, Ghatotkach.'

'Don't be disheartened. Nothing is lost yet,' replied Bhishma. 'I suggest you don't engage with Ghatotkach. You are a king and you should fight a king. Pick Yudhishthira or one of his brothers to fight. Let me handle Ghatotkach.'

Bhishma called Bhagadatta and said, 'King Bhagadatta, you are the only person who can destroy this mighty rakshasa. Take your soldiers and attack Ghatotkach with all your might and kill him. Otherwise, we'll have no option but to surrender and hand over the throne of Hastinapur to Yudhishthira.'

Bhagadatta mounted a huge elephant named Supratik, picked up a massive weapon, and hurled it at Ghatotkach. Ghatotkach laughed and grabbed the weapon mid-air and, holding it like a stick with his two arms, he struck it on his thigh and snapped it into two pieces. Bhagadatta was not deterred, though. He picked up his bow and began to shower arrows on Ghatotkach. They could hardly nick Ghatotkach's thick skin as he continued his rampage.

In the meantime, Bheem, Abhimanyu, Chediraj and the five sons of Draupadi joined Ghatotkach and helped him mow down the Kauravas. It seemed they were on the verge of a huge victory and didn't want to waste any time.

Enraged at the death of his son Iravan, Arjun launched a stupendous attack on Bhishma and Kripacharya. He no more felt reverence or pity for these Kaurava seniors. He was determined to destroy them and avenge his son's death. Bhishma and the Kauravas also showed no compassion towards Arjun and countered his attacks with equal viciousness. A fierce battle ensued between the three great warriors.

Bheem again struck Duryodhan's brothers and killed seven of them. The others gave up and fled the battle. With total dominance over the enemy, the Pandavas seemed to have a real shot at achieving a tremendous victory just on the eighth day of the battle. However, the sun god had something else in mind and decided to go down in the horizon. As the last rays of sunlight faded away, the conch shells rang out to announce the end of the day's battle. The Kauravas sighed in relief, while the Pandavas felt disappointed for not being able to finish the war once and for all. Hoping to get back into the battle the next morning, the two sides retired to their camps to get some rest.

63

Day Nine of the War

DURYODHAN WAS HAVING DINNER WITH SHAKUNI AND KARNA. THE MOOD in the tent was quite sombre. The oil lamp standing on the floor cast long shadows of the three Kaurava warriors on the tent walls as they silently ate their food. Duryodhan was hardly eating anything. Noticing this, Shakuni said, 'My dear Duryodhan, it seems you have lost your appetite. I understand you are not happy at the way this war is shaping up. But don't take it out on your food. You'll only deny yourself of the nourishment you need.'

Duryodhan was almost in tears. 'Uncle, I don't understand why our great warriors like Bhishma, Drona, Kripa, Shalya and Bhurishrava are not able to destroy the Pandavas. These old men are causing us more harm than good. Every day, we are losing thousands of soldiers. Bheem killed my brothers right in front of Drona and he did nothing but watch them die.'

Karna felt bad for his dear friend. He had been sitting idle and helplessly watching the devastation caused by the Pandavas. He tried to console Duryodhan. 'Don't lose hope, my friend,' he said. 'The moment Bhishma retires, I will enter the battlefield and finish off the Pandavas in no time. You know, Bhishma likes your cousins and will try his best not to hurt them. Besides, I don't think he has what it takes to kill these valiant warriors. I suggest you go to Bhishma and politely ask him to give up his arms and return to Hastinapur. I will take it up from there and end all your pain and misery.'

Karna's words made Duryodhan feel better. It was a mistake to make Bhishma the chief of his army. Now was the time to correct that mistake, he thought. He finished his dinner, mounted his horse and headed towards Bhishma's tent.

Bhishma had just finished his meal and was about to sit down to plan the next day's battle when Duryodhan entered the tent and bowed down to touch his feet. Bhishma was surprised to see Duryodhan's sudden expression of reverence. He asked Duryodhan to take a seat. Duryodhan obeyed, and then, with palms joined, he said, 'Grandfather, I came here to apologize and ask for your forgiveness for all the harsh words I have said to you. I should have realized long ago that age is a cruel enemy that can affect even a great warrior like Bhishma and rob him of the edge he once enjoyed. I forgot that the valour and prowess with which the young Bhishma fought his guru Parashurama cannot remain the same.'

Bhishma was quite amused to listen to Duryodhan. 'What are you trying to say? I don't have what it takes to fight this war?' he asked.

Palms still joined, Duryodhan replied, 'You are great ... And, yes, you can still destroy our enemy and kill the Pandavas in a single day, if you really want. But, from what I understand, age can rob a person of his will to fight and win. You had promised that you'd kill our enemies and make us victorious, but that day is yet to come. In the meantime, we are losing thousands of warriors every day, while my gallant friend Karna sits idle on the side lines. If he joins the battle, I am sure the tide will turn in our favour.'

Duryodhan paused to take a deep breath and, before Bhishma could respond, he said, 'Grandfather, if for whatever reason, you think it wouldn't be possible for you to kill the Pandavas, then I would request you to step down and allow Karna to fight. Trust me, I won't hold you to your promise. I will make all arrangements for you to return to the Hastinapur palace, where you can give company to my father Dhritarashtra and mother Gandhari.'

Duryodhan's words, although delivered in the sweetest tone he could muster, fell on Bhishma's ears like molten lead. Never had he felt so insulted. Had this not been his grandson Duryodhan, he would have killed him that very instant. Instead, Bhishma closed his eyes, clenched his fist and bit his lips to control his anger. Then he slowly raised his head and replied, 'I am not going to repeat what I have said a thousand times, for you will never understand. You will never understand that nobody in this world, not even the gods, can defeat the Pandavas, especially when Vasudeva Krishna is on their side. As a Kshatriya, I will never quit the battle; hence, stepping down is out of the question. So I will either emerge victorious or I will die in the battlefield. That has been my principle and it still is. Let me tell you this. Tomorrow, nobody will escape my wrath and I will fight a battle that people will remember for eons to come. Now, please leave my tent and let me get some rest.'

The next morning, as the sun rose on the eastern horizon of the Kurukshetra battlefield on the ninth day of the war, Bhishma commanded his army to create the Sarbatobhadra formation. Kripacharya, Kritavarma, Jayadrath, Drona, Bhurishrava, Duryodhan and Bhagadatta guarded the pivotal points.

On the Pandava side, Dhrishtadyumna created an impenetrable formation. Arjun came up to him and said, 'Keep Shikhandi in the lead, facing Bhishma. I will protect him.' Arjun knew Shikhandi was born a woman and Bhishma would avoid fighting him. If Shikhandi tried to engage Bhishma in a battle, Bhishma would be distracted and that might force him to cause less damage.

Soon, a mighty battle erupted. The violent clash between the two armies caused the earth to tremble. Sparks flew off the metal armaments like meteor showers. Arjun's teenaged son Abhimanyu rode a chariot drawn by four powerful yellow horses and mowed down the Kaurava Army with his incessant volley of arrows. Duryodhan called his demon warrior Alambush and said, 'What are you doing here? Go and stop Abhimanyu. Use your magic.'

Alambush approached Abhimanyu and cast his magic spell. Soon, the battlefield was cloaked in dark smoke and blinded the warriors. They couldn't see a thing and failed to tell who's a friend and who's a foe. Abhimanyu was prepared for Alambush's sorcery. He pulled out his Bhaskara weapon and launched it high in the sky. As the weapon exploded with a bright flash, the smoke cloud dissipated in an instant. With a clear view, Abhimanyu began to strike his choicest weapons at Alambush. The demon couldn't take it any more. He jumped off his chariot and ran for his life.

In another section of the battlefield, Bhishma struck the Pandavas with a ferocity they had never experienced before. As if to keep his promise to Duryodhan, Bhishma unleashed his most powerful weapons, killing thousands with each strike. Nobody could stand in front of him, not even the most skilled Pandava warriors. As the day progressed, corpses of men, horses and elephants piled up. Many of the Pandava warriors began to flee the battlefield.

When Krishna heard the news, he turned his chariot towards where Bhishma was wreaking havoc. He called Arjun and said, 'Remember, Parth, what you had promised Sanjay in the kingdom of Virat? If not, let me remind you. You said that when the Great War happened, you'd show no mercy to Bhishma, Drona, Kripacharya or to any of the Kauravas and would kill them all. If you are a true Kshatriya, rise to the occasion and do whatever is needed to keep your promise.'

'I don't know what is better: to kill these valiant men whom I adore and revere only to win a kingdom that I can't enjoy, or to quit this bloody war and spend the rest of my life in penance in a forest,' muttered Arjun almost inaudibly. Then he raised his voice and said, 'I'll do what you say, Krishna. Take me to Bhishma and I will destroy him.'

Krishna drove the chariot towards Bhishma, and soon the two great warriors faced each other. On this ninth day of the war, Bhishma was simply unstoppable. Not even Indra, the lord of the gods, could have stopped him. Bhishma's arrows covered Arjun from all sides, and he couldn't keep up countering them. A dark cloud of arrows covered Arjun's chariot and he could hardly be seen. Krishna tried his best to manoeuvre his chariot to escape Bhishma's onslaught, but nothing seemed to work. The warriors around stopped fighting and watched in amazement as the old man in a flowing white beard and white garments completely subdued the mighty warrior Arjun. Emboldened by Bhishma's prowess, the Kaurava Army launched their attack on the Pandavas with renewed vigour. Thousands of Pandava soldiers lost their lives, and it seemed that, if Bhishma continued in his devastating form, nothing could stop the Kauravas from winning the war. The Sun god was kind to the Pandavas, and soon dusk fell. Those still alive sighed in relief as they retreated to their respective camps.

In the Pandava camp, Yudhishthira summoned his brothers and trusted lieutenants to an emergency meeting. Bhishma's onslaught during the day had shattered him. He looked at Krishna and said, 'Vasudev, it was a great mistake to fight against Grandfather Bhishma.

You saw how he decimated our army today. Arjun was no match for him. If he continues like this, we have absolutely no chance of winning this war. I have been thinking about giving up and retiring to the forests. At least there we can live in peace and with dignity.'

Krishna held Yudhishthira's hands and said, 'My dear Yudhishthira, don't lose hope. I am with you. If Arjun cannot muster up the will to kill his favourite grandfather, give me the orders. I will take up arms to fight and kill Bhishma in front of the Kauravas. An enemy of the Pandavas is my enemy too, and I am willing to do whatever it takes to make you victorious. Arjun is my dearest friend, my brother-in-law, and my student. For him, I can cut off and sacrifice my flesh if needed. Yes, Arjun had promised to kill Bhishma. But if it is too costly a burden for him, then relieve him of his promise and allow me to do the job. The moment Bhishma decided to join the evil Kauravas, his days were numbered. It is only a matter of time before Bhishma falls. If you order me, I will not hesitate for a moment and join the battle tomorrow morning.'

Arjun stood behind with his head hung in shame. Yudhishthira knelt before Krishna and said, 'Pardon me, Vasudev. With you on our side, we can even defeat the gods, let alone Bhishma. I don't want you to break your promise for our sake. That would be worse than losing the war. You please stay with us as you have always done.' Raising himself from the supplicant's position, he sat next to Krishna and said, 'Bhishma once told me that although he is fighting for Duryodhan, if we ever needed his advice on how to win, he'd be glad to offer his help. I have decided: we'll ask Bhishma himself how we can kill him. When we were young kids, Grandfather never refused us anything. I am sure, even today, he won't turn us back. He would give us the right advice to ensure our victory.' Yudhishthira paused for a moment and looked at his brothers, who stood shocked. They couldn't believe their ears. Bhishma would tell them how to kill him? Wasn't that too much to ask?

Krishna stood up and said, 'You have taken the right decision, Yudhishthira. Bhishma loves you brothers more than anything else. He won't refuse you anything you want, even if it is his life. I suggest you don't waste any more time. Go to his tent right now.'

Yudhishthira turned to his brothers and said, 'You heard what Krishna said. Let's go to our grandfather and ask for one last gift.' He took off his arms belt, his armour and his helmet, and walked out of the tent. His brothers did the same and followed him. In the darkness of the night, the five brothers walked barefoot towards the Kaurava camp, while the guards and soldiers watched and wondered what their princes were up to this time.

When Yudhishthira and his brothers entered their grandfather's tent, Bhishma didn't seem surprised. His greetings sounded like he had been expecting them. 'Come in, my dear grandsons. It always gives me immense pleasure to enjoy your company,' he said.

The Pandavas touched his feet to pay their respects. Bhishma kissed their foreheads and asked them to sit down and be comfortable.

'Tell me, what can I offer you? You know there's nothing that I can't give you. So ask me what you want, and I'll do whatever it takes to make you happy,' said Bhishma.

The Pandavas sat speechless with their heads hung low. Bhishma tried to cheer up the brothers. 'Come on, don't be shy. I am your grandfather. I have never refused you anything you asked, and I won't refuse today either.'

Yudhishthira looked up at Bhishma and said, 'Grandfather, we know you won't turn us down even if we ask for what's most precious to you. And that's what makes it more difficult to ask.'

Bhishma smiled: 'As a king, you have responsibilities towards your people. If the object you ask for helps you serve your people better, don't hesitate. I told you, there is nothing in this universe that I can't give you.'

Yudhishthira stood up and said, 'You have always wished us well. You wished us victory. But with you fighting against us, it is impossible for us to win this war. When you fight, we can't find a single weak spot to strike you. You shoot with such tremendous speed that we can't even see when you pick up your arrow, when you pull your bowstring and when you release. It's all a blur. Thousands of Pandava soldiers are dying at your hands every day. If this continues unabated, nobody will be left on our side. They'd either die or flee the battlefield to escape your wrath.' Yudhishthira paused and moved close to Bhishma. He held the old man's hands in his palms and said, 'Grandfather, tell us ... how can we defeat you? How can we kill you? This is what we came here to ask from you—your life and our victory.' Yudhishthira struggled to control his tears as he uttered these words.

Bhishma slowly pulled his hands away and walked towards the window. He looked at the vast Kurukshetra battlefield while the Pandavas waited eagerly for an answer. His mind was travelling through time as his life flashed before his eyes—his promise to Satyavati's father that he'd never claim the throne and stay celibate forever; the day he turned Amba away; Amba's curse; his fight with Guru Parashurama; the arrival of the young Pandavas after Pandu's death; the game of dice and the horrible insult of Draupadi; the banishment of the Pandavas; and Duryodhan's refusal to give them their kingdom. Why was he defending the Kauravas all this while, he wondered. Was it only to defend his words, his unbreakable promise, which got him his name and fame? He remembered the thousands of insults he had to tolerate from Duryodhan, Dushasana and Karna. Still, he clung to the throne of Hastinapur with unyielding loyalty. Was it worth it? What had this loyalty given him in return? This horrible war where he must kill his favourite grandsons, the

Pandavas? He felt an unbearable feeling of disgust and self-loathing. He possessed the boon to decide when to die, which, for all practical purposes gave him the power to live for eternity. But was this life worth living? Maybe it was time to wrap up and make his grand exit, he thought. He turned back to Yudhishthira and said, 'You are right. As long I am alive, you cannot win this war. So, if you'd like to win the war, you must kill me.'

'But how?' asked Yudhishthira. 'In the battlefield, you are like the lord of death himself. When you have your bow in hand, even the gods can't beat you. And we are mere mortals.'

'Yes, when my bow is in my hand, and arrows in my quiver, nobody can touch me, let alone kill me. So, to kill me, you must make me drop my weapons,' said Bhishma.

The Pandavas didn't know what to say. How could they make Bhishma drop his weapons? Bhishma anticipated the question and said, 'Let me tell you this. I do not fight unarmed or injured men, or men who surrender to me and seek my mercy. I do not fight disabled men, or the father of a single son. And finally, I find it distasteful to fight women, or someone who was once a woman, or carries the name of a woman. You have Shikhandi, the son of Drupad, on your side. You know, he was born a woman and was later transformed into a man. Arjun, I suggest you put Shikhandi in front of you and strike me with your deadliest arrows. When I see Shikhandi, I will not strike back and will lay down my weapons. That will be your opportunity to strike and kill me. And once I am out of this battle, your victory shouldn't be too far. Now go back to your tents and get some rest. You have a big day tomorrow.'

The Pandavas were dumbfounded to hear Bhishma detail out the strategy for his own death. Tears flowed down their cheeks. One by one, they touched his feet to pay their respects and left the tent with their heads hung in shame and sorrow.

Back in Yudhishthira's tent, Arjun couldn't stay silent any longer. He blurted out to Krishna: 'I don't know how I can kill our beloved grandfather Bhishma. He was my closest friend, my guardian. I remember, when I was a child, many a times I would play with dirt and then climb up his lap to smear his face with the same dirt. He was never angry and would always laugh at my mischief. Sometimes, mistakenly, I'd call him "father". He would laugh and say, "I am not your father, Arjun. I am your father's father." Now tell me, how can I kill such a man? I'd rather let him destroy us. I don't crave for the kingdom, I don't crave for wealth, I don't crave for power. I only want my grandfather Bhishma to live. Is that too much to ask? Tell me, Krishna, where am I wrong?'

Krishna was calm. He said, 'Arjun, you know very well, it is your Kshatriya duty to kill your enemy, regardless of who he is. As far as Bhishma is concerned, his time to depart this mortal world has come. You are only an instrument to make the inevitable happen. If you refuse to do it, somebody else will. But you'll forever suffer the consequences of not executing your duty as a soldier. Remember, Arjun, if a man wants to kill you, it is advisable to kill him before he strikes.'

64

Day Ten of the War

(O)N THE MORNING OF THE TENTH DAY, THE PANDAVAS STRUCK WITH THE sole strategy of pulling out Bhishma from the Kaurava formation and killing him using Shikhandi as their shield. Shikhandi led the attack, with Arjun following closely to provide him cover. Bheem, Nakul, Sahadev, Satyaki and the other Pandava generals kept the Kauravas engaged and prevented them from distracting Shikhandi and Arjun. Bhishma knew today would be his last day of battle and unleashed his full fury on the Pandava Army. His arrows showered on the Pandavas like hail storm and killed them by the thousands. Shikhandi's chariot broke through the Kaurava Army as he raced to take down Bhishma. Shikhandi shot an arrow that hit Bhishma's armour and deflected. Bhishma glanced at Shikhandi and asked his charioteer to turn away. Shikhandi followed and kept shooting his choicest arrows at Bhishma, who said to him: 'Shikhandi, strike me as much as you want, but I won't engage. I know, God created you a woman named Shikhandini. You may look like a man to others, but to me you are still a woman. I don't fight with women.'

Shikhandi was furious. 'I don't care whether you want to fight me or not. Today, you will die at my hands,' yelled Shikhandi at the top of his voice as his chariot hurtled behind Bhishma's.

Arjun approached Shikhandi and said, 'You keep attacking Bhishma and I will protect you from the other Kauravas. Nobody will be able to come near you. Remember, if we fail to kill Bhishma today, we'll become the laughing stock of the armies.'

From behind Shikhandi, Arjun launched a vicious assault on the Kauravas. Anybody who came close and tried to defend Bhishma or attack Shikhandi was cut to pieces by Arjun's arrows. Thousands lay dead on the sides, creating a clear path for the three racing chariots—Bhishma's, Shikhandi's and Arjun's.

Duryodhan knew things were not looking good for him. He asked his charioteer to bring him close to Bhishma. When Duryodhan's chariot came near Bhishma's, he yelled, 'Grandfather, why are you running away from Shikhandi? Turn around and kill him. The Pandavas are wreaking havoc. This is not the time to remain true to your vanity of not fighting against women.'

Bhishma glanced at Duryodhan and said, 'I promised you that I'd kill ten thousand Pandava warriors a day. I have kept my word. And now I promise you, today, either I will die on the battlefield, or the Pandavas will die at my hands. Prince Duryodhan, you have taken care of me all these years. Today, I will repay my debt with my blood.'

Watching Bhishma run away from Shikhandi and Arjun, the other Pandava warriors—Bheem, Nakul, Sahadev, Ghatotkach, Satyaki, Abhimanyu, Virat, Drupad, Yudhishthira—joined the chase with the sole objective of killing Bhishma. The Kauravas tried their best to stop them and protect Bhishma. Drona called his son Aswathama and said, 'My son, I have a strong feeling something bad is going to happen today. The Pandavas are using Shikhandi as their shield, knowing well that Bhishma won't shoot at him. Arjun and his brothers will use this opportunity to kill Bhishma right in front of us. Arjun is desperate, and he will not stop at anything to achieve his goal. I advise you to stay away from him and attack Bheem, Dhrishtadyumna or any other Pandava. That way, you'll survive. I don't want my son to die before I do.'

As Bhishma's chariot raced through the battlefield with Shikhandi, Arjun, and the other Pandavas in hot pursuit, Bhishma had the same thought that has been lingering in his mind for the last few days: he was tired of this constant killing; enough was enough. He saw Yudhishthira following him at a distance. He asked his charioteer to take him close to Yudhishthira and said, 'My dear Yudhishthira, I have killed many men, elephants and horses in this battle, and I am tired of killing. I feel disgusted and don't want to carry the burden of my body any more. So, use this opportunity and ask Arjun to kill me before I change my mind.'

Bhishma's chariot veered away as Yudhishthira stood speechless. Moments later, he turned to Dhrishtadyumna and his soldiers and said, 'Go and kill Bhishma now. Arjun will protect you.' Drona, Aswathama, Kripacharya and Shalya rushed in to defend their commander. Abhimanyu, Satyaki, Dhrishtadyumna and the rest of the Pandava brothers didn't let them come anywhere near Bhishma.

Shikhandi and Arjun approached Bhishma and began to shower him with arrows. Bhishma laughed and said, 'Shikhandi, try as you might, I won't fight you. I know, Arjun is hiding behind you and these deadly arrows that are piercing my armour are from him and not from you. I enjoy fighting my beloved grandson, Arjun. You move aside and let him come and fight me.'

Neither Arjun nor Shikhandi paid attention to his words. They kept attacking Bhishma. Bhishma decided, now was the moment to end his battle forever. He asked his charioteer to stop the chariot. Then he stood up and said, 'Well, then, here I am in front of you. Strike me as much as you want.' He put down his bow and his quiver of arrows and addressed Shikhandi: 'I don't wish to fight any more. Bring on all the weapons you have. Make them pierce my armour, my body.'

Arjun was waiting for this opportunity. From behind Shikhandi, he kept shooting his fiercest arrows at Bhishma. The arrows entered Bhishma's body from the front and stuck out from his back. Soon, every inch of his body was covered with arrows from Arjun and Shikhandi. Bhishma stood there silent and absorbed all the pain without uttering a single word. Just before sunset, Bhishma couldn't stand any longer. He rolled off the chariot and fell to the ground with a loud thud. With the arrows sticking out from his back, Bhishma's body did not touch the ground. He lay suspended in air on a bed of arrows.

At that moment, the entire Kurukshetra fell silent. The great Bhishma had fallen. As the news spread like wildfire through the battlefield, everybody stopped fighting and converged upon the spot where he lay. Krishna, Arjun, Yudhishthira, Bheem, Nakul, Sahadev, and all the Pandava warriors got off their chariots and knelt before Bhishma. Duryodhan, Kripacharya and Shalya came crying. Drona fainted in his chariot. When he regained consciousness, he came to Bhishma and sat down at his feet. Soon, all the Pandava and Kaurava kings assembled around Bhishma.

Bhishma was down, but he wasn't dead. He opened his eyes and, with a faint voice, he said, 'I am pleased that you have come to see me. But I can't see you. My head his hanging in this uncomfortable position. Can somebody arrange a proper support for my head?'

Within moments, the kings brought in a variety of pillows of different sizes and shapes and tried to place them under Bhishma's head to give it support. Bhishma laughed: 'These pillows are not for me. Take them away. Where is Arjun?'

Arjun was standing nearby, tears flowing down his cheeks. He came close and said, 'Here I am, Grandfather. Tell me, what can I do for you?'

Bhishma looked at him and said, 'You are a Kshatriya warrior. You know what can provide the best support to my head. Please do something so that it goes well with my bed.'

Arjun understood what Bhishma was asking for. He bowed to Bhishma and lifted his Gandiva. Then he shot three arrows at the ground around Bhishma's head. The arrows stuck to the ground at angles and Bhishma's head rested between them.

Pleased with the arrangement, Bhishma smiled and said, 'See, Arjun gave me the best pillows. Now I can rest my head in peace.' He looked around and said, 'You know I have the power to pick my time of death. The sun is now in the southern hemisphere. I will lie here on my bed of arrows till the sun moves to the northern hemisphere and warms the earth. Then I will leave my body and depart for the heavens. Till then, please make arrangements to protect my body. Dig a moat around me such that wild carnivores don't eat me alive.'

Duryodhan had asked his healers to bring their medications to treat Bhishma's wounds and relieve him of his pain. Bhishma waved them away and said, 'I don't need any treatment. Duryodhan, please pay them their dues and ask them to leave.' Then he looked at the others and said, 'You too go back to your tents and get some rest. You still have a war to fight.'

The Kauravas and Pandavas joined hands to dig a moat around their grandfather. A canopy was erected to protect Bhishma from the elements. And after everything was completed to their satisfaction, they went back to their camps with a heavy heart. Bhishma lay alone in the battlefield on his bed of arrows, immersed in deep meditation.

65

Day Eleven of the War

B HISHMA'S FALL WAS A BIG BLOW TO THE KAURAVAS WHO THOUGHT HIM to be invincible. They still had many gallant warriors on their side, but losing Bhishma was something they couldn't grapple with. The war was far from over and the next morning the two armies would clash again on the battlefield. Duryodhan couldn't sleep. He shuffled around his tent and tried to figure out whom to pick as his army's next commander-in-chief.

Karna couldn't sleep either. His fights with Bhishma had created a bitterness between them. Enraged by Bhishma's insults, he had promised not to fight as long as Bhishma was in the battlefield. Now, when his time had come to join the battle, he felt maybe his feelings towards Bhishma were a bit too harsh. Without the blessings of the great Kaurava patriarch, he felt his mission to kill the Pandavas would never succeed. Karna mounted a horse and galloped towards the battlefield where Bhishma lay on his bed of arrows.

The sun was yet to rise when Karna got off his horse and walked towards Bhishma. He knelt next to the old man, but couldn't say a word. Tears flowed down his cheeks as he covered his mouth with his fist to control his emotions.

Bhishma opened his eyes and noticed Karna. He called his guards and said, 'Can you please leave us alone for a moment?'

The guards bowed and moved away. Bhishma extended his arm and gently touched Karna's shoulder. 'I am glad you came to see me,' he said. 'I'd have been really angry at you if you didn't come.'

Karna couldn't speak. Bhishma said, 'To tell you the truth, I was never really angry with you. I knew you are the only one who could cause real harm to the Pandavas. So, my insults and harsh words were only meant to demoralize you and distract you from your mission.' Bhishma paused to catch his breath. 'Karna, I know your true identity. I know you are Kunti's firstborn child. The Pandavas are your brothers. In my final hours, please grant me my last wish. Abandon your animosity towards the Pandavas and join them to end this battle. Let me be the last man to die in this war. Let all the kings and warriors go home and live their lives in peace.'

Karna gently freed himself from Bhishma's feeble grip and said, 'I respect your request, but I am sorry, I can't oblige. Kunti abandoned me. It was Adhirath, the charioteer, who rescued me and brought me up. And that is my true identity—son of a charioteer. Duryodhan has been kind to me and has given me the respect and honour I deserve, for which I have pledged my life to him. I cannot leave him now. Just as Krishna is determined to make the Pandavas victorious, so am I determined to destroy the Pandavas. Either I will kill the Pandavas, or they will kill me. Nothing can prevent this inevitability. Grandfather, I came here to seek your permission to join the battle. Bless me such that I emerge victorious, or die in battle and rest in peace.'

Bhishma sighed. 'I knew I wouldn't be able to sway you. Still, I tried, just as I had tried all my life to end this vicious animosity between the Kaurava and Pandava cousins and bring peace to the family. I failed. Well, then, go ahead and fight like a true Kshatriya warrior and protect the Kauravas to the best of your ability. May Dharma guide you to do the right thing.'

Karna stood up and bowed to Bhishma, and then walked away to mount his horse and race towards the Kaurava camp.

When Karna entered Duryodhan's tent, he found the Kaurava generals waiting in silence. Duryodhan rose from his seat and said, 'Here you are, Karna. We have been waiting for you. We have a difficult decision to make. I need your counsel.'

Karna bowed to Duryodhan and said, 'I hope I didn't keep you waiting for long. Please tell me, how can I help you?'

'Grandfather Bhishma's fall has created a huge void that is hard to fill,' said Duryodhan. 'His indomitable prowess on the battlefield, his wisdom and leadership as our commander for the last ten days almost took us to the verge of victory. But we haven't achieved victory yet. And for that, we need a commander-in-chief who can serve as the right successor to Bhishma. Tell me, who do you think would be the best person to fulfil that job?'

Karna looked around and saw the great Kaurava warriors—Drona, Kripacharya, Shalya, Aswathama—waiting anxiously for his opinion. Karna thought for a moment and then said, 'My dear friend, each one of the great warriors who are assembled here can serve as the commander-in-chief. But we can't give them all the title. We need to pick one—someone who is not only a great warrior, but is also revered for his prowess and wisdom. The only man who fulfils these requirements is Acharya Drona. He is not only the teacher of many who have assembled here, he is also regarded as the greatest archer alive. He is learned, experienced, and the wisest of us all. If he becomes the commander-in-chief, the Kaurava warriors would gladly accept his leadership and feel blessed to fight under his guidance.'

Duryodhan smiled: 'Karna, I couldn't agree more.' He stepped towards Drona and knelt in front of him. 'Gurudev, you have taught us how to fight and how to use our weapons. Now teach us how to win this great battle. O Gurudev, please be our commander-in-chief and lead us to victory against the Pandavas.'

Drona touched Duryodhan's head with his right palm and said, 'My King, I accept your offer. I will lead the Kaurava Army and fight the Pandavas to the best of my ability. However, I have a condition. I will kill anyone who dares to fight me, except Drupad's son Dhrishtadyumna. He was born to kill me, and I cannot change my destiny.'

Duryodhan summoned the royal priest and performed the rituals to formally ordain Drona as the commander-in-chief of the Kaurava Army. Drona was pleased with Duryodhan's display of respect and honour. He called Duryodhan and said, 'You have honoured me by giving me the responsibility to be your commander-in-chief. I want to return the favour by rewarding you. Ask me anything you want.'

Duryodhan bowed to Drona and said, 'If you want to give me something, then capture Yudhishthira and bring him to me alive, in chains.'

Drona was surprised to hear this strange request from Duryodhan. 'You must be thinking that I would never kill my beloved student Yudhishthira, right? Is that why you ask me to capture him instead? Or is it that you don't consider him to be your real enemy. Whatever the reason, it seems Yudhishthira is truly blessed.'

Duryodhan couldn't conceal his feelings any longer. He replied, 'No, Gurudev, you don't understand. Yudhishthira's death won't give me my victory. If I manage to get Yudhishthira killed, the Pandava brothers would hunt me down and kill me for sure. So here is my plan. Capture Yudhishthira and bring him to me. I will then challenge him to another game of dice and send him and his brothers back to the forest in exile for life. This way, we can achieve lasting peace.'

Duryodhan's devious plan stunned Drona. He thought for a while and then said, 'Alright. I promise to deliver you Yudhishthira in chains, only if Arjun is not around to protect him. You know, Arjun is undefeatable even by the gods. I am his guru, but he won't spare me either. It would be impossible for me to capture Yudhishthira if Arjun is guarding him. So, if Arjun can be kept busy in battle somewhere far from Yudhishthira, then consider Yudhishthira to be yours.'

Duryodhan was ecstatic. He knew, when Drona promised, he delivered. Still, to make sure Drona delivered on his promise, he made his announcement public, and the news spread like wildfire through both the camps.

When Yudhishthira heard of this, he grew anxious. He called Arjun and said, 'Did you hear about Drona's promise? We all know he is a man of his word. However, our gurudev has also given us an indication of how to make him fail. So, while Drona is alive, stay around me and defend me from his wrath. Don't let anybody lure you away from me.'

Arjun smiled: 'You have nothing to worry about. You know I can't kill my teacher Drona, but I will not let him come anywhere near you. I will stay close to you and never let you out of my sight.' Yudhishthira felt relieved. He asked Dhrishtadyumna to lead the Pandava Army to the eleventh day's battle.

Within moments, the two armies engaged in a fierce battle. Drona led the Kaurava Army in his golden chariot and began to mow down the Pandava Army with his arrows. Dhrishtadyumna tried to stop Drona, but the newly appointed Kaurava commander attacked with such ferocity that, soon, Dhrishtadyumna was left with no option but to flee. Yudhishthira and the other Pandava brothers rushed to restrain Drona and rescue the Pandava soldiers from his onslaught.

On the other side of the battlefield, Abhimanyu was engaged in a fierce encounter with Brihadbal, who jumped off his chariot to save himself from an incoming missile by Abhimanyu. The missile hit his chariot and instantly killed his horses and his charioteer. Abhimanyu jumped off his chariot and, with a machete in one hand and a shield in the other, he attacked Brihadbal. Jayadrath saw Brihadbal in trouble and wedged his chariot between Brihadbal's and Abhimanyu's. Abhimanyu shouted at the top of his voice: 'Uncle Jayadrath, get out of my way. Otherwise, today will be your last day on earth.' He jumped on Jayadrath's chariot and swung his machete at Jayadrath's neck. Jayadrath ducked to save himself and fell off his chariot, which raced away with Abhimanyu on board. Abhimanyu grabbed a mace and jumped off to chase Jayadrath, who was running for his life.

Shalya was watching the battle between Abhimanyu and Jayadrath, and felt that if he didn't intervene, Jayadrath would be a dead man in a matter of seconds. He got off his chariot with a huge mace in his hand and challenged Abhimanyu: 'My dear grandson, leave Jayadrath alone and fight me if you can. Let me see how well you have mastered the art of the mace.' He swung his humongous mace above his head and stood blocking Abhimanyu's path.

Abhimanyu paused midway through a swing: 'Don't try to stop me, Grand-uncle. You may be an expert with the mace, but I am no novice either. I learnt my skills from none other than the greatest mace warrior in the world—my uncle Bheemsen. Come, try me. My mace is eager to taste your blood.'

Shalya was amused to hear the war cry of the young lad who was still in his teens. He laughed: 'Only cowards use rhetoric in the hope of scaring off their opponents. These pompous words don't mean anything to me. Come and give me a good fight.' He stomped ahead to face Abhimanyu.

Bheem was passing by on his chariot and noticed Abhimanyu about to pounce upon Shalya with his mace. Abhimanyu might be

a great warrior, but he was no match for Shalya when it came to the mace. Shalya would crush him in no time. Bheem swerved his chariot and faced Shalya. 'Uncle, if a mace fight is what you want, then leave the boy alone and fight me,' yelled Bheem. Turning to Abhimanyu, he said, 'You take my chariot and go after Jayadrath. Let me take care of my dear uncle.' Abhimanyu obeyed grudgingly.

Shalya said to Bheem: 'It was a wise decision indeed. I would have hated myself if I had to kill the boy. With you, it is different. I look at you as my equal. Now let's fight.' Shalya swung his mace to strike Bheem. With lightning speed, Bheem lifted his mace and it struck Shalya's with a loud bang, the sound of which reverberated through the battlefield. Soon, the two warriors engaged in a deadly fight. Sparks flew off their weapons as they struck each other with enormous power. Bheem and Shalya kept striking at each other while the soldiers ran to save themselves from being crushed by the wild swings of their huge maces. The fight continued for hours until the two found themselves thrown to the ground and panting in exhaustion. Kritavarma rushed in, pulled Shalya on his chariot and left the battlefield. Bheem felt relieved that he didn't have to kill Shalya that day.

As the day progressed, the Kauravas found themselves severely pounded by the Pandavas. Drona wasn't happy at all. He didn't want his first day as the commander-in-chief turn out to be a huge disaster for the Kauravas. He tried to lift the spirits of the fleeing Kaurava soldiers: 'Don't be afraid of the Pandavas. Turn around and fight. We will be victorious.' Drona felt the only way to gain the trust of his soldiers was to make them see him keep his promise. He asked his charioteer to take him to Yudhishthira.

As soon as Yudhishthira's chariot came into view, Drona engulfed him in a volley of arrows. Yudhishthira was overwhelmed and cried out for help. The Panchal prince Kumar came to help and struck

Drona with powerful weapons. Drona deflected them all and kept up his attack on Yudhishthira. Bhagadatta and Singhasen came to protect Yudhishthira, but Drona's arrows soon took their lives. Helpless, Yudhishthira looked around for Arjun, but he was nowhere to be found. The Kaurava soldiers around grew certain that today Drona would capture Yudhishthira and the Pandavas would be forced to surrender. Hearing of Drona's imminent victory, Duryodhan asked his charioteer to take him near Drona. The other Kaurava generals followed suit.

Just as Yudhishthira was about to give up all hope, Arjun rushed in and covered the sky with thousands of arrows that hurtled towards Drona. His chariot circled Yudhishthira's and created a wall of arrows that overwhelmed Drona and his warriors. Drona knew, with Arjun around, it would be impossible for him to come anywhere near Yudhishthira. He called out to Yudhishthira: 'My dear Yudhishthira, today you were lucky to have Arjun come to your rescue. Remember, this won't happen every day.' He turned his chariot and left the battlefield.

Soon, the day ended with the sun setting in the western horizon. The warriors sighed in relief.

As dusk fell upon the vast Kurukshetra grounds, the Pandava and Kaurava soldiers dragged their tired and injured bodies to their respective tents. A visibly frustrated Drona entered Duryodhan's tent and saw the other generals assembled around Duryodhan. Drona put down his helmet and said, 'I am sorry, Duryodhan. Today I couldn't keep my promise. It was impossible to shake off Arjun from Yudhishthira's side. And as I said before, with Arjun around, we can never capture Yudhishthira alive. If you can arrange to pull away Arjun to some other part of the battlefield, I'll get you Yudhishthira.'

Susharma—the ruler of Trigarta—and his brothers were among the assembled kings. Susharma stepped forward and said, 'King Duryodhan, if you permit, we the Trigartas, can engage with Arjun and draw him away from Yudhishthira. Arjun has always treated us with disrespect, and nobody wants him dead more than we do. It will be our pleasure to kill Arjun and help you win this war. I assure you, tomorrow, either Arjun will die at our hands, or the earth will be void of the Trigartas.' Duryodhan accepted the offer with no reservations.

The Trigarta brothers—Susharma, Satyarath, Satyaverma, Satyabrata, Satyeshu and Satyakarma—assembled their warriors to prepare for the pledge ceremony. A huge sacrificial fire was lit and the Brahmins chanted hymns from the Vedas. The Trigartas, dressed in traditional costume, stood in front of the fire with joined hands and took the solemn vow: 'We the Trigartas solemnly pledge to kill Arjun in this holy war of Kurukshetra. If we fail, may we burn in hell for eternity.' Duryodhan and the other Kauravas applauded them.

'My dear Trigartas,' Duryodhan said, 'a warrior who takes such a deadly pledge is honoured by the Kshatriyas as a Samsaptak—the death-defying valiant. We all know, killing Arjun is a huge challenge and not many would dare to venture upon a mission like this. But with your courage and will, I am sure you'll succeed in achieving your objective.'

The Trigartas then moved to the edge of the battleground, just beyond the Pandava camp, and yelled insults at Arjun, daring him to fight them the next day.

Yudhishthira tried to dissuade Arjun from falling for their tactic: 'Pay no attention to their calls. This is Duryodhan's ploy to pull you away from me.'

Arjun was in a fix. He sat next to Yudhishthira and said, 'If someone challenges me to fight, how can I refuse? It's against my principles. I must fight. I beg you, please permit me to teach these arrogant Trigartas a lesson they deserve.'

Yudhishthira knew he was in a difficult position. He stood up and said, 'I understand. But you know, Drona has made it his sole mission to capture me and hand me over to Duryodhan in chains. Now, I leave it up to you to do the right thing to ensure my protection.'

Satyajit, a gallant warrior from Panchal, was standing nearby. Gesturing to him, Arjun said, 'Don't worry, Brother. While I am away, Satyajit will protect you from Drona. He is a skilled warrior, and as long as he is alive, I can assure you, Drona won't be able to touch a single strand of hair on your body.' He paused a little and continued, 'In case Drona manages to neutralize him, then don't wait. Ask your charioteer to leave the battlefield immediately.'

Satyajit was overwhelmed to be given this huge responsibility. He bowed to Yudhishthira and said, 'O King, have faith in me. I will protect you from Drona till my last breath.' Yudhishthira had no option but to agree.

66

Day Twelve of the War

THE NEXT MORNING, WITH THE SOUND OF THE CONCH SHELLS, THE TWO
sides clashed for the twelfth time in the great war in Kurukshetra.

Sticking to their plan, the Trigartas mocked and challenged
Arjun: 'Come on, Arjun. If you have the guts, come and fight us.
Today, we will show the world that all your gallantry and prowess is
nothing but hype.'

Arjun said to Krishna, 'Look at these fools. They are about to die,
yet they are laughing. Take me to them. I don't want them to wait for
their death.' Arjun picked up his Devadutta conch and blew it. The
roar of the conch shook the Trigartas to the core and, for a moment,
they were unable to move. Soon, they recovered and attacked Arjun
with full vigour. Arjun retaliated by showering deadly arrows at
them. The Trigarta soldiers began to drop like flies. Overwhelmed by
Arjun's attack, they began to flee the battlefield.

King Susharma yelled at them: 'Friends, don't panic. Have you
forgotten your pledge? If you flee, you'll be the laughing stock of
the Kshatriyas. Come back and fight like a true Trigarta warrior.'

Susharma's spirited words were not wasted. The warriors turned back and once again attacked Arjun with full force. Arjun realized that the Samsaptak warriors weren't going to give up easily. He pulled out his magical Tastra weapon built by none other than Lord Vishwakarma. The weapon created a fantastic illusion, and the Trigarta warriors saw each other as Arjun or Krishna. Bewildered by the magic, they began to strike and kill each other. Arjun took this opportunity to wipe them out with his deadly weapons. But the illusion didn't last long. Soon, the Trigartas recovered and their arrows engulfed Arjun in a dark cloud. Arjun hurled his Vayu Astra at them. The winds churned up and created a huge tornado that blew away the enemy soldiers like dry leaves.

While Arjun was busy fighting the Trigartas, Drona created the Garuda—the bird formation—and attacked Yudhishthira. The formation had Duryodhan at its head, along with Kritavarma, Kripacharya, Salwa, Karna, Jayadrath and many others at its pivotal points.

On the Pandava side, Dhrishtadyumna arranged his army in the Half-moon formation to counter Drona. Yudhishthira called Dhrishtadyumna and said, 'Make sure Drona doesn't capture me.'

'Don't worry. As long as I'm alive, Drona won't be able to come anywhere near you.' Dhrishtadyumna tried to assure Yudhishthira and then commanded his army to attack Drona.

Drona, however, didn't care for Dhrishtadyumna. His sole target was Yudhishthira. With incessant arrows flowing from his bow, he continued to mow down the Pandava soldiers and clear his path towards Yudhishthira. Satyajit stepped forward to stop Drona from reaching Yudhishthira. He fought gallantly to keep his promise, but he was no match for Drona's skills. Drona's arrows pierced his armour and killed him instantly. Yudhishthira remembered Arjun's advice. He asked his charioteer to take him away from Drona. He called out to Dhrishtadyumna and the other Pandavas: 'Give me cover. Keep Drona engaged while I leave the battlefield.'

Dhrishtadyumna, Shikhandi, Satyaki, Chetikan—they all tried their best to stop Drona, but he was simply unstoppable. Who'd have thought that this mild-mannered old Brahmin could be so fierce? They gave up and began to flee the battle along with the other Pandava soldiers.

Duryodhan noticed the plight of the Pandavas and laughed. 'Look at them running away from Drona,' he said to Karna. 'It seems our great Guru Drona will keep his promise and get me Yudhishthira.'

Karna wasn't laughing, though. He was watching Bheem fighting with his usual ferociousness and advancing towards Drona. 'Don't be so sure, my friend,' he replied. 'As long as Bheem is alive, he won't let Drona net his catch. I suggest, we go and stand by Drona to protect him from Bheemsen's wrath.' Duryodhan agreed and they turned their chariots towards Drona.

Bhagadatta rode his huge elephant and advanced towards Bheem, trampling and killing hundreds of Pandava soldiers on the way. The king of Darshan tried to stop Bhagadatta. Bhagadatta's elephant lifted him and thrashed him to the ground, killing him instantly. The Pandava soldiers panicked and ran to save their lives.

Hearing the cry of the elephant, Arjun said to Krishna: 'That was Bhagadatta's elephant. That humongous beast can tolerate any weapon you throw at him. If we don't destroy that moving mountain, it'll kill all our soldiers in no time. I must stop Bhagadatta and get rid of this menace.'

Soon, Arjun's chariot reached Bhagadatta. Bhagadatta turned his elephant to face Arjun. Krishna took advantage of the elephant's slow movements and turned the chariot to the south of the moving behemoth. 'No, Krishna,' said Arjun. 'I don't want to fight Bhagadatta from behind. Take me to his side.' Krishna pulled up the chariot parallel to Bhagadatta. With a swift volley of arrows, Arjun destroyed the elephant's armour. He then shot some of the most powerful weapons he had at the elephant, but the beast didn't budge. It trumpeted loudly and turned to attack Arjun's chariot. Bhagadatta was waiting for this moment. Just when he had Arjun in clear sight, he pulled out his Vaishnavastra—the lethal weapon of Lord Vishnu—and aimed it at Arjun. He engaged the weapon on his bow, uttered the secret mantra to activate it, and shot it at Arjun. Like a lightning bolt, the weapon left Bhagadatta's bow and zoomed towards Arjun. Before the weapon could strike, Krishna stood up to guard Arjun. The arrow struck Krishna's chest and instantly transformed into a majestic necklace on his neck.

Arjun was shocked. 'Why did you do this?' he asked. 'You promised not to participate in the battle, and now you are violating your promise for my sake. Why?'

Krishna smiled, 'This weapon, the Vaishnavastra, is one of the deadliest in existence, and no mortal can survive its strike. If it had hit you, you'd have died for sure. It was I, in my divine self, who had given this weapon to Narakasur as a gift, which in turn was given to Bhagadatta. Bhagadatta held on to this weapon only to kill you. I can't let him do that. So, I had to take back my weapon. Now Bhagadatta has nothing left to protect himself. Go ahead, kill him and fulfil your duty.'

Arjun pulled out the powerful Narach weapon and hurled it at Bhagadatta's elephant. It pierced the elephant's heart and killed the beast instantly. As his mount crashed to the ground, Bhagadatta jumped off and tried to run away. Before he could move, a half-moon arrow from Arjun struck his chest and killed him.

In the meantime, Drona and his son Aswathama were wreaking havoc amongst the Pandava warriors. Dhrishtadyumna, Bheem, Satyaki and the other Pandava stalwarts failed to control their onslaught. And when Karna and Duryodhan joined hands with Drona, things went from bad to worse. Just then, Arjun and Krishna arrived at the scene of the battle. The incessant flow of arrows from Arjun overwhelmed Drona's warriors and they got busy trying to save themselves. Each arrow shot from Drona's bow was cut down by Arjun. Karna shot his fire-belching weapon at Arjun., which he destroyed mid-air. He then killed the three brothers of Karna who were trying to give him cover. Inspired by Arjun, Bheem and Dhrishtadyumna pounced upon the Kauravas with renewed vigour. With their swords and maces, they began to destroy hundreds of Kaurava warriors, who panicked and began to flee.

Soon, the sun went down the western horizon and the conch shells rang out to signal the end of the twelfth day's battle. The warriors sighed in relief as they struggled to drag their tired and injured selves back to their respective camps to get some rest.

In the Kaurava camp, a dejected and frustrated Duryodhan was waiting for Drona, who had to go to Duryodhan but felt ashamed to do so. As he entered, Duryodhan said, 'Gurudev, today you had Yudhishthira in your grip. Yet, you didn't capture him. I kept my part of the bargain and held Arjun far away from Yudhishthira, and in the process lost many of our friends. But you failed to keep your promise. I didn't expect this from you.'

'I am really sorry, Duryodhan,' said Drona. 'I don't have to tell you how difficult it is to overcome an opponent who has Krishna on his side.'

Duryodhan wasn't happy with the answer. To appease him, the old Brahmin said, 'Don't you worry. Tomorrow, I promise to kill at least one of the Pandava giants. I will create a formation that only a handful of people know how to penetrate. Arjun is one of them. You just keep Arjun busy on another part of the battlefield while I trap the Pandavas in the formation and kill them.'

67

Day Thirteen of The War

O N THE MORNING OF THE THIRTEENTH DAY, THE SAMSAPTAKS ONCE AGAIN lured Arjun far away from the rest of the Pandavas. Arjun couldn't refuse their challenge and engaged in a vicious battle in yet another attempt to annihilate them. On the other side of the battlefield, Yudhishthira saw the Kaurava Army approaching him in a formation that had never been seen in this battle. Drona had created the invincible Chakravyuha or the Wheel formation with all the Kaurava generals, including Duryodhan, his son Lakshman, Dushasana, Karna, Shalya, Kripa, Shakuni, Jayadrath and others protecting the vantage points. Yudhishthira knew that only Arjun had the knowledge to penetrate this formation, but he was nowhere to be seen. Yudhishthira panicked and asked Dhrishtadyumna, 'What do you think we should do? Without Arjun, the Kauravas will soon engulf us in his formation and kill us all.'

Dhrishtadyumna was in a fix. 'The only way to counter Drona is to break open the formation somehow, and attack the Kauravas from inside. But it is impossible to fetch Arjun now.'

Abhimanyu, the teenaged son of Arjun, was on his chariot next to Yudhishthira. He said, 'Uncle Yudhishthira, I know how to penetrate the Wheel formation.'

Yudhishthira was surprised. 'You do? But how? You are too young to know this complicated skill.'

Abhimanyu said, 'While I was in my mother's womb, I heard my father explain the strategy. That's how I learnt the trick. But ...' Abhimanyu paused for a moment.

'But what?' Yudhishthira was impatient.

'I know how to penetrate the Wheel and get in, but I don't know how to get out of it. My mother fell asleep before my father could explain the exit strategy, and I could hear no more.'

Yudhishthira could finally see a silver lining in Abhimanyu. He said, 'Today, our survival depends on you, my boy. You break open the formation for us and don't worry about the exit. We will follow you and bring you out of the formation safe and sound.'

Bheem said, 'My son, you only open the formation for us. I, along with Dhrishtadyumna and Satyaki, will storm in and decimate the formation by killing the Kaurava guards. You will be out in no time.'

'It will be an honour to be of service to my family at this hour of crisis,' said Abhimanyu. 'I will pierce the Wheel and show Drona that I may be a teenaged boy, but I am no less than any of them.'

Yudhishthira prayed for his success as Abhimanyu drove his chariot towards Drona's army.

Abhimanyu's charioteer, Sumitra, wasn't too sure about this adventure. 'Are you sure you want to do this?' he asked Abhimanyu. 'Drona is an indomitable warrior, and he won't show any mercy towards you just because you are the son of his favourite student.'

Abhimanyu laughed. 'I am not afraid of Drona or any of the Kaurava warriors. I am skilled enough to take on anybody, even Lord Indra if he wants to fight me. Now stop worrying and take me to the head of the formation. That's where I plan to pierce the wheel and tear apart Drona's army.'

Within moments, the sixteen-year-old boy broke through Drona's impenetrable formation with ease. Nothing could stop him. Once inside, Abhimanyu launched a fierce attack on the Kauravas and began to kill hundreds of warriors. Duryodhan called upon all his generals and said, 'Abhimanyu has entered our formation, but we won't let him get out alive. Attack him with all your might.'

Drona, Kripa, Aswathama, Shalya and Karna along with Duryodhan and Dushasana, the seven great charioteers encircled Abhimanyu and launched their attack. But they could hardly contain him. Abhimanyu's arrows hit Shalya's helmet and knocked him out. Shalya's brother tried to replace him, but Abhimanyu cut him to pieces in no time.

Drona was thrilled to witness Abhimanyu's gallantry. He called Kripa and said, 'Look how that young lad is fighting. I haven't seen such a skilled warrior before. I am sure he'd soon surpass his father Arjun.'

Duryodhan was furious to hear these words. He looked at Dushasana and Karna and said, 'Drona doesn't want to kill his favourite student's son. Don't wait for him. Let us finish off the boy as soon as possible.'

Dushasana said, 'Leave Abhimanyu to me. I'll kill him.' He stormed ahead to face Abhimanyu.

Abhimanyu laughed at Dushasana and said, 'Welcome, dear uncle. Today you'll pay for your sins.' Just as he finished his words, he hurled a spear at Dushasana, who dropped unconscious on the chariot floor. As Dushasana's charioteer turned around to take him to safety, Karna and his brother stepped in to fight Abhimanyu. Abhimanyu's arrows soon decapitated Karna's brother, and overwhelmed Karna who had to turn away to save himself.

While the young boy was fighting the Kauravas inside, the rest of the Pandavas were struggling to enter the wheel. Immediately after Abhimanyu broke through the formation, Jayadrath closed the entrance behind him and stood guard with his soldiers. Bheem, Satyaki, Dhrishtadyumna, Shikhandi and Drupad, along with the other Pandava warriors, tried their best to get past Jayadrath, but failed miserably. A few years ago, when the Pandavas were in exile, Jayadrath had made a failed attempt to abduct Draupadi. Bheem had caught him and beat him severely, but spared his life. Deeply hurt, Jayadrath had went on a long penance to appease Lord Shiva to help him kill the Pandavas. Shiva didn't oblige, but gave him the boon that, except for Arjun, he'd be able to defeat the rest of the Pandava brothers for one day in his life. Today was the day. Jayadrath stood tall and fought with such vigour that none could enter the formation and Abhimanyu was left alone inside, fighting the great Kaurava warriors.

Abhimanyu's arrows killed Brihadbal, Shalya's son Rukmarath, and Duryodhan's son Lakshman. Losing his favourite son to Abhimanyu made Duryodhan desperate. He commanded his generals: 'I want to see Abhimanyu dead. Kill him by hook or by crook.'

The seven charioteers surrounded Abhimanyu and attacked him from all sides, but with little effect. Admiring the boy's valour, Drona said, 'If his arrows kill me today, I will die happy. He is indeed the greatest warrior I have ever seen.'

Karna was bleeding all over. His eyes bloodshot, he said, 'I am badly wounded, and I need immediate medical attention. Yet, I am here only to serve my friend Duryodhan. Tell me, Gurudev, how can I win over Abhimanyu.'

Drona looked at him and said, 'I don't think you can pierce his armour from the front. It is indestructible, since he used the same technique to wear it as I had taught his father Arjun. If you want to beat him, strike him from behind. First destroy his bow, and then his chariot. That's the only way to get him.'

Karna immediately turned his chariot around to position himself behind Abhimanyu while the others kept him busy in the front. In quick succession, Karna cut down Abhimanyu's bow and killed his charioteer and his horses. As the chariot came to a crashing halt, Abhimanyu jumped off with a machete and shield in hand. Drona shot an arrow at Abhimanyu that sliced off the machete at the grip. Abhimanyu picked up a discuss and ran towards Dushasana. Drona cut it down to pieces. Abhimanyu looked around and found a mace lying nearby. He picked it up, whirled it around his head and ran towards Duryodhan. Dushasana's son swung his chariot behind Abhimanyu and struck his head with his mace. The huge blow knocked him out and the boy lay unconscious on the battlefield with blood gushing out of his cracked skull. The seven charioteers circled him and struck him continuously with deadly arrows to make sure the boy was dead. Duryodhan let out a great cry of joy. The others joined him, except for Drona, who sat silently in his chariot.

When the news of Abhimanyu's fall reached the Pandavas, panic struck the soldiers. They felt the Pandavas had no hope against Drona and began to flee in hordes. Yudhishthira tried to reason with them. 'Don't panic, my friends,' he said. 'Abhimanyu was killed in an unfair battle by the seven cowards. Yet, he fought gallantly and died like a true Kshatriya warrior, and has gone to the heavens. We should not cry for him. Rather, we should feel inspired to fight like him for the victory of the rightful heirs to the throne of Hastinapur.' The words calmed the warriors, but deep inside, Yudhishthira felt as if a part of him had died. The pain and guilt he felt for not being able to keep his promise and protect Abhimanyu burnt his soul. He looked at the sky and prayed, 'How long, O Lord, do you wish to punish me? For how long?'

Soon, the shadows grew on the battlefield as the sun went down, ending the thirteenth day of the war. The Pandavas returned to their tents in deep silence and fought hard to control their tears.

Arjun Vows Revenge

Yudhishthira entered his tent and collapsed to the ground. Abhimanyu's death had caused a deep void in him, and he felt as if all his strength had drained out. His brothers stood behind him but none could utter a word. The terrible blow left them dumbfounded.

Yudhishthira, tears flowing down his face, said, 'It was for me that my boy Abhimanyu broke through Drona's formation, only to be killed by the Kauravas. I promised him, we'd follow and rescue him from that death trap. I failed. It was my fault. Now what am I going to say to Arjun and Krishna? No words can console them. No words can console me. Winning this war seems meaningless to me. The throne, the kingdom, the heavens, nothing makes sense to me any more.'

At that moment, the great sage Vyasa appeared. He held Yudhishthira's hand and pulled him up on his feet. 'Get up, my son,' he said. 'A wise man like you should not lament the death of a gallant warrior like Abhimanyu. He had a glorious death that a Kshatriya deserves. Death is inevitable for any living being. So, no point in crying over it.'

Yudhishthira asked, 'Why? Why is death inevitable?'

Vyasa responded, 'Let me tell you a story Narada once told the great King Akampan.

'There was this king named Akampan who had a valiant son named Hari. When Hari died in a battle, King Akampan was devastated. He lost all interest in ruling his kingdom and his subjects suffered. Rishi Narada visited him and narrated this story to him: "After Lord Brahma created life, he faced a huge problem. The living beings were multiplying indiscriminately and the earth soon became overpopulated. Frustrated and enraged, Brahma created a huge fire that began to destroy everything on earth. Shiva came to him and said, 'What are you doing? Why are you destroying your own creation?'

"Brahma replied, 'What could I do? The Earth couldn't bear the weight of the living. I was angry at myself, and my anger burst into flames and began to devour the earth.'

"Shiva said, 'Have pity on your children. They are suffering for no fault of theirs. I am sure you can find some solution.'

"Shiva's plea helped Brahma calm down and the fire subsided, sparing the lives of millions. He sat in meditation, trying to find a solution to his problem. From Brahma's body emerged a goddess. Her skin was like fire, her face was red like hot iron, and her eyes blood shot. She stood in front of Brahma her palms joined and said, 'O lord, please tell me what is the purpose of my existence?'

"Brahma said, 'You are death. I command you to go to earth and kill the living beings.'

"Lady Death was shocked to hear this. She asked, 'Lord, you created me a woman. Why do you give me such a cruel duty? I will always be hated and cursed by the loved ones of the deceased. Please save me from committing such a grave sin.'

"Brahma ignored her plea and said, 'Go and perform your duty.'

"Death refused to follow his orders. She went to Rishi Dhenuk's hermitage and began to lead a life of austerity with the aim to please Brahma. Pleased with her perseverance, Brahma offered her a boon.

"Goddess Death said, 'Lord, I can't kill happy, healthy living beings for no reason at all, and bear their curse. I will only kill them if they commit sins like lust, greed, anger, envy and cruelty.'

"Brahma said, 'So be it. You can enter the bodies of living beings as a disease and cause their death. You won't be held responsible for performing your duty without any bias or discrimination.'

"Since then, death has been taking away the lives of all beings, without discrimination. Death is inevitable for any living being. So, stop lamenting. Remember, when somebody dies, their senses leave the mortal body in an invisible form. When they fulfil their Karma, the fine self returns to earth in a new body."'

'Abhimanyu's soul has left the earth and is now in heaven with his ancestors. He is happy. Don't cry for him.' Saying this, Vyasa disappeared.

Arjun was in a distant corner of the battlefield, fighting the Samsaptaks. At sunset, when the conch shell rang out announcing the end of the day's battle, Krishna turned his chariot to return to the Pandava camp. Arjun experienced a strange feeling. His heart fluttered, and his mouth felt dry. He said, 'Krishna, I don't feel good. I have this feeling that something bad has happened. Tell me, are my brothers safe?'

Krishna said, 'Don't worry, I am sure they are all fine.'

'No, Krishna, something is not right,' Arjun insisted. 'I've never had this feeling before. Take me to our camp as soon as possible.' Krishna tugged the reins of the horses, and the chariot raced towards the Pandava tent.

When the chariot stopped at the camp, no bells nor conch shells rang out to welcome them. An eerie silence engulfed the entire camp. Arjun and Krishna jumped off the chariot and entered the tent and were met with a strange sight—the Pandava brothers sitting on the floor with their heads down. They looked drained of all strength and didn't even look up to greet them. Arjun was anxious. 'Why are you sitting like this? What happened?' None spoke. He looked around and said, 'Where is Abhimanyu? I don't see him. I heard Drona had formed the Chakravyuha today. Among you, only Abhimanyu knows how to break open the Wheel formation. Was he able to penetrate it?' The Pandavas didn't answer.

Arjun's anxiety grew further. 'I taught him how to breach the formation but not the technique to get out. Was he able to exit it?' Nobody answered. Arjun was getting impatient. He almost yelled, 'Tell me, was he able to get out? Or did he get killed inside the wheel?' The entire camp was silent.

Arjun cried out, 'Why don't you answer me? Is my son alive or was he killed in battle? Tell me! What am I supposed to tell his mother Subhadra ... his wife Uttara?' Yudhishthira looked up at Arjun, tears streaming down his cheek. Arjun knew instantly what had happened to his dear son. He felt his head spinning, his legs losing all strength. He grabbed Krishna's arm to prevent himself from collapsing. Then he slowly stepped towards Yudhishthira, held his shoulder and asked, 'Abhimanyu fought his enemies till his last breath, right? He died a glorious death deserving of a gallant Kshatriya, right? When Karna, Drona struck him with their fierce weapons, did he cry out for help? While those cruel Kaurava warriors surrounded him and struck him again and again, did he cry out—Father, where are you, help me ... did he? Of course not. How could he? He is my son, Krishna's nephew, he can't cry like that. Tell me, Krishna, can he?'

Krishna held Arjun in his arms and said, 'Calm down, Arjun. Like a true Kshatriya warrior, Abhimanyu has died in battlefield and entered the heavens. All warriors dream of such a death. Don't mourn him. You are the greatest warrior alive. You can't afford to break down like this. Your grief is making your brothers weak. Stop lamenting and console your brothers. They need your support.'

Arjun looked at his brothers and said, 'Dear brothers, tell me, how did my son Abhimanyu die? Did the Kauravas trick my son and kill him in an unfair battle? How could the enemy kill him with you around? Ah, it was my fault that I left him under your watch and went to another side of the battlefield. What good are you that you couldn't protect my teenage boy? All your gallantry, your so-called skills and might—they are nothing but hollow words. You are good for nothing!' Arjun stood with his nostrils flared, his eyes bloodshot, and body trembling in rage.

Yudhishthira slowly stood up and said, 'After you left us to fight the Samsaptaks, Drona created the Wheel formation and attacked us. We were overwhelmed and were forced to send Abhimanyu to break open the Wheel. We planned to follow Abhimanyu into the formation and fight the Kauravas, but Jayadrath stopped us at the entrance. We tried our best to get past him, but with Shiva's boon, he was indomitable today, and we failed to beat him. Inside the Wheel, Drona, Kripa, Karna, Aswathama, Brihadbal, Kritavarma and Dushasana surrounded Abhimanyu and attacked him from all sides. Abhimanyu fought valiantly and killed Brihadbal, along with thousands of Kaurava warriors. But Karna disarmed him, and Dushasana's son struck him from behind and killed him ...'

Arjun collapsed unconscious on the floor. The Pandava brothers rushed to help him. A little later, he regained consciousness and stood up, shaking off the dirt from his armour. He looked around at his brothers' faces and then at Krishna. In a sombre voice, he said, 'With all of you as my witness, I take a vow that unless Jayadrath surrenders to us, or to Krishna, tomorrow I will kill him. I also promise that if I fail to kill him tomorrow before sunset, I will step into a fire pit and kill myself. Nobody, not even the gods can save Jayadrath.'

Arjun pulled the string of his Gandiva bow, and Krishna blew his Panchajanya conch shell. The sound reverberated throughout Kurukshetra and the Kauravas knew the next day's battle will be a costly one for them.

When the news of Arjun's vow reached Jayadrath, he panicked and ran to Duryodhan. 'My brother, did you hear the news? Arjun has vowed to kill me by sunset tomorrow. I must leave Kurukshetra immediately and hide some place far away.'

Duryodhan was busy preparing for the war next day. He looked up at Jayadrath and said, 'My dear brother-in-law, today you fought a magnificent battle. None of the Pandava warriors could get past you. You stopped everybody—Yudhishthira, Bheem, Dhrishtadyumna. Everybody spoke highly of your gallantry and you made me proud. And now you want to run away? How could a valiant warrior like you even think of such a cowardly act?'

Jayadrath sat down and wiped the sweat off his forehead. 'Duryodhan, you may say whatever you want, but the truth is, I am scared. If I stay here, Arjun will kill me for sure,' he was almost in tears.

Duryodhan held Jayadrath's arm and said, 'Don't worry. I cannot let my sister become a widow, can I? We will protect you with all our might. Arjun won't be able to touch a strand of hair on your body. Leave all your worries to me. Now go to your tent and get some rest.'

Jayadrath left, but clearly Duryodhan's words didn't give him enough confidence. Instead of returning to his tent, he walked towards Drona's.

Drona was discussing the war strategy with few of his generals. When he saw Jayadrath, he asked the generals to leave. Jayadrath touched Drona's feet and said, 'I am sure you can guess why I am here.'

Drona replied, 'Yes. But you shouldn't ...'

Jayadrath didn't let him complete the sentence. He asked, 'Gurudev, you have taught both Arjun and me the skills of warfare. Was there any difference between what I learnt and what Arjun did?'

Drona paused a little and then said, 'I never discriminate between my students. I taught you and Arjun the same skills. With rigorous practice, perseverance and indomitable will, Arjun has made himself a superior warrior. I can't claim any credit for that.'

Jayadrath couldn't stand any longer. Fear consumed his body. He lost all strength and was about to fall. Drona caught him and said, 'Gather yourself, Jayadrath. A valiant warrior like you shouldn't display such weakness. Besides, we are with you and will protect you with all our resources. Let me tell you this. Tomorrow, I plan to create such a difficult formation that even Arjun won't be able to break in. You stay inside the formation and fight to the best of your ability. That is your best bet to survive Arjun's wrath.' He paused a little and then said, 'Remember, Jayadrath, none of us is immortal. So don't be afraid of death and face it with courage and grit.'

Drona's reassuring words calmed Jayadrath. He felt much better and walked back to his tent to prepare for the battle next day.

Krishna was concerned about his dear friend Arjun as his rash decision could cost the Pandavas the throne. He turned towards Arjun and said, 'It wasn't wise of you to make such an outrageous promise without consulting with me. I hope we don't become the laughing stock amongst Kshatriyas. My sources tell me that the Kauravas are working on a plan to protect Jayadrath. Karna, Bhurishrava, Aswathama, Brishasen, Kripa and Shalya—these six gallant warriors will stick to Jayadrath. Without defeating these warriors, you won't be able to reach Jayadrath.'

Arjun replied, 'Krishna, the combined strength and skills of those six warriors is not even close to half of mine. Tomorrow, you'll see how I decapitate Jayadrath in front of Drona and all his warriors. With you by my side, and my Gandiva bow in hand, nothing can stop me.'

Krishna was glad to see the confidence and determination in Arjun's countenance. He left Arjun and went to Darook to prepare the chariot for the next day's battle. Darook bowed to him and said, 'O Krishna, I am scared. All of us are. Please ask Arjun to withdraw his vow. We know Arjun is the greatest warrior alive, but if by any chance he fails to kill Jayadrath, then it will be a disaster.'

Krishna held Darook's hand and said, 'I understand your concern. But don't worry. Tomorrow, I will do whatever it takes to make sure Arjun kills Jayadrath. Arjun is my dearest friend. I can do anything to ensure his success and keep him alive. Now go and prepare my chariot for the battle tomorrow. I need four strong and fresh horses to draw my chariot. Load the chariot with my Kaumadiki mace, my Chakra and other weapons.'

68

Day Fourteen of the War

ON THE MORNING OF THE FOURTEENTH DAY OF THE WAR, DRONA CREATED the Chakra-Shakata or the Wheel-Cart formation with his massive army. Within this formation, he created the Lotus formation, which in turn included the Needle formation. Drona asked Jayadrath to stay within the needle, with Bhurishrava, Karna, Aswathama, Shalya, Brishasen and Kripacharya guarding the pivotal points. 'Stay here, and Arjun will never be able to reach you. We will protect you from all sides,' said Drona to Jayadrath, leaving him rather relieved.

Arjun looked at Drona's formation from a distance and said, 'Krishna, take my chariot to the point where Duryodhan's brother Dumarshan is on guard with his elephant army. That's where I'd like to break open the formation.'

The moment the conch shells rang out to announce the beginning of the day's battle, Krishna raced his chariot towards Dumarshan, with Arjun hurling his deadly weapons from his Gandiva. Dushasana rushed in to help his brother, but Arjun's onslaught overwhelmed him. He turned away and took shelter behind Drona.

When Arjun met Drona, he bowed to him and said, 'Gurudev, I am your pupil. Help me keep my promise. Stand aside and let me pierce open this impregnable formation of yours.'

Drona smiled: 'Arjun, this is a battlefield, and here, I am your opponent. You cannot get past me without defeating me.' As soon as he finished his words, he hurled a volley of arrows at Arjun, only to be destroyed mid-air. Soon, a fierce battle broke out between the teacher and his pupil.

Krishna was impatient. He looked back at Arjun and said, 'Don't waste your time on Drona. You have to find and kill Jayadrath.'

Arjun agreed and moved away from Drona. Seeing Arjun leave the fight, Drona yelled at him, 'Arjun, where are you going? You can't run away without defeating your enemy.'

Arjun looked at him and said, 'You are not my enemy, Gurudev. Besides, nobody can defeat you.' Arjun raced towards the Kaurava Army, unleashing a deadly barrage of weapons and killing thousands of warriors at a time. Srutayudh, the king of Kamboj, hurled his heavy mace at Krishna. It bounced off him and ricocheted right back at Srutayudh, killing him instantly. Many others tried to stop Arjun, but everybody failed. The Kaurava Army panicked and began to flee in hordes.

Duryodhan was worried. He ran to Drona and said, 'Gurudev, how could you allow Arjun to get past you? I promised Jayadrath that with Gurudev guarding the formation, Arjun won't be able to come anywhere near you. It seems you are not keeping your end of the bargain. Aren't you compensated enough for your services to the throne? Is this how you express your gratitude to the Kuru dynasty?'

The harsh words pained Drona. Yet, he smiled and replied, 'My dear Duryodhan, you need to understand—I am getting old. I cannot match the speed and agility of Arjun. I promised to capture Yudhishthira for you. How can I abandon my promise and chase Arjun? Why don't you fight Arjun and stop him?'

Duryodhan was dumbfounded to hear Drona's words. 'Are you out of your mind? You ask me to stop Arjun, whom you failed to hold?'

Trying to pacify his pupil, Drona said, 'Come to me. Let me strap this impregnable armour on you. Lord Shiva gave this armour to Indra, and later, due to my good fortune, I was blessed to have it. Neither Arjun nor Krishna would be able to pierce this armour. Put it on and fight Arjun without any fear.'

Duryodhan wore the armour and drove his chariot towards Arjun.

Arjun and Krishna were racing towards Jayadrath, killing whoever came in their way. Time was running out and Arjun could feel his horses slowing down because of injuries and fatigue. He said to Krishna: 'The horses need rest. They need water. Stop the chariot and tend to the horses while I fight on foot.'

Krishna agreed and stopped the horses. Arjun jumped off the chariot and shot an arrow to the ground. The arrow pierced the ground and water gushed out and collected in a basin. The horses drank the water. Krishna tended to their injuries and soon the horses recovered their strength. The chariot again raced through the Kaurava formation while Arjun mowed down the soldiers to clear their path.

Duryodhan met Arjun on his path and attacked him with all his weapons. Krishna said, 'Arjun, it seems your luck is favouring you today. Duryodhan has come to you to sacrifice himself. Kill him and end this war once and for all.'

An intense battle broke out between Duryodhan and Arjun. No matter which weapon Arjun hurled at Duryodhan it bounced off his armour, leaving him unscathed.

Krishna was surprised. He said, 'What's happening, Arjun? It seems either you or your Gandiva have lost strength. Are you tired?'

'I think it is the armour on Duryodhan,' replied Arjun. 'Drona must have given him this armour and tied it himself. Don't worry, I can still take care of him.'

Arjun then targeted Duryodhan's charioteer and horses and killed them all. He then proceeded to cut off Duryodhan's bow, leaving him helpless. Just then, Karna, Bhurishrava, Kripa and Shalya arrived to save their king. They surrounded Arjun and attacked him from all sides.

Arjun knew it would be difficult for him to free himself and reach Jayadrath in time. He needed help. Arjun plucked the string of his Gandiva several times with the hope that the sound would reach the Pandavas. Krishna blew his Panchajanya conch to attract their attention too.

The Pandavas were busy fighting Drona on the other side of the battlefield. Hearing the Panchajanya and the Gandiva, Yudhishthira knew Arjun was in trouble and needed help. Satyaki was by his side to protect him from Drona. Yudhishthira asked him to go and help Arjun.

Satyaki said, 'Arjun has assigned me to protect you. He said I should never leave you alone. I can't disobey him. And don't worry about Arjun. All the Kauravas together don't even have half the strength and prowess he possesses.'

Growing impatient, Yudhishthira said, 'I still think you should go and help Arjun. Don't worry about me. Bheemsen is here, and so are

Ghatotkach, Virat, Drupad—they are all close by. If needed, they will come to help me. You go now.'

Satyaki bowed to Yudhishthira, 'My king, I can't ignore your orders. Stay safe.' Satyaki veered his chariot and made his way through the Kaurava Army.

Before he could go far, Drona stopped him. 'Arjun ran away from me without giving me a good fight. Are you planning to do the same?' he asked.

'I don't intend to fight you either,' replied Satyaki. 'I am only following Yudhishthira's orders to go and help Arjun.'

'I appreciate your concern, but I can't let you go past me.' Drona attacked Satyaki with full force. Other Kaurava warriors joined him. But that day, Satyaki was unstoppable. His arrows killed king Jalasandha and Sudarshan. He then killed Drona's charioteer, making the bewildered horses run in all directions. A helpless Drona tried to control them. The Kaurava warriors left Satyaki and turned to help the tired old man and take him to safety.

Satyaki continued his journey towards Arjun while mowing down whoever tried to stop him. The ferocious barbarian soldiers of Duryodhan attacked in hordes with their fierce weapons. Soon they lay dead in the dust behind Satyaki's chariot. The Kauravas panicked and ran for shelter.

When Drona saw Dushasana hiding behind him, he asked, 'What happened? Why are you fleeing the battle? Is Jayadrath still alive?'

Dushasana replied, 'He is, but the rate at which Satyaki is destroying our army and disintegrating our formation, it won't be long before Jayadrath gets exposed to Arjun.'

'Shame on you, Dushasana!' Drona could no longer conceal his anger. 'Didn't you once say that the Pandavas are a bunch of incompetent cowards? Then why are you hiding from them now?

What happened to your Kshatriya valour?' Dushasana was in no mood to argue. He turned around and ran away from Drona.

Drona knew that as the commander-in-chief, it was finally his responsibility to defend the Kauravas from this carnage. The eighty-five-year-old man put his armour back on and once again joined the battlefield and began to fight like a sixteen-year-old. In quick succession, he killed three major Pandava warriors—Brihat-kshatra, Shishupal's son, Dhrishtaketu, and Dhrishtadyumna's son, Kshatra Verma. The Pandavas realized that while Drona was alive, the battle would be far from over.

The Killing of Jayadrath

As the day progressed, Yudhishthira's anxiety rose. He hadn't heard the loud twang of Arjun's Gandiva for a while. From time to time, he could hear the deep and sonorous boom of Krishna's Panchajanya conch, but nothing from his dear brother Arjun. He called Bheem and said, 'I haven't seen Arjun in a while ... Haven't heard his Gandiva either. I am worried he might have been killed and Krishna is fighting the Kauravas alone. Do you hear his conch? It doesn't sound right. This must be his distress call. They need our help. Go and help them.'

Bheem was busy smashing the skulls of the Kaurava warriors who dared to attack him. He glanced at Yudhishthira and said, 'I am sure they are fine. Nobody can harm them. However, since you asked, I'll go and see what's keeping them busy.' He called Dhrishtadyumna and said, 'I leave Yudhishthira under your protection. Don't let Drona come anywhere near him.'

Dhrishtadyumna assured him, 'As long as I am alive, I won't let a fly come near Yudhishthira. You go and, on the way, kill as many Kauravas as you can.'

Bheem turned his chariot towards the direction from where the sound of the Panchajanya was heard. The Somak and Panchal soldiers accompanied him.

Once again, Drona's chariot intercepted Bheem's. 'You have to defeat me before you can pass,' said Drona as he shot a powerful arrow at his former pupil. The arrow bounced off Bheem's armour and fell to the ground.

'Gurudev, I am not as kind as Arjun and I won't spare you just because you happen to be my teacher. If you don't get out of my way, I'll punish you just the way I punish any other enemy.' Bheem hurled his huge mace at Drona. It hit Drona's chariot, shattering it and killing the charioteer. Drona tumbled down to the ground, but in the next instant he jumped into a passing chariot and left the battlefield.

Bheem continued his journey and, on the way, he killed four of Duryodhan's brothers—Binda, Anubinda, Subarma and Sudarshan. Soon, he could see Arjun and Krishna fighting the Kauravas at a distance. Delighted to see Arjun alive and well, Bheem let out a thunderous roar. Arjun and Krishna also yelled in joy. The sound reached Yudhishthira and, along with the other Pandavas, he felt relieved and pounced upon his opponents with renewed vigour.

Before Bheem could go anywhere near Arjun, Karna stopped him: 'Where do you think you are going, Bheem?'

Bheem tried to ignore him and tried to swerve his chariot away. Karna yelled, 'Stop running away like a coward and fight me if you can.'

Intolerant to taunts and insults, especially from someone like Karna, Bheem replied, 'Come on, Karna. Today I will teach you a lesson.' Bheem turned his chariot around and hurled a giant mace at Karna, who ducked, making the mace fly above his head. Soon, a ferocious battle broke out between the two warriors. Several brothers of Duryodhan came forward to help Karna. They all succumbed to Bheem's wrath.

Karna had been taking this fight quite lightly. He toyed with Bheem and kept him busy. It was quite clear that Bheem was no match for Karna in archery skills, which is essential when fighting from a moving chariot. One by one, Karna shattered Bheem's bow, killed his horses, and then his charioteer. Bheem's chariot came to a crashing halt. He jumped off his vehicle and attacked Karna with a giant machete, a shield in the other hand. Karna shred his shield to pieces. Bheem hurled his machete at Karna. It cut Karna's bow into pieces. Karna smiled and picked up another bow and began to shower Bheem with his arrows. Bheem took shelter behind the fallen elephants and horses, but the incessant flow of arrows from Karna overwhelmed him, and he almost lost consciousness. As Karna engaged a deadly weapon to finish off Bheem, he remembered his promise to Kunti: except for Arjun, he would not kill any of her other four sons. Karna put down his weapon and came near Bheem, who was sitting on the ground, leaning against a dead elephant. He poked Bheem with the end of his bow and said, 'Hey fatso, get up and go back to your kitchen. That's where you belong, you greedy glutton. Go and cook for your brothers and your wife. That's all you are good for. You are not fit to fight a warrior like me.'

Bheem looked at Karna with groggy eyes and said, 'Don't be so proud, Karna. Come down from your chariot and wrestle with me. I'll tear you apart the way I tore apart Keechak.'

In the meantime, Arjun turned around his chariot and began to shoot arrows at Karna to distract him. Karna left the area to join Duryodhan. Satyaki picked up Bheem on his chariot. Just as he was about to go back to Arjun, Bhurishrava waylaid him. Bhurishrava was a great warrior and soon Satyaki was left with no weapons to fight.

Satyaki jumped off the chariot to find a weapon. Bhurishrava came to him and kicked him to the ground. Then he jumped off his chariot with a sword in hand. Satyaki was lying unconscious on the ground. Bhurishrava held Satyaki by his hair and pulled him up. Just as he was about to strike with his sword, an arrow struck his right arm and cut it off from his elbow. Bhurishrava cried in pain and turned to the direction from where the arrow had come. It was Arjun. Krishna drove the chariot towards Bhurishrava and circled him. Bhurishrava said, 'Why did you do such a heinous thing, Arjun? I wasn't fighting you. I was fighting Satyaki. You shouldn't have listened to that low life Krishna and abandoned your Kshatriya code.'

'Don't lecture me about the Kshatriya code. You were about to kill an unarmed man,' said Arjun. 'And where was your Kshatriya code when you killed Abhimanyu like a coward?'

Bhurishrava realized his end was near. He ignored Arjun and sat on the floor to meditate. Arjun wasn't sure what to do of him. Just then, Satyaki woke up and saw Bhurishrava sitting in mediation. He couldn't control himself. He pulled out a machete and ran to kill Bhurishrava.

Arjun yelled at him, 'Stop, Satyaki. Don't kill an unarmed, meditating man.' The other warriors around tried to stop him too, but Satyaki didn't listen. With a single blow of his machete, he decapitated Bhurishrava.

Everybody around was stunned. They couldn't believe that a righteous man like Satyaki could do such a horrible thing. Satyaki yelled at them: 'Stop judging me. Where were you and your righteousness when they mercilessly killed that young boy Abhimanyu? Besides, I had promised that I'd kill anybody who disrespects me and kicks me. I killed Bhurishrava, and I did the right thing.'

Arjun glanced at the sun racing to dip into the horizon. 'Krishna, we don't have much time,' he said. 'Take me to Jayadrath as soon as you can.' Krishna veered his chariot and drove in the direction where the Kaurava warriors were assembled to face the final assault.

Duryodhan called Karna and said, 'The day will end soon. If we manage to protect Jayadratha a little longer, Arjun will have no option but to kill himself. And if he dies, his brothers will follow. The Pandavas will be wiped off the face of the earth and we will rule without any obstacles. Let's make sure we fight with all our might to make this a reality.'

Duryodhan, Karna, Vrishasen, Shalya, Aswathama and Kripa surrounded Jayadrath to protect him for these final moments.

Arjun began his final onslaught with a barrage of arrows, mowing down the Kauravas on his path. Satyaki and Bheem gave him close cover. Duryodhan, Karna and Kripa tried to stop Arjun from all sides, but soon they gave up and took cover to save themselves from Arjun's wrath. Arjun chased Jayadrath. His arrows hit Jayadrath's charioteer and shattered his chariot mast. But Jayadrath escaped Arjun's arrows and remained unharmed.

Krishna was concerned. He said to Arjun: 'Six of the greatest Kaurava warriors are protecting Jayadrath. To kill him, we need to either defeat them or deceive them. Listen to me carefully. I will use my powers to cover the sun. When the sky turns dark, the Kauravas will think the sun has set and they are out of danger. Jayadrath will no longer feel the need to hide behind the warriors and will reveal himself. At that moment, you must kill him.' Arjun agreed.

Krishna closed his eyes and, within moments, a dark shroud began to engulf the sun. The sky darkened and the Kauravas shouted in joy. Jayadrath couldn't believe his luck. He stood up on his chariot and looked up at the sky to make sure the sun wasn't visible. Krishna called Arjun: 'Look, there is Jayadrath looking at the sky and searching for the sun. This is the moment we've been waiting for. Kill him now.'

Through the darkness and dust, Krishna drove his chariot through the rejoicing Kaurava soldiers. When they arrived close to Jayadrath, Krishna stopped the chariot and said, 'Arjun, the sun will be down soon. You must act fast. But listen to me carefully before you shoot. When Jayadrath was born, his father Vriddhakshatra was told by the gods that his son will be decapitated in the battlefield. Angry Vriddhakshatra cursed his son's murderer saying that the person who drops his son's head to the ground would end up with his head bursting at the same instant. Jayadrath's father now lives the life of a sage in the forest of Samanta Panchak, and is in deep meditation. Arjun, make sure that you use a weapon that will carry Jayadrath's head all the way to his father and drop it on his lap. For, if you drop the head to the ground, your head will burst, causing your death. I hope you understand what I'm saying.'

Arjun nodded and thought for a moment. He then picked a weapon, aimed it at Jayadrath, uttered a mantra and released it. The weapon flew like a missile and in an instant separated Jayadrath's head from his body. And then, instead of dropping to the ground, the weapon flew high up in the sky, with the head hanging on its tip. Arjun hurled a few more arrows to the head, and it kept flying towards the Samanta Panchak Forest. Arjun turned his attention to the battlefield and continued killing the rejoicing Kaurava soldiers.

The arrow with Jayadrath's head went flying until it reached the place where Vriddhakshatra was meditating. The arrow stopped and the head dropped straight on his lap. The startled old man stood up and his son's head dropped from his lap to the ground. Vriddhakshatra's head exploded instantly, and the man fell dead next to his son's head.

In the battlefield, Krishna raised his hand and pointed towards the sun. The shroud dispersed slowly and the battlefield lit up again. The Kauravas found Jayadrath's headless body lying on the ground and knew once again that Krishna's divine power had saved the Pandavas from disaster. Krishna, Arjun, Bheem and Satyaki blew their conch shells to declare their victory. The roar of the conch reached Yudhishthira, and he knew that Arjun had kept his promise. Jayadrath was dead.

The Fall of Ghatotkach

Jayadrath's death struck a severe blow to Duryodhan's confidence. He had promised to protect his brother-in law and failed miserably. He went to Drona and said, 'Gurudev, I understand I am not the righteous kind of man to whom you'd lend your support. I also understand that Arjun is your favourite student, and you can't kill him. But instead of individuals, you should think about your loyalty to the throne that supported you all your life. If you want, I can go and kill myself right now. The throne is bigger than me or any other individual. Show some respect to the throne.'

Drona was tired of listening to Duryodhan's complaints. 'Stop bickering, Duryodhan,' he said. 'You don't have to teach me about my responsibilities. You, along with six of the greatest Kaurava warriors, failed to protect Jayadrath. Still, you blame me. Let me tell you this: I won't take off my armour till I have finished the last of the Pandava warriors. That's all I can promise. And for that, today, the battle will not stop even after sunset. It will continue as long as necessary. Now let me go and fight.'

Drona raised his bow and instructed his charioteer to take him to the middle of the battlefield. Karna overheard Duryodhan's conversation with Drona. He pulled his chariot near Duryodhan's and said, 'My friend, you must not blame Drona. The poor Brahmin is old and has lost his touch. He no longer possesses the vigour and skill that once made him a great warrior. Don't you worry. I alone will defeat the Pandavas and make you victorious.'

Kripacharya was passing by. He stopped and laughed at Karna. 'If words could have won battles, then I am sure you would succeed in bringing victory to Duryodhan. In all your previous battles with the Pandavas, you lost miserably and had to run away to save yourself. Now stop boasting and go, fight.'

Karna was furious. He yelled at Kripa, 'How dare you insult me? Do you have any idea about my strength and prowess? I have in my possession the deadly Shakti weapon of Indra. No mortal can escape it. I have been saving it, for I plan to use the weapon to kill Arjun. And when I hurl the weapon, not even Krishna can save him. So, keep your mouth shut and watch me do my job. For if you utter one more word of insult, I will cut off your tongue.'

Drona's son Aswathama heard this and couldn't control himself. He pulled out his sword and ran towards Karna. 'How dare you threaten my uncle?' he yelled. 'Who do you think you are? Where were you when Arjun killed Jayadrath? Where was your so-called Shakti weapon? You are nothing but a fraud. You deserve to die.' Aswathama raised his sword to strike Karna. Duryodhan and Kripa jumped ahead to stop him.

'Control yourself, Aswathama,' said Duryodhan. 'My friend Karna had no ill-intention. Please forgive him.'

Aswathama was still angry. 'I will forgive him only if Uncle Kripacharya forgives him.'

Kripa said, 'We all are on the same side. We shouldn't be fighting amongst ourselves. I forgive you, Karna. But remember, Arjun won't be so kind, and he will not tolerate your arrogance.'

Karna bowed to Kripa and asked his charioteer to take him to the middle of the Pandava Army. There, he launched the most ferocious attack one could imagine. None of the Kauravas had taken such a devastating toll on the Pandava soldiers so far. Thousands were killed and Karna's bow seemed to be spitting out an endless stream of deadly arrows.

The sun went down on the western horizon, but no conch shells rang out to declare the end of the day's battle. The fighting continued and, in the darkness of the night, one could only hear the death cries of the soldiers, the sound of racing chariots, the galloping of horses and the cries of stampeding elephants. The generals on both the sides asked the warriors to carry lamps and torches. Each elephant carried seven torches, each chariot carried ten, each horse two, and the infantry men carried one torch each. The thousands of dancing torch lights gave the battlefield an eerie look that was never witnessed before.

Unable to counter Karna's onslaught, the Pandava Army began to scatter and flee the battlefield. Yudhishthira knew that if Karna wasn't checked, tonight might be the last night of the war. He asked his charioteer to take him to Arjun. Yudhishthira's charioteer skilfully drove the chariot through the darkness to reach Arjun. Yudhishthira stood up on his chariot and yelled, 'Arjun, what are you doing here? Go stop Karna. He is killing thousands of Pandava soldiers every instant. Our warriors and generals are fleeing the battlefield. You must kill Karna today.'

Arjun knew Yudhishthira was serious. 'Krishna, take me to Karna. Tonight, either I'll kill Karna, or he'll kill me.'

Krishna said to Yudhishthira: 'Don't worry. We'll take care of Karna. Go to your tent and get some rest.' Krishna tugged the reins of his horses and the chariot moved forward.

Arjun was perplexed. 'What are you doing, Krishna? Take me to Karna.'

Krishna stopped the chariot and said, 'Listen to me carefully. Karna has with him a deadly weapon called the Shakti. Lord Indra gave him this weapon. When struck, nobody can survive it. Karna has been saving this weapon with the sole objective of using it against you. He has been waiting for the right moment to strike. After Jayadrath's fall, he is under tremendous pressure to do something. So, I don't think it would be wise for you to face him now.'

'I can't hide from Karna just because he has this weapon,' said Arjun. 'You know very well that only I can stop Karna and defeat him. No other person can kill him.'

'Right. No other warrior can defeat Karna. But a rakshasa can,' said Krishna. Arjun was baffled. Krishna elaborated. 'Bheemsen's son Ghatotkach is an indomitable fighter. He has a wide array of weapons at his disposal, and he possesses magical powers. He should be able to overpower Karna and defeat him. Let me summon him.'

As soon as Krishna thought of Ghatotkach, the giant rakshasa appeared before him. He bowed to Krishna and said, 'Please accept my regards, Krishna. Tell me, what can I do for you?'

Krishna smiled and said, 'My dear Ghatotkach, I have heard that you've killed thousands of enemy soldiers and wreaked havoc among the Kauravas. Now you have something greater to do. Karna is giving lot of trouble to your uncles and your relatives. His arrows are killing thousands of Pandavas and our warriors and generals are fleeing the battlefield in hordes. You must use your powers to stop and destroy Karna. I know your powers amplify during the night. So, this is the best time to exercise your strength and your magic.'

Arjun said, 'I regard you as the greatest of the Pandava warriors—the same as Bheemsen and Satyaki. I want you to engage with Karna tonight. Satyaki will give you cover.'

Ghatotkach bowed to Krishna and Arjun: 'Thank you for placing your trust in me. Tonight, I'll fight a battle that nobody has seen before. I won't spare anybody. Victory will be ours.' Ghatotkach jumped on his chariot and drove in the direction of Karna.

Karna wasn't prepared for this sudden attack by the huge and grotesque rakshasa, Ghatotkach. With his eyes bloodshot, beard dyed yellow, teeth sharp as steel swords and a brass armour on his body, Ghatotkach rode a chariot driven by a hundred horses. On top of the mast sat a hungry vulture who'd tear apart the flesh of Ghatotkach's victims in seconds. Karna was startled for a moment, but then responded to Ghatotkach with full force. Ghatotkach used his magic to create thousands of ferocious rakshasa soldiers who attacked Karna's army using spears, machetes, boulders, chains and what not. Ghatotkach used all sorts of tricks to confuse Karna. Sometimes he'd disappear, and then suddenly attack from behind. Sometimes he'd fly up in the sky and attack from above and at the next instant, emerge from the ground below and hurl a spear at Karna. Karna wasn't fooled, though. He riddled Ghatotkach with arrows and soon he resembled a porcupine. Suddenly, Ghatotkach split himself into several wild animals like lions and tigers and snakes, and pounced upon Karna. Karna killed them all. But Ghatotkach was indomitable. Alayudh, another rakshasa from the Kaurava side, attacked Ghatotkach. Ghatotkach severed his head and threw it at Duryodhan. Then Ghatotkach's illusory rakshasa army began to kill thousands of Kaurava soldiers. Karna was finding it difficult to keep up with his never-ending tricks. Karna knew, at this rate, Ghatotkach alone could annihilate the entire Kaurava Army.

Duryodhan came to Karna and said, 'What are you doing, Karna? Kill Ghatotkach immediately, or we are doomed.'

'I am trying my best,' said Karna as he shot another volley at Ghatotkach. 'It seems he is indestructible.'

'Use your Shakti weapon on Ghatotkach. It'll kill him for sure, right?'

'Yes, but I have been reserving that weapon for Arjun. It can be used only once.' Karna was hesitant.

Duryodhan grew impatient. 'Forget Arjun. If we can't kill Ghatotkach now, the war will end tonight. Don't hesitate. Use the weapon and kill Ghatotkach—now!'

Karna knew Duryodhan was right. Ghatotkach must be eliminated to keep alive any hopes of victory. He pulled out the deadly Shakti weapon, aimed it at Ghatotkach, uttered a mantra and released it. The weapon shot ahead with a loud roar, fire streaming from its tip, and before one could blink an eye it struck Ghatotkach's chest and exploded with a loud bang.

Ghatotkach stumbled at the impact of the weapon. He knew instantly that his final moment had arrived. Wanting to cause maximum damage to the Kauravas even during his death, he used his magical powers to expand and become as huge as a mountain. As he died, his body crashed to the ground, killing thousands of Kaurava soldiers who were gathered underneath.

The Kauravas who survived rejoiced at the death of Ghatotkach. They praised Karna for his gallantry and his prowess. The Pandavas were heartbroken at the death of Bheemsen's son.

Krishna, however, didn't seem upset at all. When the news of Ghatotkach's demise reached him, he jumped in joy and hugged Arjun. Arjun was surprised, to say the least. 'Krishna, what are you doing? Bheemsen's son, my nephew Ghatokach has been killed. And you are dancing in joy?' he asked, hurt by Krishna's reaction.

Krishna laughed. 'Yes, I am happy—indeed, very happy—for you. Karna has spent his Shakti weapon—which he had intended to use on you—on Ghatotkach. That's why I sent Ghatotkach to fight Karna—to save you. Now you can kill Karna without any fear.'

Arjun was stunned to hear this. 'How could you be so cruel?' he asked.

Krishna smiled. 'I have done this only for you, for it is through you that I want to rid the world of evil and build a righteous world. For you, I have killed Jarasandh, Shishupal and Ekalavya. If they weren't dead, they'd have joined Duryodhan and caused your defeat. For you, I caused the deaths of villains like Hirimb, Bak, Kirmir and now Ghatotkach. It's good that Karna killed Ghatotkach and gave him a glorious death. If not, one of these days I might have had to kill him.'

'You would've killed Ghatotkach?' Arjun couldn't believe his ears.

'Ghatotkach is your nephew, and he has treated you and your family with respect. But I know that he was a Brahmin hater and a ferocious creature who plundered many hermitages and yagnas, tortured the sages and hermits, and killed many innocent people. I had been hearing a lot of complaints about him, but didn't take any harsh action only because of you. Now, he has died a warrior's death and will be respected forever. So, stop lamenting and get ready to fight.' Krishna tugged at the reins of his horses, and the chariot began to roll. With a heavy heart, Arjun picked up his Gandiva and prepared to face the enemy once again.

69

Day Fifteen of the War

IT WAS PAST MIDNIGHT. THE SOLDIERS WERE TIRED AND COULDN'T STAY UP any longer. They dropped their weapons and lay down to get some sleep wherever they could—some on horseback, some atop elephants and some lay down on the ground, behind the dead animals. Arjun realized that without some rest, the soldiers won't be able to fight at all. He called his soldiers and said, 'Brothers, I know you are tired, and it is difficult for you to fight in the darkness. I suggest you suspend fighting and try to get some sleep. We'll resume the battle when the moon rises and lights up the battlefield.' The Pandava soldiers sighed in relief.

The Kaurava soldiers were tired too, and when they heard of Arjun's announcement, they approached Duryodhan and Karna, and said, 'O King, the Pandavas have announced a temporary ceasefire to give their soldiers some rest. We pray you let us take some rest too.' Duryodhan agreed. Soon, the entire battlefield went to sleep, and a dead silence engulfed Kurukshetra.

After a couple of hours, a full moon rose and lit up the night sky. The soldiers woke up refreshed and the battle commenced once again. Drona took a huge contingent of the army and launched a ferocious attack on the Pandavas. It seemed as if the old man had regained his youth. His chariot raced through the battleground, leaving a trail of dead Pandava soldiers behind. Soldiers from Chedi, Kekay, Srinjay and Matsya were devastated by Drona's arrows. King Drupad and King Virat, along with their armies, tried to stop Drona. Drupad was an old enemy of Drona, and a vicious fight broke out between them. Three of Drupad's grandsons came forward to help their grandfather. Drona killed them all. Then Drona attacked Drupad and Virat. He hurled a spear at Virat. It struck his chest and killed him instantly. Drupad shot several arrows at Drona to counter his attack. Drona dodged them all, and hurled another huge spear at Drupad. Drupad tried to cut the spear with his arrows, but failed. The spear hit Drupad and decapitated him.

The sun rose on the eastern horizon on the fifteenth day of the war. The soldiers worshipped the Sun God and continued the battle. Drona continued his rampage.

Something had to be done to check Drona. Krishna took Yudhishthira and Bheem aside and said, 'Look, as long as Drona has a bow in his hand, nobody can defeat him. If we can make him abandon his weapons, it is possible to kill him.'

'What do you suggest we do?' asked Yudhishthira.

Krishna paused for a moment, then said, 'I think, if we give Drona the news of his son Aswathama's death, he'll drop his weapons and stop fighting. Someone should go and give him this news.'

'But Awathama is alive!' Arjun sounded confused.

Krishna didn't answer, but his silence was enough. Arjun was visibly upset. 'You want us to lie to our teacher Drona?' he said scornfully.

'It's time to focus on winning this war rather than be the most righteous side, else Drona alone will kill you and end this war.'

Bheem thumped his chariot and said, 'Krishna is right. Drona wasn't righteous when he and his generals killed Abhimanyu. Why should we?'

Yudhishthira was in a fix. He knew, this was possibly the only way to neutralize Drona. Yet, in his heart he was reluctant to tell an outright lie, especially when he was known as a person who never lied. He said to Bheem: 'I agree with you, Bheem. The Kauravas abandoned righteousness in this battle the day they killed Abhimanyu. Still, we cannot stoop to their level. We must find a way such that we don't fall from our path, yet we succeed in deceiving Drona.'

'I know what to do,' Bheem cried out. He didn't wait any longer and drove away his chariot into the battlefield. Everybody was puzzled. Only Krishna smiled.

Indravarma, the king of Malav, had an elephant named Aswathama. Bheem decided to kill the elephant and tell Drona that Aswathama had died. That should do the trick, he thought. The moment Bheem saw Indravarma's elephant, he picked up a huge mace, swung it above his head and hurled it at Aswathama's head. The mace struck the elephant right between the eyes and crushed its skull. The huge beast stumbled and fell dead to the ground with a heavy thud. Bheem cried out: 'Aswathama is dead!'

He turned his chariot and drove it close to Drona while yelling at the top of his voice: 'Aswathama is dead! Aswathama is dead!'

Drona was fighting Dhrishtadyumna. When he heard Bheem's cry, he froze for a moment. Aswathama, dead? His only son, his gallant son ... dead? How was this possible? There were very few warriors in the world who could kill a warrior like Aswathama. Bheem must be bluffing to demoralize him, he thought. He ignored Bheem and attacked Dhrishtadyumna with such ferocity that within moments Dhrishtadyumna's horses were killed and his chariot shattered into pieces. Bheem picked up Dhrishtadyumna in his chariot and said, 'Only you can kill Drona. So get up, gather yourself, and attack again.'

As Bheem's chariot veered away with Dhrishtadyumna, Drona drove his chariot near Yudhishthira's. He stood up and asked, 'Yudhishthira, I heard Bheem yell "Aswathama is dead". Is this true? I couldn't believe Bheem. But if you say it's true, I'd believe it.'

Yudhishthira was dumbfounded and didn't know what to say. He stammered and said, 'Gurudev, I am not sure if Aswathama has been killed. Let me find out.'

Yudhishthira asked his charioteer to take him to Bheem. When he arrived near Bheem, Krishna and Arjun were there too. Yudhishthira asked, 'Bheem, Gurudev said you've been claiming that Aswathama is dead. Is that true?'

Bheem said, 'Yes, it is true. Indravarma, the king of Malav, had this huge elephant named Aswathama. He was trampling and killing hundreds of our soldiers. So, I killed him. Now if you tell Drona that Aswathama is dead, he would think that his son has been killed and he would quit fighting.'

Krishna said, 'My dear Yudhishthira, for our sake, you must say this little white lie. Remember, a lie to save lives isn't a sin.'

Yudhishthira had no option but to agree. He asked his charioteer to take him close to Drona, but not too close. From a distance, he yelled, 'Aswathama is dead ...' Then he dropped his voice and, in an almost inaudible whisper, he continued, 'the elephant, that is.' In the noise of the battlefield, those trailing words were lost and couldn't be heard even by his charioteer. Yudhishthira was the only man on earth who had never lied in his life. For this virtue, he enjoyed a special gift from the gods. His chariot wheels never touched the ground and always floated a few inches above the ground. The moment he uttered those words, his chariot dropped, and the wheels touched the ground like any other.

When Drona heard Yudhishthira claim that Aswathama had been killed, his arms became numb. His bow slipped off his hand, and his legs couldn't bear his body weight any longer. Drona stumbled down on his chariot in a stupor and stared at the battlefield with a vacant look. 'Duryodhan, Karna, Kripa, I can't fight any more,' he said. 'You keep fighting to the best of your ability and protect the throne.' Saying this, Drona went into a deep meditation.

Dhrishtadyumna was waiting for this opportunity. The moment he saw Drona drop his bow, he jumped off his chariot and ran towards him, an open sword in his hand. Arjun yelled to him: 'Dhrishtadyumna, don't kill Drona. Capture him and bring him alive.' Dhrishtadyumna paid no heed to his words. To kill Drona was the sole purpose of his existence. He climbed on Drona's chariot, held the old man by his hair and, with a quick swish of his sword, Dhrishtadyumna beheaded the old Brahmin. Then, with a blood-curdling holler, he tossed Drona's head in the middle of the Kaurava fighters, while his body rolled off the chariot to the battleground below. The Pandavas were shocked to see such savage display of vengeance by their commander-in-chief, and hid their face in shame and sorrow. Only Bheem congratulated Dhrishtadyumna with a warm embrace and said, 'Good job. When Karna and Duryodhan die, I'll embrace you again.'

With the death of Drona, the Kaurava Army was thrown into complete disarray. Duryodhan tried to calm them, but they were too scared to listen to words of reason. The Kaurava generals looked around for Drona's body, but with thousands of decapitated bodies strewn all around, they failed to identify their commander-in-chief.

Drona's son Aswathama was busy fighting Shikhandi. When he noticed the Kaurava soldiers fleeing, he guessed that something had gone wrong. He went to Duryodhan and asked, 'Why are our soldiers running away?' He didn't get an answer. Aswathama turned to Karna. He too looked away. Aswathama asked, 'Why are you so morose? Did something bad happen? Did any of our generals get killed?'

Kripacharya held Aswathama's hand and broke the news to him. In vivid detail, he narrated how the Pandavas had tricked Drona to believe that Aswathama was dead, and how Dhrishtadyumna had killed him like a savage.

As Kripa's words entered Aswathama's ears, he turned red with rage and grief. He stood like a stone wall and tried to control himself. Then he wiped his tears and said, 'To die in a fair battle is something one should not feel sorry about. But when one kills an unarmed man by pulling his hair and beheading him in front of thousands of warriors, I call that cowardice and savagery. I can never forgive the way Yudhishthira—the champion of truth and righteousness—used a filthy lie to deceive my father, his guru. They will have to pay for this. Dhrishtadyumna will have to pay for this.' He then looked around at the Kaurava generals and said, 'Listen to me. I have in my possession a weapon that will destroy them all. None of the Pandavas, not even Krishna, is aware of this weapon. Lord Narayan gave this weapon, the Narayanastra, to my father. The lord instructed my father to use this weapon only in extreme circumstances for, once unleashed, the weapon won't stop until it destroys all its enemies. Nobody can survive unless they drop their weapons and surrender. Today, I will use the Narayanastra and destroy the Pandavas.'

Aswathama pulled out the Narayanastra and engaged the weapon. Lightning began to strike, gale-force winds began to blow, and dark clouds covered the sky. The Kaurava soldiers cried out in joy. They began to play their drums and bugles and marched to the battlefield.

When Yudhishthira heard the joyous cries from the Kaurava side, he asked Arjun, 'When Drona was killed, the frustrated and scared

Kauravas fled the battlefield. Why are they returning? What makes them rejoice? Who made them re-join the battle?'

Arjun was still trying to deal with his teacher's death and wasn't in a good mood at all. He replied scornfully: 'I am sure it is Aswathama who motivated the Kaurava Army to avenge his father's death. The way Dhrishtadyumna humiliated and killed my guru is something that no son would ever forgive, let alone a gallant warrior like Aswathama. You are equally responsible. Gurudev trusted you to speak the truth. You deceived him and committed a grave sin. Aswathama is no weakling, and he will kill us all. For the sake of winning the kingdom, the throne, we gave up our virtue and stooped to the lowest of the low. We deserve to die.'

Bheem was furious to hear such discouraging words from Arjun. 'Shame on you, Arjun,' he said. 'You sound like a forest-dwelling hermit and not a Kshatriya warrior. Remember, the Kauravas stole Yudhishthira's rightful kingdom and tricked us into thirteen years of exile. They humiliated Draupadi by pulling her hair and tried to disrobe her in a full court. Don't you think they ought to be punished for their crimes? If you don't want to fight, get out of the way. I alone will kill the Kauravas with my mace.'

Dhrishtadyumna said, 'A Brahmin's duty is to acquire and disseminate knowledge to his students and preach the laws of dharma. Did Drona ever follow the traditions of a Brahmin? Instead, he took up arms like a Kshatriya and was bent upon destroying us using his terrible weapons. I don't understand what's the big deal if we had to take a crooked path to kill him. Remember, I was born of the sacrificial fire with the sole objective of killing my father's greatest enemy. I have succeeded in my mission. You should be congratulating me. Nobody complained when you killed Bhishma. If that wasn't a crime, why is my achievement one? I have a clear conscience and can claim proudly that I haven't committed any sin, neither did Yudhishthira.'

Arjun spit on the ground in disgust. 'Shame on you, Dhrishtadyumna. I despise you.'

Satyaki was boiling with anger. 'I am not sure why somebody is not killing this insolent Dhrishtadyumna,' he yelled. 'This man doesn't even have the intelligence to distinguish between the killings of Bhishma and Drona. Try to understand, you fool, Bhishma himself told us how to kill him, and it was your brother Shikhandi who was responsible for his fall. So, keep your mouth shut, else I will crush your skull with my mace.'

Dhrishtadyumna laughed: 'Satyaki, you have committed the most heinous crime yourself by killing a disarmed and helpless Bhurishrava, and now you judge me? You are the most sinful of all. Now shut up and get back to battle.'

Satyaki couldn't control himself any longer. He picked up his mace and rushed to strike Dhrishtadyumna. Bheem stepped in and stopped Satyaki. 'Don't behave like a child, Satyaki,' he said. 'The war is not over. We shouldn't be fighting amongst ourselves.'

Krishna held Dhrishtadyumna and Satyaki's arms and said, 'Bheem is right. We still have a long way to go. Let's try to forget our differences and focus on Aswathama, who is bent upon destroying us. Get back to your chariots and prepare to counter his attack.'

On the battlefield, the Pandava soldiers were being massacred by Aswathama. His Narayanastra tore through the enemy like a tornado. The weapon unleashed thousands of lethal armaments like missiles, maces, spears, fire balls and chains, and killed whoever came in its path. It seemed the weapon would spare nobody and annihilate the entire Pandava Army within a matter of minutes.

Krishna, however, knew the secret of the Narayanastra. He raced his chariot through the Pandava soldiers and yelled at the top of his voice, 'Drop your weapons, everybody. Get off your chariots, horses and elephants, and surrender to Aswathama's weapon. That is the only way to survive the Narayanastra.'

The soldiers dropped their weapons and knelt on the ground with their palms joined. Bheem was not convinced. 'Don't surrender. Don't drop your weapons. I will stop the weapons with my arrows.' Bheem picked up his bow and raced towards Aswathama on his chariot. Aswathama laughed and riddled Bheem with his arrows.

Krishna and Arjun ran to Bheem and pulled him down from his chariot. 'Why are you doing this? The only way to stop the Narayanastra is to surrender to the weapon. Listen to me. Stop fighting. Drop your weapons and get down.' Arjun snatched his bow from Bheem and threw it away. Krishna held him down on his knees and asked him to keep his head down.

The entire Pandava Army, all the warriors, the generals, everybody was on the ground, weapons lying next to them. The Narayanastra slowed down and then returned to its abode in the heavens.

The Pandavas rose and prepared to fight again. Duryodhan asked Aswathama, 'What's happening? Why did your weapon fail?'

'Krishna knew how to escape from the Narayanastra. It has been disabled,' said Aswathama as he prepared to launch another attack.

'Then release it again,' commanded Duryodhan.

'Sorry, Duryodhan, that's not possible. The Narayanastra can be used only once. If I use it again, it will turn back and kill me.' Saying this, Aswathama drove his chariot to join the battle. Before the sun went down on the fifteenth day of the battle, Aswathama killed thousands of Pandava soldiers, including Sudarshan, the king of Malay Briddhakshatra of the Puru dynasty and the crown prince of Chedi.

Soon, the conch shell rang out to announce the end of the day's battle. Having fought continuously for two days, the soldiers were glad to return to their camps and get some rest before waking up for battle the next day.

Karna, the New Army Chief

When the fifteenth day of the war concluded with the sun setting in the western horizon, Duryodhan returned to his chamber and called for an urgent meeting with his generals. With the fall of Drona, he had to select a new commander-in-chief of his army—and this time, he was determined not to pick anyone who sympathized with the Pandavas. Although Bhishma and Drona were the best warriors on the Kaurava side, they were old and always had special feelings for the five brothers. This was their greatest weakness, and that is what caused their fall. They willingly gave away their lives to make sure the Pandavas won the war. Today, Duryodhan was determined not to lose his temper and not to pick someone just because of his age and experience. He had to select not just a gallant warrior, but also someone who hated the Pandavas from the core of his heart.

The generals assembled in Duryodhan's tent. He addressed them calmly: 'My dear friends, we all know what kind of a dire situation we are in. But it is still not too late. With your help, we can, and we will, defeat the Pandavas. I'd request you all to speak your mind and together let's figure out a plan to win this war.'

Aswathama stood up and said, 'O King, both Grandfather Bhishma and my father Drona were gallant warriors, and they have done their part. We should not give up, for with strong will and resolve, we can carve out our destiny. We still have many great warriors amongst us who can lead us to victory. I suggest you appoint the great warrior and the king of Anga, our friend Karna, as our new commander-in-chief. Nobody in the Kaurava or the Pandava camp can match his skills in weaponry and warfare. I am sure he can easily defeat the enemy and make us victorious.'

'Aswathama, you spoke my mind,' said Duryodhan as he stood up and walked towards Karna, extending his hand towards him. 'My dear friend, you are the most capable warrior amongst us who can defeat the Pandavas. I know, when Arjun finds you leading our army, he'd leave the battlefield in fear, never to return. I request you to accept my offer to take over the Kaurava side as our commander-in-chief.'

Karna held Duryodhan's hand and said, 'My friend, my king, I accept your offer. Please rest assured, tomorrow I will destroy the Pandavas once and for all, and bring you victory.' Duryodhan called the priests and formally consecrated Karna as the Kaurava commander-in-chief.

70

Day Sixteen of the War

ON THE MORNING OF THE SIXTEENTH DAY, KARNA APPEARED ON THE Kurukshetra battlefield in his heavily armed chariot drawn by four powerful horses. He arranged the Kaurava Army in the Makara or Crocodile formation, with his chariot at the top. The other Kuru generals covered the rest of the vantage points.

Yudhishthira watched the Kaurava Army and called upon Arjun. 'My dear brother, most of the gallant warriors of the Kauravas are dead,' he said. 'Now, only the inferior ones are left, except for Karna. Kill Karna, and victory will be ours.'

Arjun created the crescent moon formation with Bheem on the left, Dhrishtadyumna on the right, and Yudhishthira in the centre. Arjun, Nakul and Sahadev stood behind Yudhishthira to provide him cover.

With the sound of the conch shells ringing out across Kurukshetra, the two armies clashed for the sixteenth time. The soldiers pounced upon each other like fierce animals, and soon the battlefield was littered with body parts. Bheem rode on a huge elephant and attacked

Khemdhurti, the king of Kumut. Khemdhurti commanded his army to surround Bheemsen from all sides. Bheem's elephant trampled and killed them like ants. Then he hurled a huge mace at Khemdhurti and knocked him off his elephant. Aswathama attacked Bheem from his chariot. Bheem got off the elephant and jumped into a chariot to match Aswathama's speed. The gallant warriors then engaged in a wild battle using their most fierce weapons. Warriors around stopped fighting and watched the two giants clash and praised their skills. Soon, both Bheem and Aswathama were riddled with each other's arrows and fell unconscious on their respective chariots. The charioteers quickly drove them out of the battlefield to give them some time to recuperate.

After a little rest, Aswathama asked his charioteer to take him back to the battlefield. He saw Arjun fighting the Samsaptaks at a distance. He raised his voice and yelled at Arjun: 'Leave those weaklings alone and fight me if you dare. Let me see what you've learnt from my father.'

Krishna turned the chariot and drove Arjun close to Aswathama. 'Aswathama, here, I've brought my friend Arjun to you,' said Krishna. 'Try to strike him hard and be prepared to be struck back equally hard. This is your time to pay back your Kuru masters, to make the best use of it. Remember, Brahmins fight with words, but you've chosen to pick up arms like a Kshatriya. So let your weapons decide your fate.'

'So be it,' said Aswathama and, in quick succession, struck both Krishna and Arjun with his arrows. Arjun laughed and rapidly shot hundreds of arrows at Aswathama and overwhelmed him. The kings and warriors from Anga, Banga, and Kalinga came riding their elephants to attack Arjun and help Aswathama. But Arjun's arrows were too much for them to handle and they soon gave up and fled the battle.

Aswathama, however, was not rattled by Arjun's incessant attack. Using the skills he had learned from his father Drona, he struck Arjun and Krishna with deadly weapons and forced them to retreat. Arjun was reeling from Aswathama's attack and was struggling to stand on his feet. Krishna circled the chariot back and said, 'Focus, Arjun. Focus on Aswathama. You've been taking him too lightly. Remember he is your guru Drona's son, and he is as skilled as you are. Aswathama is looking for revenge, and you must use all your power to stop him.'

Arjun wiped off the blood from his face, engaged a few of his fiercest arrows on the Gandiva, and aimed at Aswathama. Within moments, Aswathama's hands, his chest, his head, and his thighs were riddled with arrows. Arjun struck Aswathama's horses, and the animals ran berserk, dragging the chariot away from Arjun.

In another section of the battlefield, Nakul was busy decimating the Kaurava Army. His sharp and deadly arrows killed thousands and the soldiers began to flee for their lives. When Karna heard this, he veered his chariot to face Nakul.

Nakul welcomed Karna with a laugh and said, 'The gods have granted me my wish after a long time and sent you here. You are the cause of all this mess. It is because of your unwise advice that we cousins are killing each other. This war won't end until you die. And today, I'll fulfil my duty by killing you.'

Karna lifted his bow and said, 'My dear Nakul, only fools boast more than they fight. Stop babbling and fight me with all your might. Let's see what you've got.'

Nakul was furious. He pulled out his deadly weapons and hurled them at Karna while circling his chariot. Karna laughed and, with the skilful use of his arrows, he intercepted all and destroyed them while in flight. Nakul continued shooting arrows at Karna, who kept dodging them. And then Karna began to shoot at Nakul. The incessant flow of arrows from Karna's bow covered the sky like a dark cloud. Nakul was overwhelmed. He tried his best to deflect them, but soon lost his horses and his charioteer. Karna's bows shattered Nakul's chariot and Nakul fell to the ground. He grabbed a sword and stood up to defend himself. Karna shattered his sword with a single shot from his bow. Nakul was scared. He began to run for his life. Karna chased Nakul with his chariot and soon caught up with him. Karna extended his arm and grabbed Nakul's neck with his bow. Nakul struggled to free himself, but Karna held him tight and said, 'Now tell me what you were saying then? You wanted to kill me, right?' Nakul couldn't speak. Karna pulled him close and said, 'My boy, you picked the wrong person to show your prowess. You should only fight those who are equal to you and avoid the mighty Kaurava warriors. I can kill you now, but I won't. Go back to your tent and tend to your injuries.' Karna released Nakul in order to honour his promise to Kunti. Freed from Karna's bow, Nakul tried to catch his breath while he jumped on a chariot and left the battlefield.

The Samsaptaks continued their mission of keeping Arjun engaged in battle. Arjun kept killing them, but they kept attacking him in hordes. It seemed they were bent upon dying at the hands of Arjun. The leader of the Samsaptaks, King Susharma, continued motivating his army by reminding them of their oath. His brother Satyasen hurled a spear at Krishna. It pierced Krishna's left arm, making the reins slip off his hands. Krishna pulled out the spear and picked up the reins to control the chariot. Arjun was furious. He pulled out a fierce weapon from his chariot and, with a loud cry, hurled it at Satyasen. The weapon killed him instantly. Arjun then engaged the deadly Indrastra on his Gandiva, chanted the activating mantra and released it. The weapon went high into the sky, split into thousands of deadly arrows and zoomed down towards the enemy soldiers around him and killed them all.

In another section of the battlefield, Duryodhan was engaged in an intense battle with Yudhishthira. Yudhishthira was at his best and demonstrated that he was no less than his brothers Bheem and Arjun. He attacked Duryodhan with such ferocity that the Kaurava king found it difficult to keep up with him. Yudhishthira's arrows killed Duryodhan's charioteer and his four horses, and shattered his bow and his mast. Duryodhan couldn't keep his balance and stumbled onto the ground. Karna, Aswathama and Kripa saw their king in distress and came to save him from Yudhishthira's onslaught. Watching Yudhishthira being outnumbered, the Pandava brothers surrounded Yudhishthira to protect him. Duryodhan didn't give up. He jumped on an empty chariot and riddled Yudhishthira with arrows. Yudhishthira laughed and said, 'Duryodhan, your arrows are nothing more than pinpricks to me. Don't you have anything more powerful?' Duryodhan growled in anger and looked for more potent weapons in the chariot. Yudhishthira took this opportunity to hit him with a volley of arrows that cut through his armour. Duryodhan began to bleed. Duryodhan knew, bows and arrows were not his forte. He picked up his favourite weapon, the mace, and jumped off the chariot. With a thunderous roar, he swirled the mace over his head and ran towards Yudhishthira. Yudhishthira engaged a fierce weapon that glowed like a red-hot iron and fired it at Duryodhan. The weapon shot through the air like a blazing meteor, struck Duryodhan on his chest and knocked him out. Yudhishthira pulled out his sword and jumped off the chariot to finish off his arch enemy when Bheem blocked him with his chariot.

'Stop!' said Bheem. 'Don't slay Duryodhan. He is not for you to kill. I have promised to kill him and will do so when the time arrives. Till then, you must leave him alone and help me keep my promise.'

Yudhishthira remembered the ill-fated day of the game of dice when a furious Bheem vowed to crush Duryodhan's thigh and kill him. He said to Bheem: 'Thank you for reminding me. I'll leave Duryodhan for you.'

Yudhishthira stepped back into his chariot and drove away as the sun began to dip behind the western horizon. The conch shells rang out, announcing the end of the sixteenth day of the battle. The exhausted soldiers dropped their weapons and lay down on the ground in relief.

71

Day Seventeen of the War

AT DAWN, WHEN THE TWO SIDES WERE BUSY PREPARING FOR THE seventeenth day's battle, Karna stepped into Duryodhan's tent. Duryodhan was putting on his armour with the help of some of his attendants. Karna said, 'O King, may I have a word with you?'

Duryodhan asked his attendants and guards to leave and then said, 'Yes, Karna. Tell me, how can I help?'

Karna looked right into Duryodhan's eyes and said, 'My friend, I promise you, today either I will kill Arjun, or he will kill me. Since the beginning of the war, Arjun and I've hardly met on the battlefield. Both of us were busy fighting other warriors. Today, I will attack him right from the beginning and won't stop till one of us falls. I am a superior warrior than Arjun. My Vijaya bow, which was gifted to me by my guru, Parashurama, is superior to Arjun's Gandiva. With that bow in my hand, Arjun won't be able to harm a single hair on my body. However ...' Karna paused a little.

'However?' an impatient Duryodhan asked.

'I think it would only be fair to mention the areas where Arjun is better equipped than I am,' said Karna. 'Arjun has in his possession his never-ending quivers and his indestructible chariot from Agni. To top it all, he has Vasudev Krishna as his charioteer, who not only drives him around but also advises him when needed. It is because of Krishna that Arjun remains undefeated.'

'I can provide you the best chariot we have, as good as Arjun's, and I will have you followed by multiple chariots who'd provide you with an endless supply of weapons,' said Duryodhan. 'As far as your charioteer is concerned, I cannot get Krishna for you. If you have anybody else in mind, let me know. I'll make sure you have him as your charioteer.'

'King Shalya of Madra is an expert pilot. He is also extremely knowledgeable about horses. And he is as wise as Krishna. If you can convince him to be my charioteer, I am sure nobody will be able to save Arjun from my arrows.'

Duryodhan held Karna's hand and said, 'Come with me.' Then he stepped out of his tent and walked towards Shalya's camp with Karna following him.

When they arrived outside Shalya's tent, Duryodhan turned towards Karna and said, 'You wait here. Let me do the talking.'

Shalya was having his meal when Duryodhan entered his tent. 'Good morning, my dear nephew,' said Shalya. 'What brings you here?'

Duryodhan nodded and said, 'Uncle Shalya, I have a favour to ask. I hope you won't turn me down.'

'I have agreed to fight on your behalf instead of joining my true nephews, the Pandavas. What more can I do?'

'You know, the source of Arjun's strength is his charioteer, Krishna. It is because of Krishna's advice and shrewdness that Arjun is still alive and undefeated. Karna feels, if you take up the reins of his chariot, then he can easily defeat Arjun. On behalf of my dear friend and our commander-in-chief Karna, I'd like to request you to be Karna's charioteer.'

Shalya's face turned red with rage. 'How dare you make such an insulting proposal? I am a high-born Kshatriya. I'd never serve the low-caste son of a charioteer. If you try to force me, I'll immediately leave and go back to my kingdom.'

'Uncle Shalya, please try to understand,' pleaded Duryodhan. 'You are the only person who is wiser than Krishna. Only you can guide Karna the way Krishna guides Arjun. With you at the helm, nobody will be able to stop Karna and victory will be ours.'

Shalya thought for a moment. He remembered his promise to Yudhishthira—when the time comes, he'd keep Karna distracted with spiteful taunts and insults, such that Karna fails to focus on Arjun. Shalya said, 'You said in front of everybody that I am wiser than Krishna. For that, I forgive your insolent behaviour, and I accept your proposal.'

Duryodhan was ecstatic. He called Karna who was waiting outside, 'Come in, my friend. I have great news to share.'

Karna stepped in and, with joined palms, bowed to Shalya, who raised his hand to bless Karna and said, 'I will be your charioteer, but I have a condition.'

Karna said, 'To have you as my charioteer and guide, I can accept any condition.'

Shalya said, 'While I am your charioteer, I can say whatever I like, and you'll have to listen and tolerate it. Do you accept?'

Before Karna could answer, Duryodhan said, 'Of course we accept. What do you say, Karna?'

Karna bowed and said, 'To have the great Shalya as my guide, I am willing to accept any condition.'

Shalya smiled. 'Well, then, let's go pick our horses and load our chariots. We have a war to fight.'

Duryodhan arranged for the best chariot for Karna and said,
'Karna, you have all that you asked for. Now go and fetch me my
victory.'

Karna mounted the chariot and said, 'Don't you worry, my friend.
I will keep my promise.' He looked at Shalya who was holding the
reins of his horses and said, 'O King Shalya, take me to the battlefield.
Today, the Pandavas will see what I am made of. My arrows will kill
them all and make my friend Duryodhan victorious.'

Shalya laughed: 'Don't be so sure, my friend. Maybe you haven't
yet learnt your lesson from the numerous defeats you suffered at
the hands of the Pandavas. When Arjun's Gandiva rings out in the
battlefield and his arrows cover the sky like a dark cloud and kill your
soldiers in hordes, you won't feel so exuberant.'

Karna's face turned red with anger, but he remembered Shalya's
condition and decided to exercise restraint. He picked up his bow
and in a calm but stern voice, said, 'Let's go.'

As Karna's chariot rolled out, the Kauravas shouted in joy. 'Long
live Karna,' they said. 'Karna will destroy the Pandavas and bring us
victory!'

Karna said to Shalya: 'You hear them? Remember, at this stage of
the war, if anybody can bring victory to the Kauravas, it is I.'

Shalya smirked: 'Victory? Really? In all your past encounters, did
you ever defeat Arjun? Remember the time when the gandharvas
imprisoned Duryodhan? You were the first to flee that battle. It
was Arjun who freed Duryodhan from them. When you, along with
Bhishma and Drona, went to steal Virat's cattle, Arjun thrashed you
as well as the rest of the Kauravas. There's no comparison between
you and Arjun. He is the best warrior the world has ever seen.'

Karna was furious. 'Stop praising Arjun,' he growled. 'How could
you keep praising our enemy? If you like the Pandavas so much, what
you are doing in the Kaurava Army? The Pandavas must have planted

you to create dissent amongst us, make us weak. You are Duryodhan's uncle. Otherwise, I'd have killed you this very moment. Just keep quiet and take me to Arjun.'

Shalya laughed: 'When a man nears his end, he loses his senses. I am afraid, that's why you have lost your mind too. Otherwise, you wouldn't underestimate the strength of the Krishna-Arjun pair. Nobody in this world can defeat them. If you have the slightest wisdom left in you, I suggest you surrender to Krishna and seek his blessings.'

'I am fully aware of Krishna's and Arjun's might and power,' said Karna. 'Still, for my friend Duryodhan's sake, I will fight them. I am not afraid of anybody, be it God or human. If my chariot wheels don't get stuck in the ground, Arjun won't be able to escape.'

'Wheels stuck in the ground?' Shalya was surprised.

'Yes,' said Karna. 'Once, while practising my archery, I accidentally killed a Brahmin's cow. The angry Brahmin cursed me—during my final war, my body will become so heavy that my chariot wheel will sink into the ground and get stuck. I offered him wealth, cattle, gold ... but he refused to withdraw his curse. King Shalya, I know you despise me. Still, I am telling you all this to let you know that despite the curses, I am not afraid to fight Arjun. Remember, Karna never fights for riches or for the throne. Karna only fights for his honour, and that's what I will do.'

While Shalya was busy trying to distract Karna, the battle was raging. Yudhishthira saw Karna from a distance and asked his charioteer to take him there. 'Karna, it seems you are too eager to fight Arjun,' he said. 'Before you meet Arjun, fight me. Let's see what you've got.'

Yudhishthira hurled a series of deadly weapons at Karna. A distracted Karna was caught by surprise. The weapon struck his left shoulder and threw him down on his chariot. For a few moments, he lost consciousness, but he recovered soon and picked up his bow. In quick succession, Karna killed Yudhishthira's guards. His next arrow pierced his armour. Yudhishthira cried out in pain and pulled out the arrow from his chest. Blood gushed out of his wound, but Yudhishthira ignored the pain and hurled a spear at Karna. It whizzed past Karna's head, leaving him unscathed. An angry Karna struck back vehemently. Yudhishthira's body was riddled with arrows. With each strike, Yudhishthira writhed in pain. Karna was careful not to kill him. He destroyed Yudhishthira's chariot. Yudhishthira fell to the ground and screamed in pain. 'A chariot. Send me a chariot,' he yelled.

A Pandava charioteer heard his cry and brought his chariot to Yudhishthira, who scrambled up the vehicle and panted: 'Take me away, or Karna will kill me.'

Before he could leave, Karna brought his chariot next to Yudhishthira and held his shoulder. 'Yudhishthira, are you not a Kshatriya? How can you flee the battlefield? The truth is you are not fit to be a Kshatriya warrior. You have mastered the Vedas and the scriptures better than your weapons. You are more of a Brahmin than a Kshatriya. I advise you to quit fighting and practise meditation, for that suits you best. Send Arjun to fight me—he is the only one worthy of fighting me.' He shoved Yudhishthira back on the chariot and let him go.

Arjun was busy fighting the Samsaptaks. They surrounded Arjun and Krishna like bees and stung them from all sides. A few of them held Krishna's hands and hung from them. Krishna swung his arms, and they flew off the battlefield. Arjun fired his Serpent weapon at the Samsaptaks. Thousands of serpents emerged and entangled the feet of the Samsaptak warriors. Their king, Susharma, shot the Garuda weapon to scare off the snakes.

Krishna said, 'Arjun, let's not waste our time with the Samsaptaks. We must attack Karna and neutralize him.'

'You are right,' agreed Arjun. 'Take me to Karna.'

Krishna turned his chariot, but before he could leave, Aswathama attacked Arjun with a volley of arrows. Arjun cried out, 'Get out of my way, Aswathama. I have no time to fight you.' Aswathama didn't listen and kept up the attack.

Krishna glanced back at Arjun and said, 'Don't show any mercy to Aswathama. Take care of him now.'

Arjun shot some of his deadliest weapons at Aswathama and shattered his chariot. Drona's son stumbled to the ground and, before he could get up and gather himself, Arjun's chariot sped away.

On the other end of the battlefield, Karna was busy decimating the Pandava Army. From his Vijaya bow, he fired the Bhargavastra—a deadly weapon that bloomed into thousands of arrows and covered the sky before raining down on the enemy.

From a distance, Arjun watched the spectacle and said, 'Look, Krishna, Karna has fired the Bhargavastra. I can't stop it now. It will cause immense damage to our army. What should I do?'

Krishna thought for a moment. He knew, Arjun needed a little rest and a boost of motivation to kill Karna. Besides, Karna was at the peak of his fighting spirit right then. Later in the day, he'd have worn out a bit—a good time to finish him. He said to Arjun: 'I hear our king Yudhishthira has been seriously injured by Karna. Let's go to his tent and see how he is doing. I'm sure he'd like to hear some words of assurance from you. We can return later and take care of Karna.' Arjun agreed and Krishna turned his chariot towards the Pandava camp.

In his tent, Yudhishthira was lying on the bed, with multiple injuries on his body. The healers and medics were busy cleaning his wounds and applying healing emollients on them. When Yudhishthira saw Arjun, he jumped up on his bed with expectation. 'Oh, how happy I am to see you!' he said. 'You must have come here with good news, right? Tell me, how did you kill Karna? That evil man almost killed me today. It is because of him that Duryodhan dares to fight us. It was he who instigated Dushasana to drag Draupadi to the court and insult her in front of all the Kurus. Now that the horrible man is lying dead on the battlefield, I can sleep in peace.'

Arjun didn't know what to say. He never expected Yudhishthira to interpret their visit thus. He had to tell him the truth. 'My king, I think you have misunderstood my visit,' he said. 'I haven't killed Karna yet. He is still fighting, and brother Bheem is defending our army. I heard you were seriously injured and got anxious. I thought I'd pay you a visit and see for myself how you are doing.'

Yudhishthira's face turned red with anger. 'You came to see me? Or was it that you were scared to see Karna's might and fled the battlefield? Shame on you, Arjun. We have been depending on you to kill Karna and make us victorious. And now you disappoint us by running away from your enemy? If you are so scared of facing Karna, hand over the Gandiva to some other Pandava warrior. Let him take care of Karna while you stay in hiding.'

Arjun's blood began to boil. His face turned purple, his nostrils flared, sweat beads covered his forehead. He ran out of the tent and dropped on his knees. Breathing heavily, he took off his helmet and hurled it on the ground. Then he got up, pulled out his sword and turned back towards Yudhishthira's tent. And there he saw Krishna standing. 'What happened, Falguni?' asked Krishna. 'You came here to see Yudhishthira and he is doing fine. You should be happy. Why are you angry and why have you pulled out your sword?'

'I will kill Yudhishthira,' blurted Arjun.

'Kill Yudhishthira? Are you out of your mind?' Krishna was shocked.

'I had promised that if anybody told me to give up my Gandiva, and that too to some other warrior, I'd decapitate him immediately. King

Yudhishthira insulted me and asked me to hand over my Gandiva to another warrior. To keep my oath, I must kill Yudhishthira. Isn't that the right thing to do?' asked Arjun.

'Shame on you, Arjun.' Krishna sounded quite upset. 'You have been blindly following Dharma without knowing its true intent. Killing any life for no good reason is not Dharma. And you want to kill your brother for a silly promise you made? I'd say, it is better to tell a lie than to kill. There was once a Brahmin sage named Kaushik. One day, a few men and women came running to his hermitage to take shelter from a band of dacoits. They hid behind the bushes in the hermitage. When the dacoits came and asked Kaushik if he knew where the men were hiding, the sage showed them the bush, for he would never lie. The dacoits pulled the men and women out and killed them mercilessly. The poor Brahmin didn't know the real intent of Dharma and for this sin he had to suffer in hell. Dharma means to hold and protect. And to protect somebody, if one has to lie, so be it.'

Arjun was confused. 'Krishna, I get your point, but what am I supposed to do now? If I don't honour my oath, I'll commit a grave sin. You tell me, what should I do to protect Yudhishthira and save myself too?'

Krishna replied, 'Whatever Yudhishthira said was caused by his pain and frustration. Besides, he must have thought, a little insult can stoke your anger and motivate you to go after Karna and kill him.' Krishna paused a little and then said, 'This is what I suggest you do: a respectable man is killed in spirit when he is insulted. You say some insulting words to Yudhishthira, and that would hurt him enough to feel like death. Then you can apologize for your behaviour and make amends. The wise king Yudhishthira wouldn't mind, and would accept your apology.'

Arjun agreed. He placed the sword in its case and stepped inside Yudhishthira's tent. Krishna followed him. Arjun stood in front of

Yudhishthira, his eyes bloodshot, his nostrils flaring. In a hoarse voice, he said, 'Yudhishthira, you have no right to insult me. Sitting here in the safety of your tent, far away from the battlefield, you have no idea what is going on. You are weak and you are cruel. You cannot hurt anybody with your weapon—all you can do is hurt us with your caustic words. You have no right to blame me or anybody for what's happening in the war. It is your foolish decision to play the game of dice that has put us in this terrible situation. It is because of that irresponsible act of yours that thousands are dying. Still, we have been defending you. But you keep accusing us and blaming us for not performing our duty. Shame on you!' Arjun blurted out all that he had kept hidden in his chest in one breath.

Yudhishthira was stunned. Before he could say anything, Arjun pulled out his sword and swung it above his head. Krishna stepped forward and held Arjun's hand. 'What are you doing? Why have you pulled out your sword again?'

Arjun replied, 'I have done the most heinous crime—I insulted my brother King Yudhishthira. I have no right to live. Let go of my hand.'

Krishna laughed. 'Moments ago, you were about to kill your brother. Now you want to kill yourself for saying these harsh words? What would you have done if you had really killed him?' Krishna was serious now. 'Remember, you would commit a graver sin by killing yourself than killing your own brother. But I understand your feelings. Listen to me. Go to Yudhishthira and sing your own praise to him—tell him how great you are. Self-praise and boasting is equivalent to suicide.'

Arjun put down his sword and said, 'King Yudhishthira, listen to me. I am the greatest warrior that ever lived. I am next to nobody, except lord Shiva. If I wish, I can destroy the world in a moment. I have the knowledge of using the most powerful weapons. It was I who brought down all the kings to their knees and made them submit to you for your Rajasuya Yagna. It was because of me that you could amass your wealth, build your grand palace, and become the emperor of the world. In this great war of Kurukshetra, it is I who killed more than half of our enemy soldiers. When I am in the battlefield with my Gandiva in hand, nobody can defeat me—not even Karna. And I promise you, today Karna will die at my hands. Nothing can stop me.'

Arjun stopped to catch his breath while Yudhishthira sat on his bed, dumbfounded. Arjun then suddenly sank to his knees and, with his head bowed, said, 'Oh my king, my brother, forgive me for all that I have said. Someday, you'll understand the reason for all this. Now allow me to return to the battlefield.'

Yudhishthira stood up from his bed and said, 'You have said nothing wrong. Indeed, I am the cause of all this misery. I have put you all—and thousands of warriors and soldiers—in grave danger. My foolishness and irresponsible behaviour have caused immense pain and destruction. I don't deserve to live. Kill me and relieve me of this burden.'

Krishna came forward and held Yudhishthira's hand. 'Don't feel bad, my king,' he said. Krishna then explained the reason for Arjun's behaviour and said, 'Arjun acted on my advice. You know the laws of Dharma better than anybody. Pardon me if I made any mistake.'

Yudhishthira bowed to Krishna and said, 'You have saved us from a grave crisis, O Vasudev. Without you as our guide, we'd be blind.' He then turned to Arjun and said, 'Forgive me, Arjun, for what I said. Trust me, I didn't mean a single word.' The brothers embraced each other with tears flowing down their cheeks.

Arjun then turned to Krishna and said, 'My friend, I have a promise to keep. Take me to Karna. Today will be his last day on earth.'

Krishna and Arjun stepped into their Kapidhwaj chariot and sped away towards the battlefield.

The Fall of Karna

As Arjun's chariot raced towards the battlefield, Krishna said, 'My dear Arjun, no doubt you are the greatest warrior alive in this world. But don't you ever ignore the might of Karna. Today, on the seventeenth day of the war, most of the warriors from both sides have succumbed and left for the heavens. Still, the Kauravas have five of the most valiant generals alive—Aswathama, Kripacharya, Kritavarma, Shalya and Karna. Aswathama is your guru Drona's son, Kripa is your guru, and you have family ties with Kritavarma and Shalya. It is possible you have a soft corner for them, but you must not show any mercy to Karna. It was he who encouraged Duryodhan to do all the evil things against you. You must kill him today.'

While Arjun was heading towards the battlefield, Bheem was busy fighting the Kaurava Army. He hurled a huge mace at an incoming Kaurava chariot and shattered it into bits, killing all its riders. Bheem turned to his charioteer Vishoka and said, 'I don't see Arjun. Yudhishthira went back to his tent after being injured. I wonder if they are alive. Whatever it may be, I will continue my rampage and destroy the Kauravas. Tell me, do I have enough weapons in my cache?'

Vishoka peeped inside the chariot and said, 'Don't worry, Bheemsen. You have enough armaments to kill your enemies. You keep firing as much as you want.'

Assured of his stash of weapons, Bheem continued his killing spree. A little later, Vishoka said, 'Lord, I think I can hear the twang of Arjun's Gandiva bow.' He stood up on his chariot, gazed in the direction of the sound, and said, 'There! I can see Arjun's chariot mast. He is coming.'

Bheem was elated. 'You have given me the greatest news today,' he said. 'For this, I'll reward you handsomely.'

Soon, Arjun's chariot approached Bheem. 'How is Yudhishthira?' asked Bheem. 'Is he alive and well?'

'Yes, he is fine and recovering from his wounds,' replied Arjun. 'There is nothing to worry about. You keep fighting. I'll go and engage with Karna.'

Hearing the good news, Bheem attacked the Kaurava Army with renewed vigour. Watching Bheem slaughtering his soldiers, Dushasana came to stop him. With a volley of arrows, Bheem shattered Dushasana's bow, and then killed his charioteer. Dushasana didn't give up. He picked up the reins with his left hand and drove the chariot on his own. With his right hand, he hurled a spear at Bheem and knocked him out. Before Dushasana could strike him again, Bheem jumped up on his chariot and cried out loud: 'Dushasana, today I'll kill you and drink your blood.'

Dushasana laughed and hurled the mighty Shakti Astra at Bheem. In response, Bheemsen picked up his huge mace, whirled it above his head and threw it towards Dushasana. It shattered Dushasana's Shakti Astra and then struck him on his head and flung him far from his chariot. Dushasana cried out in pain.

Bheem remembered the day when Dushasana had dragged Draupadi to the court by her hair and then tried to disrobe her in front of the Kuru clan. His blood boiled at the thought. He jumped off his chariot and walked towards Dushasana, who was writhing in pain. Bheem stopped in front of Dushasana, pulled out his sword and cried out, 'Listen to me, you Kaurava warriors. Now I will kill this evil man Dushasana and avenge Draupadi. Stop me if you can.' With his knee, Bheem squeezed Dushasana's neck and plunged the sword into his chest. Blood gushed out of Dushasana's chest. Bheem collected the blood in his palms and drank it the way a man drinks from a mountain spring to quench his thirst. With his hands and face smeared with blood, he looked around and cried out, 'This is the most delicious drink I've ever had. No other drink has been able give me so much peace, so much pleasure.'

Watching this ghastly scene, the Kaurava soldiers panicked. Some fell unconscious, others began to flee. Krishna and Arjun brought their chariot near Bheem and were shocked. Bheem said to them: 'Why are you looking at me like that? I have killed Dushasana the way I said I would. I kept my promise. Next, I'll kill Duryodhan by crushing his thigh. Only then can I rest in peace.' Saying this, Bheem walked back to his chariot and sped away.

When the news of Dushasana's horrific death reached Duryodhan, he was devastated. But that wasn't all. Soon, another messenger came in with the news that Bheem had killed ten more of his brothers. Duryodhan could feel the war slipping away from his hands. Karna was his last hope. He asked the messenger to tell Karna to focus all his attention on Arjun and kill him as soon as possible.

Karna, however, was not waiting for Duryodhan's instructions. When he learnt that his favourite son Vrishasen had been killed by Arjun, he was furious. He said to his charioteer Shalya: 'Take me to Arjun. Today, I'll kill both Krishna and Arjun, and end this battle once and for all.' Shalya veered the chariot in the direction where the death cries of the Kaurava soldiers were emanating from.

Soon, Karna's and Arjun's chariots faced each other and a fierce battle broke out. Streams of arrows spewed from their bows, killing thousands of soldiers on both sides. They hurled their fiercest weapons, especially reserved for this battle, at each other. The earth rumbled as their chariots circled each other. Explosions rocked the battlefield and lit up the sky. The warriors ran to save themselves from the wrath of the two giants. The gods in the heavens came out to witness this great battle and took sides—some supported Arjun and some Karna.

Aswathama rushed to Duryodhan and pleaded, 'Duryodhan, stop this madness. This war is helping nobody. Declare a ceasefire and bring the Pandavas to the table and negotiate a peace treaty. I am sure the Pandavas will listen to you and agree to any respectable arrangement.'

Duryodhan sighed. 'It's too late, Aswathama. How can I live in peace after witnessing the horrible death of my dear brother Dushasana in the hands of that monster Bheem? The Pandavas won't trust me either. But don't you worry. Arjun is tired and, soon, Karna will overpower him.'

Arjun and Karna kept shooting their most powerful weapons—the fire, the wind and the water weapons. But neither of them budged an inch. Arjun shot his deadly Indrastra—the weapon he had received from Lord Indra. Karna halted it mid-air with his Bhargavastra.

Bheem was angry. 'What's the matter with you, Arjun?' he asked. 'Your weapons seem to have lost their power and Karna is devastating our army. If you think you are unfit to fight Karna today, let me know. I'll kill that charioteer's son with a single strike of my mace.'

Krishna too was disappointed with Arjun's performance. 'Gather yourself, Arjun,' Krishna chastised him. 'None of your weapons are able to break through Karna's defence. Karna is destroying them all mid-fire. It seems you've lost your sharpness. Are you in a trance? Wake up and focus your attention. You have a job to do—kill Karna. If you don't think you are up to it, let me know. I'll decapitate that evil man with my Sudarshan Chakra.'

Krishna's rebuke woke up Arjun. He picked up a deadly arrow—the Brahmastra—and said, 'Krishna, thank you for pulling me out of my daze. Now, if you'd allow me, I'll shoot this Brahmastra at Karna and destroy him.'

'Do whatever you need to,' said Krishna. 'Just kill him.'

Arjun engaged the Brahmastra on his Gandiva, chanted the activation mantra sequence and released the weapon. With a sonorous roar, the arrow shot out of the bow and flew towards Karna at lightning speed. Karna was prepared. He shot a series of counter measures and deflected Arjun's Brahmastra.

From a nearby chariot, Bheem yelled, 'Try again, Arjun. Don't let that evil man get away.'

Arjun released another Brahmastra. The weapon shot out and spewed out thousands of smaller arrows and struck the enemy soldiers. Once again, Karna destroyed the weapon before it could cause any significant damage. Arjun's mighty pull broke the bowstring of the Gandiva. As he scrambled to replace it, Karna took the opportunity to strike him. Karna's arrows pierced Arjun's armour and cut through his flesh. Karna struck Krishna with multiple arrows, making him bleed. Seeing the blood on Krishna's body, Arjun roared like a lion. With a new bowstring in place, he covered the sky with thousands of arrows, which fell back to the earth, killing thousands and injuring both Karna and Shalya. The Kaurava warriors panicked and began to flee.

Ashwasen, whose mother, the Takshak serpent, had died when Arjun burnt down the Khandava Forest, was lying deep underground. The rumbling of the chariots, the thumping of the elephants and the explosions of the weapons woke him up. He came up to the surface and saw Arjun fighting Karna. This was the right time to extract revenge. He slipped into Karna's quiver and took the shape of an arrow. Karna, not aware of Ashwasen, picked the serpent as his arrow and engaged him on his bow to shoot Arjun. Shalya noticed this and realized that it will be impossible for Arjun to survive this weapon. Remembering his promise to Yudhishthira, he said to Karna, 'Don't use that weapon. It won't cut Arjun's neck. Try some other weapon.'

Karna, while aiming at Arjun, said, 'I never reengage my arrow. I picked this weapon, and this is what I'll use.' Saying this, Karna released the weapon.

The serpent weapon shot out of Karna's bow like a meteor and hurtled towards Arjun. The moment Krishna noticed the weapon, he knew that if it strikes Arjun, he'd die for sure. In an instant, he stood up and pressed down on the chariot floor. The wheels immediately sunk into the ground, almost an arm's length, and the weapon struck Arjun's helmet and knocked it off, saving Arjun's life.

A frustrated Ashwasen returned to Karna and revealed himself. 'You fired the weapon without knowing it was me you were shooting,' he said. 'That's why I failed to kill Arjun—the man who burnt my mother alive. Shoot me once again, and this time I won't fail.'

'Ashwasen, I understand your pain, but I can't accept your offer,' said Karna. 'I want to kill Arjun with my own might. I don't need help from anybody.'

Angry Ashwasen jumped up in the sky and hurled himself towards Arjun to avenge his mother's murder. Krishna warned Arjun. 'Look up, that is Ashwasen the serpent coming to kill you to avenge his mother's death. Strike him now.' With six arrows shot in quick succession, Arjun cut the serpent into pieces. Krishna jumped off the chariot and, with his bare hands, pulled the chariot wheels out of the ground.

Once again, Arjun launched a fierce attack on Karna. This time, he didn't give Karna any opportunity to defend himself. Arjun's arrows shattered Karna's helmet, cut open his armour, and pierced into his flesh. Karna reeled in pain as blood gushed out of his wounds. His bow dropped off his hand and he stumbled on the chariot and grabbed the mast to prevent himself from falling. Arjun felt pity for Karna and stopped shooting at him.

'Why did you stop?' asked Krishna. 'Karna is tired, and you must take this opportunity to finish him off.'

'He is wounded and is unarmed,' said Arjun. 'It's not right to kill an unarmed man.'

'A warrior never offers relief to his enemy,' said Krishna. 'That is foolishness. Strike him now before he recovers and strikes back.'

Arjun picked up his Gandiva to shoot at Karna, but he was late. Karna had already recovered and launched his counter attack. The sky was once again covered with the arrows from Karna and Arjun while Shalya and Krishna drove their chariots in a zigzag maze.

Suddenly, Karna felt that his chariot was not moving. He said to Shalya: 'What happened? Why aren't we moving?'

Shalya looked down and said, 'It seems our chariot wheels are stuck in the ground. Let me try to get them out.'

Instantly, Karna remembered the Brahmin's curse—when his time comes, his chariot wheels would get stuck in the ground. Karna wasn't afraid. He said, 'King Shalya, try to get the chariot out. I'll use some of my deadliest weapons and keep Arjun at bay.'

Karna tried to pick a weapon, but he couldn't remember any of his special weapons. Guru Parashuaram's curse was coming true. Still, he didn't despair. He kept shooting his ordinary arrows at Arjun and cut his bowstring several times. While Arjun repaired his bowstring, Shalya tried to extricate the chariot wheels from the mud.

Arjun then picked up a deadly ironclad arrow and aimed it at Karna. Karna dropped his bow and stood up on the chariot, waving his hands. 'Arjun, you see I am unarmed. You know it better than anybody, it is unfair to strike an unarmed warrior. Give me a moment to pull out my chariot. We can engage in our battle after that. You are an honourable man, and I am sure you know that it is the right thing to do.'

Before Arjun could respond, Krishna yelled at Karna, 'Don't you lecture us about right and wrong, and about honour. Where were your ethics and your righteousness when you joined in the fun with Dushasana, Duryodhan and Shakuni to drag Draupadi into the court and tried to disrobe her? Where was your righteousness when that evil Shakuni defeated a naive Yudhishthira in an unfair game of dice? Where was your moral code when you and your Kaurava generals encircled that boy Abhimanyu and killed him in the most unfair and cowardly manner? Stop lecturing us about righteousness and pay the price for your sins.'

Karna had no answer. He stooped down in shame and tried to gather himself. Then he suddenly picked up a deadly arrow laced with poison and shot it at Arjun. The arrow struck Arjun's arm and he cried out in pain. His head began to spin and his Gandiva fell from his hand. Karna took this opportunity and jumped off his chariot and tried to pull out the wheels that were stuck deep in the ground. The more he tried to pull, the more the wheels sank. Karna struggled and struggled more, but to no avail.

Arjun regained consciousness and picked up his Gandiva. Krishna said, 'Do not hesitate, Arjun. Finish off Karna. Now!'

Arjun picked up the fierce Anjalik weapon and engaged it on his Gandiva. 'If I have treated my elders with respect and have their blessings, if I have worshiped the gods and received their blessings, if I have been well-mannered to my friends and family, then let this weapon take the life of my enemy.' Saying these words, Arjun released the weapon. Like a bolt of lightning, the Anjalik cut through the air and sliced off Karna's head.

As Karna stumbled to the ground, the onlookers saw a bright light emanate from his headless body, rise to the sky, and merge into the sun. The Kauravas cried in despair and the Pandavas hollered in joy.

Duryodhan was devastated when he heard the news. The loss of
Dushasana and Karna on the same day was too much for him to bear.
Shalya and Aswathama tried to console him. However, their words
didn't have any effect on him.

Krishna and Arjun went back to Yudhishthira's tent to give him
the news. A delighted Yudhishthira embraced them and asked them
to take him to the battlefield where Karna lay. Seeing Karna's lifeless
body, Yudhishthira said, 'Krishna, how can I ever thank you? Without
your inspiration and guidance, we could never have achieved this.'
Then he turned to Arjun and said, 'My dear brother, you kept your
promise. I might have said some harsh words to you in the past, but
never did I doubt your prowess and I always knew you are the greatest
warrior of all. Because of you and Krishna, tonight I'll sleep in peace.'

72

Day Eighteen of the War

URYODHAN WAS SITTING ALONE IN HIS TENT, CONTEMPLATING. Seventeen days had passed, and in those handful of days he had lost three of his greatest warriors—Bhishma, Drona and Karna. He had embarked upon this war depending solely on the might of these three, but the Pandavas had shattered his dreams. Bhishma and Drona were old, and neither of them gave their best to fight the Pandavas. Their death didn't perturb Duryodhan as much as the loss of his dearest friend. With Karna's fall, Duryodhan knew, the war had already slipped away from his grip. It was only a matter of time before Yudhishthira and his brothers would claim complete victory and take over the throne of Hastinapur. Duryodhan felt lonely, and a deep feeling of despair overwhelmed him as tears rolled down his cheeks.

Just then, Kripacharya, Aswathama, Shalya and Kritavarma entered his tent. Duryodhan was in no mood to welcome them. He sat still, with his head bowed. Kripacharya broke the silence: 'My dear Duryodhan, I think, the time has come to revisit our options. Kshatriya dharma says that a warrior should never give up. He must fight till the end. However, the scriptures also dictate that when one is weakened in battle, it is advisable to negotiate a truce with the enemy. If we declare a ceasefire and request the Pandavas, I am sure Yudhishthira would accept you as the king. Maybe that is our best option at this moment.'

Duryodhan stood up slowly and faced Kripacharya. 'You speak like a wise man, and your advice is well-intentioned. Every word you speak is for my good. However, I cannot accept your proposal. Surrender to Yudhishthira and live on his charity? Never. Even if he accepts me as the king of Hastinapur, I'll have to bow to him forever because of his generosity. It is better to die a glorious death in a battle than to live like a slave. Besides, why would Yudhishthira agree to such a proposal? Especially after all that we've done to them?' Duryodhan paused for a moment and said, 'Listen to me: tomorrow we will fight with all our might. We have gallant warriors like you, and I believe we still have the capability to win. Now we need to find us a commander-in-chief. Aswathama, tell me, who do you think should lead us to battle tomorrow?'

Aswathama bowed to Duryodhan and said, 'O King, in my opinion, King Shalya would be the best person to be our next commander-in-chief. He is not only a valiant warrior, but has proved his loyalty to you by abandoning his own nephews and joining your side.'

Duryodhan was pleased with the suggestion. He walked towards Shalya with folded hands and said, 'Dear Uncle, now is the time to test who is our friend and who our foe. You are strong, and skilled in using various weapons. You are as powerful as Bhishma and Drona, and as wise as Krishna. Now, you are our only hope. I pray you lead us in the battle as our new commander-in-chief.'

Shalya was delighted with the praise. He touched Duryodhan's head and said, 'My dear Duryodhan, I am pleased and honoured to have won your trust and confidence. I accept your offer to lead the Kaurava Army. Tomorrow, you'll witness my true might when I destroy the Pandavas.'

Duryodhan called in the priests to conduct the rituals and ceremony to appoint Shalya, the king of Madra, as the next Kaurava commander-in-chief.

When the news reached the Pandava camp, Yudhishthira stepped into Krishna's tent and asked, 'Duryodhan has appointed our uncle, the great warrior, King Shalya, as his commander-in-chief. How do you suggest we defeat him?'

Krishna smiled. 'Shalya is indeed extremely powerful and could prove to be quite dangerous. He is stronger than most of our Pandava warriors. However, I feel you are the best person—perhaps the only person—who can kill the Madra King. If you don't go soft on him because he is your uncle, then I am sure tomorrow Shalya will die at your hands.'

The next morning, the Kaurava generals—Kripa, Kritavarma, Aswathama, Shalya and Shakuni—met with Duryodhan and decided that none of them would engage in a one-on-one combat with the Pandavas. During the battle, they'd always cover and protect each other, and won't allow the Pandavas to break through their defense.

With the ringing of the conch shells, the two armies clashed again for the eighteenth time in the great war of Kurukshetra. The death of Karna boosted the confidence of the Pandavas manifold and they pounced upon the enemy with such ferocity that the Kauravas felt overwhelmed. Nakul killed Karna's two sons, Chitrasen and Satyasen. Sahadev killed Shalya's son. Bheem attacked Shalya and killed his horses. Shalya struck back at Bheem by hurling a huge spear at him, piercing his armour. Bheem pulled out the spear and hurled it back at Shalya. The spear hit Shalya's charioteer and killed him. Shalya and Bheem fought each other like men possessed, till both were exhausted. Kripacharya came to Shalya's rescue and took him away from Bheem.

Yudhishthira called his brothers and said, 'You have demonstrated your prowess by killing the mightiest of Kaurava warriors. Now, I'd request you to leave Shalya to me. Today, either I will kill him, or he will slay me. Satyaki, Dhrishtadyumna, Bheem and Arjun—all of you protect me from any attacks from the sides and my back. But do not interfere when I fight my uncle.'

With the Pandava brothers supporting and surrounding him along with Satyaki and Dhrishtadyumna, Yudhishthira attacked Shalya. Krishna's encouragement on the previous night gave Yudhishthira's confidence a big boost. He pounced upon Shalya with such aggressiveness that the Pandava soldiers around him were stunned. That the softspoken and kind man, who was regarded as the personification of Dharma himself, could turn out to be such a valiant and fierce warrior was something they could never imagine. Yudhishthira's arrows killed Shalya's horses and his charioteer. Aswathama came running to rescue him. Yudhishthira continued killing Shalya's warriors with his favourite weapon, the spear.

Moments later, Shalya returned in a new chariot and, in rapid succession, killed Yudhishthira's horses and his charioteer. Bheem couldn't control himself. He hurled his mace at Shalya and destroyed his chariot. Shalya jumped off the vehicle with a machete and a shield in his hands, and ran towards Yudhishthira. Bheem shot a sharp arrow at Shalya and cut the handle of his machete.

Yudhishthira knew this was his moment to kill Shalya. He stood on his horseless chariot and pulled out a ferocious arrow from his quiver and engaged it to his bow. He aimed the weapon at Shalya and said, 'Uncle Shalya, you abandoned the path of Dharma and joined the evil Kauravas. And for that sin, my arrow will kill you now.' Saying this, he released the weapon. The arrow zoomed at lightning speed and struck Shalya's chest, tearing it apart. Shalya's lifeless body crashed to the ground.

Bereft of a commander-in-chief, the Kaurava Army was in total disarray. They began to flee in hordes, while the Pandavas went on a killing spree. Duryodhan tried to persuade them to come back: 'The war is not over yet. We have great warriors—Aswathama, Kripacharya, Kritavarma—we can still win the war ...'

King Salwa, from the lands beyond the northern mountains, rode a huge elephant that belonged to Duryodhan and attacked the Pandava soldiers. The elephant trampled the soldiers while Salwa showered them with arrows. Dhrishtadyumna tried to stop the elephant by shooting spears and arrows at it but the weapons hardly penetrated the beast's thick skin. Salwa drove the elephant towards Dhrishtadyumna to crush him. Dhrishtadyumna jumped off his chariot to save himself but as soon as he made his escape, the elephant crushed the chariot along with his charioteer and four horses. Bheem, Shikhandi and Satyaki tried to kill the beast by shooting their fiercest weapons at it, but they bounced off the animal, leaving it unscathed. Dhrishtadyumna picked up a huge mace, jumped up and struck a huge blow to the temple of the elephant. Instantly, the elephant collapsed and crashed to the ground, dead. Salwa tried to run away, but Dhrishtadyumna hurled a spear and beheaded him.

The Pandavas kept ravaging the Kaurava Army. One by one, their generals and warriors who stood up to fight the Pandavas died at the hands of Bheem, Arjun, Nakul and Sahadev. Shakuni and his son Uluk, along with their followers, tried to launch a bit of resistance and fought valiantly against Sahadev. Sahadev hurled a spear at Uluk and decapitated him. Furious at the loss of his son, Shakuni shot a fierce weapon at Sahadev, who destroyed the weapon in mid-flight and hurled another spear at Shakuni in retaliation. The spear pierced Shakuni's chest and killed him instantly.

It was clear to Duryodhan that he had no hope against the Pandavas. His army had been totally decimated, his generals all killed. He was sure to be the next to face the wrath of the five brothers. He picked up his mace and quietly leaving the battlefield moved towards Lake Dwaipayan. Upon arriving at the lake, Duryodhan dove into the water and looked for a place to hide. He found a secret cove hidden behind a wall of water. Duryodhan slid into the cove and lay down in the cool waters and thought about what to do next.

Aswathama, Kripacharya and Kritavarma noticed Duryodhan leave. They were busy fighting the Pandavas and couldn't join him at first. As the sun descended towards the western horizon, Aswathama said to Kripacharya and Kritavarma: 'There is no point in fighting the Pandavas any more. Let's find Duryodhan. He might need our help.' The three warriors mounted their horses and galloped towards the direction where Duryodhan was last seen.

As dusk fell on the grounds of Kurukshetra, it was clear that the war had finally come to an end. The soldiers who were still alive, dragged themselves back to their tents and prepared to depart for their homes. But for Yudhishthira, as long as Duryodhan was alive, the war was far from over. He ordered his men to find him, but they failed to find him anywhere near the battlefield.

Aswathama, Kripacharya and Kritavarma arrived near the banks of Lake Dwaipayan and looked around for Duryodhan. They knew that this was the best place for him to hide. Aswathama called out, 'O King Duryodhan, where are you? Come out of hiding and join us. Together, we'll fight Yudhishthira and his brothers and win back your kingdom. Or else, we'll die and depart for the heavens.'

Duryodhan answered from his secret cove: 'I am glad you are still alive. I appreciate your concern and your willingness to fight for me. But I am tired and wounded. Let me rest. Maybe tomorrow I'll regain my strength and join you to fight the Pandavas.'

As Duryodhan was speaking, a band of tribal hunters were passing by. When they heard Duryodhan, they ran to the Pandava camp and informed Yudhishthira about the hiding place.

Yudhishthira was elated. He called his brothers and said, 'Let's go to Lake Dwaipayan and finish the war.' The Pandavas, along with Krishna, mounted their chariots and left for the lake.

When Aswathama heard the rumble of the Pandava chariots, he said, 'King Duryodhan, the Pandavas have found your hideout. We must leave now.' With Duryodhan's permission, the three Kaurava warriors mounted their horses and galloped away.

Yudhishthira arrived and looked around. He knew Duryodhan was hiding in the lake. He called out: 'Duryodhan, come out of hiding and fight. You caused the destruction of your family, and now you want to flee? That's not the right thing to do for a Kshatriya. Have you lost all your pride? Don't be afraid. Come out and fight. Defeat us and rule the world, otherwise, die a glorious death and go to the heavens.'

Duryodhan answered, 'I am not hiding. I only want to rest a while. Don't you worry. When I am refreshed, I will come out and fight you. However, if you are so impatient, go ahead and rule my kingdom. With my family dead, I have lost all interest in the throne. Take it and let me live in peace in the forest. You enjoy the throne of Hastinapur.'

Yudhishthira, however, was not willing to give up easily. He stepped towards the lake and said, 'Who are you to give us the kingdom? I don't want to accept your charity. You remember, when I had asked for five villages for us five brothers, you said that without a fight, you wouldn't give us even a speck of land one could lift on a needle? Now let us fulfil your wish. Come out and fight. We'll defeat you and win the throne with our might.'

Duryodhan tried to stall. 'I can fight, but I don't have chariots, armours and helmets. Besides, you are five and I am alone. It will not be a fair fight.'

'You talk about a fair fight?' asked Yudhishthira. 'Where was your sense of fairness when seven of you warriors surrounded the young Abhimanyu and killed him?' Duryodhan didn't answer. Yudhishthira continued, 'This is what I offer you: we will give you whatever you need to fight us. You may pick any weapon of your choice and choose to fight any one of us five brothers. If you kill the person whom you choose to fight, the kingdom is yours. Do you agree?'

'I agree. I will pick the mace as my weapon. You can assign anybody to fight me. Nobody can defeat me with my favourite weapon.'

Krishna was furious at Yudhishthira. 'How could you make such a foolish proposal?' he said. 'Select any one of your brothers to fight? What if he selects you or Nakul or Sahadev? Duryodhan is not only strong, but he is also the most skilled mace warrior in the world. Nobody can defeat him in a fair mace fight. Bheem may be stronger than him, but as far as skill is concerned, Duryodhan is far superior.'

Bheem stepped forward and said, 'Brother Yudhishthira, allow me to fight Duryodhan. I have promised to kill him and I want to honour it.' He addressed Krishna: 'Krishna, don't you worry. I know how to defeat Duryodhan. I will kill him for sure.'

Duryodhan stepped out of the lake with his huge mace in hand. Yudhishthira gestured towards his chariot and said, 'Put on your armour and helmet and prepare to fight. Bheemsen will fight you on our behalf.'

Duryodhan strapped on a heavy armour and put on a helmet to protect his head. Then he walked towards Bheem and said, 'Today I will fulfil your wish to fight me. You'll die at my hands. Now pick up your mace and fight me.'

Bheem flared his nostrils and roared at the top of his voice. 'Prepare to die, you evil man. Today, my mace won't rest until it tastes your blood.' He thumped the ground with his feet and the earth trembled as if an earthquake had struck the area.

At that moment, Krishna's brother Balram arrived with a huge plough on his shoulder. He had been visiting several pilgrimages, and when he heard the news that his student Duryodhan was engaged in a mace fight with Bheem, he couldn't leave. Yudhishthira and Krishna welcomed him, and he sat down to watch the fight.

Bheem and Duryodhan faced each other like two huge giants. Swinging their maces and thumping their chests, they hurled vicious insults at each other. They moved in circles to find the right moment to strike. Suddenly, Bheem swung his mace at Duryodhan's head. Duryodhan ducked and avoided the blow. In the next instant, he struck Bheem on his chest and left him breathless. Bheem took a couple of minutes to recover and then attacked Duryodhan with a huge blow on his left side. Duryodhan reeled to absorb the impact and then bounced back. The fight continued with such savagery that gods in the heavens assembled to watch the spectacle. The maces of the giants struck each other with loud bangs, and sparks flew into the sky. Soon, Duryodhan and Bheem were covered in blood, their armours shattered, helmets broken.

Arjun turned to Krishna who sat next to him and asked, 'Who do you think is the better warrior? Who do you think will win this fight?'

Krishna looked concerned. 'Bheem is stronger than Duryodhan. But the latter is more skilled with the mace. To beat him, Bheem cannot stick to the rules.' He paused and looked at Arjun meaningfully. 'During the game of dice, when Duryodhan made the obscene gesture at Draupadi by slapping his thighs, Bheem had promised to kill him by breaking his thighs. Maybe Bheem has forgotten his promise and needs to be reminded.'

Arjun understood. He moved to a position where he could have direct eye contact with Bheem. Arjun then suggestively patted his thighs with his right palm and Bheem knew what to do. He crouched and ran towards Duryodhan to strike him. Duryodhan jumped up into the sky to let Bheem pass under him. The moment Bheem crossed Duryodhan, he turned back and swung his mace to strike a terrible blow to Duryodhan's thighs, mid-air. Duryodhan cried out in pain and crashed to the ground with both his thigh bones shattered to smithereens. Bheem began squashing Duryodhan's head under his feet and said, 'You evil man, do you remember how you and your brother Dushasana insulted Draupadi? I kept my promise by drinking Dushasana's blood. And now I honour the second one by breaking your thighs.' Angry Bheem then pressed Duryodhan's head harder to crush it.

Yudhishthira ran up to him and said, 'Stop, Bheem. You have crushed Duryodhan's thighs and kept your promise. You don't have to humiliate him further. Leave him alone and let him suffer for his sins.'

Balram leapt out of his seat with his hands flung out. 'Unfair! This is unfair,' he yelled. 'Bheem hit my pupil Duryodhan below his navel—this is against the rules. I will punish him.' Balram lifted his huge plough over his head and rushed to strike Bheem.

Krishna wrapped his arms around Balram and said, 'Calm down, Brother. Bheem did what he did only to keep his promise. Duryodhan may be your pupil, but he is the enemy of our allies, the Pandavas. He committed heinous crimes and now has to suffer for his sins.'

Balram was not happy with Krishna's logic. 'Whatever you may say, I still can't support what Bheem did to Duryodhan. Bheem will have to suffer for this.' Saying this, Balram stepped into his chariot and left.

Duryodhan tried to lift his torso with his hands and cried out in pain. 'Krishna, you are responsible for my misfortune. It was you who reminded Bheem of his promise. Don't think I didn't notice you talking to Arjun and Arjun gesturing to Bheem. You have been playing dirty all along. It was you who used Shikhandi to kill Bhishma. It was you who spread the lie about Aswathama's death to kill Drona. It was you who compelled Arjun to kill an unarmed Karna. If you had played fair, the Pandavas could have never defeated us.' Duryodhan couldn't stay up any longer. He fainted and collapsed to the ground.

Duryodhan's criticism made the Pandavas uncomfortable. Unable to counter his arguments, they stood with their heads hung in shame. Krishna smiled and said, 'Don't pay attention to Duryodhan's whining. It isn't unusual to leverage unconventional strategies to win a battle. For ages, people and gods have resorted to deception and other means to defeat a more powerful enemy. You would have never been able to kill Bhishma, nor Drona, in a fair and straight battle. That's why I suggested a little trickery to expose their vulnerability and they fell for it. At the end of the day, we succeeded and they failed. We won and they lost. Now enjoy your victory and prepare for the days ahead.'

The Pandavas mounted their chariots and headed back to their camp, leaving behind an unconscious Duryodhan by the banks of Lake Dwaipayan to die a gruesome death.

73

Aswathama's Revenge

Aftⁿer the Pandavas had left, Aswathama, Kripacharya and Kritavarma returned to the banks of Lake Dwaipayan, where Duryodhan lay unconscious. Aswathama brought some water from the lake and sprinkled it on Duryodhan. Gently, he cleaned the blood and grime from his face and body. Slowly, Duryodhan regained consciousness and, as his senses became active, he cried in pain.

Aswathama could not hold back his tears. The heir to the throne of Hastinapur, the great King Duryodhan, was lying helpless in the dust and writhing in pain, with nobody to care for him. He could never have imagined witnessing such a horrific and tragic scene.

Aswathama said, 'O King, my heart breaks to see you in such a condition. Tell me, how can I be of any service to you?'

With great difficulty, Duryodhan lifted his torso using his elbows as support. 'The Pandavas tricked me and defeated me using unfair means. Avenge me if you can—that's all I ask of you.'

'If you allow me, tonight I will kill the Pandavas and the Panchals. That is a promise,' said Aswathama, fuming.

Duryodhan turned towards Kripacharya and said, 'Gurudev, please fetch a pot of water. I want to consecrate the appointment of Aswathama as the next commander-in-chief of the Kaurava Army.'

Kripacharya brought some water in an earthen pot, and Aswathama was appointed as the next commander-in-chief. 'Go and fulfil your promise,' muttered Duryodhan while trying to hide his pain. 'I pray you return victorious.'

Aswathama bowed to Duryodhan and mounted his horse. Kripacharya and Kritavarma followed him, and the three warriors galloped towards Kurukshetra, leaving behind Duryodhan awaiting his death.

At nightfall, they reached a dense forest and decided to rest awhile and work out a plan to attack the Pandavas. They sat down under a huge banyan tree and, within moments, Kripacharya and Kritavarma fell asleep. Aswathama, however, couldn't sleep. He racked his brain thinking about ways to overpower and kill the Pandavas and the Panchals. Suddenly, he heard the crows in the branches overhead crying out loud and fluttering their wings. Aswathama looked up and saw a huge black owl on one of the branches. The owl attacked the crows' nests, and was killing their sleeping babies at will. The crows woke up and tried to defend their children, but the ruthless owl was on a killing spree and within minutes killed numerous birds before merging into the night sky.

The scene gave Aswathama goosebumps—this was the way to destroy his enemy. He'd attack the Pandava camp at night while they were asleep. He'd enter the camp and kill the sleeping Panchals and the Pandavas and keep his promise. He woke up Kripacharya and Kritavarma and told them the details of his plan.

Kripa and Kritavarma were flabbergasted and couldn't speak for a few moments. Kripa stood up and said, 'This is an outrageous plan! I don't know how you could even think of such a cowardly act. This is so unlike you. I suggest you have a good night's sleep and clear your head. Tomorrow we'll think of something more honourable to achieve victory.'

Aswathama was furious. 'How can I sleep when my king lies in his deathbed and cries in pain,' he yelled. 'I cannot rest without avenging King Duryodhan. I cannot rest without killing Dhrishtadyumna. You need to understand, tomorrow the Pandavas and Panchals will be protected by Krishna and Arjun, and we won't be able to touch even a strand of their hair.'

Kripa tried to say something, but Aswathama stopped him. 'Fine, you don't have to enter the camp and do anything. I will do whatever is necessary, and if I need to, I will suffer the consequences with no regrets.' Aswathama mounted his horse and galloped away towards the Pandava camp.

Kripacharya and Kritavarma stood perplexed for a while, not knowing what to do. Kripa said to Kritavarma, 'I think we shouldn't leave him alone. We don't have to enter the camp with him, but outside the camp we should protect him from any attacks.' Kritavarma agreed. They mounted their horses and followed Aswathama at a distance.

Yudhishthira was despairing that evening. What had the war given him? Victory of course, but at what cost? People whom he loved, respected, people whose company he enjoyed, were all dead. With whom could he share his glory? He said to his brothers: 'Tonight, I don't feel like sleeping in the camp. I want to go somewhere peaceful—maybe by the banks of the river—and sleep under the open sky. Would you like to join me?' The brothers agreed. Krishna agreed to accompany them too. They mounted their chariots and went to a peaceful place by the riverbank and lay down to rest on the sand.

Aswathama stood on the margins of the Pandava camp and looked for the right place to enter. It seemed the Pandavas, having been assured of victory, hardly had any guards around the camp. Only one man stood at the entrance. The rest of the camp was silent. Aswathama decided to enter the camp right from the main entrance. At that moment, Kripacharya and Kritavarma arrived and stood next to him. 'Good that you've decided to come,' whispered Aswathama. 'You stay outside, and if anybody tries to escape, kill them.'

Aswathama alighted from his horse, covered his head in a cloak and walked towards the camp with an open sword in hand. Quietly, he arrived at the gate and, with a quick swish of his sword, killed the half-asleep guard. He then entered the camp and looked for Dhrishtadyumna's tent. The Panchal prince's tent wasn't difficult to find. Aswathama stepped into the tent and found Dhrishtadyumna sleeping on his bed. Looking at his father's killer peacefully asleep, Aswathama's blood boiled. He held Dhrishtadyumna by his hair and yanked him off his bed. Dhrishtadyumna woke up but, before he could raise an alarm, Aswathama placed his feet on his mouth and pressed hard. Dhrishtadyumna realized his time had come. He held Aswathama's feet and muttered, 'Kill me with your weapon and let me go to the heavens.'

'Never! You don't deserve to go to the heavens,' growled Aswathama. He placed his hand on Aswathama's chest and pressed so hard that Dhrishtadyumna's chest got crushed, which killed him instantly.

Aswathama then saw the five brothers sleeping. He was elated at the idea of killing the brothers together. He yanked one of the brothers by his hair and, with a swift strike, decapitated him. The noise woke up the other four, and Aswathama realized they weren't the Pandava brothers but the sons of Draupadi. But that didn't stop him. Before the startled brothers could defend themselves, Aswathama killed them all.

By then, the word about Aswathama's raid had spread inside the camp and the warriors scrambled to defend themselves. But Aswathama was indomitable. Like death himself, he killed them indiscriminately. Those who tried to flee the camp got killed by Kripacharya and Kritavarma's arrows. Aswathama continued his rampage inside the camp. He then went to the stable and killed all the horses and elephants without any mercy. Finally, when there was nobody left to challenge him, Aswathama walked out of the camp, mounted his horse and, along with Kripacharya and Kritavarma, rode back towards the Dwaipayan Lake where Duryodhan lay wounded.

Duryodhan was still alive when Aswathama arrived. He was spitting out blood while frantically trying to shoo away the hungry predators. Aswathama knelt before him and said, 'My king, I wasn't able to kill the Pandavas, but I have killed the five sons of Draupadi. I have also killed Dhrishtadyumna and many other Panchal and Pandava warriors. I know, this is not enough, but at least I could avenge my father.'

Duryodhan was overjoyed to hear this. 'You have achieved what our great warriors like Bhishma, Drona and Karna have failed to achieve,' he said trying hard to raise his head. 'Now I can die in peace.' And then Duryodhan stopped speaking and dropped dead on the banks of the lake.

The messengers ran to Yudhishthira and delivered the terrible news of the massacre. Yudhishthira's knees buckled and he collapsed to the ground unconscious. His brothers, overwhelmed with grief, gathered around and tried to console him. A little later, Yudhishthira regained consciousness. Tears rolling down his eyes, he said, 'We won the war, yet we lost. Our sons escaped the wrath of great warriors like Bhishma, Drona and Karna, but succumbed to Aswathama. It is our fault that we left him alive.' He paused to catch his breath, and then said, 'I don't know how Draupadi is going to take this news. Nakul, you go and fetch Draupadi to the camp. The rest of us will leave right now.'

When Yudhishthira stepped into the camp and saw the dead bodies of his sons and friends strewn all around, he almost collapsed again. With great difficulty he controlled himself and sat down in a corner with his brothers. Krishna stood by his side, but didn't utter a single word.

Draupadi came running and the moment she saw her sons' decapitated bodies lying on the ground, she fell to the ground. Bheem helped her get up. Draupadi touched each of her sons' bodies. They were still warm. She turned towards Yudhishthira and wiped off her tears. 'What price for victory, my king?' she said. 'You were too complacent with your victory and forgot that you haven't yet completed your job. Now listen to me. If you can't kill Aswathama by the end of the day, I will fast unto death.'

Yudhishthira tried to reason with Draupadi, 'Don't lament for your sons or your brother. They died an ideal Kshatriya death and have gone to the heavens.'

'Don't give me any excuses,' said Draupadi. She turned towards Bheem and said, 'Bheemsen, Aswathama carries a gemstone embedded in his forehead. Kill him and bring me the gemstone. I know only you can, and you will do this for me.'

Bheem immediately mounted his chariot and left to find Aswathama, with Nakul as his charioteer.

After Bheem left, Krishna said to Yudhishthira: 'Why did you let Bheem go alone? You and Arjun should've accompanied him.'

Yudhishthira was confused. 'You know Bheem. Aswathama is no match for him. I am sure he'll find Aswathama and kill him.'

Krishna wasn't happy with the answer. 'You underestimated Aswathama, and for that you had to pay a high price. His father Drona taught him to use the deadly Bhrahmasir weapon. When fired, it can destroy the entire earth. Drona also taught the use of this weapon to Arjun. Drona, of course, had instructed both his students not to use this weapon ever, especially on humans, but I doubt a desperate Aswathama would abide by his father's words. I think it would be wise of you and Arjun to go and help Bheem. If Aswathama uses the Bhrahmasir weapon, only Arjun can counter it.' Yudhishthira and Arjun mounted Krishna's chariot and the three drove in the direction where Bheem went.

Soon, they caught up with Bheem and joined him in his frantic search for Aswathama. They found Aswathama sitting on the banks of River Ganga with a group of sages. When Aswathama saw Bheem and Arjun, he panicked. He had no weapons in hand, but to activate the Bhrahmasir, he didn't need any physical weapon. He remembered his father had told him not to use this weapon against any human, but he had no option. He ripped out a blade of grass from the ground, uttered a mantra, and threw it up, saying, 'Let the Bhrahmasir destroy the Pandavas.' The weapon flared up and, with a huge roar, it blasted towards the sky to launch a strike against the Pandavas.

Screaming at the top of his voice, Krishna said, 'Arjun, fire your Bhrahmasir now and counter Aswathama's strike. Otherwise, we all will die along with thousands of your people.'

Arjun picked up an arrow, loaded it on his bow and shot it up in the sky, activating the Bhrahmasir by uttering the mantra. The arrow transformed into a ball of fire and shot up into the sky to counter Aswathama's weapon.

The gods and the sages panicked. Vyasa appeared between the two weapons and stalled them. Angry at Aswathama and Arjun, he said, 'Why did you fire the Bhrahmasir? Didn't you know it is a crime to fire it against humans? Retract your weapons immediately.'

'I fired it to counter Aswathama's strike and to protect our people,' said Arjun. 'However, I can't disobey you. I will retract my weapon. Please ask Aswathama to do the same.' Arjun uttered a mantra to retract the Bhrahmasir.

Aswathama said, 'I was scared to see Bheem and Arjun, and fired the weapon only as a last resort to protect myself.'

'Hand over the gemstone on your forehead to Bheem and they will let you live,' said Vyasa. 'But before anything, you must retract your weapon.'

Aswathama nodded and said, 'O great Rishi Vyasa, this gem is more precious than my life. However, I can't disregard your command, and I will give my gem to Bheem. But I don't know how to retract the Bhrahmasir weapon. So it needs to strike something. I will retarget it at the wombs of the Pandava women, and it will kill their unborn children.'

Vyasa agreed, but the Pandavas and Krishna were furious.

Krishna said, 'You are a coward, Aswathama. You have committed several sins, and now you want to kill unborn babies? I curse you, you'll live for 3,000 years, but your life will be one of endless pain and suffering. And let me tell you this: your weapon may kill the unborn children in the wombs of the Pandava women, but I will revive Abhimanyu's wife Uttara's child, and he will rule the Kuru kingdom for sixty years.'

'I accept your curse, Krishna,' said Aswathama. He pulled out his knife, cut out the gemstone from his forehead and gave it to Bheem. Then he stood up and walked away to live a long and painful life of 3,000 years.

Yudhishthira, Bheem, Arjun and Krishna returned to the camp. Bheem handed the gem to Draupadi and said, 'We defeated the murderer of your sons. Here, take Aswathama's gemstone. I hope it gives you peace.'

Draupadi stood up with the gem in hand and said, 'Thank you, Bheem.' Then she turned to Yudhishthira and said, 'O King, I'd like you to wear this gem on your crown to remind everybody that the Pandavas never forgive those who harm their family.' Saying this, Draupadi broke down in tears. The Pandava brothers stood by silently.

74

The Mourning

WHEN THE BLIND KING DHRITARASHTRA HEARD ABOUT THE DEATH OF his favourite son Duryodhan, he fell from his throne and fainted. His attendants took him to his bedroom and sprinkled water on his face to revive him. Dhritarashtra woke up and the moment he thought of his son's death, he fainted again. He woke up again and began to cry. Sanjay stood next to him and said, 'O King, please don't lament. It won't do you any good.'

Dhritarashtra lay on his bed and sobbed inconsolably. 'I lost all my sons, my friends, my family. I have nobody left who can help me. I lie here powerless like an old bird with broken wings. I have no use for my life anymore.'

Hearing of Dhritarashtra's condition, Vidura came to see him. 'Get up from your bed, Dhritarashtra,' he said in a firm voice. 'Death is the final destiny for all mortal beings. You may cry as much as you want, but your sons are not coming back. So, stop crying and get back to the business at hand.'

The great sage Vyasa came to console his son. 'Try to get a hold on yourself, my son. If you keep lamenting like this, Yudhishthira might kill himself in shame and sorrow. I advise you to overcome your grief and welcome Yudhishthira to Hastinapur and accept him as the king. He is kind and will treat you with respect.'

The next morning, Dhritarashtra left for Kurukshetra along with Gandhari, Kunti and the other Kuru widows. Thousands of others followed. On the way, they met Kripacharya and Kritavarma and heard the news of the death of Dhrishtadyumna, and the five sons of Draupadi.

When Dhritarashtra arrived in the Kaurava camp, Yudhishthira, along with his brothers, Draupadi and Krishna came to visit. Yudhishthira and his brothers bowed to Dhritarashtra to touch his feet. Reluctantly, Dhritarashtra embraced Yudhishthira and looked around. 'Where is Bheem? I am eager to meet him,' said the blind king as he groped around in the darkness.

Bheem stepped forward, but Krishna stopped him and gestured him to step aside. He then pushed a life-size iron statue of Bheem towards the blind king. Duryodhan used to practice his mace fighting skills on this statue. Dhritarashtra put his arms around the statue in a tight embrace, and the Pandavas watched in awe how the old man crushed the iron Bheem with his bare arms, powered by his hatred and rage. As the statue shattered into pieces and fell to the ground, Dhritarashtra was filled with remorse.

'Oh, what have I done!' cried the old king. 'I have killed my beloved Bheem.' Dhritarashtra dropped to his knees and covered his face to hide his shame.

Krishna came forward and said, 'O King, don't worry. You haven't killed Bheem. You have only destroyed his iron statue. Grief had detracted you from the path of Dharma, and that's why you were motivated to kill Bheem. Remember, killing Bheem won't bring your sons back. You have studied the scriptures and are well-versed in the laws of Dharma. Why do you have to behave like this? When you had the opportunity, you didn't listen to my advice and gave your sons a free run. Now you are suffering for those poor decisions.'

Dhritarashtra sighed. 'You are right, Krishna. My blind love for my sons is the cause for my suffering.' Then he said, 'Bheem, I am sorry for my behaviour. Please come to me. I'd like to touch you. My sons are all dead. Now, Pandu's sons are my sons.' Dhritarashtra embraced Bheem and kissed his forehead to bless him.

The Pandavas then proceeded to meet Gandhari. Gandhari, with her blindfold on, was fuming. Before Yudhishthira could meet Gandhari, the great sage Vyasa appeared. He knew that Gandhari won't be able to control her anger, and her wrath would be too much for Yudhishthira to handle. He stood next to Gandhari and said, 'My dear Gandhari, you shouldn't express your anger towards the Pandavas. During the war, whenever Duryodhan came to you and asked for your blessings, you'd say, "Let victory come to those who follow the path of Dharma." That's what has happened, and your blessings have come true. The Pandavas have always followed the right path, and that's why they won. You must control your anger and pardon them.'

Gandhari knew that the Pandavas were in the room with her. She turned towards them and said, 'My lord, I know my sons are responsible for their loss. Their greed and arrogance caused their downfall. But I can't say the Pandavas have always followed the right path either. Bheem struck Duryodhan below the navel, and that too in the presence of Krishna. How is that right by any law?'

Bheem stepped forward and said, 'I know what I did was wrong, but I did it only in self-defence. I pray you forgive me. Let me also remind you, it was your sons who defeated Yudhishthira in an unfair game of dice and refused to give his kingdom back even after we completed our time in exile. It was your sons who dragged Draupadi into the court and humiliated her in front of everybody. Duryodhan patted his thighs and made lurid suggestions to Draupadi. It was then that I promised to break Duryodhan's thighs and that's what I did. Now that he is dead, we have no animosity towards anybody in the Kuru dynasty.'

'You killed my son Dushasana mercilessly and drank his blood. No human can perform such a horrendous act. How do you justify that?'

Bheem knelt in front of Gandhari and said, 'Mother, trust me, I did not drink Dushasana's blood. Dushasana is my brother, and his blood is my own blood. How can I drink my own blood? Yes, the blood touched my lips and teeth, but I didn't swallow a single drop. I killed Dushasana to keep my promise that I had made when he dragged Draupadi by her hair to the court. Mother, your sons have done terrible things to us and caused us irreparable harm. You never stopped them. You cannot blame us now.'

Gandhari sighed. 'Couldn't you have let one of my sons survive to serve us during our final days?'

Bheem stayed quiet.

Gandhari turned away from Bheem and asked, 'Where is Yudhishthira?'

Yudhishthira was trembling like a leaf. He touched Gandhari's feet. 'Mother, here I am, the killer of your sons. Punish me.'

Overcome with rage, Gandhari couldn't say a word. She stayed silent and tried to control her anger. Through the bottom of her blindfold, her eyes fell upon Yudhishthira's fingertips, and instantly his nails turned black. Yudhishthira cried out in pain and retracted his hands. Gandhari felt bad that she hadn't been able to control herself and inadvertently caused harm to Yudhishthira. She pulled Yudhishthira close and embraced him. She called Bheem, Arjun,

Nakul, Sahadev and Draupadi, and embraced them all. Krishna stood on the side and sighed in relief.

Gandhari, Dhritarashtra and the other women then went to visit the Kurukshetra battlefield. The macabre scene of the battlefield, with dead bodies and body parts strewn all around, the ghastly scenes of dogs and vultures fighting to devour the flesh of humans and animals, was too much for the women folk to handle. Many fainted. Others cried out loud and ran to search for the bodies of their loved ones.

Gandhari, though blindfolded, could see the battleground with her inner eye. She said, 'Krishna, I can see my beloved son Duryodhan lying dead in a pool of blood with his mace in his hand. I can see my daughters-in-law frantically searching for their husbands' bodies. Can you listen to their wails, Krishna? There, I see Karna's wife lying unconscious next to her husband's half-eaten body. I see Uttara sitting next to Abhimanyu's body and caressing him. I see Dushala crying like a mad woman and running around, searching for Jayadrath's head. So much pain, so much destruction ... Tell me, Krishna, why did you let this happen? If you wanted, you could have stopped this destruction, the destruction of my family.' Krishna didn't answer.

Gandhari continued, 'I curse you, Krishna. Just as you caused the destruction of my family, you will also cause the destruction of your family, of your clan. For thirty-six long years, you'll live alone, without any friends or family, and then die a dishonourable death.'

Krishna smiled. 'O Queen, I know my fate. What you say is exactly what's going to happen. I will be the destroyer of my clan, the Yadavas and the Vrishnis. Nobody else can destroy them; they will destroy themselves.'

Yudhishthira ordered his men to set up funeral pyres to cremate the dead. Soon, the sky was filled with smoke from the thousands of pyres, along with the sound of the chanting of the priests and the wailing of the women.

When the fire subsided, Yudhishthira and his brothers stepped into the river to offer their prayers to the dead. Suddenly, Kunti stepped forward and said, 'My sons, wait. Offer your prayers to the man who was killed by Arjun, and who was known to the world as Karna, for he was your elder brother. Karna was born of my womb, fathered by the Sun god.'

Yudhishthira and his brothers were dumbfounded. With tears flowing down his eyes, Yudhishthira said, 'Why didn't you tell us this before? The man whom we dreaded the most, our most powerful enemy was our brother and you kept this a secret? Why? Mother, this news has pained us more than anything in this war. If we had Karna with us, nothing in this world would have been unachievable, and this war wouldn't have happened either.' The Pandavas huddled together and cried while offering their prayers to Karna.

After completing the last rites for the departed souls, preparation began for the consecration of Yudhishthira to the throne of Hastinapur. The priests performed yagnas and other rituals. Yudhishthira sat on the golden throne with Krishna and Satyaki in front of him. Bheem and Arjun sat on either side. Kunti, Nakul and Sahadev sat on ivory thrones nearby. Priest Dhaumya conducted the fire sacrifice with Yudhishthira and Draupadi. Krishna poured holy water from his Panchajanya conch shell. Musicians played songs in praise of Yudhishthira and the Pandavas. The people of Hastinapur poured in to witness the celebration, and hailed Yudhishthira as the king of Hastinapur. Yudhishthira greeted them with generous gifts of gold and silver.

The Pandavas began to rule their kingdom with blessings from the subjects. Yudhishthira appointed Bheem as the crown prince and the next in line to the throne. Arjun was appointed as the minister of defence, Nakul as the chief of the army, and Sahadev as Yudhishthira's personal guard and assistant. Vidura was appointed as the chief advisor, and Sanjay was in charge of finance. The people of Hastinapur were happy to see their favourite king back on the throne. However, Yudhishthira was not happy. A constant feeling of guilt bothered him as he blamed himself for the death of his near and dear ones. No words or scriptures could provide him any relief from his misery.

Yudhishthira went to Krishna for advice. 'Tell me, Krishna, how can I serve my people with this enormous feeling of guilt inside me?' he asked. 'I feel lost and find no joy in ruling the kingdom.'

Krishna held his hand and said, 'Yudhishthira, you have your greatest advisor, your mentor, Pitamaha Bhishma, still alive. You should go to him and ask for his guidance before he leaves us. I am sure he'll give you the right advice.'

The next morning, Yudhishthira left for Kurukshetra to meet Bhishma, who was happy to see Yudhishthira. Yudhishthira paid his respects to the great Kuru patriarch and asked, 'Grandfather, time and again you have helped us stay on the path of Dharma. With your blessings, we have won the war and the throne of Hastinapur. For this, we had to pay a steep price. We lost all our near and dear ones, our friends, our family, and I have lost all interest in ruling the kingdom. Please tell me, how can I motivate myself to serve my people the right way?'

Bhishma smiled. 'I don't think I need to tell you anything as you are well-versed in the laws of Dharma. But I can see that grief has clouded your judgement and you can't seem to find your path. I will try to dispel your doubts and maybe help you recover from your malaise.'

Bhishma then delved into his deep reservoir of experience and enlightened Yudhishthira on the ways of leadership and gave him several tips on how to be a good ruler. Yudhishthira felt much better. He bowed to Bhishma and said, 'Thank you for your advice. I will try to follow them to the best of my ability.'

'I am happy to be of help. You should now let go of your sorrow and focus on making your people happy and prosperous. Come back to me when the sun begins to travel towards the northern hemisphere and bid me farewell.' Yudhishthira mounted his chariot and sped towards Hastinapur to begin a new journey.

Fifty-eight days after he fell from his chariot, when the sun began to move towards the northern hemisphere, Bhishma decided to leave his mortal body. In the presence of Yudhishthira and his brothers, Kunti, Dhritarashtra, Gandhari, Krishna, Vyasa, and many others, Bhishma bid farewell to everybody and closed his eyes. The priests chanted mantras from the Vedas and everybody around watched in awe as Bhishma's soul left his body, and like a lightning bolt, shot up to the sky and disappeared behind the clouds, leaving Bhishma's lifeless body limp on the arrows.

With a heavy heart, Yudhishthira and his brothers performed the last rites of their dear grandfather and left Kurukshetra.

75

Yudhishthira: The King of Hastinapur

YUDHISHTHIRA HAD BEEN TRYING HIS BEST TO SERVE AS THE KING OF Hastinapur, but despite all the words of wisdom from his elders, his guilt kept tormenting him. Vyasa visited him and said, 'Stop acting like a child, Yudhishthira. It seems you've forgotten all you have learnt from the scriptures. All the advice we offered seems to have fallen into deaf ears. So, I don't know how to help you.' Vyasa paused for a moment and watched Yudhishthira who sat still, with his face hanging low. It was clear, words couldn't help Yudhishthira. He needed to take some action to get out of his depression. Vyasa said, 'My son, if you strongly feel that you need to cleanse yourself of your sins, then you should perform the Aswamedha Yagna. Like Lord Rama, perform the horse sacrifice and donate generously to the Brahmins, and you'll rid yourself of the sin of killing your friends and relatives.'

Yudhishthira's face lit up, but not for long. He sighed. 'My lord, I know that the horse sacrifice can help free us from our sins, but the yagna requires a lot of wealth. The war has drained all our resources and my coffers are empty. I can't perform the yagna now.'

Vyasa thought for a while and said, 'Maybe I can help you. Many years ago, King Marutta had amassed a huge amount of wealth in gold to donate to Brahmins. He stored the gold in a secret place in the Himalayas. I will tell you the location of this gold and you can go and fetch it. With that wealth, you should be able to fill up your coffers and perform the yagna.'

Yudhishthira stood up and said, 'O Lord Vyasa, how can I thank you? I will send my men to the Himalayas to fetch Marutta's gold. Once we get it, I will begin the preparations for the horse sacrifice.' Vyasa gave Yudhishthira the details of the location and disappeared.

While Yudhishthira was preparing for his expedition to the Himalayas, Krishna came to him and said, 'My dear Yudhishthira, it's been a long time since I left Dwarka. I miss my father and my family. Please allow me to go back to Dwarka.'

Yudhishthira embraced Krishna. 'I understand. Go back to Dwarka and pass our regards to your father. But don't forget to come back when I perform the Aswamedha Yagna.' Krishna agreed.

Krishna bid farewell to Dhritarashtra, Gandhari and his aunt Kunti, and mounted his chariot for Dwarka. His sister Subhadra accompanied him. Bheem, Arjun, Vidura and others followed him for some distance until Krishna's chariot vanished beyond the horizon.

On an auspicious day, Yudhishthira, along with his brothers and a small contingent of soldiers, left for the Himalayas to fetch Marutta's gold. On reaching the location, he set up a camp and offered prayers to Lord Shiva. He treated the locals to food and drink and asked their permission to begin digging the ground. The diggers started their work and cut through the rocks and boulders, and soon hit upon a huge store of gold, silver and gemstones. The Pandavas piled the treasure on elephants, camels, horses and carts, and returned to Hastinapur, taking multiple rest stops along the way. The Hastinapur coffers once again was filled to the brim, and Yudhishthira began to prepare for the Aswamedha Yagna.

As promised, Krishna arrived in Hastinapur to join the yagna. But, soon, disaster struck the Pandava family. Uttara, the widow of Arjun's son Abhimanyu, gave birth to a still-born boy. Aswathama's curse had come true. His Bhrahmasir weapon had changed course to kill all Pandava babies in their mothers' wombs. Kunti came crying to Krishna and said, 'You are the only one who can save the Kuru clan from total annihilation. Revive Uttara's son as you had promised.'

Subhadra, Krishna's sister and Abhimanyu's mother, cried and said, 'Brother, I beg you—please make my grandson live again. They say you are the supreme lord, and you can perform miracles. If you can't help us now, what good are you?'

Uttara was holding the dead baby in her arms and crying inconsolably. She looked up at Krishna and said, 'Aswathama's weapon did its job and killed my baby. I wish the weapon had killed me rather than my child. Shame on my fathers-in-law for failing to destroy Aswathama and his weapon. What good is their victory if they failed to protect their children? Uncle Krishna, I hear you had promised that you will make sure Aswathama's weapon fails, and my child lives. What happened to your promise? Look, my baby is dead in my arms.'

Krishna picked up the baby in his arms and said to Uttara: 'Don't cry, my child. My words can never go wrong.' He gently rocked the baby in his arms, and slowly his heart began to beat. His pale face regained its colour, and the child began to breathe. And in the next moment, the baby let out his first cry. Uttara, Subhadra, Kunti, all cried out in joy and bowed to Krishna, who passed the baby to its mother, Uttara, and said, 'Here, take your son Parikshit. He will grow up to be a strong and powerful king and rule the earth for many years.'

A month after Parikshit's birth, the Pandavas began preparing for the Aswamedha Yagna. A strong and powerful horse was selected for the sacrifice. The horse would roam around freely through several kingdoms. A huge army would follow the horse. If any king dared to capture the horse, he would have to face the wrath of the Pandavas and their army. If he let it roam free, it meant that he accepted Yudhishthira as his king, and was an ally.

In the presence of Vyasa, Krishna, Dhritarashtra and the rest of the Pandavas, the horse was consecrated by the priests and released. Arjun followed the horse with a huge contingent of well-equipped soldiers. Before Arjun mounted his chariot, Yudhishthira said to him: 'My brother, I am tired of wars and battles, and would like to avoid death and destruction at any cost. If any king challenges you, try to talk to him with all humility and persuade him to avoid any confrontation. Tell him, we seek his friendship and invite him to the yagna.' Arjun agreed.

The horse trotted along through forests and meadows and passed through several kingdoms. Most kings didn't dare to stop the horse until it reached the kingdom of Trigarta. During the Kurukshetra war, Arjun had killed thousands of Trigartas who had declared themselves to be Samsaptaks and vowed to kill Arjun. Their sons and grandsons captured the horse and attacked Arjun to extract their revenge. Arjun tried to reason with them, but the Trigartas didn't budge and attacked Arjun with all their might. But they were no match for Arjun's might, and soon fell to his feet and prayed for his pardon. Arjun let them go and invited them to the yagna.

When the horse reached Pragjyotishpur, the land of King Bhagadatta whom Arjun had killed in the war, Bhagadatta's son

Vajradatta attacked Arjun riding a huge elephant. Arjun killed the elephant, and Vajradatta crashed to the ground. Arjun picked up Vajradatta and said, 'Vajradatta, don't be scared. I won't kill you. I am here to invite you to King Yudhishthira's Aswamedha Yagna.' Vajradatta humbly accepted the invitation.

The people of Sindh were angry with Arjun for killing their king Jayadrath. So, when the horse reached Sindh, they attacked Arjun's army but were summarily defeated by Arjun. Jayadrath's wife Dushala came to Arjun with her grandson and said, 'Brother Arjun, please have pity on my grandson. His father—my only son Surath—is dead, and I am the only one to take care of him. Forget the misdeeds of Jayadrath and Duryodhan if you can, and let my grandson live.'

Arjun was deeply saddened to hear this. He blessed Surath's son and invited Dushala to attend the yagna in Hastinapur.

Then one day, the horse arrived in the kingdom of Manipur, the land ruled by Arjun's wife Chitrangada. Overjoyed at the news of Arjun's arrival, his son Babruvahan arrived to greet him with garlands and flowers. Arjun wasn't happy to see him, though. He said to Babruvahan sternly: 'Shame on you, Babruvahan. This is not how a Kshatriya welcomes an invader. Fight me and defend your land if you can.'

Babruvahan was perplexed and didn't know what to do. The serpent princess Ulupi, the other wife of Arjun, appeared in front of Babruvahan and said, 'My son, I am your step-mother Ulupi. Go, fight your father Arjun with all your might. That will make him happy.'

Babruvahan went back to the palace, put on his armour and helmet, picked up his weapons, and attacked Arjun with full force. Arjun was pleasantly surprised and fought back his son with a volley of arrows. It was soon evident that young Babruvahan was no less of a warrior than Arjun himself. His arrows pierced Arjun's armour, broke his helmet, and shattered his weapons. Arjun couldn't take it any longer and dropped unconscious from his chariot.

Babruvahan was shocked to see his mighty father fall. He was racked with guilt and questioned why he had obeyed his father's orders in the first place. Babruvahan's head began to spin, and he too fell from his chariot and fell unconscious on the ground next to Arjun.

Queen Chitrangada came running. 'Ulupi, why did you provoke Babruvahan to fight his father?' she screamed. 'You are responsible for their death, and you must revive them with your serpent magic. Otherwise, I will sit here and fast unto death.'

Ulupi smiled and said, 'Don't worry, dear sister. They are not dead. Give me a moment, and I'll revive them both.' Ulupi pulled out a gem and touched it on Babruvahan's and Arjun's forehead, and they both woke up.

Arjun embraced Babruvahan and said, 'I am proud of you, my boy. You have proven yourself and have rightfully conquered me.' He then looked at Chitrangada and Ulupi, and said, 'I invite you all to the Aswamedha Yagna celebrations. Now I have to leave and follow King Yudhishthira's horse.'

The horse then travelled back west through Magadh, Koshal, Banga, Pundra and then turned south. From there, the horse turned back again and went towards the west coast, to Dwarka, the kingdom of the Yadavas and the Vrishnis. The horse then travelled north to the land of the five rivers, and from there to the province of Gandhar. A few of the kings, like Shakuni's son, the king of Gandhar, and the King of Magadh, challenged Arjun, but failed to defeat him. Arjun invited them all to the yagna.

Finally, after many months, Arjun returned to Hastinapur with the horse, and the preparations for the yagna began. Thousands of kings, princes and Brahmins from far and near arrived to attend the celebrations. A huge fire was lit, and the priests sat all around and chanted mantras. Yudhishthira, Draupadi and the rest of the Pandava brothers sat in front of the fire and followed the instructions of the priests. Finally with loud music and drums playing in the background, the horse that roamed the country was sacrificed to the gods. The Pandavas offered the horse meat to the yagna fire and the smoke spread around the city, purifying the earth. Yudhishthira donated huge amounts of gold and land to the Brahmins and sages. Vyasa embraced Yudhishthira and said, 'Now you have cleansed yourself of all your sins and have nothing to repent for. Rule your kingdom with a clean heart and make your people happy.'

76

Vanaprastha and the End of the Yadavas

FOR FIFTEEN YEARS FROM THE DAY YUDHISHTHIRA ASCENDED THE THRONE of Hastinapur, the Pandavas treated Dhritarashtra and Gandhari as their own parents. Yudhishthira consulted Dhritarashtra before taking any important decision. 'Please make sure our uncle Dhritarashtra never feels like he is neglected,' he instructed his brothers. 'He has lost his sons in the war and he feels lonely and dispossessed. But he is kind to us and loves us like his own sons. We should treat him like our own father.'

Bheemsen didn't agree, though. 'How could you forget the way he treated us?' he asked Yudhishthira. 'It was because of his indulgence that Duryodhan defeated you in that rigged game of dice, sent us to the forests for thirteen years, and then refused to give us our kingdom back. Dhritarashtra never did anything to stop his son. And now you want us to treat him like our father?'

'Let us try to forget our past animosity, my dear brother,' replied Yudhishthira. 'I hold no grudge against him and I want you all to do the same. Make sure he is treated with respect and enjoys all the facilities that he is used to. Spare no expense to ensure that he has nothing to complain about.'

Bheem didn't argue any further, but he didn't make any attempts to conceal his resentments either. For fifteen years, Dhritarashtra tried to ignore Bheem's insolence, thinking about Yudhishthira's kindness and the respect he and his other brothers showered on him. But when Bheem clapped his hands in front of the blind king and boasted, 'With these hands I killed Duryodhan and his friends,' he couldn't take it any longer. He decided to leave the palace.

The next morning, when Yudhishthira came to pay his respects to Dhritarashtra and Gandhari, Dhritarshtra said, 'My dear Yudhishthira, you have treated us with respect and kindness all these years. You took care of all our needs, and never let us feel unwanted or neglected. However, the time has come for us to take the next step in our lives. Gandhari and I want to leave the palace and live like monks in a forest hermitage and spend the rest of our days in meditation and prayers. Please grant us our wish.'

Yudhishthira was shocked to hear this. 'How could you say such a thing?' he cried. 'Did I do anything wrong? Did anybody in the palace disrespect you? Please tell me.'

Dhritarashtra tried to console Yudhishthira. 'Try to understand, my son,' he said. 'A man has to pass through four phases in his life—Brahmacharya, Grihastha, Vanaprastha and Sannyas. It is time for our Vanaprastha and Sannyas. Please let us go.'

Yudhishthira was deeply saddened to hear this and kept pleading with Dhritarashtra to stay. 'I am willing to give up the throne and make anybody you wish the king. You can be the king if you'd like. Please don't leave us as orphans once again.'

At that moment, the great sage Vyasa appeared. 'Let him go, Yudhishthira,' said Vyasa. 'Let them perform their worldly duties by spending their remaining days like monks. That's the right thing to do. You should not feel bad about their decision.' Yudhishthira was left with no option but to agree.

On an auspicious day, Dhritarashtra and Gandhari prepared to leave the palace. Yudhishthira and the rest of the Pandavas assembled to bid them farewell. Kunti stepped forward and said, 'My sons, I too have decided to accompany them to the forest. Please do not stop me.'

Yudhishthira was devastated. Bheem cried and held Kunti's feet. 'Mother, if all you wanted was to leave us and go to the forests, then why did you make us fight this war and kill thousands of people?' he asked.

Kunti touched Bheem's head and said, 'My son, I didn't want you to be cheated and deprived by your cousins and live your life in poverty. That's why I encouraged you to fight and win back what was rightfully yours. When my husband was alive, I have enjoyed enough luxury and have no repentance. So, let me go and let me do what my heart desires.'

The Pandavas tried their best to stop Kunti, but she was adamant. Finally, Yudhishthira and his brothers had to agree. Vidura and Sanjay also decided to accompany Dhritarashtra to the forest.

Dhritarashtra, Gandhari, Kunti, Sanjay and Vidura began their journey on foot. In Kurukshetra, they met the saint, King Satayup. Satayup greeted them and said, 'O King Dhritarashtra, I would like to invite you to my hermitage in the forest. You can spend the rest of your life with me and my fellow monks.' Dhritarashtra agreed.

In Satayup's hermitage, they discarded their royal garments and put on clothes made of tree bark and began their life of penance. Vidura sat in deep meditation for days and nights without having any food or drink. His body turned into a skeleton. Termite mounds grew on his body. The monks in the hermitage tried to persuade him to break his meditation and have something to eat. Vidura didn't budge. He continued with his penance. Then one day, his soul left his body and went to the heavens. The monks in the hermitage, along with Dhritarashtra, Gandhari, Kunti and Sanjay, were deeply saddened. When they began preparing for cremation of Vidura's body, Vyasa appeared and said, 'Do not cremate his body. Let him stay where he is.'

Several years had passed since Dhritarashtra left for the forest. Yudhishthira was busy with the affairs of his kingdom, but he'd often think of his mother, uncle and aunt. One day, Narada visited Hastinapur. He went to Yudhishthira and said, 'My son, I have been travelling a lot. While returning, I thought I'd pay you a visit.'

Yudhishthira was glad to see him. He greeted Narada and offered him food and drinks. Later, he asked, 'O great saint, during your travels, did you get a chance to meet my father Dhritarashtra? Did you meet my mothers Kunti and Gandhari? How are they doing?'

Narada placed his hands on Yudhishthira's shoulder and said, 'That's why I am here: to inform you about your parents. My son, Dhritarashtra, Gandhari, Kunti and Sanjay were engaged in severe penance. Dhritarashtra ate nothing but air, Gandhari survived only on water, Kunti ate only once a month and Sanjay once every five days. Then one day, a forest fire broke out. Dhritarashtra, Gandhari and Kunti were too weak to escape. Dhritarashtra called Sanjay and said, "You are strong enough to run away. Go, save yourself. We will sit here in meditation and let the fire devour us." Sanjay was reluctant to leave them, but he couldn't disobey Dhritarashtra's orders. He ran out of the forest, while the fire engulfed the other three.'

Yudhishthira and his brothers were devastated to hear this. Yudhishthira cried and said, 'Shame on us! We failed to protect our parents. How ungrateful is the fire god Agni! Arjun had once burnt the Khandava forest to please him. And this is how he pays us back ... by devouring our mother, Kunti!'

Narada replied, 'Don't blame Agni. Dhritarashtra was not killed by a freak accident. Rather, he sacrificed himself to the fire. The monks had performed a yagna and threw the burning cinders into the forest which then turned into a forest fire. So, you can say, your parents were consumed by the yagna fire. You should not feel sorry for them.'

Yudhishthira and his brothers then visited the burnt hermitage and performed the last rites of their parents, and returned to Hastinapur with a heavy heart.

For thirty-six years after Yudhishthira's ascension to the throne, the Yadavas and the Vrishni dynasties in Dwarka had fallen into decadence and corruption. They were busy killing and robbing each other, and had no regard for authority. One day, the great sages Vishwamitra, Kanwa and Narada visited Dwarka. A few of the Yadavas, lead by Krishna's step-brother Saran, got drunk and decided to play a prank on the sages. They dressed up Krishna's son Samba as a pregnant woman, took him to the mystics and asked, 'Lords, it is said that you can see the future. Can you tell us whether this lady would give birth to a boy or a girl?'

The sages weren't fools and they caught their deception right away. Angered at their insolent behaviour, they said, 'Shame on you, Yadavas. You have lost all dignity and will suffer for your behaviour. This woman is Krishna's son Samba in disguise, and he will give birth to an iron club, and the club will be the cause for your destruction—for all of you, except Krishna and Balram. Balram will die in the oceans and Krishna will succumb to an arrow shot by a tribal hunter, Jara.'

The next day, Samba did give birth to an iron club. King Ugrasen ordered the club to be crushed and dumped into the ocean. To bring back order to the city, Ugrasen banned the production and consumption of alcohol in the city of Dwarka. Anybody who defied his orders would face the death penalty, he announced.

The Yadavas, the Vrishnis and the Andhakas tried to be cautious. Several bad omens were seen around the city. Ominous-looking, huge, dark, bald men were seen roaming the city and causing destruction. They were impervious to arrows and other weapons. Krishna knew, the final days of the Yadavas and the city of Dwarka were afoot. He announced, 'Dear Yadavas, you should all leave Dwarka and go to Pravas.'

The Yadava men grabbed this opportunity and went to Pravas along with their concubines, and tons of food and liquor to escape Dwarka. In Pravas, they partied continuously and drank copious amounts of wine and liquor. They didn't even care for Krishna. Satyaki and Kritavarma got into a quarrel and soon it turned into a bloody fight. Satyaki blamed Kritavarma for helping Aswathama kill the sons of the Pandavas in their sleep. Kritavarma fought back, but Satyaki pulled out his sword and beheaded Kritavarma. Soon, a battle broke out between the Bhojas, the Vrishnis and the Andhakas. They began to strike each other with whatever they could lay their hands on.

Krishna knew the time for the destruction of his clan had arrived. He picked up a fistful of grass and it turned into a bunch of maces. He hurled the maces at the Yadavas and the blow killed many. The remaining picked up the maces and began to kill each other. The tall grass around the fighting men magically transformed into maces, and the Yadavas used them to kill each other mercilessly. Father killed his son, son killed his father, friend killed his friend. Soon nobody was left alive. Daruk, Krishna's charioteer, came to Krishna and said, 'Let's leave this place and visit Balram.' Krishna agreed.

Krishna and Daruk looked around for Balram. Finally, they found him sitting quietly under a tree by the seaside. Krishna knew, Balram was preparing to leave his mortal body, which meant that his own death wasn't too far. He turned to Daruk and said, 'Go to Hastinapur and ask Arjun to come to Dwarka and protect the women and children. He should take everybody with him since Dwarka will soon be swallowed by the ocean.' Daruk left for Hastinapur.

Balram was sitting with his eyes closed. From his mouth emerged a thousand-headed serpent which slowly disappeared into the ocean, leaving behind the lifeless body of Balram. Krishna roamed around in the forest for a while and then sat under a tree behind some bushes. He mulled over Gandhari's curse. At that time, a hunter named Jara was looking for a kill. From behind the bushes, he saw Krishna's legs and mistook them for a deer. The hunter shot at his target and the arrow pierced Krishna's feet. When Jara saw that it was Lord Krishna himself whom he had shot, he fell at his feet and prayed for mercy. Krishna blessed him and said, 'This was my destiny, my friend, and this was your destiny too. So don't feel bad.' Krishna closed his eyes, and his soul left his body and departed for the heavens.

Daruk arrived in Hastinapur and informed the Pandavas about the misfortune that had struck the Yadava clan. Then he passed on Krishna's message to Arjun, who prepared to leave for Dwarka right away.

When Arjun arrived in Dwarka, he could only hear the wails and cries of the Yadava women and children. Krishna's father Vasudev held Arjun's hand and said, 'I never dreamt of witnessing such a terrible day. Arjun, you are our only saviour. Krishna told me to send all the women and children with you to Hastinapur. And we have to do it fast, since the city of Dwarka will be devoured by the sea soon.'

The next morning, Arjun prepared to leave Dwarka with a huge caravan, carrying thousands of Yadava women and children. He pleaded with Vasudev to come with him, but he remained adamant: 'Leave me, Arjun. I want to die here. That is my wish.' Arjun didn't push any further.

As Arjun's caravan left the city, the sea waters rose and began to flood the city. Soon, no trace of Dwarka could be seen, except for miles of sea water.

While Arjun travelled through the province of the five rivers, a band of dacoits attacked the caravan with sticks and stones to steal the Yadava women. Arjun warned them, but they didn't listen and began to pull the women off their chariots and carts. Arjun picked up his Gandiva bow, but it felt too heavy. With great difficulty, he strung his bow, but then he could not remember any of his divine weapons. He tried to shoot arrows at the raiders, but they missed their targets. He then tried to strike the dacoits with his Gandiva, but the raiders laughed and ran off with the women. Arjun was devastated. He knew, he no longer possessed the strength and skills of the greatest warrior on earth. With the remaining women and children, he arrived in the city of Indraprastha. There, he appointed Vajra, the grandson of Krishna, as the ruler and asked him to take care of the women. He then paid a visit to Rishi Vyasa's hermitage.

Vyasa said, 'What happened, Arjun? It looks like you've been sapped of all your strength.'

Arjun narrated the story about the destruction of the Yadava clan, the death of Balram and Krishna, and finally his failure to protect the Yadava women. 'Why did all this happen?' he asked Vyasa. 'I have lost my strength and I don't know how I can live like this any longer.' Arjun was crying.

'Don't feel bad, my son,' Vyasa tried to console him. 'Sooner or later, all good things have to end. The Yadavas died of their own fault, and Krishna knew that the end had to happen. That's why he left too. You have done great deeds, but I am afraid, your time has come too. Now you too must prepare for your departure.'

Back in Hastinapur, Arjun narrated his experiences to Yudhishthira, who said, 'Time consumes everyone and we are no exception. Let us prepare for our next journey.'

77

The Final Departure

YUDHISHTHIRA PERFORMED THE LAST RITES OF KRISHNA AND BALRAM. He then appointed Abhimanyu's son Parikshit as the king of Hastinapur. He called Subhadra and said, 'From now on, your grandson Parikshit will rule the kingdom. I have appointed Kripacharya as his teacher. I have also appointed Krishna's grandson Vajra as the ruler of Indraprastha. He will take care of the remaining Yadavas.'

He then assembled his subjects and his ministers and announced, 'My dear people of Hastinapur, for the last thirty-eight years, I have been privileged to serve you as your king. Now I'd like to step down. My brothers and I have decided to leave the palace and the kingdom, and proceed on foot towards the heavens. Our grandson Parikshit will take good care of you.'

The citizens were stunned to hear this. They cried, 'Please don't leave us. We'll be orphans without you.'

Yudhishthira didn't listen.

On an auspicious day, the Pandavas and Draupadi discarded their expensive royal costumes and put on simple clothes made of tree bark—the kind worn by monks. They worshipped the gods and then left the palace on foot. The people of Hastinapur followed them and pleaded with them to turn back. The Pandavas kept walking. After a while, the subjects gave up and returned to their homes. Only a dog kept following them.

The Pandavas walked towards the east and crossed many provinces, until they reached the banks of the Lohitya Lake. Arjun carried his Gandiva along as a habit. Suddenly, one day, the fire god Agni appeared to him and said, 'Arjun, you helped me burn the Khandava Forest and cured me of my illness, and for that I fetched the Gandiva from Varuna and gifted you the bow. You don't need it anymore. Please return it to Varuna.' Arjun took off his Gandiva and threw it into the waters of the lake. The bow sank and returned to Varuna.

The Pandavas continued their trek. They walked past the submerged city of Dwarka and moved north towards the Himalayas.

They crossed the foothills of the Himalayas and gradually entered rough terrain that was full of rocks and boulders. The Pandavas no longer had the strength of their youth. The journey felt more arduous than they had imagined. From the rocky terrain, they moved into a snow-covered region. The climb was getting steeper and steeper as the five brothers, Draupadi and the dog continued their hike. Blizzard winds swept across the mountain side, making it extremely difficult to walk.

Yudhishthira led the team as he trudged forward with a staff in his hand, with Draupadi struggling at the tail end. Bheem offered to carry her, but she refused. Suddenly, Draupadi couldn't take it any more. She collapsed to the ground. Snow began to cover her body. Bheem tried to scramble behind to help her, but Yudhishthira stopped him. 'Let go, Bheem. No need to pick her up,' he said.

Bheem was shocked to hear this. 'Panchali never committed any sin. She always followed the path of righteousness. Why did she fall?'

'Draupadi was biased towards Arjun and loved him more than any of us. And that's why she fell.' Yudhishthira kept walking without showing any emotion.

The five brothers and the dog continued their journey. Suddenly, Sahadev collapsed. Bheem asked, 'Yudhishthira, why did Sahadev fall? He was the nicest of all, and never expressed any pride. He always took care of us, and respected us.'

Yudhishthira said, 'Sahadev thought he was the wisest of all. His pride was the cause of his downfall.'

A little later, Nakul collapsed. Bheem asked again, 'Nakul never did anything wrong. He always obeyed us and kept on the path of Dharma. Why did he fall?'

'Nakul thought he was the most handsome and good-looking man,' replied Yudhishthira. 'Bheem, leave him alone and follow me.'

Arjun was walking with great difficulty. The fall of Draupadi and his brothers deeply saddened him. He was thinking about them when suddenly his foot got stuck in a crevice and he collapsed to the ground. Bheem was shocked. He asked, 'Yudhishthira, Arjun had no vice. He never ever uttered a lie, not even as a joke. How could he fall?'

Yudhishthira looked ahead and solemnly answered, 'Arjun proudly claimed that he could destroy all his enemies in a single day. He couldn't do so. Besides, he always looked down upon and underestimated the prowess of other archers. He shouldn't have done that.'

A little later, Bheem fell too. With great difficulty, he raised his head and asked, 'Why me?'

Yudhishthira replied, 'You were a glutton and ate too much. Besides, you were too proud of your strength and never appreciated the strength of others.' Yudhishthira didn't look back and continued his journey ahead with only the dog as his companion.

Suddenly, with a huge roar, a golden chariot descended from above and halted in front of Yudhishthira. From the chariot, the king of the gods, Indra, stepped out and said, 'Yudhishthira, I have come to take you to the heavens. Come, get into the chariot.'

Yudhishthira bowed to Indra and said, 'O lord, thank you for your kindness. Please allow me to take my brothers and my wife with me on your chariot. They are lying here in the snow.'

Indra smiled and said, 'You don't have to worry about them. They have died and are already in heaven. Come with me, and you'll see them.'

Yudhishthira was about to mount the chariot, but suddenly his eyes fell on his companion, the dog. He said, 'Lord, this dog is my follower. I wish to take him with me to the heavens.'

Indra was surprised. 'You wish to take this dog? You should be glad that you can enter heaven in your mortal body. No human has ever achieved this feat. Forget the dog.'

Yudhishthira was adamant. 'This dog has been following me since I left Hastinapur,' he said. 'He has suffered with us, but never abandoned us. I cannot abandon him now and go to the heavens to enjoy myself.'

'Yudhishthira, try to understand. Dogs are not allowed in heaven,' said Indra. 'They can ruin religious rituals, yagnas, and spread filth and dirt. I cannot allow him to enter heaven.'

'Then I won't go to the heavens either,' said Yudhishthira. 'This dog is my friend, and I cannot leave him here.'

The dog had been listening to the conversation. Suddenly, he transformed into Lord Dharma himself and said, 'Yudhishthira, you are indeed a remarkable person. You were willing to give up the heavens for a dog. Nobody would do such a thing, not even in the heavens. You deserve to enter the heavens in your mortal body. Go with Indra and enjoy eternal bliss with your loved ones.'

Yudhishthira mounted the chariot and Indra drove him to the heavens. Narada welcomed Yudhishthira with open arms. 'Yudhishthira, we have been waiting for you,' he said excitedly as soon as Yudhishthira entered. 'You are the best of the Bharata clan and indeed the most fortunate. I have never heard of a live mortal enter the heavens. You are the only one.'

Yudhishthira looked around and said, 'I don't see my brothers around. Where are they? I wish to be with them. Please take me there.'

Indra smiled and said, 'You have come to the heavens; yet you haven't let go of your earthly attachments. You should live where you deserve to live. Your brothers didn't earn the same rights as you did.'

Yudhishthira bowed to Indra and said, 'O lord, I am what I am, and I cannot abandon my brothers and my wife. I wish to live where they are. Please take me to them.'

Indra then asked one of his assistants to take Yudhishthira to his loved ones. Yudhishthira followed the angel who took him through a dark and smelly tunnel. Putrid smoke emanated from the fires around and filled the surroundings. The tunnel led Yudhishthira to the hells where sinners rotted in terrible pain. Yudhishthira asked, 'How long do I have to travel on this horrible path? Where are my brothers?'

Indra's assistant answered, 'Are you tired? The lord asked me to take you back the moment you felt exhausted.'

Yudhishthira felt he couldn't take it any more. Just when he was about to turn back, he heard voices, 'O King Yudhishthira, please stay a few more moments. Your presence has brought us peace and solace and our pain has subsided.'

Yudhishthira asked, 'Who are you? Why are you here?'

The voices replied, 'I am Karna ...', 'I am Arjun ...', 'I am Bheem ...', 'I am Nakul ...', 'I am Sahadev ...', 'I am Draupadi ...'

Yudhishthira was dumbfounded. How could this be true? What sins had caused them to suffer in hell, he wondered. He cried out to the assistant, 'Go back and tell your lords, I won't leave my loved ones. I will stay here and won't return.'

The assistant went back and reported this to Indra, who came to Yudhishthira. In a moment, all darkness disappeared. Indra smiled and said, 'Yudhishthira, don't be upset. All kings need to visit hell. All human beings commit sin sometime in their life. Those who sin less, visit hell first and then enter the heavens. You lied to Drona about Aswathama's death, and for that you had to make this short trip through hell. Your brothers, Draupadi, and the rest of your family members have all been to hell and now are back in the heavens. Come with me and join them.'

Indra took Yudhishthira to the heavens, where he saw Karna, Bheemsen, Arjun, Nakul, Sahadev and Draupadi waiting for him. His father, Pandu, was there too. So were Kunti and Madri. Bhishma and Drona stood next to them. Yudhishthira smiled and walked towards them with his arms spread wide.

Bibliography

1. Ganguli, Kisari Mohan, trans. *The Mahabharata of Krishna-Dwaipayana Vyasa*, Ved Vyasa. Calcutta: Pratap Chandra Roy, 1883-1896.
2. Basu, Rajsekhar. *Krishna Dwaipayana Vyasa's Mahabharata* Calcutta: M.C. Sarkar & Sons Private Limited, 1986.
3. Debroy, Bibek. *The Mahabharata.* India: Penguin, 2015.
4. Pattanaik, Devdutt. *Jaya: An Illustrated Retelling of the Mahabharata.* India: Penguin, 2010.
5. Dharma, Krishna. *Mahabharata: The Greatest Spiritual Epic of All Time.* US: Torchlight Publishing, 1999.
6. Brook, Peter, trans. *The Mahabharata*, Jean-Claude Carriere. India: Bloomsbury Publishers, 2006
7. Easwaran, Eknath. *The Bhagavad Gita.* US: Nilgiri Press, 2007.

About the Author

Sudipta Bhawmik is an award-winning playwright who has written nearly forty plays in both Bengali and English. His plays have been produced and staged across the US, the UK, India, and Bangladesh, and they have been translated into Hindi, Marathi, and Tamil. He has also authored four books. Sudipta holds a Ph.D., a Master's degree, and a Bachelor's degree in Electronics and Computer Engineering from IIT Kharagpur. He currently resides in New Jersey, USA.

30 Years *of*

 HarperCollins *Publishers* India

At HarperCollins, we believe in telling the best stories and finding the widest possible readership for our books in every format possible. We started publishing 30 years ago; a great deal has changed since then, but what has remained constant is the passion with which our authors write their books, the love with which readers receive them, and the sheer joy and excitement that we as publishers feel in being a part of the publishing process.

Over the years, we've had the pleasure of publishing some of the finest writing from the subcontinent and around the world, and some of the biggest bestsellers in India's publishing history. Our books and authors have won a phenomenal range of awards, and we ourselves have been named Publisher of the Year the greatest number of times. But nothing has meant more to us than the fact that millions of people have read the books we published, and somewhere, a book of ours might have made a difference.

As we step into our fourth decade, we go back to that one word – a word which has been a driving force for us all these years.

Read.

Harper
Collins

HARPER
PERENNIAL

HARPER
BUSINESS

HARPER
BLACK

हार्पर
हिन्दी

HarperCollins
Children'sBooks

HARPER
DESIGN

HARPER
VANTAGE

Harper
Sport